ENTICK v CARRINGTON: 250 YEARS OF THE RULE OF LAW

Entick v Carrington is one of the canons of English public law and in 2015 it is 250 years old. In 1762 the Earl of Halifax, one of His Majesty's Principal Secretaries of State, despatched Nathan Carrington and three other King's messengers to John Entick's house in Stepney. They broke into his house, seizing his papers and causing significant damage. Why? Because he was said to have written seditious papers published in *The Monitor*. Entick sued Carrington and the other messengers for trespass. The defendants argued that the Earl of Halifax had given them legal authority to act as they had. Lord Camden ruled firmly in Entick's favour, holding that the warrant of a Secretary of State could not render lawful actions such as these which were otherwise unlawful.

The case is a canonical statement of the common law's commitment to the constitutional principle of the rule of law. In this collection, leading public lawyers reflect on the history of the case, the enduring importance of the legal principles for which it stands and the broader implications of *Entick v Carrington* 250 years on.

Volume 9 in the series Hart Studies in Comparative Public Law

Entick v Carrington

250 Years of the Rule of Law

Edited by
Adam Tomkins and Paul Scott

·HART·
PUBLISHING
OXFORD AND PORTLAND, OREGON
2017

Hart Publishing
An imprint of Bloomsbury Publishing Plc

Hart Publishing Ltd	Bloomsbury Publishing Plc
Kemp House	50 Bedford Square
Chawley Park	London
Cumnor Hill	WC1B 3DP
Oxford OX2 9PH	UK
UK	

www.hartpub.co.uk
www.bloomsbury.com

Published in North America (US and Canada) by
Hart Publishing
c/o International Specialized Book Services
920 NE 58th Avenue, Suite 300
Portland, OR 97213-3786
USA

www.isbs.com

HART PUBLISHING, the Hart/Stag logo, BLOOMSBURY and the
Diana logo are trademarks of Bloomsbury Publishing Plc

First published in hardback, 2015
Paperback edition, 2017

British Library Cataloguing-in-Publication Data
A catalogue record for this book is available from the British Library.

ISBN: PB: 978-1-50991-832-4
HB: 978-1-84946-558-8

Typeset by Compuscript Ltd, Shannon
Printed and bound in Great Britain by
Lightning Source UK Ltd

To find out more about our authors and books visit www.hartpublishing.co.uk. Here you will
find extracts, author information, details of forthcoming events and the option to sign up for our
newsletters.

Contents

Notes on Contributors

Denis Baranger is Professor of Public Law at the Université Panthéon-Assas (Paris II).

Timothy Endicott is Professor of Legal Philosophy at the University of Oxford and Fellow of Balliol College.

David Feldman is Rouse Ball Professor of English Law at the University of Cambridge and Fellow of Downing College.

Tom Hickman is a Barrister at Blackstone Chambers and Reader in Public Law at University College London.

Tom Mullen is Professor of Law at the University of Glasgow.

Jacob Rowbottom is Associate Professor of Law in the Faculty of Law, University of Oxford, and Fellow of University College.

Paul Scott is Lecturer in Public Law at the University of Southampton.

Adam Tomkins is John Millar Professor of Public Law at the University of Glasgow.

Introduction

ADAM TOMKINS AND PAUL SCOTT

*E*NTICK *v CARRINGTON* is one of the canons of English public
law. In 2015 it is 250 years old. In 1762, the Earl of Halifax, one
of His Majesty's Principal Secretaries of State, despatched Nathan
Carrington and three other of the King's messengers to John Entick's house
in Stepney. They broke into his house and opened his boxes, chests and
drawers, seizing his papers and causing significant damage. Why? Because
he was said to have written seditious papers published in *The Monitor*.
Entick sued Carrington and the other messengers for trespass. The defendants argued that the Earl of Halifax had given them legal authority to act
as they had. Lord Camden, Chief Justice of the Common Pleas, ruled firmly
in Entick's favour, holding that the warrant of a Secretary of State could
not render lawful actions such as these—entering and ransacking private
property—which were otherwise unlawful.

Entick v Carrington is widely agreed to be a leading statement of the
common law's commitment to the constitutional principle of the rule of
law. One could collect from the law books a vast number of testimonies
to its significance: ECS Wade called it 'perhaps the most important of all
cases to be found in the law reports of England',[1] while FH Lawson said it
was 'the case to take to a desert island'.[2] And yet the unarguable consensus
as to the importance of *Entick v Carrington* masks a series of disagreements
as to what exactly the case decided and, in turn, how the common law
manifests its commitment to the rule of law ideal. Some even suggest that
it is another aspect of the case which makes it worth reading in the twenty-
first century. This collection—remarkably, the first of its kind on this great
case—considers these matters and others. It does so by reflecting on the
history of the case, including the febrile political and social context within
which it was decided, on the enduring importance of the legal principles
for which it stands and on the broader implications of *Entick v Carrington*
250 years on.

The chapters in this book approach the case from three main vantage
points. The opening three contributions, from David Feldman, Tom Hickman

---

[1] ECS Wade, 'Liability in Tort of the Central Government of the United Kingdom' (1954) 29
New York University Law Review 1416.
[2] See RFV Heuston, *Essays on Constitutional Law*, 2nd edn (London, Stevens, 1964), 35.

and Jacob Rowbottom, illuminate the eighteenth-century context of the case. In focusing on the politics and the people of *Entick v Carrington*, Feldman reminds us that, as well as resounding with great constitutional principle, the case was also a politically inspired battle, fiercely fought between rival camps of government and opposition. His chapter allows us to understand the role of the various individuals implicated in the political disputes out of which *Entick* emerged—their relationships to the case and, just as importantly, to each other. Hickman focuses on the legal background to the case and, especially, on the law of seditious libel, its institutions and its mechanisms of enforcement. His careful reconstruction of the development of the law of seditious libel in the decades before *Entick v Carrington* enables him to challenge the influential account of the case given by Sir William Holdsworth. While Hickman invites us to reflect on *Entick* as a case about state security, Rowbottom's account focuses on the liberty of the press and on the extent to which the dispute at the heart of the case was about propaganda, its uses and its control. By explaining the 'propaganda wars' which formed the backdrop to the case and the skirmishes in the battle for press freedom which took place in the years after *Entick*, he teaches us much about the role of the press in the political process at this point in history and the law's contribution to the environment in which it operated.

The next three chapters focus on legal doctrine and assess the propositions of law for which *Entick v Carrington* may be regarded as authority. Timothy Endicott asks the following questions: if *Entick* is a landmark of the common law, what sort of guide is it and to what sort of legal landscape? The answer he offers emphasises the peculiar marriage of continuity and change which is so central to Lord Camden's judgment, as it is to the common law method generally. Paul Scott argues that one of the many ways in which we might come to appreciate the richness of the case and the exact nature of its contribution to the common law rule of law ideal is to read it as a case about property. For that reason, he contextualises *Entick v Carrington* within the considerable body of common law rules which protect property against interference by both public and private actors. Adam Tomkins seeks to locate *Entick* in the variety of overlapping and sometimes conflicting claims that public lawyers make of the rule of law. In particular, he addresses the specific issue—of which the courts have made little sense in recent years—of the legal powers enjoyed by Ministers of the Crown, and the limits which exist on them, using *Entick v Carrington* to argue for a broad conception of the rule of law ideal and a correspondingly limited role for the Crown's common law powers.

The final chapters in the book move away from the detail of the doctrine and offer broader reflections on the case's legacy. Denis Baranger reflects on what *Entick* has to tell us about liberty and power in the modern state, arguing that the case captures an important moment in the historical process by which law and power came to be rationalised. That the process in question did not result in an all-encompassing legal entity known as 'the state' has granted to the quite particular notion of the state reflected in *Entick* an ongoing significance. Finally, Tom Mullen reminds us that it is not only in the law of England and Wales that *Entick* enjoys authority: his survey of the varied uses made of *Entick* in Scots law offers a nuanced view of the ways in which Scots law both reflects and diverges from English legal understandings of the constitutional relationship of public power to individual liberty.

Most of the chapters collected here were presented in draft at a workshop held at the School of Law, University of Glasgow in January 2014. The workshop was generously funded by the School of Law Tercentenary Fund, and we are grateful to Professors Rosa Greaves and Mark Furse for their support. Jenny Crawford and Rona Cameron helped in numerous and invaluable ways with the running of the workshop, and we thank them. Thanks also to all those who attended the workshop, offering constructive comments on the papers and adding hugely to the conviviality of the proceedings: especially James Chalmers, Margit Cohn, Lindsay Farmer, Chris McCorkindale, Aileen McHarg, Marcelo Neves and Stephen Tierney. Finally we thank our publishers for allowing us to include as an appendix to this volume the full report of *Entick v Carrington* contained in *Howell's State Trials*.

1

The Politics and People of Entick v Carrington

DAVID FELDMAN

I. THE HISTORICAL CONTEXT

RITAIN IN THE mid-eighteenth century was in political ferment. The government, embroiled in the Seven Years' War and colonial expansion abroad and beset by divisions at home, faced serious political unrest. In their efforts to maintain order and security, governments were accused of arbitrary disregard for liberty at home and a lack of patriotism in foreign relations. Ministers branded the opposition as seditious and even treasonous. A sense of insecurity was fuelled by mutual suspicion between Roman Catholics and Anglicans, between English and Scots, between Hanoverians and Jacobites, and between Whigs and Tories, contributing to social, religious and political tension internally, and diplomatic and military confrontation externally. Ministers and their opponents used political propaganda, parliamentary proceedings, law and litigation as campaign weapons. *Entick v Carrington* was just one skirmish in a long-running series of battles stretching back to the English Reformation of the sixteenth century, taking in the upheavals of the seventeenth century, the union of England and Scotland in the early eighteenth century, and threats to the Hanoverian monarchy from Jacobite and Tory challenges.

A. The Crown and Parliament, Anglicanism and Roman Catholicism

When King Henry VIII established the Church of England in the 1530s as independent of the Papacy and the Roman Catholic Church, he ensured that two problems would underlie English, and later British, politics for several hundred years. First, religion would be taken as an important indication of political loyalty. The country's confessional allegiance was to be tied to that of the monarch for the remainder of the sixteenth century—

Protestant under Henry VIII and his son, Edward VI, Roman Catholic under Mary I and Philip, and Protestant again under Elizabeth I—and opposition to the prevailing faith would be treated as entailing disloyalty to the monarch.[1] England's foreign relations reinforced the link between loyalty and religion. The Holy Roman Empire and the recently united Spanish Kingdoms of Aragon and Castile applied diplomatic and military pressure to protect English Roman Catholics and force England back to the Church of Rome. English monarchs quite reasonably saw religious non-conformists as enemies within the realm.

Second, by using Acts of Parliament to establish the Church of England and authorise action against dissenters, King Henry VIII and his Protestant successors handed previously unimagined authority to the two Houses of Parliament. This led to friction when Parliament, and particularly the House of Commons, started to flex its muscles over matters such as taxation and foreign affairs under Queen Elizabeth I.[2] A struggle for dominance over government between Parliament and the monarch descended into civil war and, briefly, a republican Commonwealth in the mid-seventeenth century. After James II of England (and VII of Scotland), who had converted to Roman Catholicism in or about 1668, tried to use the royal prerogative to mitigate the effects of anti-Catholic legislation on his co-religionists and to bring leading Roman Catholics into prominent positions at court and in the country, a politico-religious backlash forced him to leave England precipitately in 1688. Opposition to the King came not only from Whigs, who opposed royal claims to divine right and any hint of Roman Catholicism, but also from many Tories, who were committed to the Crown and, usually, the Church of England, and found they could not tolerate a king who embodied one but not the other.[3]

The English political elite, seeking a replacement for James II, plumped in 1688–89 for a Dutch Protestant, William, Duke of Orange, and his wife Mary. They had respectable dynastic credentials. Mary (born 1662) was the Protestant elder daughter of James II and his first wife, Anne Hyde. William, born in 1650, was a nephew of Charles II and James II and a grandson of Charles I. Mary died childless in 1694, so on William's death in 1702, the crown passed to Mary's Protestant younger sister Anne. Anne's only child,

[1] See AG Dickens, *The English Reformation* (London, Fontana, 1967) 161–75; GR Elton, *England under the Tudors* (London, Methuen, 1962) 102–37, 369–78; J Guy, *Tudor England* (Oxford, Oxford University Press, 1988) 131–38; P Williams, *The Later Tudors: England 1547–1603* (Oxford, Oxford University Press, 1995) 465–76.
[2] JE Neale, *Elizabeth I and Her Parliaments*, 2 vols (London, Jonathan Cape, 1965) graphically shows how Queen Elizabeth and her ministers had to manage Parliament to maintain royal, including religious, authority and revenues.
[3] JR Western, *Monarchy and Revolution* (London, Blandford Press, 1972) chs 6–9; J Hoppitt, *A Land of Liberty? England 1689–1727* (Oxford, Oxford University Press, 2000) 13–50. James II henceforth lived in France as a guest of King Louis XIV, dying in 1701.

William, Duke of Gloucester, had died in 1700, aged 11, at which point the English political elite had foreseen the risk that both William III and his heir presumptive, Anne, would die without issue. The Act of Settlement 1701 therefore provided that, should that happen, the crown would pass to Sophia, Electress of Hanover, and her descendants. Sophia (born in 1630) was the twelfth, and only surviving, child of Elizabeth, the younger sister of Charles I, and Frederick V, Elector Palatine. The Act further required any future ruler to be a communicant of the Church of England. Sophia's son George (born 1660), who succeeded his father as Elector of Hanover, proved himself a vigorous and effective military leader and a clear-headed ruler.

Its role in settling the succession showed that henceforth a monarch would have to be acceptable to Parliament. Parliamentarians were cautious, however, about asserting, let alone regularly exercising, a power to rein in a serving monarch. In 1689, William III retained considerable independence, not least in his choice of ministers. The 'Glorious Revolution' restricted his freedom to use certain controversial aspects of the royal prerogative, but Parliament did not yet control the executive; nor was there a belief that the monarch's ministers should be chosen by, or even principally accountable to, Parliament.[4] This was to change over the first half of the eighteenth century. In 1714, as Basil Williams wrote: 'George I appointed his first ministers, but he could not have kept them in office had not his first parliament of 1715 supported them; he dismissed Townshend in 1717, but the strength of Townshend and of his brother-in-law Walpole, who had thereupon resigned, was so great in parliament that he was obliged to reinstate them three years later.'[5] By 1756, when William Pitt became Prime Minister by popular demand, regardless of the will of George II and with only limited aristocratic connection, not only were ministers accountable to Parliament but the will of the people in the choice of a leader also had to be respected by both Parliament and monarch.[6] The effectiveness of an appeal to 'the people', over the heads of both Parliament and monarch, and control over the means of making such an appeal were central to the political movements which in the 1760s generated the litigation of which *Entick v Carrington* was part.

B. Britishness, War and Patriotism

Despite the Act of Settlement, succession to the throne after the death of Queen Anne in 1714 was open to doubt. James II had died in 1701 still

---

[4] See Western (n 3) ch 10; Sir G Clark, *The Later Stuarts 1660–1714*, 2nd edn (Oxford, Clarendon, 1956) 144–53; E Wicks, *The Evolution of a Constitution: Eight Key Moments in British Constitutional History* (Oxford, Hart Publishing, 2006) ch 1.

[5] B Williams, *The Whig Supremacy 1714–1760*, 2nd edn, CH Stuart (ed) (Oxford, Clarendon, 1962) 32.

[6] Williams (n 5) 375–76.

claiming to be king and maintaining his successors' claim to the throne. James Francis Edward Stuart, son of James II and his Roman Catholic second wife Mary (daughter of Duke Alfonso IV of Modena), was recognised by Jacobites as King James III of England and VIII of Scotland. Dynastically, James was the senior male who could claim descent in the male line from the children of King Charles I. As a Roman Catholic, however, he was unacceptable to most of the British political elite and population, which regarded him as a 'pretender' to the throne. (He has become known as the 'Old Pretender' to distinguish him from his son, Charles Edward Stuart, the 'Young Pretender'.) Nevertheless, on Queen Anne's death, a relatively small but significant Jacobite faction among the Tories wanted to proclaim him as King notwithstanding the 1701 Act. More realistic Tories, however, even if they sympathised with the sentiment, saw that it would be futile, so George, Elector of Hanover, succeeded fairly peacefully to the throne.[7]

George I's position on his accession was complicated by cross-cutting nationalisms. The first concerned the identity of the realm. In 1707, the Kingdoms of Scotland and England had merged. The Treaty of Union created a new Kingdom of Great Britain, with a loss of Scottish national sovereignty which was resented by many Scots, some of whom retained an attachment to the Stuart cause.[8] Many English people, in turn, came to resent the increased influence of Scots in matters and institutions affecting England. Tension between the English and the Scots over the nature of the state and their roles within it naturally spawned a degree of suspicion concerning patriotic loyalties.

Second, many English and Scots suspected that George I and his son, George II, German-speaking Hanoverians and principally concerned with their continental possessions and interests, pursued foreign policies more closely aligned with the European interests of Hanover than those of Britain as a colonial world power. The 'otherness' of the first two Hanoverian monarchs fuelled such suspicions. They never fully integrated into British society. George I in particular made himself unpopular, even with those who had approved of or acquiesced in his accession, by his attitude to his British court and subjects, and alienated the Tories by excluding them from his government.

The Hanoverian monarchs in their turn were not unreasonably suspicious of some of their leading Tory subjects. Early in the reign of George I, riots erupted around England. Growing disorder encouraged some Jacobite Tories to plot a coup. The Duke of Ormond, an Anglo-Irish Jacobite Tory, having been accused of treason, went to France and took charge of plans for an invasion bankrolled by the King of Spain. However, the Secretary of State for the North, William Stanhope, first Earl of Harrington, quickly

---

[7] See ibid 150–64 on the political aspects of the succession.
[8] See Wicks (n 4) ch 2.

had matters under control, countering the plot and maintaining an army in England in expectation of invasion. The 'Old Pretender', known to his supporters as King James III, landed an army in Scotland in 1715 and made some headway, but was defeated when he reached England. Nevertheless, the invasion and the support it received from some Tories, Scots and Roman Catholics damaged trust in those groups for half a century or more. Suspicion was reinforced by periodic flurries of Jacobite activity and deepened in 1745 when James' son, 'Bonnie Prince Charlie' or the 'Young Pretender', launched a further, ultimately unsuccessful, invasion in an attempt to take the throne. Whilst the relative ease with which the government crushed the 1745 rebellion showed that British people, Scots as well as English and Welsh, were generally content with the way in which government was being conducted, the government still faced cross-cutting tensions over nationalisms and military and colonial policy. Fears about loyalty and security led George I and George II to govern through Whig ministers for virtually all of the 46 years of their reigns.

Politics were dominated by three major Whig figures. Thomas Pelham-Holles, the first Duke of Newcastle, was an experienced and accomplished politician (though without the personal characteristics which might have made him a respected statesman), who marshalled support for the government through judicious use of patronage.[9] Newcastle's brother, Henry Pelham, was an honest, decent man and 'an authentic political and parliamentary heavyweight' whose 'command of patronage was extensive' and who was adept at managing elections, and whose 'right to the title of Prime Minister matches that of Walpole, North and Pitt'.[10] The third dominant politician was Sir Robert Walpole, often regarded as the first true Prime Minister. He, too, made extensive use of patronage for political advantage; he was thought to have benefited personally from corruption in office, but he was exceptionally successful in stabilising public finances (reducing the national debt and greatly extending the system of excise duties), re-establishing economic stability after the collapse of the South Sea Company and supporting British industries.[11] By and large, during the long period of Whig government, these three dominant figures did a creditable, if broadly non-interventionist, job in keeping the state secure and allowing the economy to develop.

For much of the period, and particularly after 1739, their task was complicated by the fact that Britain was almost continuously involved in wars on several fronts, not only on the European mainland but also in the British

---

[9] P Langford, *A Polite and Commercial People: England 1727–1783* (Oxford, Oxford University Press, 1989) 226.

[10] ibid 205–06. Langford notes that the two brothers often quarrelled about policy matters; the Lord Chancellor, Philip Yorke, Earl of Hardwicke, usually acted as peace-maker. (The title of Prime Minister, rather than First Lord of the Treasury, belongs properly to those who led government from, and through control of, the House of Commons.)

[11] Williams (n 5) 180–93.

colonies in North America, the Caribbean and India. The so-called Seven Years' War (1754–63, although most of the military action took place from 1756) was fought on a vast scale, involving disputes with France over far-flung colonies and a shifting tangle of alliances in Europe, and was correspondingly expensive and controversial. Domestic politics were complicated by differences of opinion as to Britain's war aims. A strong body of public opinion supported the war as a means of extending British commercial interests internationally, but disliked fighting and paying for wars which seemed to benefit only the European interests of Hanover. Ministers were targets of vitriolic criticism from Tories, among whom William Pitt was prominent, when their policies were thought to reflect insufficient mercantile patriotism. As the cost of the wars rose, the Crown's increasing dependence on parliamentary taxation inhibited its military strategy. Managing the two Houses of Parliament became a priority, but was complicated by a split among Whig ranks, which Pelham was instrumental in containing.

George II proved adept at attracting first-class parliamentary managers to his service despite their conflicting personalities and principles. In 1757, he brought Pitt, a notably able statesman, into his ministry alongside Newcastle. Pitt was a highly principled and inflexible politician who had great influence among independent members in the House of Commons, who respected his intellect and integrity. Pitt had previously opposed Newcastle's management of the war, building an unexpectedly powerful campaign in Parliament and, more particularly, in the country by calling for the government to act patriotically, ie, to pursue British colonial and commercial expansion vigorously through its diplomatic and military activities, departing from the more pragmatic, less aggressive policy of previous years. He now took responsibility for the vigorous conduct of the war, and his influence over the Commons and the people was crucial. Newcastle continued to manage the House of Lords through a mixture of astute pragmatism and patronage. Newcastle and Pitt mistrusted each other and were reluctant to work together (although Pitt sat for a pocket borough controlled by Newcastle), yet they shared the King's wish for a successful conclusion to the wars and for some time enjoyed considerable success alongside each other.[12]

George II died in 1760. He had arranged for the next generation to be brought up in England, so that his son, Prince Frederick, saw himself as British rather than Hanoverian. Whilst bolstering the long-term acceptability of the Hanoverian dynasty, however, this caused friction at court. Frederick used his patriotism to distance himself from his father and let it be known that he disapproved of the King's policies, ministers and morals, particularly corruption and the use of patronage to maintain political support. Frederick's court at Leicester House became a magnet for critics of the King's court and government, predominantly Tories, who were able to

---

[12] Langford (n 9) 230–34; Williams (n 5) 355–70.

present themselves as standing up for British patriotism against the Crown's ministers. In 1751 Frederick predeceased his father, but he had imbued his son George, then aged 12, with his views. The young Prince's Scottish tutor, John Stuart, third Earl of Bute, who had Tory sympathies, reinforced this prejudice.

George III therefore saw himself as being on a moral crusade, as well as wanting revenge on those Whigs whom he regarded as having been his father's enemies. He was not inclined to tolerate any behaviour from ministers which he regarded as inappropriate. Nevertheless, he did not immediately dismiss his grandfather's ministers. He recognised that the partnership between Pitt and Newcastle was good for the country; each offered something that the state needed. George III allowed them to continue, while replacing some Whigs with members of his own circle when opportunities arose. In March 1761, Bute (the King's former tutor) became a Secretary of State alongside Pitt, and Lord Halifax, of whom we will hear more later, became Lord Lieutenant of Ireland. In the same year, Bute acquired the means of exercising great influence, acquiring a fortune on his father-in-law's death and becoming leader of the 45 Scottish MPs and nine Scottish peers when the previous leader, the Duke of Argyll, died (the new Duke having no interest in politics).

Vigorously prosecuting the war increased its cost rapidly. Rising debt added to tensions between ministers. Pitt made total victory a condition for peace and wanted to declare war on Spain over Gibraltar while Spanish finances were strained. His colleagues, concerned at the political impact of the rising cost of the war, demurred. Pitt, intolerant of contradiction, resigned in October 1761. Without his mastery of the Commons, the government struggled. Its position worsened in 1762 when negotiations with Spain over Gibraltar broke down and war was declared, but by then (as Pitt had foreseen) Spain had replenished its war chest. Meanwhile, Prussia, encouraged by Russia's new neutrality, wanted to intensify its military campaign against Austria with British financial support, while British interests favoured using Prussia's new position of strength as a favourable basis for peace negotiations. This made it impossible for Newcastle to maintain solidarity within his own government for seeking an additional £1 million in credit to continue to pay a previously agreed subsidy to Prussia. Opposed by two members of his own Treasury Board, Newcastle resigned. Bute took over from him, and George Grenville, an abrasive, self-opinionated politician and brother-in-law of Pitt, became Secretary of State.

Bute's main task was to make peace on terms which would be accepted by the country and the two Houses of Parliament. With Pitt and Newcastle sidelined, it should have been possible for the government to distance Britain from Prussia and make peace with Spain. Grenville, however, insisted on peace demands which Bute thought were unachievable. In the in-fighting which occupied the summer of 1762, Bute tried to persuade

Newcastle to come back as a pragmatic compromiser, while Grenville tried to persuade Pitt to return to office. Both overtures failed. So effective was the opposition press, with John Wilkes's *The North Briton* allied with *The Monitor* in attacking Bute's administration, that localised anti-Scottish and anti-Catholic riots erupted in many parts of England. Nevertheless, with the help of Henry Fox in the Commons, Bute succeeded in guiding the government and Parliament towards accepting the Treaty of Paris, which ended the Seven Years' War in 1763. But he resigned that year, exhausted by the effort. Grenville succeeded him and approved the treaty, and at once became the target of vicious criticism from Tories led by Pitt and including Earl Temple, Grenville's brother, who felt that the Treaty was insufficiently advantageous to British interests.

Out in the country, Pitt's criticisms were reinforced by John Wilkes, who owed his parliamentary seat to Earl Temple. Their anti-government propaganda provoked riots against Bute and then Grenville. To show his authority, Grenville 'judged it necessary to cow those who had stirred up such violence in the country against Bute. Pitt and Temple were the leading exponents of this covert demagogy, and Temple's most effective agent, because the most violent, had been John Wilkes'.[13] This precipitated a legal assault on the opposition press, which responded by using litigation and parliamentary proceedings for both defence and attack. The course was set to *Entick v Carrington*.

II. PEOPLE AND INSTITUTIONS: LAWYERS,
JUDGES AND POLITICIANS

A. The Intermingling of the Small Worlds of Law and Politics

There are two points to bear in mind about the relationship between bar, bench and politics in the eighteenth century. First, judicial independence of government was far less well established and institutionalised in the mid-eighteenth century than it became subsequently.[14] The Act of Settlement 1701 limited the monarch's prerogative powers over the judiciary, providing in law for the first time that judges held office during good behaviour, could not have their stipends reduced while in office and could be dismissed only on an address of both Houses of Parliament, but appointments were still in the gift of the monarch on the advice of ministers. In the first half of the

---

[13] J Steven Watson, *The Reign of George III 1760–1815* (Oxford, Clarendon, 1960) 98.
[14] See generally D Lemmings, 'The Independence of the Judiciary in Eighteenth-Century England' in P Birks (ed), *The Life of the Law: Proceedings of the British Legal History Conference, Oxford 1991* (London, Hambledon Press, 1993) 125–49.

century, virtually every judge owed his appointment to either Walpole or Newcastle. In addition, until 1760, a judge's commission from the monarch lasted only for the reign of that monarch; on the demise of the Crown, the commission lapsed, together with the judge's competence to act and right to be paid. The next monarch could choose whether to re-appoint the same judges or replace them with people more to his or her taste politically, and on his accession in 1714 King George I replaced Tory judges with Whigs.[15] This was changed by the Commissions and Salaries of Judges Act 1760, 1 Geo III c 23, passed at the personal request of the young King George III to provide for judges' commissions and salaries to continue on the demise of the Crown.

What is more, a significant proportion of the judges had been MPs at a time when finding a parliamentary seat depended in large part on being supported by influential people and finding a great deal of money to pay for favours. Quite frequently, a judgeship followed a period as Attorney General or Solicitor General, the government's chief legal advisers and representatives in litigation. This meant that there was no meaningful separation of powers between the judiciary and other branches of government. In the circumstances, the record of most judges of robust independence from political pressure in their decisions reflects well on them and on governments.

Second, the English legal and political elite was very small. The population of the British Isles as a whole in 1760 has been estimated at around 11 million people (of whom 6.5–6.75 million were in England and Wales, 1.25 million in Scotland and 3.25 million in Ireland).[16] The population of England and Wales was about three-quarters of today's population of London, and 1.5 times the current population of New Zealand. The pool of educated, professional, politically active people was actually even smaller than this; women, constituting half the population, were excluded, and men wanting to buy their way into public office or politics needed access to a great deal of money and to an influential patron. Nevertheless, the core, elite group was not hermetically sealed. Talented individuals could rise meteorically if they attracted the attention of influential sponsors. Despite this, the pool from which the political and professional elite was drawn remained tiny by comparison with that of modern Britain. It is not surprising, then, that (as in small jurisdictions today) able individuals tended to move between, or even combine, roles at the apex of politics, government and law. Members of this elite were closely connected. Many were long-standing friends, colleagues and rivals who had been at the same schools or universities. The English were dominant; Scots were, relatively speaking, outsiders, but could achieve considerable influence and status if they could overcome English suspicions of them.

---

[15] ibid 136.
[16] Steven Watson (n 13) 10.

B. The Judges: Common Pleas

The Lord Chief Justice of Common Pleas at the time of *Entick v Carrington*, Sir Charles Pratt (1714–94), exemplifies the close connection between law, government and politics.[17] His father was an MP who became Lord Chief Justice of the King's Bench. Pratt was a friend of Pitt at Eton and went on to graduate from King's College, Cambridge, where he became interested in the idea of the constitution as guardian of liberty. Called to the Bar in 1738, he was initially unsuccessful, but with help from the more senior barrister Robert Henley (later Lord Chancellor), he eventually prospered, making his mark in cases like that involving Alexander Murray, whom he defended on a charge of libel, arguing that the jury should be the arbiters not only of the fact of publication but also of whether it was libellous. Pratt maintained his friendship with Pitt, through whom he became associated with the anti-Whig Leicester House party and Attorney General to Prince George. When Pitt agreed to join Newcastle in government in 1757, part of the price which he extracted was that Pratt should be appointed Attorney General, the government's chief Law Officer and legal adviser, leapfrogging Richard Yorke (second son of Philip Yorke, Earl of Hardwicke, the Lord Chancellor and a long-standing ally of Newcastle), who had been, and remained, Solicitor General. Pitt entered Parliament as MP for the notoriously corrupt burgage borough of Downton, in Wiltshire. As Attorney General, Pratt worked well with Yorke. Their opinion of 24 December 1757 on the rights of the Crown in relation to colonies, distinguishing between territories acquired by conquest and those acquired by treaty, was a foundation for the constitutional law of the British Empire. He also conscientiously prosecuted John Shebbeare (later to be one of the authors of *The North Briton*) for seditious libel, while still insisting that it was for the jury, not the judges, to decide whether the publication was libellous. Appointed Lord Chief Justice of Common Pleas in 1762, he presided over some of the most politically controversial cases of the 1760s. In 1766, when George III asked Pitt to form a ministry, Pratt became his Lord Chancellor, being raised to the peerage as Lord Camden, and continued under Grafton until 1769, when he resigned because he could not accept the ministry's decision to have Wilkes expelled from Parliament after the Middlesex elections. In opposition, he generally continued to follow the course set by Pitt (now Lord Chatham) and asserted the right of the American colonists to resist the imposition by the Westminster government and Parliament of excise duties.

The other judges of the Court of Common Pleas in the 1760s included some who seem to have owed their advancement at least in part to political

---

[17] For biographical information on Pratt, see PDG Thomas, 'Pratt, Charles, First Earl Camden (1714–1794)' in *Oxford Dictionary of National Biography* (Oxford, Oxford University Press, 2004; online edn, 2008).

and social connections rather than respect for their professional qualities. Sir Edward Clive (1704–71) became an MP in 1741 for St Michael's Borough, or Mitchell, a rotten borough in Cornwall, through the patronage of Thomas Scawen, son of a former Governor of the Bank of England, but made no impression during his four years in the Commons. He gave up the seat on his appointment as a Baron of the Exchequer in 1745, and in 1753 he was appointed a justice of Common Pleas and knighted. He retired in 1770, having left as little mark on the law as he had on politics.[18]

Sir Henry Bathurst (1714–94) was educated (like Pitt) at Eton and Oxford (at Balliol College). He went into Parliament in the family's seat for Cirencester and as an MP initially opposed Walpole's government. He started to support the government, however, when it awarded his father, the first Earl Bathurst, an office. After his father's dismissal in 1744, he transferred his allegiance to the anti-Whig faction centred on the Leicester House court of Frederick Prince of Wales, serving as his Solicitor General and then Attorney General, and after Frederick's death (as Pratt was later to do) as Attorney General to the young Prince George. Resuming his support for the Whig government, he was appointed a justice of Common Pleas in 1754 and later became Lord Chancellor. He was regarded as being an honest judge but no great lawyer; he usually deferred to the Chief Justice when sitting *en banc* and tried to avoid deciding points of law when sitting alone.[19]

William Noel (1695–1762) was a Tory MP for Stamford from 1722 until 1747, opposing Walpole. In his practice at the Bar, however, he prosecuted a number of Jacobites for their involvement in the 1745 rising, and he moved closer to the Whigs in politics, becoming aligned with Pelham's ministry by the time of the 1747 election. Always active in seeking advancement through patronage, he was appointed a justice of the Court of Common Pleas in 1757 through the influence of Lord Hardwicke, but was not knighted, Noel was not considered to be a particularly strong judge. He died in office in 1762.[20]

It would be wrong, however, to suggest that all the judges of Common Pleas owed their positions to political influence. Pratt was, on any view, a good lawyer, and Sir Henry Gould (1710–94), who replaced Noel in Common Pleas and sat from 1762 until his death 32 years later, was regarded as a sound lawyer and a good judge who had not been active in politics.[21]

---

[18] JH Baker, 'Clive, Sir Edward (1704–1771), Judge' in *Oxford Dictionary of National Biography* (n 17); E Foss, *A Biographical Dictionary of the Judges of England from the Conquest to the Present Time 1066–1870* (London, John Murray, 1870) 170–71.

[19] NG Jones, 'Bathurst, Henry, Second Earl Bathurst (1714–1794)' in *Oxford Dictionary of National Biography* (n 17).

[20] AA Hanham, 'Noel, William (1695–1762), Judge' in *Oxford Dictionary of National Biography* (n 17).

[21] JA Hamilton, rev Robert Brown, 'Gould, Sir Henry (1710–1794), Judge' in *Oxford Dictionary of National Biography* (n 17).

Nevertheless, the justices of Common Pleas tended to be politically engaged rather than jurisprudential heavyweights.

C. The Judges: King's Bench

The Court of King's Bench was rather different. Lord Mansfield CJ was politically involved but was also a fine lawyer who exemplifies the ability of outsiders to break into the English legal and political establishment.[22] William Murray (1705–93) was a Scot whose family included leading Scottish Jacobites; his father had supported the Old Pretender, and one of his brothers took a prominent position at the court of 'King James III' in France and Italy. Suspicions of Jacobitism were to haunt Murray as he developed his career in England. At the age of 13, he rode unescorted from his family home at Scone, near Perth in Scotland, to London, and enrolled at Westminster School. His time at Westminster, where the headmaster had Jacobite sympathies and connections, was formative; later in life he benefited from the brotherhood of former Westminster pupils and in turn supported other members of it. One of his fellow-pupils was Thomas Foley, whose father, the first Baron Foley, generously supported William financially in order to allow him to pursue a career at the Bar. After Westminster, Murray went to Christ Church, Oxford, where he alienated Pitt (with whom, as a supporter of Newcastle, Murray later clashed in the House of Commons) by beating him in a prize competition for Latin verse in 1727. Despite popular suspicion that he harboured Jacobite sympathies, he maintained connections with both Tories and Whigs. In 1742 the Whig First Lord of the Treasury, Lord Newcastle (another former pupil at Westminster), appointed him Solicitor General and put him into Parliament as MP for Boroughbridge. In 1745, with the Attorney General, Sir Dudley Ryder, he had to prosecute the leaders of the 1745 rising, including people who were connected with his family, and he did his job conscientiously. In 1753, a former schoolfriend accused him of having proposed a toast to the Pretender when at Westminster, but he was eventually exonerated (rightly or wrongly) after an inquiry and a parliamentary debate. In 1754, Ryder was elevated to the Bench, and Murray succeeded him as Attorney until 1756, when, following Ryder's death, Murray succeeded him as Chief Justice of the King's Bench and was ennobled as Lord Mansfield. Through his opinions as a Law Officer and as a judge, he greatly influenced the development of public international law and English commercial law, and, despite his somewhat

---

[22] Biographical information on Murray is largely drawn from NS Poser, *Lord Mansfield: Justice in the Age of Reason* (Montreal, McGill-Queen's University Press, 2013); and J Oldham, 'Murray, William, First Earl of Mansfield (1705–1793)' in *Oxford Dictionary of National Biography* (n 17).

authoritarian inclinations (perhaps influenced by a desire to avoid stoking suspicions about his Jacobite connections), he was committed to administering law rather than politics and made some notably liberal decisions in cases concerning slavery, the ability of women to enter into contracts and the constitutional position of the colonies.

Most of the justices who sat with Lord Mansfield CJ in the Court of King's Bench in our period owed their advancement mainly to professional quality rather than political service. Sir Thomas Denison (1699–1766) was the son of a Leeds merchant who went directly from Bar to Bench in 1741 on the strength of his professional ability, apparently without having been involved in politics. He retired in February 1765 without having made a lasting impression on the law, and might be regarded as one of the less impressive justices from a jurisprudential point of view, but Mansfield is said to have had a high opinion of his learning.[23] Others left stronger legacies. Sir Michael Foster (1689–1763) matriculated at Exeter College, Oxford in 1705, although there is no record of his having taken a degree. He practised at the Bar mainly in Bristol, becoming Recorder of Bristol, before being appointed a justice of the King's Bench in 1745. He published a significant work touching on the law of treason among other matters[24] and was regarded as a learned, upright judge and an outstanding authority on Crown (ie, criminal) law. He died in office in November 1763.[25]

Sir John Wilmot (1709–92) had attended Westminster School like Mansfield and had then gone to Trinity Hall, Cambridge. His father refused to allow him to become an academic theologian and forced him to go into law. A deeply learned, wise lawyer, he was a retiring country-lover by inclination, but was eventually persuaded to become a justice of the King's Bench. He enjoyed a cordial, mutually respectful relationship with Mansfield, and displayed integrity and amiability on the bench. He later agreed to become Chief Justice of Common Pleas, but consistently refused invitations to become Lord Chancellor.[26]

Sir Joseph Yates (1722–70) was from a legal family. He had a weak constitution but great ability. Appointed to the King's Bench in 1764, he was known as much for his integrity, industry and refusal to be influenced by the Crown or government as for his liking for fashionable dress and *belles lettres*. He transferred to Common Pleas in 1770, but died only months later.[27]

[23] Foss (n 18) 216.
[24] Sir M Foster, *A Report of some Proceedings on the Commission of Oyer and Terminer and Goal [sic] Delivery for the Trial of the Rebels in the Year 1746 in the County of Surry and of other Crown Cases. To which are added Discourses upon a few Branches of the Crown Law* (Oxford, Clarendon, 1742).
[25] Foss (n 18) 278–79.
[26] J Oldham, 'Wilmot, Sir John Eardley (1709–1792), Judge' in *Oxford Dictionary of National Biography* (n 17).
[27] J Oldham, 'Yates, Sir Joseph (1722–1770), Judge' in *Oxford Dictionary of National Biography* (n 17).

Sir Richard Aston (1717–78) was educated at Winchester College and was called to the Bar by Lincoln's Inn in 1740. In 1761 he was made Chief Justice of Common Pleas in Ireland and in 1665 he returned to England to become a justice of King's Bench. Though perhaps less learned than his brethren, he was regarded as a sound judge and as being immune to governmental influence, although there were rumours that he had been bribed by supporters of Wilkes to hold the writ of outlawry against him to be formally invalid.[28]

All in all, then, Mansfield was the intellectually powerful leader of a strong Court of King's Bench, whose members respected each other as outstanding lawyers; the extraordinarily high level of unanimity throughout Mansfield's period of leadership is a tribute to his ability to build consensus, although it probably owes something to his powerful intellect and personality, which must have discouraged dissent. By contrast, Pratt was clearly the dominant legal mind and personality in the more political, Tory Court of Common Pleas. This is why Pitt's supporters tended to bring cases against the ministers and agents of government in the Common Pleas rather than the King's Bench, which was the forum for cases involving the Crown.

D. The Bar

Naturally, the Bar from whose ranks the judges were drawn had its fair share of members with links to government and opposition. The Earl of Halifax, the Secretary of State who issued the warrants for arrest of those concerned in producing *The Monitor* and *The North Briton*, together with his Under-Secretary, Robert Wood, and the King's Messengers who executed the warrants, were naturally defended by successive Attorneys General and Solicitors General, the Law Officers to the Crown, who were MPs: Sir Charles Yorke; Sir Fletcher Norton; and William De Grey. Also representing the defendants at various times were six of the 12 or so Serjeants-at-Law, the inner circle of barristers with exclusive rights of audience in the Court of Common Pleas, from whose ranks judges were drawn (even if they were appointed Serjeants only so that they could immediately be elevated to the Bench).[29] Serjeants Davy, Hewitt, Nares, Whitaker and Yeates also represented the defendants at various times. They were instructed by the Treasury Solicitor, Philip Carteret Webb MP, a man of modest abilities. For the plaintiffs,

---

[28] J Oldham, 'Aston, Sir Richard (1717–1778), Judge' in *Oxford Dictionary of National Biography* (n 17).

[29] The Order of Serjeants-at Law existed as early as the twelfth century. Their monopoly of the right to plead in the Court of Common Pleas ended in 1834. They were regarded as the judges' brethren, the foremost of whom could be appointed King's Serjeant. See JH Baker, *The Order of Serjeants at Law* (London, 5 Selden Society Supplementary Series, 1984).

Serjeant John Glynn was the main counsel for John Wilkes, and he and Serjeant Leigh appeared for John Entick. Other counsel for Wilkes were John Dunning, Mr Recorder Eyre, and Messrs Stow, Wallace and Gardiner. Serjeant Burland[30] appeared on both sides at different times, representing the plaintiff in *Huckle v Money*, then, having been appointed a King's Serjeant, acting for the defendants in *Entick v Carrington*.[31]

Several of these counsel were tied into politics as practising politicians or advisers to government, or both. On the Crown's side, the Attorneys General and Solicitors General were their governments' Law Officers and MPs. Charles Yorke (1722–70) was the son of Philip Yorke, first Earl of Hardwicke, who had risen from relatively humble, provincial origins to become an outstanding lawyer and politician, protégé of the Duke of Newcastle. As Lord Chancellor from 1740 to 1756, he had established equity as a precedent-based discipline, worked hard to ensure that justice was done and exercised a powerful influence over the development of equity. In politics, he was a key supporter of Henry Pelham and his brother Newcastle. Charles, his second son, was educated at Corpus Christi College, Cambridge. He was called to the Bar in 1746 and entered Parliament in 1747, where he quickly made an impact. He was, however, inclined to be verbose and found it difficult to make decisions. In 1756 he was made Solicitor General, but the next year found himself being leapfrogged by Charles Pratt, a protégé of Pitt, who was brought into Parliament and made Attorney General over him. When Pratt became Chief Justice of Common Pleas in 1762, Yorke became Attorney General, advising on the issues of general warrants, whether parliamentary privilege protected Wilkes from arrest, and the seizure of goods from Entick. However, when his mentor Newcastle left office, instead of loyally following him, he hesitated and prevaricated. Eventually pressure from Newcastle forced him to resign, but by then he had lost the confidence of all parties, being left in the invidious position of supporting Grenville's government without being a member of it. In 1770, Grafton offered Yorke the post of Lord Chancellor. Pressed by King George III, Mansfield CJKB and Wilmot CJCP to accept, but by Hardwicke and Rockingham to refuse

---

[30] John Burland (1724–76) was a highly respected lawyer. He was made a serjeant in 1762 and King's Serjeant in 1764. In 1774 he was appointed a Baron of the Exchequer. See P Polden, 'Burland, Sir John (1724–1776)' in *Oxford Dictionary of National Biography* (n 17).

[31] *Huckle v Money*: Serjeant Burland for the plaintiff and Serjeant Whitaker for the defendant; Wilkes' application for habeas corpus: Serjeant Glynn for Wilkes, and Serjeants Hewitt, Whitaker, Nares and Davy for the King; *Wilkes v Wood*: Serjeant Glynn, Mr Recorder Eyre, Stow, Wallace, Dunning and Gardiner for Wilkes, Solicitor General Norton and Serjeants Nares, Davy and Yeates appeared for the defendant; *Beardmore v Carrington*: the King's Serjeants appeared for the defendants to argue (unsuccessfully) for a new trial on the ground that damages were excessive; *Leach v Money*: Dunning for the plaintiff and Solicitor General De Grey and, later, Attorney General Yorke for the defendants; *Entick v Carrington*: Serjeant Leigh and Serjeant Glynn at different stages for Entick, and Burland and Nares, both King's Serjeants, for the defendants.

and support his friends, Yorke at first refused and then accepted, with a peerage as Lord Morden of Cambridgeshire. Three days later, however, he died suddenly after a violent argument with his brother.

Fletcher Norton (1716–89) was a successful barrister who took Silk in 1754, was elected to Parliament in 1756 and was appointed Solicitor General in Bute's government in 1762. Of 'a choleric disposition',[32] he was elected Speaker in 1770, but his ill temper caused a falling out with the King and the government. As a result of his opposition, he was defeated in an election for Speaker at the start of the 1780 Parliament. When Rockingham formed his second government in 1782, he insisted on the King's elevating Norton to the peerage as Baron Grantley of Markenfield.

William De Grey (1719–81) made his way through legal ability; he became a politician only after being appointed a Law Officer. He was the son of a landowning MP and went to Trinity Hall, Cambridge, without taking a degree. Called to the Bar in 1742, he married the daughter of a MP, was appointed King's Counsel in 1758 and became Solicitor General to Queen Charlotte in 1761, taking a seat in the Commons as MP for Newport in Cornwall and later for the University of Cambridge. At the Bar, he was an accomplished lawyer. In Parliament he supported the government and was appointed Solicitor General in December 1763 and Attorney General in 1766. In 1770 he became Lord Chief Justice of Common Pleas and was knighted. In 1780 he resigned and was created the first Baron Walsingham.[33]

Of the other counsel for the defendants, most progressed in the profession through their professional abilities and did not take part in politics. Mr Serjeant William Whitaker was an extremely experienced, highly professional counsel, who by dint of seniority was the leader of the English Bar as the senior King's Serjeant at the time of his death in 1777.[34] Mr Serjeant William Davy was an excellent trial lawyer with sharp repartee and strength in cross-examination rather than a great legal scholar. He was called to the Bar in 1745 and was created a Serjeant-at-Law in 1755 after only 10 years in practice. He became a King's Serjeant in 1762, and was leader of the Bar as senior King's Serjeant, in succession to Whitaker, from 1770 until he died in 1780.[35]

Mr Serjeant Joseph Yates, or Yeates (1722–70), was the son of a barrister in Manchester. His family fell on hard times and he was supported at Queen's College, Oxford by Mr Serjeant Bootle, a relative. He had a weak

[32] P Laundy, 'Norton, Fletcher, First Baron Grantley (1716–1789)' in *Oxford Dictionary of National Biography* (n 17).
[33] G Goodwin, rev MJ Mercer, 'Grey, William de, First Baron Walsingham' in *Oxford Dictionary of National Biography* (n 17).
[34] HW Woolrych, *Lives of Eminent Serjeants-at-Law*, 2 vols, (London, WH Allen, 1869) ii, 562–66.
[35] JH Baker, 'Davy, William (d 1780), Serjeant-at-Law' in *Oxford Dictionary of National Biography* (n 17); Woolrych (n 34) ii, 605–33.

constitution but great ability and succeeded rapidly after being called to the Bar in 1753. In 1761 he was appointed King's Counsel for the Duchy of Lancaster and was a member of the defence team in *Wilkes v Wood*, the hearing of which on 6 December 1763 was one of his last appearances at the Bar before being knighted and appointed a Justice of the Court of King's Bench, in which capacity he sat with Lord Mansfield CJ on some of the later cases involving Wilkes. In 1770 he was transferred to Common Pleas, but died shortly afterwards.[36]

King's Serjeant James Hewitt (?1709/1715–89) came from a respectable trading family in the Midlands. His father, a milliner and draper, became Mayor of Coventry. James was employed by an attorney, took articles and was called to the Bar in 1742. Hewitt was known as a highly accurate, skilful lawyer. He became a serjeant in 1755 and a King's Serjeant in 1759. He won the parliamentary seat for Coventry in 1761. In 1766 he was appointed a Justice of King's Bench and from 1768 until his death in 1789 served as Lord Chancellor in Ireland, being given an Irish peerage at first before being created the first Viscount Lifford in 1781.[37]

King's Serjeant George Nares (1716–86) also had a respectable but fairly humble background, being a younger son of the steward to the second and third Earls of Abingdon. Educated at Magdalen College School and New College, Oxford, he was called to the Bar in 1741, practising mainly in criminal courts. In 1751 he married the daughter of Sir John Strange, the Master of the Rolls. He was appointed a serjeant in 1759 and a King's Serjeant later that year. Later, in 1768, he became MP for the city of Oxford, supported by the Duke of Marlborough, and supported the government in moving to expel Wilkes from the Commons in 1769. He was appointed a justice of Common Pleas in 1771 and was knighted.[38]

For the plaintiffs, Mr Serjeant John Glynn, or Glyn (c 1722–79), was one of the most learned men at the Bar and was a passionate campaigner for liberty, which he considered to have been guaranteed in the Anglo-Saxon constitution but lost under the Norman yoke and needing to be progressively rediscovered and re-asserted.[39] Glynn was a Cornishman who matriculated at, but did not graduate from, Exeter College, Oxford, and was called to the

[36] J Oldham, 'Yates, Sir Joseph (1722–1770), Judge' in *Oxford Dictionary of National Biography* (Oxford, Oxford University Press, 2004).

[37] A Lyall, 'Hewitt, James, First Viscount Lifford (d 1789), Lord Chancellor of Ireland' in *Oxford Dictionary of National Biography* (n 17).

[38] GFR Barker, rev Anne Pimlott Baker, 'Nares, Sir George (1716–1786), Judge' in *Oxford Dictionary of National Biography* (n 17).

[39] This historical (though ahistorical) understanding of English constitutional history was common among those who asserted political freedom and the primacy of Parliament and the people over the Crown in the sixteenth to eighteenth centuries. See JP Reid, *The Ancient Constitution and the Origins of Anglo-American Liberty* (DeKalb, Ill., Northern Illinois University Press, 2005) esp ch 5 ('Forensic Techniques of Ancient Constitutionalism').

Bar in 1748.[40] He was appointed Serjeant-at-Law in 1763, in which year he became counsel to John Wilkes, thereafter being associated legally and politically with him and other radical critics of the government. In 1768 he was elected an MP for Middlesex at a by-election soon after Wilkes's election, and in the House he challenged the decision to deprive Wilkes of his seat. Outside Parliament and the courts, too, he was a leading campaigner for Wilkes. He and Wilkes were not friends, however. It has been written that: 'A man of moral and political rectitude, Glynn had never found Wilkes a kindred spirit.'[41] Lord Eldon recorded that Wilkes told King George III that Glynn was his counsel, not his friend: 'he loves sedition and licentiousness, which I never delighted in. In fact, Sir, he was a Wilkite, *which I never was*'. The King, according to Eldon, 'said the confidence and the humour of the man made him forget at the moment his impudence'.[42]

John Dunning, another of Wilkes's counsel, was a West Countryman, educated at his local grammar school and trained in the office of his father, an attorney in Ashburton, Devon, before being called to the Bar in 1756. In London he was associated with populist campaigners Lloyd Kenyon and John Horne Tooke, and worked alongside Glynn, getting a break when Glynn was taken ill and handed his cases to Dunning. He was not, however, anti-authoritarian or straightforwardly libertarian. He agreed to become Solicitor General in 1768 in the Rockingham-Grafton ministry which combined Pittites with Whigs, and entered Parliament, supporting Lord Camden (then Lord Chancellor) against attacks by Burke and Grenville in the Commons. Dunning resigned in 1770, being unable to support the government's decision, against his advice, to move for Wilkes' expulsion from the Commons without giving him an opportunity to defend himself against accusations of seditious libel. In opposition, he opposed the government's policy towards American colonists and supported their right to resist the government. In 1780 he defeated the North government on the motion that 'the influence of the Crown has increased, is increasing and ought to be diminished'.[43] Nevertheless, he was even-handed in his legal practice. For example, in 1772 Dunning appeared (ultimately unsuccessfully) for the slave owner, Stewart, to defend habeas corpus proceedings brought by Glynn and a team of counsel acting pro bono on behalf of the escaped slave, Somerset, whom Stewart had recaptured and detained on a ship on the Thames with a view to returning him to America.[44]

---

[40] For biographical outlines, see PDG Thomas, 'Glynn, John (bap 1722, d 1779), Lawyer and Politician' in *Oxford Dictionary of National Biography* (n 17), Woolrych (n 34) ii, 605–33.

[41] Thomas (n 40).

[42] H Twiss (ed), *The Public and Private Life of Lord Chancellor Eldon, with Selections from His Correspondence*, 3 vols (London, John Murray, 1844) vol 2, 356, quoted in PDG Thomas, *John Wilkes: A Friend to Liberty* (Oxford, Oxford University Press, 1996) 219.

[43] J Cannon, 'Dunning, John, First Baron Asburton (1731–1783), Barrister and Politician' in *Oxford Dictionary of National Biography* (n 17).

[44] *Somerset v Stewart* (1772) Lofft 1; 98 ER 499. Francis Hargrave, junior counsel for Somerset, made the decisively effective submission on the second hearing. See Poser (n 22) 292–97; P Byrne, *Belle: The True Story of Dido Belle* (London, William Collins, 2014) ch 10.

Of other counsel who appeared for the plaintiffs in the litigation, James Wallace subsequently became Solicitor General and then Attorney General in North's government in 1783, going into Parliament. James Eyre (baptised 1734, died 1799), who was from a clerical background, was educated at Winchester College and St John's College, Oxford. Called to the Bar in 1755, he practised as counsel to the City of London, which was dominated by supporters of Pitt, until the Council elected him Recorder of London in 1763, a position he held when he appeared for Wilkes against Wood in 1763. In that role he made a powerful submission against general warrants. However, he became less inclined to stand against governmental measures, being willing to support exceptional measures to preserve public order during the Wilkite riots in 1770. In 1772 he was appointed a serjeant, knighted and given a commission as a Baron of Exchequer. In 1793 he became Lord Chief Justice of Common Pleas. In his judicial roles, he showed great severity in not only imposing but also, with above-average frequency, recommending the execution of death sentences. In the 1790s he tried to expand liability for treason through his rulings.[45] It seems that his argument for Wilkes was partly a reflection of a politic attachment to Pitt's party and partly sheer professionalism; by inclination he was no bleeding-heart liberal. Who paid for this stellar assemblage of legal luminaries? In the case of the defendant ministers and King's Messengers, the Crown footed the bill. For the plaintiffs, the funding was substantial and was politically motivated. The cost was borne in the form of loans made by Lord Temple, supporter of Pitt, encourager of Wilkes, and the brother of George Grenville, who had initiated the clampdown on the opposition press which led to the litigation.[46] The loans were to be reimbursed out of damages and costs obtained at trial or, failing that, by Wilkes personally. This again highlights the intimacy and interconnectedness of the political and legal elite in the 1760s.

E. Concluding Reflections

To sum up, the foremost counsel, judges and politicians were drawn from a small group, whose members were not necessarily well connected (though some were) or scions of legal families, but made their way mainly through their professional abilities. The leaders of the Bar often became parliamentarians,

---

[45] D Hay, 'Eyre, Sir James (bap 1734, d 1799), Judge' in *Oxford Dictionary of National Biography* (n 17).
[46] WJ Smith (ed), *The Grenville Papers: Being the Correspondence of Richard Grenville, Earl Temple, K.G., and the Right Hon: George Grenville, Their Friends and Contemporaries,* 4 vols (London, John Murray, 1852–53) ii, 57 (letter from Wilkes to Earl Temple, 25 May 1763 seeking a loan of £200); 59–60 (same to same, 5 June 1763: Wilkes has paid Beardmore's account of £150, and Beardmore wants £250 more; Wilkes requests £400 or £500 from Earl Temple); 142–43 (Earl Temple to Wilkes, 20 October 1763, enclosing promissory note for £500 to pay off expenses).

although in most cases they entered Parliament either when they were appointed as a Law Officer or as something of a sideline. They might provide legal advice to the government or opposition, though if they were appointed King's Serjeant, they were allowed to act only in the interests of the Crown. Many went on to hold senior judicial offices, in which they were usually respected for the way in which they performed their duties. In a few cases they returned to Parliament with a peerage later, particularly if they became Lord Chancellor, taking on an overtly political role. Even when they were political or legal opponents, the small size of the group made it important to be able to get on with each other. One example suffices. During the trial of actions on 6 and 7 July 1763 brought by journeymen printers wrongly arrested for involvement in producing *The North Briton* No 45, the Attorney General strongly attacked both *The North Briton* and Wilkes, who was present. But, as Wilkes reported: 'He was personally very civil. The Solicitor General very decent, and in his way polite, except to the jury.'[47]

III. POLITICAL PROPAGANDA AND THE LAW

During the 1750s and 1760s, weekly newspapers were instruments of populist politics, whereby politicians appealed to ordinary people for support against, and over the heads of, ministers and Parliament. Pitt's supporters in particular were seeking to exploit the strength of their support in the country. Pitt, who campaigned against what he saw as the corrupting effect of patronage and sought to put English commercial interests at the heart of British foreign policy, enjoyed a strong following in the City of London (where the Common Council was solidly behind him) and other commercial centres. When roused by Pitt's rhetoric and the savage satire of the opposition press, crowds could be brought to the point of violence against the government and its supporters. As George Rudé showed, rioters were predominantly relatively respectable labourers, and violence tended to be against property and the propertied class, foreigners and Catholics, and in favour of popular causes or slogans such as 'Wilkes and Liberty'. Criminal ne'er-do-wells were in the minority.[48] The press helped to keep feelings running high among people whose commercial interests and notions of patriotism were engaged, and it scared the government.

In 1755, a new weekly paper, *The Monitor, or British Householder*, was established to support the efforts made by Pitt and his supporters in Parliament to force the Whig government, led by Newcastle, to pursue British

---

[47] Smith (n 46) ii, 72. The Attorney General was Sir Charles Yorke; the Solicitor General was the notoriously curmudgeonly Sir Fletcher Norton.

[48] G Rudé, *The Crowd in History 1730–1848*, rev edn (London, Lawrence & Wishart, 1981) ch 3, esp 60–63.

interests more vigorously in the Seven Years' War and to challenge corruption in government. According to information which Jonathan Scott laid in 1762 before Edward Weston JP, an assistant to the Earl of Halifax (Secretary of State for the North), Scott, Arthur Beardmore (an attorney), John Shebbeare, John Entick and several other men met at the Horn Tavern. They agreed that Shebbeare and Entick would each receive £200 a year for writing and editing the paper, which was to be funded by subscription. Scott would take any profits. However, according to Scott, Shebbeare wrote relatively little and received only £50 as part payment of his first year's entitlement, after which he was excluded. Beardmore and Entick took the money that came in. It could well have been a grievance over this that led Scott to lay the information against Beardmore and Entick. The first issue appeared on 9 August 1755 and the paper quickly established itself as a highly effective thorn in the government's side.

The authors had colourful backgrounds. Shebbeare had practised as a physician in Bristol and styled himself 'Dr' (though his medical qualification was doubted). He turned to political satire as being more profitable. By 1755, he had already been the subject of legal action by the government over his first novel, *The Marriage Act* (1754). This attacked Lord Hardwicke's Marriage Act, passed the previous year, which Shebbeare portrayed as upholding the interests of the propertied elite by allowing them to force their children to marry for the purpose of social and financial advantage, despite their feelings being engaged elsewhere. He was arrested for contempt of Parliament, but was released. The following year he published *Lydia*, a romantic novel which attacked Newcastle's government for inadequately defending British interests in North America against French aggression. Also in 1755, he published *Letters on the English Nation*, a satirical work which claimed to be a translation of an assessment by an Italian Jesuit criticising the decline of British morals, and *A Letter to the People of England*, the first of a series of pamphlets criticising the government for its handling of the Seven Years' War with France, which was just beginning. Shebbeare argued that the government's support for George II's Hanoverian interests in Europe caused it to sacrifice Britain's commercial and imperial interests in North America, and alleged that the Whigs were using the war to consolidate their hold on power. In the third *Letter*, he praised Pitt to the skies, but after moving on from *The Monitor*, he became less supportive of Pitt and John Wilkes. In 1758, by which time Pitt had gone into government with Newcastle, Shebbeare was arrested again for seditious libel in his sixth *Letter to the People of England*. Prosecuted by Charles Pratt, the Attorney General (previously, like Shebbeare, an opponent of the government, but now part of it), and convicted after a trial before Lord Mansfield CJ in the Court of King's Bench, he was sentenced to pay a fine of £5, to serve three years' imprisonment and to stand in the pillory at three locations in London, as well as being required to find sureties for his good behaviour for seven years to the value of £1,000. This caused great hardship to him and his family.[49] He never forgave Pitt for having failed to protect him against the consequences of his publication and became a supporter of King George III and Bute, and attacked Wilkes.[50]

The other main author of *The Monitor*, John Entick, had a more conventional background. In the late 1720s he had published learning aids for students of Latin and Greek and a book on the evidence for Christianity. *The Monitor* seems to have been his first foray into political satire.[51] Nevertheless, he was very effective in attacking the government, particularly after Pitt resigned from it in 1761. In numbers 357, 358, 360, 373, 376, 378 and 380 of *The Monitor*, he stung the government of Bute by his allegorical discussion of the first-century Roman politician 'Sejanus' (Lucius Aelius Seianus, a friend of the Emperor Tiberius who used his political influence to strengthen his own position in government and have his opponents removed). The government assumed, rightly, that Entick intended readers to associate Sejanus' relationship to Tiberius with Bute's hold over King George III.

Bute used both law and propaganda in his attempt to counter this. However, the government-sponsored journal, *The True Briton*, largely written by Thomas Smollett, could not match the popularity and entertainment value of *The Monitor*. The publicity war moved further against the government in 1762, when a new publication, *The North Briton*, was founded specifically to attack Bute (the 'North Briton', ie, Scot, of the title) and support Pitt's criticisms of Bute's ministry. Largely written by John Wilkes, with contributions by Charles Churchill, *The North Briton* launched sustained, scurrilous attacks on the King and his ministers. Wilkes and Churchill were true rabble-rousers. Wilkes was from a prosperous trading family and (despite being unusually unattractive to look at) caught the eyes of a number of influential people as a result of his charm, intelligence and wit. One such person was Thomas Potter, a lawyer, political associate of George Grenville and MP for Aylesbury. He introduced Wilkes to the 'Medmenham Monks', a group of libertines who held blasphemous orgies in a parody of the Catholic mass.

---

[49] When he stood in the pillory, however, the under-sheriff in charge was Arthur Beardmore, his former collaborator. Contrary to normal practice, Beardmore raised the upper board of the pillory so that Shebbeare was able to stand upright. The Attorney General, Pratt, brought proceedings against Beardmore for contempt of court, and Lord Mansfield CJ fined Beardmore £50. J Almon, *Biographical, Literary, and Political Anecdotes, of Several of the Most Eminent Persons of the Present Age*, 3 vols (London, Longman and Seeley, 1797) i, 373–76, cited in Poser (n 22) 268–69.

[50] G le Grys Norgate, 'Shebbeare, John (1709–1788)', *Dictionary of National Biography*, vol xviii, 1–4; M John Cladwell, 'Shebbeare, John (1709–1788), Physician and Political Writer' in *Oxford Dictionary of National Biography* (n 17).

[51] Alongside it he was writing *A New Naval History*, published in 1757, in which he styled himself 'the Rev. John Entick, M.A.', although there is no evidence to support his claim to holy orders or a degree. J Humphreys, rev P Wilson, 'Entick, John (c 1703–1773), Author' in *Oxford Dictionary of National Biography* (n 17).

Potter admired Wilkes' *Essay on Woman*, an obscene parody of Pope's *Essay on Man*, for which Wilkes was to be prosecuted for obscene libel in 1763. In 1757, he induced Wilkes to pay about £7,000 for an arrangement whereby Pitt moved from Okehampton to a Bristol constituency, Potter moved to be MP for Okehampton, and Wilkes was elected for Aylesbury. To pay for this, Potter introduced Wilkes to moneylenders who, according to Potter's biographer, were to ruin Wilkes financially.[52] In the meantime, however, Wilkes became a demagogic supporter of Pitt and from 1762 was a prime mover in the production of *The North Briton*, for which he wrote in his customary, uncompromisingly vitriolic style.[53]

Charles Churchill, Wilkes's collaborator on *The North Briton*, managed to fit a world of dissolution into his short life. A vicar's son, Churchill was a promising scholar at Westminster School, but as a teenager was party to a 'Fleet marriage'[54] with a woman who was to bear him three children. Ordained in 1754, he succeeded his father as curate and lecturer of St John's, Smith Square, in London after his father's death in 1758, but was short of money and narrowly avoided arrest for debt. Churchill and his wife separated in 1761, the year in which he achieved financial success as author of a satirical poem, 'The Rosciad'. This allowed him to pay off his creditors in full and give his wife an allowance. He was extravagant and dissipated, despite being a clergyman. In 1762, he and Wilkes embarked on *The North Briton*, which Churchill edited, and, though writing fewer than half as many numbers as Wilkes, was said by the printer, Kearsley, to have taken all the profits. Churchill became a member of the Medmenham Monks and was a womaniser. In 1763, he seduced and eloped with the 15-year-old daughter of his landlord. In 1764, perhaps to avoid the risk of arrest for assaulting his printer, Dryden Leach, he visited Boulogne to see Wilkes, who had decamped to France following his arrest for libel, and died there, aged 32.[55]

Notwithstanding their authors' questionable morals, *The Monitor* and *The North Briton* were effective in stirring anti-government feelings and causing more than annoyance to the King. The ministry resorted to law in order to combat them. Treason, which had been widely interpreted in the seventeenth century, was regarded by the mid-eighteenth century as involving more than mere words; some act to give effect to threats against the Crown had to be proved (although, as noted earlier, one of the counsel for the Wilkites, Mr Recorder Eyre, was to argue in the 1790s for a far

[52] RDE Eagles, 'Potter, Thomas (1718?–1759)' in *Oxford Dictionary of National Biography* (n 17).

[53] Thomas (n 42) 3–22.

[54] 'Fleet marriages' were relatively informal, without the need for bans, and so were popular with eloping couples. They became unlawful under Lord Hardwicke's Marriage Act in 1754, the measure which Shebbeare attacked, with dire consequences for him.

[55] J Sambrook, 'Churchill, Charles (1732–1764)' in *Oxford Dictionary of National Biography* (n 17); Thomas (n 42) 20–26, 59.

wider definition). Seditious libel was far easier to invoke. It was a loosely defined common law offence. In describing Wilkes's alleged sedition, the House of Commons referred to insolence and contumely towards the King, gross aspersions on both Houses of Parliament, defiance of the authority of the legislature, and tending to alienate the affections of the people from the King, induce them to disobey the law and to excite insurrections against the government. This fairly reflects the common law. In the sixteenth and seventeenth centuries, the crime had been used to inflict severe punishments merely for speech against the monarch or government, but during the first half of the eighteenth century, David Cressy tells us that governments were increasingly willing to ignore mere speech. 'The state no longer felt imperilled by dangerous words'; however, Cressy adds a telling caveat: 'so long as those words were not distributed through writing'.[56] *The Monitor* and *The North Briton* crossed that line.

Nevertheless, it proved difficult to secure evidence against the authors and publishers. The government thought that its chance had come when, on 11 October 1762, Jonathan Scott, who had been selling *The Monitor* at the Black Swan in Pater Noster Row, deposed before a Justice of the Peace that the issue published on 22 May 1762, which contained the article concerning 'Sejanus' (understood to refer to Bute), had been printed from a manuscript which had been written in the hand of David Meredith, clerk to Arthur Beardmore.

On receiving the information, Lord Halifax[57] on 3 November 1762 wrote to the Attorney General, Sir Charles Yorke, and the Solicitor General, Sir Fletcher Norton, enclosing copies of *The Monitor, or British Householder*, Nos 357, 358, 360, 373, 376 and 378, and seeking their opinion as to 'how far the Contents of these papers or any of them maybe held to be libellous in the Eye of the Law, and subject the Authors, Printers and Publishers of them to Prosecution'.[58] On 4 November, the Law Officers replied that they

---

[56] D Cressy, *Dangerous Talk: Scandalous, Seditious, and Treasonable Speech in Pre-modern England* (Oxford, Oxford University Press, 2010) 235 and 242–44.

[57] George Montagu Dunk (1716–71). George Montagu was the son of the first Earl of Halifax and was educated at Eton and Trinity College, Cambridge, where he was reputed to be a very brilliant student. Succeeding to his father's title in 1739, he married Ann, daughter of William Richards, afterwards Dunk, who had inherited the estate of Sir Thomas Dunk on condition that he and his male heirs thereafter took the name 'Dunk'. He was a Whig, but opposed Walpole, and held office in the household of the Prince of Wales; however, he later sided with Henry Pelham and his brother Newcastle. As a notably hard-working President of the Board of Trade, he sought to exercise control over colonial appointments, but the Seven Years' War thwarted his efforts to reform colonial affairs and he resigned when his plans were blocked. In 1761 he was appointed Lord Lieutenant of Ireland in succession to Bute and was well liked there, combining the post in 1762 with that of First Lord of the Admiralty. In September 1762 he became Secretary of State for the North, in which role he became embroiled with *The Monitor* and *The North Briton*. In 1763 he moved to be Secretary of State for the South, but left office on the fall of Grenville's government in 1765 and died six years later.

[58] BL Add MS 22131, f 4.

'are humbly of Opinion, that the same are Libels, in consideration of Law, and that the Authors, Printers, and publishers are liable to be prosecuted'.[59] Halifax accordingly issued warrants on 6 November, requiring the King's Messengers in Ordinary to search for Beardmore and Entick as people implicated in the production of those numbers of *The Monitor*, and to seize them and their books and papers and take them to Halifax to be examined. Both warrants were in the same form. That for Beardmore read:

> [Seal] George Montague Dunk, Earl of Halifax, Viscount Sunbury and Baron Halifax, one of the Lords of His Majesty's Most Honorable Privy Council, Lieutenant General of His Majesty's Forces, Lord Lieutenant General and General Governor of the Kingdom of Ireland, and Principal Secretary of State, & cᵃ.

> These are, in His Majesty's Name, to authorise and require you, taking a Constable to your Assistance, to make strict and diligent search for Arthur Beardmore, the Author, or one concerned in the writing of several Weekly very seditious Papers, entituled, The Monitor, or British Householder, No. 357 358 360 373 376 379 and 380—London, printed for J. Wilson and J. Fell, in Pater-Noster Row, which contain gross and scandalous Reflections, and Invectives, upon His Majesty's Government, and upon the Houses of Parliament; And Him, having found, You are to seize and apprehend, and to bring, together with his Books and Papers, in safe Custody, before me, to be examined concerning the Premises, and further dealt with according to Law: In the due Execution whereof all Mayors, Sheriffs, Justices of the Peace, Constables and all other His Majesty's Civil and Military, and loving Subjects whom it may concern, are to be aiding and assisting to you, as there shall be Occasion. And for so doing, This shall be your Warrant. Given at Sᵗ James's the Sixth Day of November 1762 in the Third Year of His Majesty's Reign.

> [Signed] Dunk Halifax
> To Nathan Carrington,
> James Watson, Thoˢ: Ardran, &
> Robert Blackmore Four of His
> Majesty's Messengers in Ordinary.[60]

On 11 November 1762, the four King's Messengers in Ordinary[61] executed the warrants. They visited the home of John Entick in the parish of St Dunstan in Stepney, now in the East End of London, entered by force and stayed for four hours. They searched several rooms and looked in a bureau, a writing-desk and several drawers, reading and examining several papers.

---

[59] ibid f 22.

[60] ibid f 24.

[61] The term 'in Ordinary' signifies that they occupied substantive offices rather than being employed on an ad hoc basis. The King's Messengers were employed both to carry messages and to arrest state prisoners.

They found nothing seditious, but detained Entick and took away some of his books and papers. At Beardmore's house, they searched his private and public office, arrested him, removed books and papers, and detained him and his clerk, David Meredith, at the messengers' house for six days, during which time Beardmore could not conduct his business as an attorney, before they were released on giving recognisances for their good behaviour and to appear before the King's Bench.[62] The Messengers also went to the premises of the booksellers and printers, Wilson and Fell, against whom warrants were issued, and took them and some of their books and papers into custody.

IV. THE CAMPAIGNS IN THE COURTS
AND PARLIAMENT

A. Litigation Arising from Action Taken against *The Monitor*

In the Court of Common Pleas, Entick brought separate actions against the King's Messengers for trespass to land and goods and against the Earl of Halifax for false imprisonment. Beardmore and the printers Wilson and Fell brought similar actions. Meredith sued the Earl for false imprisonment. It is at least possible that the inspiration for claiming against Halifax as well as the Messengers came from Lord Temple.[63]

As already noted, it was unusual for politically controversial cases to be tried in the Court of Common Pleas. King's Bench was the forum for actions brought by or against the Crown, as most political cases were. The Court of Common Pleas, which heard cases between subjects, was open because the action was, in form, brought against the Secretary of State and the King's

---

[62] They were discharged from their recognisances on 22 June 1763, no charges having been brought against them. *Annual Register*, vol 6 (1763) 82.

[63] The actions against Lord Halifax seem to have been something of an afterthought. On 24 July 1763, a few days after the journeymen printers arrested on general warrants issued in connection with *The North Briton* No 45 had secured large damages against the King's Messengers who had detained them, Earl Temple wrote from Stowe to Wilkes, 'On talking over the business of the Devils [ie, printer's men], your friends, it is a Q. here whether it may not be right for them to bring provisional actions with notice against the Secretaries of State; for in case the Bill of Exceptions should prevail, the six months will be elapsed, and their worships, the sage Secretaries, will escape the Devils scot free.' (Smith (n 46) ii, 78–79) On 26 July, Wilkes replied: 'I have sent to Mr. Beardmore [attorney for the plaintiffs, but also plaintiff in his own right in connection with *The Monitor*] to give him the full idea of what is proposed, that he may lay it before the Sergeant [Glynn] and Mr. Dunning' (ibid 80–81). It does not seem that Leach's men took up Temple's suggestion, but on 2 September 1763 Wilson and Fell, the printers of *The Monitor*, together with Beardmore and Entick, commenced actions against Halifax as well as the King's Messengers for false imprisonment: *Annual Register*, vol 7 (1764) 98. (Entick and Beardmore had already started actions against the King's Messengers alone for trespass to land and goods.)

Messengers as individuals. This Court was the more attractive forum to supporters of Pitt, given Pratt CJ's personal and political closeness to Pitt. In the Court of King's Bench, by contrast, Lord Mansfield CJ had links to Newcastle and the Whigs going back to his days at Westminster School.

The legal issues raised by the warrants concerning *The Monitor* were not straightforward. The authorisations for arrests, being directed against named individuals, were not amenable to the constitutional argument against general warrants. In actions for false imprisonment, the questions were whether Halifax was competent to issue the warrants, either as a justice or conservator of the peace or as Secretary of State, and whether the King's Messengers were protected by the warrant at common law or under the Constables' Protection Act 1750. In actions for trespass to goods, in respect of which the warrants were general in the sense that they left an almost unlimited discretion to the Messengers as to what books and papers to take, the issues were whether such warrants were valid and whether the Messengers were protected by them if they were acting in accordance with them.

There was a good deal of procedural manoeuvring in these cases. On 29 February 1764, at a hearing at The Guildhall in relation to the actions brought by Beardmore, Pratt CJ agreed to try both those against the King's Messengers and that against Lord Halifax together, and set 4 May for the trial. But it seems that counsel for Halifax decided not to cooperate, probably to increase the number of hearings and hence the costs accumulating for the plaintiff. At any rate, only Beardmore's action against the King's Messengers was heard on 4 May. Pratt CJ directed the jury that the arrest of Beardmore and seizure of his papers was unlawful, apparently because they had been taken before Lovell Stanhope for examination, rather than Lord Halifax in person as the warrant had instructed; however, he counselled the jury to moderation when assessing damages, pointing out that the Messengers 'were nothing but servants, and consequently could not be considered as materially culpable in the intent'. Despite this, the special jury returned a verdict for Beardmore with damages of £1,000.[64] Some weeks later, on a motion to set aside the verdict because the damages were excessive, there were two days' argument, during the course of which Beardmore offered to give up the verdict if Lord Halifax would agree to have the action between them tried and abide by the outcome; however, counsel for the Messengers were not authorised to agree to that on behalf of Halifax and the verdict was affirmed.[65]

On 21 June 1764, on a writ of enquiry determined at The Guildhall before Mr Bennet, Secondary (assistant) to the Wood Street Compter (a Serjeant-at-Law, exercising a function equivalent to the King's Bench Masters) and a special jury consisting of one person from each ward of the City of London, damages were assessed in the actions brought by Wilson and Fell against the

---

[64] *Annual Register*, vol 7 (1764) 72–73.
[65] ibid 73; *Beardmore v Carrington* (1764) 2 Wils KB 244; 95 ER 790.

King's Messengers in the sum of £300 for each plaintiff, with total costs of £24 10s, subject to a writ of error being sought.[66]

A month later, on 20 July, in the Court of Common Pleas at Westminster, Pratt CJ presided over the trial of *Entick v Carrington*, in which Entick sued the King's Messengers for trespass by forcible entry and seizing papers, and for false imprisonment. The special jury on this occasion was willing to bring in a special verdict, awarding damages of £300 and the remarkably small sum of £2 costs to the plaintiff if the judges should decide that, on the facts which the jury found, the Messengers had acted unlawfully.[67]

There followed a long delay before the legal implications of the special verdict were decided. In the interim, the Court of Common Pleas tried the actions for false imprisonment brought by Beardmore, Wilson, Fell, Meredith and Entick against Lord Halifax. On 11 December 1764, a special jury awarded Beardmore damages of £500 (in addition to the £1,000 which he had already been awarded in his action against the King's Messengers). The next day, before four different special juries, Wilson was awarded £40 in damages, Fell £10, and Entick £20 (sums which took account of the £300 which they had each already been awarded in their actions against the King's Messengers). Meredith, Beardmore's clerk, who had not previously been awarded damages, received £200.[68] (A rule of court had provided that the action 'shall abide the Event of the ... Cause Beardmore agst. The Earl of Halifax'.)[69]

Six more months passed before the Court of Common Pleas finally got round to hearing argument on the legal implications of the special verdict delivered the previous July in *Entick v Carrington*. On 18 June 1765, Serjeant Leigh represented Entick, and Burland, King's Serjeant, represented the King's Messengers. Pratt CJ asked counsel to consider in a second day or argument whether a justice of the peace who issues a warrant which there was no power to issue or a person executing a warrant who seizes items which lie outside the scope of the warrant could rely on the protection of the statute: 'I desire that every point of this case may be argued to the bottom; for I shall think myself bound, when I come to give judgment, to give my opinion upon every point in the case.'[70]

The hearing resumed in Michaelmas Term 1765, with Serjeant Glynn for Entick and Nares, King's Serjeant, for the defendants. After further exhaustive argument, the court offered the defendants a further day of argument, but counsel for the defendants declined the favour,[71] and judgment was reserved. On 27 November 1765, on behalf of the whole court, the Lord

[66] *Annual Register*, vol 7 (1764) 80–81.
[67] ibid 87.
[68] ibid 112–13.
[69] See the note 'A State of the Causes ag[st]. the late Secretaries of State and the Messengers', f 1, in the bundle of Treasury Solicitor' papers in TNA TS 11/3237, Part I, probably late autumn 1765.
[70] (1765) 2 Wils KB 275, 286; 95 ER 807, 814.
[71] See the note 'A State of the Causes ag[st]. the late Secretaries of State and the Messengers' (n 69) f 1.

Chief Justice, speaking for two hours and 20 minutes, delivered judgment for the plaintiff.[72] Two reports of the judgment are extant. One, published more or less contemporarily, was by Serjeant Wilson in his King's Bench and Common Pleas Reports. This was based on Wilson's note of the judgment and is clearly far from complete.[73] The fuller version was published in 1776 by Francis Hargrave, in his 11-volume collection of *State Trials from Henry IV to 19 George III* which was to form the basis of what we know as *Howell's State Trials*. Hargrave used Wilson's report of the arguments, but instead of his report of the judgment, he used what he said was a copy of the carefully prepared text from which Pratt spoke when giving judgment. This is the text which now appears in volume 19 of *Howell's State Trials*. How did Hargrave come upon this text? The report in *Howell's State Trials* includes Hargrave's explanatory note, which illustrates both the meticulous care which he devoted to pioneering the publication of legal manuscripts and the prolixity and tortuousness of his style to which Professor Sir John Baker has drawn attention.[74] Hargrave explains that, while most of his report is drawn from Serjeant Wilson's report, he:

> ... has the pleasing satisfaction to present to the reader the Judgment itself at length, as delivered by the Lord Chief Justice of the Common-Pleas from written notes. It was not without some difficulty, that the copy of this Judgment was obtained by the Editor. He has reason to believe, that the original, most excellent and most valuable as its contents are, was not deemed worthy of preservation by its author, but was actually committed to the flames. Fortunately, the Editor remembered to have formerly seen a copy of the Judgment in the hands of a friend; and upon application to him, it was immediately obtained, with liberty to the Editor to make use of it at his discretion. Before, however, he presumed to consult his own wishes in the case, the Editor took care to convince himself, both that the copy was authentic, and that the introduction of it into this Collection would not give offence. Indeed, as to the authenticity of the Judgment, except in some trifling inaccuracies, the probable effect of careless transcribing, a first reading left the Editor's mind without a doubt on the subject. But it was a respectful delicacy due to the noble lord by whom the Judgment was delivered, not to publish it, without first endeavouring to know, whether such a step was likely to be displeasing to his Lordship; and though from the want of any authority from him, the Editor exposes himself to some risk of disapprobation, yet his precautions to guard against it, with the disinterestedness of his motives, will, he is confident, if ever it should become necessary to explain the circumstances to his lordship, be received as a very adequate apology for the liberty thus hazarded.[75]

Several facts make it likely that Hargrave's text was indeed a copy of the text which Pratt had prepared and, probably, circulated to his brothers

---

[72] *Annual Register*, vol 8 (1765) 146. The justices of Common Pleas who heard the case were Clive, Bathurst and Gould JJ.

[73] (1765) 2 Wils KB 275, 288–92; 95 ER 807, 815–18.

[74] JH Baker, 'Hargrave, Francis (1740/41–1821)' in *Oxford Dictionary of National Biography* (n 17).

[75] (1765) 19 St Tr 1029, 1029–30.

Clive, Bathurst and Gould JJ for their comments and approval before he delivered it in court. First, Hargrave was closely connected with the cast of characters involved in the litigation. He was a colleague of Serjeant Glynn and Mr Dunning. Although his practice was primarily in chancery matters, he acted in some notable common law cases. For example, in 1772, the year in which he published his volumes of *Howell's State Trials*, he appeared pro bono in the King's Bench, before Lord Mansfield CJ, for the slave in *Somerset v Stewart*, persuading the court that a slave who escaped after being brought to England could not lawfully be retaken in England by his former owner. He was led in the case by Mr Serjeant Glynn, but it was Hargrave whose argument was thought to have been decisive. (Dunning was against him on this occasion.) Second, Hargrave was a meticulously scholarly historian of the law, who pioneered the collection and archiving of modern legal manuscripts, and whose collecting of books and manuscripts brought him and his wife into straitened circumstances until the House of Commons voted in 1813, on a petition by his wife, to buy his collections for the nation for £8,000. (They are now in the British Museum.) There is no reason to doubt his account.

B. The Government Acts against *The North Briton*

The litigation concerning the government's action against *The Monitor* did not proceed in a vacuum. It ran alongside and was overtaken by events connected with John Wilkes and No 45 of *The North Briton*, published on 23 April 1763. Halifax, purporting to act as a justice or conservator of the peace, issued warrants requiring King's Messengers to search for and arrest the unnamed responsible for the publication of that issue of *The North Briton* and to seize their papers. On the morning of 30 April 1763, the four King's Messengers named in the warrant (Watson, Blackmore, Money and Man) went to Wilkes' house, accompanied by a constable (Chisholm). After three hours' searching, Wilkes was taken away to appear before Lord Halifax. Immediately thereafter, Robert Wood, a scholar, traveller and MP who was then an Under-Secretary of State to Lord Halifax, and Mr Lovell Stanhope (who was to become an Under-Secretary to Halifax the following year) arrived. Wilkes claimed that Wood had actively participated in searching his house, although this was disputed.

Three of the King's Messengers (Money, Watson and Blackmore) also entered the premises of a printer, Dryden Leach, and arrested him and about 12 of his journeymen. This was a serious mistake; the printer was actually one Kearsley. The error was probably that of the Treasury Solicitor, Philip Carteret Webb, who knew that Wilkes and Leach were regularly in touch with each other and may have jumped to the conclusion that Leach and his employees must have been printing No 45 of *The North Briton*. It was an expensive mistake, since it meant that the warrant, even if legal, did not authorise their arrest. Leach was detained in prison for five days. Huckle, one of the journeymen, was held for about six hours by Money, who treated him to beefsteaks and beer.

Wilkes sought habeas corpus in the Court of Common Pleas before Pratt CJ and his colleagues. For Wilkes, Serjeant Glynn advanced three grounds for challenging the arrest and detention: first, that the Secretary of State's warrant was illegal because he had had no power to issue it; second, that the warrant was formally invalid because it did not specify the words which were alleged to be seditious; and, third, that as a Member of Parliament while Parliament was sitting, he was protected from arrest by parliamentary privilege in all matters other than treason, felony and breach of the peace. After reserving judgment for three days, Pratt CJ, speaking for the Court, rejected both grounds of challenge to the validity of the warrant, but upheld Wilkes's claim to parliamentary privilege, holding that privilege protected members from legal process except in respect of treason, felony and breach of the peace. Sedition, he decided, was not a breach of the peace, though it tended towards one, and it was clearly neither treason nor felony.[76] This restrictive understanding of parliamentary privilege surprised the government and at least some judges. The Lord Chancellor, Lord Henley, who was presiding over another court in Westminster Hall at the time, whispered to another judge: 'By God! Pratt is mad.'[77] Wilkes was released to cries of 'Wilkes and Liberty!' from his supporters.

C. Ministers Turn to Parliament

The ratio for Pratt's decision brought a triangular tension into play between the privileges of the two Houses of Parliament, the powers of the government in matters of national security and law enforcement, and the competence of ordinary courts to decide the scope of Parliament's privileges. These issues divided parliamentarians along party lines; those who supported Grenville's government favoured a restrictive view of parliamentary privilege, while Wilkes' supporters, who were mainly followers of Pitt, took a wider view. The government responded to the judgment by moving the issue into Parliament. On 15 November 1763, the Chancellor of the Exchequer laid before the House of Commons a copy of No 45 of *The North Briton* together with the information showing Wilkes to be the author of it,

---

[76] *The Case of John Wilkes, Esq* (1763) 2 Wils Rep 150, 159–60; (1763) 19 St Tr 981, 990.
[77] Thomas (n 42) 31.

'His Majesty being desirous to show all possible Attention to the Privileges of the House of Commons, in every Instance wherein they can be supposed to be concerned'. The Commons resolved *nemine contradicente* that:

> ... the Paper intituled, 'The *North Briton* No 45' is a false, scandalous, and seditious Libel, containing Expressions of the most unexampled Insolence and Contumely towards His Majesty, the grossest Aspersions upon both Houses of Parliament, and the most audacious Defiance of the Authority of the whole Legislature; and most manifestly tending to alienate the Affections of the People from His Majesty, to withdraw them from their Obedience to the Laws of the Realm, and to excite them to traitorous Insurrections against His Majesty's Government.

> *Resolved*, that the said Paper be burnt by the Hands of the common Hangman.

On 24 November, after debates which divided members on party lines (the Whigs opposing the resolution), the House of Commons resolved, by 258 votes to 133, 'That Privilege of Parliament does not extend to the Case of writing and publishing seditious Libels, nor ought to be allowed to obstruct the ordinary Course of the Laws, in the speedy and effectual Prosecution of so heinous and dangerous an Offence'.

On 29 November, the House of Lords resolved by a large majority to agree with the Commons as to the scope of privilege, but 17 dissenting peers argued at length that there was no precedent for treating libel as falling outside a Member's privileges.[78] Two days later, the Lords resolved to agree with the Commons that the paper should be burnt by the common hangman on 3 December at the Royal Exchange in the City of London. As Thomas observes, this was either 'unthinkingly obtuse or deliberately provocative', but either way 'the result was predictable'. The City mob, solidly for Pitt and Wilkes, did not allow the burning to take place. A crowd, throwing mud and shouting 'Wilkes and Liberty', prevented it, and the Lord Mayor and his officials made no attempt to contain them.[79] Nevertheless, on 19 January 1764, the House of Commons went further, resolving 'That it appears to this House that the said *John Wilkes* Esquire is guilty of Writing and Publishing the Paper ... which this House has voted to be a false, scandalous and seditious Libel' and 'That the said *John Wilkes*, Esquire be, for his said Offence, expelled this House'.[80]

From this point, the opposition, feeling that it was on stronger grounds arguing the legality of general warrants as a matter of principle than it had been when debating the merits of *The North Briton*, claimed to disapprove strongly of Wilkes, but pursued the issue of privilege as a protection for Parliament against the Crown and attacked general warrants as unlawful

---

[78] *The House of Commons Journals*, vol xxix, 667, 675; *The House of Lords Journals*, vol xxx, 426; (1763) 19 St Tr 981, 994–1000.

[79] Thomas (n 42) 45.

[80] *The House of Commons Journals*, vol xxix, 723.

weapons of arbitrary government. Supporters of Newcastle and Pitt complained that the actions of Halifax's Under-Secretary Robert Wood MP, Treasury Solicitor Philip Carteret Webb MP and three of the King's Messengers were breaches of privilege. The hearing of the complaint in the House of Commons began on 13 February 1764, being adjourned at midnight, and continued the next day. Countering the claim that general warrants were illegal, the King's Messengers presented examples going back over 100 years, including some issued by Pitt as Prime Minister (though Pitt retorted that he had used them only in wartime and not in respect of libels). Ultimately, in the early hours of 15 February, the government won a vote to acquit the five defendants. The debate on a further motion to resolve 'That a general warrant for apprehending and seizing the authors, printers and publishers of a seditious libel, together with their papers, is not warranted by law' was adjourned until 17 February, when Attorney General Fletcher Norton moved to postpone the matter for a further four months to avoid prejudicing pending litigation, though he remarked that, were he a judge, he would pay no more attention to such a resolution 'than that of so many drunken porters'. But the opposition had strong support from those who saw the matter as an issue of liberty rather than of support for Wilkes. Even Charles Yorke, who had been Attorney General when Halifax had issued the warrants, asserted that they were illegal, claiming that he had not been consulted before they were issued. Once again, debate continued through the night, with the government narrowly carrying a motion to adjourn the House at 7.25 the next morning.[81]

D. Meanwhile, Back in Common Pleas, Civil Actions Had Begun over *The North Briton* No 45

The first actions to be tried were those brought by Leach's journeymen. They were the simplest to litigate because it was clear that they had not printed No 45 of *The North Briton*, so their arrests had been outside the warrant and no complex legal issues arose. On 6 July 1763 at Guildhall, before Pratt CJ and a special jury, Huckle, the journeyman printer who had been held for only six hours and very well treated, was awarded the vast sum of £300 damages, to the consternation of the government and its legal advisers.[82] The Court of Common Pleas (Pratt CJ and Bathurst J) rejected

---

[81] The issue was raised again in Parliament in 1766, when Yorke and Norton, now in opposition, said that they regarded general warrants of arrest as illegal, adding that they had not been able to express that view at the time of the *North Briton* warrants because they had not been consulted in time. See generally Thomas (n 42) 33–56.

[82] *Annual Register*, vol 6 (1763) 88.

an application to set the verdict aside on the ground that the damages were excessive.[83]

On the following day, Lindsay, another journeyman printer, was awarded £200, which by agreement between the parties was taken to determine 12 of the other 17 actions pending by journeymen.[84] As Wilkes, who was present, reported to Earl Temple, who was bankrolling the litigation, Pratt CJ followed the urgings of counsel for the defendants who wanted the jury to bring in special verdicts, which would have allowed the court to decide issues of law. Despite this, the City of London jury, solidly for Pitt, insisted on delivering general verdicts, thus keeping the initiative away from the judges. 'The trials', wrote Wilkes, '... have demonstrated to me where the strength of our cause really lies; for the merchants, as I had ever the honour of submitting to your Lordship, are firm in the cause of liberty.' As Wilkes noted, the scope of the decision was narrow, but an obiter dictum was more far-reaching.

> The cause only determines that a warrant of that nature, illegally executed, entitles to damages; but Pratt declared that he would not consider the Secretaries either as Justices or Conservators of the Peace. The origin of their power, he said, was uncertain; he believed it rested on prescription.[85]

Carried away with success, Wilkes now made a serious tactical error. Installing a printing press in his house, he secured the assistance of a printer, Williams, to reprint *The North Briton* in volumes and to print the *Essay on Woman*. Before the consequences of this could become clear, however, Wilkes enjoyed personal success in his action against Wood for trespass to goods, namely Wilkes' papers which had been seized in the search under the general warrant, allegedly on Wood's orders. Wood pleaded both the general issue and a special justification relying on Halifax's warrant.[86] The trial took place on 6 December 1763, before Pratt CJ and a special jury, starting at 9 am. Late that night, Pratt CJ summed up. He noted that the

---

[83] *Huckle v Money* (1763) 2 Wils KB 205; 95 ER 768.

[84] *Annual Register*, vol 6 (1763) 88. In the end, a settlement was reached whereby the 13 journeymen awarded £200 and costs agreed to accept £120 each and bear their own costs. Huckle, who had been awarded £300, accepted £175 and bore his own costs. *Annual Register*, vol 7 (1764) 81 (21 June 1764). This settlement does not seem to have been taken into account in the list of damages awarded in the litigation against Halifax, Wood and the King's Messengers in the bundle of papers of the Treasury Solicitor, TNA TS 11/3237.

[85] Wilkes to Temple, Saturday, 9 July 1763, in Smith (n 46) ii, 71–72.

[86] Initially Wood pleaded only the general issue, but four days before the date set for trial applied to withdraw that plea and instead to plead both the general issue and the special justification, also seeking a delay in the trial. For Wilkes, Serjeant Glynn objected that the delay would bring the trial into the parliamentary session, when Wood would be entitled to claim parliamentary privilege. Wood offered to waive privilege, but Glynn objected that it was the privilege of the House, not of the member. The Court of Common Pleas refused to believe that the House would insist on the privilege in such a case and allowed the change of plea: *Wilkes v Wood* (1763) 2 Wils KB 204; 95 ER 767.

warrant specified neither the goods nor the persons to be seized. This gave a discretion to the King's Messengers 'to search wherever their suspicions may chance to fall'. If a Secretary of State had and could delegate such a power, 'it certainly may affect the person and property of every man in this kingdom, and is totally subversive of the liberty of the subject'.[87] The trial ended at 11.20 pm with the jury bringing in a general verdict for the plaintiff on both the general issue and the special justification, and awarding the enormous sum of £1,000 in compensatory and exemplary damages. The Solicitor General, Sir Fletcher Norton, offered to prefer a bill of exceptions, but Pratt CJ refused to accept it, saying it was too late.

A few days later, on 10 December, Pratt CJ presided over the trial of Dryden Leach's action of trespass and false imprisonment against the three King's Messengers who had broken into his premises and imprisoned him when wrongly relying on the warrant. For Leach, it was argued that the warrant was invalid on account of its generality, as it specified neither the people nor the papers to be taken, nor the premises to be searched. The jury returned a general verdict for the plaintiff, with damages of £400 for Leach. Counsel for the next five plaintiffs, the journeymen Mosman, Bigg, Hill, Thomas and Booth, who had been arrested by the King's Messengers at once announced that 'as they had had the happiness of fee[l]ing vindicated, asserted, and maintained, all the great and constitutional points of liberty, which had been solemnly debated and determined, they were willing to accept nominal damages (which carry costs of suit) ... which generous proposition was readily acquiesced in by the council for the crown, commended by the court, and applauded by the whole audience'.[88]

Six months later, judgment was signed in Leach's case for damages of £400 and costs of £51 16s 8d. The defendants then brought the case before the King's Bench by writ of error. The case was argued on 18 June 1765 before Lord Mansfield CJ, and Wilmot, Yates and Aston JJ. At the end of the day's argument and anticipating that there would be further argument, all the judges gave it as their opinion that an arrest warrant which did not name or describe the person sought was illegal and void for uncertainty, and, in view of the unanimity, Lord Mansfield CJ said that this issue need not be dealt with again at the second argument, although the question as to whether the Secretary of State was a justice or conservator of the peace for the purpose of the Constables' Protection Act remained alive. Yates J pointed out first that to take advantage of the Act, the plaintiff in error would have to show that the Messengers had acted in obedience to the warrant and, second, that if the Secretary of State was for the purposes of

---

[87] *Wilkes v Wood* (1763) Lofft 1, 18; 98 ER 489, 498.

[88] *Annual Register*, vol 6 (1763) 115 (10 December 1763). The journeymen accepted £5 each: see the Treasury Solicitor's list of damages awards among the bundle of papers in TNA TS 1/3237 Part 1.

the Act a justice of the peace, the plaintiff below (defendant in error) might have to be nonsuited because, contrary to the statute's requirements, he had not joined the justice as a defendant.[89] When the second argument began on 8 November, the Attorney General, Sir Richard Yorke, conceded that, regardless of the validity of the warrant, he could not show that the King's Messengers had acted in obedience to it, so the judgment was affirmed.[90]

But meanwhile Wilkes was being made to suffer by the application of the criminal law. His rash re-publication of No 45 of *The North Briton* and his publication of the *Essay on Woman* in volumes led to his conviction in the Court of King's Bench on charges of, respectively, seditious libel and obscene libel. The prosecution had difficulty in proving that Wilkes was the author of No 45, so relied instead on his having given a copy of it to his printer, Williams, this being held to constitute publication.[91] On 26 July that year, just five days after the trial of *Entick v Carrington*, Kearsley, the original printer of *The North Briton*, was convicted of seditious libel on account of No 45, and Williams, who reprinted it at Wilkes's house, was convicted of republishing it. As the *Annual Register* noted, there had been seven successful prosecutions for libel since Christmas 1763, of which five (Wilkes for publishing and then republishing No 45, as well as for publishing the *Essay on Woman*; Kearsley for publishing the original of No 45; and Williams for publishing the reprinted version) were aimed directly at Wilkes and *The North Briton*.[92] As a result of his convictions, Wilkes (as we have seen) was expelled from Parliament, outlawed, and spent some years in grave personal and financial difficulty.[93] As the printer and publisher John Almon, sending Earl Temple a highly critical account of Lord Mansfield's performance when presiding over the libel trials, observed:

> The carrying this favourite point of convicting the *North Briton* in the City, has struck such a panic into the printers, &c., that I am afraid I now stand alone in the resolution to publish with spirit; however, I am determined to persevere, and whatever may be my fate, I hope that in case of persecution (which I hear is threatened me, with the addition of the heaviest vengeance of the Administration), I shall have the assistance and support of all those who call themselves friends to the liberties of their country; at least, I will endeavour to deserve it, by acting with that prudence, firmness, and fidelity, which can never injure a good cause, nor hurt them who shall choose to be my friends.[94]

---

[89] *Money v Leach* (1765) 3 Burr 1742, 1766–68; 97 ER 1075, 1088–89; also 1 Black W 555, 561–63; 96 ER 323-24. See too (1765) 19 St Tr 1002. Additional details are supplied in the Treasury Solicitor's note of the judges' remarks: TNA TS 1/3237 Part 1, which also contains in separate documents the Attorney General's argument, a note of Mr Dunning's argument for the defendant in error and the Attorney General's reply.

[90] (1765) 3 Burr, 1768; 97 ER 1075, 1089; 1 Black W 563; 96 ER 324.

[91] *Annual Register*, vol 7 (1764) 50 (21 February 1764).

[92] ibid 87–88.

[93] Thomas (n 42) chs 4–6.

[94] Smith (n 46) ii, 428–31 at 430 (14 August 1764).

V. ENVOI

If this chapter has a theme, it is that we misunderstand the actors in the litigation surrounding *The Monitor* and *The North Briton* if we think of them as being involved only in pursuit of legal and constitutional principles. They were political agitators. Their actions, both those which gave rise to the litigation and in the course of it, had political goals and implications, were orchestrated and paid for by politicians, and had grave political repercussions in Britain and elsewhere. Constitutional principles mattered to some, perhaps many, of our actors, but for others, perhaps most, they were important as instruments of political opposition to, or bolstering of, government. This should not surprise us; we see similar alliances between lawyers and politicians today, both in and against government and Parliament. Nor should it disappoint us. If what we call constitutional law is to be important, it has to be allied to and affect practical politics. The stories outlined in this chapter, and examined in greater depth in other chapters, show how constitutional law is at its most vibrant when it acts on and is influenced by the politics of the constitution which it seeks to challenge or uphold. The most intractable but exciting dilemmas flow not from the clash of good and evil, but from conflict between conceptions of the good.

2

Revisiting Entick v Carrington: *Seditious Libel and State Security Laws in Eighteenth-Century England*

TOM HICKMAN*

I. INTRODUCTION

L IKE MANY GREAT cases, *Entick v Carrington & three other Messengers in ordinary to the King* (hereinafter *Entick v Carrington*), which is 250 years old this year, repays analysis from a variety of different perspectives: the protection of property, restriction of prerogative power, the emerging recognition of press freedom, the law of search and seizure and even, with justification, the evolving conception of the rule of law. Rather than adopting any of these perspectives, this chapter examines the case from the perspective of state security laws in the eighteenth century. It does so by locating the case in the context of the law of seditious libel, its function, development and practical operation. At the time of *Entick v Carrington*, the law of seditious libel was the principal tool available to the state not only to punish but also to deter and disrupt the dissemination of written material regarded as subversive of state institutions or of the King and his ministry.

Entick v Carrington is placed in this context in two principal ways. First, the chapter explains the importance of the law of seditious libel in the eighteenth century and the way in which it was developed by the courts, both in its substantive aspect and in relation to the powers of enforcement enjoyed by Secretaries of State, as a conscious judicial policy to aid the government in maintaining the security of the government and the state. Adopting this perspective sheds considerable light on the judgment of the Common Pleas

* I am very grateful to Lindsay Farmer, David Feldman and Ian Williams for commenting on a draft of this chapter.

in *Entick v Carrington*, embodied in the famous speech of Lord Camden CJ, by showing the degree to which the court departed from previous judicial policy and practice in interpreting the laws relating to seditious libel in a manner that enhanced their effectiveness for government purposes. This perspective also allows us to appreciate that the judgment of the court in *Entick v Carrington* was more limited in its legal consequences than has sometimes been thought. In particular, this chapter challenges the influential account of the case given by Sir William Holdsworth, which presented it as having decided that the Secretaries of State did not enjoy any power to arrest or commit for seditious libel, on the basis of which conclusion Holdsworth said the case stood alongside the greatest advances in the protection of individual liberty, such as the abolition of the Star Chamber and the Habeas Corpus Act 1679. In fact, as will be shown, *Entick v Carrington* actually *affirmed* the power of the Secretaries of State to arrest and commit for seditious libel. But in exposing how courts (and in particular the Court of King's Bench) had, over time, made substantial inroads into individual liberty, in cases that Lord Camden said he was nonetheless bound to obey, Lord Camden's judgment can be seen not only as a departure from previous judicial policy but also as a radical challenge to the legitimacy of existing (and no less binding) authority. Lord Camden justified his approach by saying that the public deserved that the court examine all the issues raised by the case to their foundations. In doing so, he explained to the public how their liberties had gradually been eroded by the courts without parliamentary approval.

The second way that this chapter places *Entick v Carrington* in the context of the law of seditious libel is by examining the manner in which the law of seditious libel was *actually used* by the government, through the adjectival powers of arrest, search and seizure. It does so by setting the case in its immediate factual context by explaining its relation to the action taken by the government against two anti-government periodicals, *The Monitor, or The British Freeholder* (hereinafter *The Monitor*), which was part-authored by John Entick, and *The North Briton*, the mouthpiece of John Wilkes. As will be explained, the action taken against the two publications was inextricably linked. Examining the action taken against these periodicals requires us to look beyond the narrow facts of Entick's case, and it provides a vivid insight into how the law of seditious libel was utilised by the government against its critics and the reality of the power afforded by the law.

These two perspectives converge in the examination of a series of celebrated legal proceedings which arose from the action taken against the publications, of which *Entick v Carrington* is but one. This immediate legal context, also explored in this chapter, is particularly significant because the timing of the litigation meant that Entick's case against the Messengers fell to be determined after most of the other claims had been tried and because Lord Camden, then Chief Justice Pratt, himself presided over most of the trials. It will be explained how these cases were influential in terms of the way in which Lord Camden approached and decided *Entick v Carrington*, perhaps decisively so. For instance, it sheds light on Lord Camden's decision to rule on all the points of importance to the public, despite these going far beyond what was necessary to decide the case; and we are able to appreciate how Lord Camden was able so keenly to dissect the defence's arguments in *Entick v Carrington* by exposing the true implications of the claimed power of search and seizure of property, the extent to which such power was open to abuse by the government and the absence of protections for the individual.

Whether or not the reader ultimately agrees with the author that a sound understanding of Lord Camden's judgment in *Entick v Carrington* and its significance to our legal history requires an understanding of the context of the law of seditious libel, both its development and its use, it is hoped that it will at least have been shown that *Entick v Carrington* merits recognition as a case concerning state security powers in which the judiciary broke with the deferential and government-minded approach that had characterised the development of the law in that area.

II. SEDITIOUS LIBEL AND STATE SECURITY LAWS IN THE EIGHTEENTH CENTURY

A. The Law of Seditious Libel

In the first half of the eighteenth century, the law of seditious libel had become the most effective, or perhaps more accurately the least ineffective, tool at the government's disposal for controlling what it perceived to be threats to the realm from the dissemination of subversive writings.

For most of the seventeenth century, the government had had the benefit of prerogative and later statutory licensing laws that enabled prosecutions to be brought against the authors of critical material. Unlicensed publication was the essence of the crime under these laws and therefore there was no need to be troubled by whether seditious meaning was present or whether the facts alleged were true. But the licensing laws expired in 1695 and were not renewed.

The two other laws directed at the security of the state that were available for controlling seditious writing were the law of treason and the law of Scandalum Magnatum. Both were medieval in origin and had been the principal means for dealing with subversion before the sixteenth century.[1] But, for different reasons, neither provided a useful means of controlling subversive writing at the time of *Entick v Carrington*.

---

[1] RB Manning, 'The Origins of the Doctrine of Sedition' (1980) 12(2) *Albion* 99, 111.

The law of treason was based on the medieval statue 25 Edward III (1352), which rendered it treasonable to imagine or compass the death of the King or to aid his enemies. Whilst an overt act was required, extensions of the law made clear that this could include writing.[2] The law of treason was, however, blunt and unwieldy. Since it carried the penalty of death, it was far too heavy-handed to charge save in the most extreme cases. Moreover, the chances of embarrassing and problematic acquittals had been made more likely by the Treason Trials Act of 1696, which had granted rights to defendants in treason cases in particular permitting them defence counsel at trial.[3] The law of treason was not therefore an effective means of curbing the forms of anti-government literature that had previously been capable of control under the licensing laws.

The law of Scandalum Magnatum was contained in a series of medieval statutes that criminalised the spreading of 'false news' that could lead to discord between the King and his subjects or lead to the overthrow of the Crown.[4] The two main difficulties with this law were, first, that it could only be used in the case of 'news' and, second and far more significantly, that it was a defence to show that the news was true. This later defect raised the inevitability of trials of the accuracy of criticism levelled against the King or his Ministers or other great figures of state and even the prospect of acquittals by mischievous juries, none of which could be contemplated and which therefore rendered the laws effectively redundant as a state security power.

The ability to prosecute for seditious libel thus became by a process of default the main legal tool available to the government for preventing the dissemination of subversive material or subversive utterances. Seditious libel was centrally concerned with prohibiting dissent of government that challenged its authority, whether expressly or impliedly. It reflected the established and prevailing ideology that the ruler was 'regarded as the superior of the subject as being by the nature of his position presumably wise and good'. As such, any dissent, however politely expressed, was to be viewed as subversive and dangerous.[5]

---

[2] Although seditious utterances and prophesies had been prosecuted under the medieval law, the Act of Treason 1534 (26 Hen 8 c 13) expressly extended the law to slanders and libels and the Act against Prophesies 1542 (33 Hen 8 c 14) did likewise for prophesies. See, eg, *R v Stayley* (1678) 6 St Tr 1501 and also Manning (n 1) 103–06.

[3] (7&8 Will 3 c 3). See P Hamburger, 'The Development of the Law of Seditious Libel and the Control of the Press' (1985) 37 *Stanford Law Review* 661, 717–23, who argues that this put an end to the government's flirtation with the idea of using the law of treason to fill the gap left by the demise of the licensing laws at a time when the Jacobite threat was substantial, something evidenced, Hamburger argues, by the successful 'test case' brought against William Anderton, a Jacobite writer, in 1693: *R v William Anderton* (1693) 12 St Tr 1245. On the act, see JH Langbein, *The Origins of Adversary Criminal Trial* (Oxford, Oxford University Press, 2003).

[4] 3 Edw 1 c 34 (1275); 2 Ric 1 c 5 (1378); 12 Ric 2 c 11 (1388); 1&2 P & M c 3 (1554); 1 Eliz 1 c 6 (1559).

[5] JF Stephen, *History of the Criminal Law of England*, (Macmillan & Co, 1883) ch XXIV 299–300; Sir WS Holdsworth, *A History of English Law* (London, Methuen & Co Ltd, 1924) vol VIII, 338; vol IV, 672–73.

The law of seditious libel is customarily traced back to the case of Lewis Pickeringe in the Star Chamber.[6] Pickeringe had authored a derogatory rhyme about Archbishop John Whitgift which he provided to a friend, who copied it and had it sung at the Archbishop's funeral. The Star Chamber accepted that a libel against a magistrate or public person was 'a greater offence' than against a private person, for there could be no greater scandal of government than the imputation that the King had appointed corrupt or wicked men to govern his subjects. It was also said that whereas a man who finds a private libel may burn it, if a libel of a public official is found, it must be reported to a magistrate. Despite these distinctions between libel and seditious libel, the law of seditious libel was not articulated as a separate doctrine. The greater doctrinal innovations—themselves extraordinary— made in *Pickeringe's case* were the findings that: (1) an action for libel would lie irrespective of the truth of the words used; (2) it would lie even if the person defamed were dead (as Archbishop Whitgift obviously was); and (3) it did not matter that Pickeringe had not printed and distributed the libel—publication was established by mere provision to a third party. Each of these doctrinal innovations had obvious and deliberate advantages for the use of libel by the government as a means of controlling the dissemination of subversive writings: first, the prospect of trials of the truth of criticisms of public officers was negated; second, it was recognised that the interests of the state and the government were perpetual; and, third, critics of the government could not shelter behind the absence of publication or ferment their discontent in private.

The traditional account of the law of seditious libel found in Stephen, in Holdsworth and in Siebert is that seditious libel was thereafter widely used by the government and the common law's acceptance of Star Chamber doctrine reflected the acceptance of the prevailing political ideology that to criticise government, however respectfully, was a crime against the state.[7] Philip Hamburger has, however, challenged the view that seditious libel was widely used before the eighteenth century, arguing that the availability of the licensing laws meant that seditious libel was only resorted to when

---

[6] Reported by Edward Coke, who argued it as Attorney General, as the *Case de Libellis Famosis* (1605) 5 Coke 125; 77 ER 250.

[7] Stephen (n 5) 313; Holdsworth (n 5) vol VIII, 340; F Siebert, *Freedom of the Press in England 1476–1776* (Champaign, IL, University of Illinois Press, 1952) 269. The principal reported cases in the seventeenth century were: *R v Dover, Brewster & Brooks* (1663) 11 St Tr 540 (a printer, bookseller and bookbinder prosecuted for publishing speeches of the regicides and a book called the *Phoenix*); *R v Pym* (1664) 1 Sid 110; 82 ER 1068 (a handwritten message to a parson asking him to bewail failings of the magistrate); *R v Barnardiston* (1684) 9 St Tr 1333 (a fine of £10,000 for critical opinion in a letter to a friend); *R v Baxter* (1685) 11 St Tr 494 (a theological book said to criticise the English bishops); *R v Eades* (1686) 2 Show 468; 89 ER 1046 (where the defendant pleaded guilty to verbally commending a book containing seditious libels); the *Seven Bishops' Case* (1688) 12 St Tr 183 (bishops prosecuted for challenging the King's right to suspend the laws in declaring toleration for Roman Catholics).

such laws were not available.[8] He contends that the courts, particularly the King's Bench under Holt LCJ, in fact made significant doctrinal innovations in the early eighteenth century reflecting the new importance of seditious libel as a state security power after the demise of the licensing laws. As he states, 'The bench appears to have understood that the seventeenth century law, as inherited from Coke, would have to be modified if it were to suit its eighteenth century function' as the chief means of prosecuting the printed press.[9] Several cases in this period did later come to be regarded as having significantly developed the law, although the degree to which they did so is a matter of debate.[10] But from our perspective, the point is not of great consequence because there is no doubt that the law of libel was articulated and set out in a series of cases in a manner that was expressly linked to the judiciary's perceived need to ensure the law was suitable for the government as a state security tool given Parliament's refusal to renew the licensing laws. Furthermore, this pro-government approach had long been a facet of the law relating to seditious libel, as reflected in *Pickeringe's case* itself.

The most significant case in this period was *R v Bear* in 1702. Giving a special verdict, the jury acquitted Bear of all but writing down and collecting libellous poems. His counsel sought an arrest of judgment before the King's Bench on the basis that what had been found was folly rather than a crime. The court did not agree. Holt LCJ held that the writing-down and collecting of libels was 'highly criminal' and of 'dangerous consequence to the Government' because they could subsequently be published; even if the collector had no ill intent, they might 'fall into such hands as might be injurious to the Government; therefore men ought not to be allowed to have such evil instruments in his keeping'.[11] The reasoning was expressly based on policy and the need for the law of seditious libel to be an effective tool in protecting the government from abuse that might incite rebellion. This is shown with particular clarity in an unreported record of the case. Holt LCJ, seeking to address the objection that the judgment was not based on legal authority, stated:

> [T]his Opinion that We now give is no Novelty in the World. It is founded upon the principle of the preservation of All Government, and Safety of all Civil

---

[8] Hamburger contends that resort was only had to seditious libel actions proper when the licensing acts could not be relied upon, such as in periods when they were not in effect or in the absence of publication: Hamburger (n 3) 697–99 and Appendix.

[9] ibid 725.

[10] The degree to which the cases departed from rather than restated previously accepted law is disputed. *cf* Stephen (n 5) 316–43; Hamburger (n 3) 725–58.

[11] *R v Bear* (1702) Holt KB 422, 423; 90 ER 1132, (1702) Carthew 407; 90 ER 836; and (1698) 2 Salkeld 417; 91 ER 363. This had been prefigured in *R v Paine* (1696) 5 Modern 163; 87 ER 584, in which the court held the defendant guilty on a special verdict for having transcribed an epitaph on Queen Mary and fetched it to be read aloud with a friend. It was not clear from the report whether the court had rested its judgment on publication by reading aloud or the mere act of writing-down.

Society: And if it Should be no Crime to Write Libels, the Government & Magistrates, must be Exposed to the Malice & discontent of Disaffected persons.[12]

In *Entick v Carrington*, Lord Camden certainly regarded *R v Bear* as having been a significant case altering previous doctrine.[13] He saw the justification for *Bear's case* in the Star Chamber principle[14] that obliged individuals in possession of seditious libels to deliver them to a magistrate, reversing previous authority that held that this was only punishable in the Star Chamber[15]—which had been abolished in 1641. The case was undoubtedly informed by Star Chamber practice[16] and probably owed something to this principle, but since writing down appeared still to be required if publication was not alleged, rather than mere collection alone, the explanation is incomplete.

The development of seditious libel as a separate law, based on broad policy concerns about the need to empower the government to prevent dangerous dissent, is also apparent from *R v Tutchin*. The defendant stood accused of seditious libel for alleging corruption in the army and navy, in a paper called 'The Observator'. Holt LCJ expressed the opinion that a seditious libel could be committed against the government in general and not just individual public officers.[17] The reasons for this referred directly to the idea that the safety and wellbeing of a country depended upon the government being above reproach: 'If men should not be called to account for possessing the people with an ill opinion of the Government, no Government

---

[12] The unreported record is in Hardwick Papers BL Add MS 35981 f14 (with quote at f22). By reference to this report, Hamburger argues that there was no plausible precedent for the case: 'Holt deliberately allowed himself to depart from precedent in *Bear's case* because the law of libel of magistrates had always been designed to protect the government (albeit solely by protecting individual officials from defamation); and now that it was the only effective law against seditious libels of pamphlets, the reason for that law seemed all the more clear. It was the law for protecting the government from seditious writings, and that purpose, rather than the more precise requirements of precedent, shaped Holt's decision' (Hamburger (n 3) 741, also 731). In my view, Hamburger's view of Holt's methodology draws support from *Ashby v White* in which Holt LCJ famously stated that: 'the law consists ... not in particular instances and precedents, but on the reason of the law': (1703) 2 Ld Raym 938, 957; 92 ER 126, 138. The contrasting legal philosophy of Lord Camden in *Entick v Carrington* is clear: 'If it is law, it will be found in our books. If it is not to be found there, it is not law.' *Entick v Carrington* (1765) 19 St Tr 1029, 1066.

[13] ibid 1072.

[14] *Case de Libellis Famosis* (n 6); *Lake v Hatton* (1691) Hobart 252; 80 ER 398.

[15] In *Anonymus* (1669) 1 Ventris 31; 86 ER 22.

[16] Holt referred expressly to cases in the Star Chamber.

[17] This was not entirely novel and was certainly a logical extension of existing law. In *R v Dover, Brewster & Brooks* (1663) 6 St Tr 564, Hyde LCJ had stated to the jury that publishing a reproach of King and government is a libel and in the *Seven Bishops' Case* (n 7) two judges, Wright LCJ and Allibone J, had accepted the government's argument that anything that shall disturb the government is a seditious libel, although this case was not regarded as a secure authority because of the extraordinary and political nature of the case: see *The Case of John Wilkes Esq, on a Habeas Corpus, Common Pleas ('Wilkes' habeas case')* (1763) 19 St Tr 981, 990 (Lord Camden); Holdsworth (n 5) vol VII, 344; Stephen (n 5) vol II, 315; Hamburger (n 3) 699.

can subsist; for it is very necessary for every Government, that the people should have a good opinion of it.' No government, he said, can be safe unless expression of ill opinion against it is punishable.[18]

The preparedness of the courts to ensure that seditious libel was effective for use to curb dissent also underpinned the view in the judiciary as to the respective role of the judge and jury in relation to judging seditious meaning and intention. The point took on significance only after the demise of the Star Chamber, which operated without a jury, and after the ending of the licensing laws, under which seditious meaning and intention had been irrelevant. Holt LCJ took the view that the question whether the words were or were not seditious, from which malicious intent was inferred, was a matter of law for the trial judge rather than for the jury.[19] The consequence was that whilst juries might be asked to determine the meaning of words used and any question of irony, they did not determine whether the words were seditious or malicious. The principal issues determined by the jury were authorship or publication and juries were therefore required to return a verdict of guilty even if they thought the writing harmless. But had seditious meaning and intent been an open matter for the jury, this would have meant that what constituted acceptable dissent of the government would have been left to the vagaries of juries, which, as the courts recognised, would have greatly reduced the utility of the law of seditious libel to the government as well as greatly weakening the courts' own power over state security.

The courts followed Holt. Lord Mansfield (LCJ from November 1756 to 1788) is said to have regarded it as necessary 'to avoid anarchy' for the issue of sedition not to be put to the jury.[20] In Dean of St Asaph's Case, R v Shipley, Lord Mansfield stated: 'The licentiousness of the press is a Pandora's

[18] R v Tutchin (1704) Holt 424; 90 ER 1133.
[19] R v Bear, accepting that the power to judge the effect of a man's words must be left to the law and for this reason must be set out in the indictment—the alternative, it was contended, 'would be of very dangerous consequene'; see also R v Drake (unreported), for which, see discussion in Hamburger (n 3) 729, 736–38. Hamburger argues convincingly that seditious intention and malice were rebuttable in the seventeenth century: Hamburger (n 3) 703–08; cf Holdsworth (n 5) 842–45. James Oldham has pointed out that Hamburger's articulation of the law in the seventeenth century is supported by Helmholz's work in the civil context: RH Helmholz, 'Civil Trials and the Limits of Responsible Speech' in RH Helmholz and TA Green (eds), Juries, Libel, and Justice: The Role of English Juries in Seventeenth and Eighteenth Century Trials for Libel and Slander (Los Angeles, University of California Press, 1984) 24–25; James Oldham, English Common Law in the Age of Mansfield (Chapel Hill, University of North Carolina Press, 2004) 215.
[20] Oldham (n 19) 219 and 221. NS Poser, Lord Mansfield—Justice in the Age of Reason (Quebec, McGill-Queen's University Press, 2013) 244 states that: 'As a prosecutor and then as a judge, Mansfield believed that vigorous enforcement of the seditious libel laws as a way of supporting the government and arresting what he saw as a decline in the moral condition of the country'. Heward criticised Mansfield's contention that he was merely following established authority as having been cover for his judicial preference that it would be 'safer to leave things … in the hands of the judges', as the question was one of judicial practice and not the subject of binding authority: E Heward, Lord Mansfield (Chichester, Barry Rose Law Publishers Ltd, 1979) (2nd impression, 1998), 133.

box, the source of every evil ... What is contended for? That the law shall be in every particular cause what any twelve men, who shall happen to be the jury, shall be included to think ... subject to no review, and subject to no control, and under all the prejudices of the popular cry of the day.'[21] The point, however, was not conclusively determined and defence counsel, including Charles Pratt before his elevation to the bench, continued to invite juries to acquit if seditious intention was not proved—and just occasionally the jury would do so.[22]

B. Powers of Committal, Arrest, Search and Seizure

The preparedness of the courts to develop the law to provide an effective tool for the government to use against the dissemination of subversive writings can also be seen in the judiciary's approach to the powers of the Secretaries of State to arrest, seize and commit for seditious libel.

During the eighteenth century, the office of Secretary of State was shared between two of the King's Ministers. Foreign affairs were divided between them on a geographical basis, whereas domestic affairs were shared ad hoc. Although their domestic duties were not numerous, it has been said that a Secretary of State 'had the pulse of the people of this country in his hand', which if 'quickened to an unusual degree' would prompt him to take measures to restore tranquility.[23] By the eighteenth century, it had become established practice for Secretaries of State to issue warrants for the arrest of persons suspected of certain crimes against the state, namely, treason, coming out of France without leave and seditious libel, and for their committal to prison pending trial, although issuing such warrants was by no means

---

[21] (1783–84) 21 St Tr 847, 1040.

[22] *R v Owen* (1752) 18 St Tr 1203, in which defence counsel were Barnard Ford and Charles Pratt. This was a position Camden 'maintained ... throughout his life' and he argued it in the House of Lords during the passing of Fox's Libel Act 1792: Holdsworth (n 5) vol X, 681. In 1764 Serjeant Glynn at the trial of John Williams for republishing No 45 of *The North Briton* is said to have asserted that the jury had the full right to determine whether the defendant had published with intent. Lord Mansfield, presiding, interjected that: 'If Serjeant Glynn asserted that doctrine again, he [Lord Mansfield] would take the opinion of the twelve judges upon it.' Not wanting to lose the point, which he was sure to do, Glynn didn't press it. The jury returned the verdict of 'Guilty of publishing the North Briton 45', but Mansfield simply took this to be a verdict of guilty and Williams was put in the pillory. (The case is not reported, but James Oldham has identified an account in J Almon, *Biographical, Literary, and Political Anecdotes, of Several of the Most Eminent Persons of the Present Age*, 3 vols (London, TN Longman and LB Seeley, 1797) vol 1, 236–37 and in Lord Mansfield's manuscripts: Oldham (n 19) 224). Despite this, 10,000 people gathered to cheer Williams, shouting 'Truth in the Pillory', 'Wilkes and liberty!' (etc) and beheaded an effigy of Lord Bute: AH Cash, *John Wilkes—The Scandalous Father of Civil Liberty* (New Haven, Yale University Press, 2006) 179. Parliament eventually changed the law by Fox's Libel Act 1792.

[23] *Calendar of Home Office Papers, 1760–1775* (hereinafter *Cal HOP*) I, preface iv, Joseph Redington, 19 February 1878.

a regular part of their activities.[24] Since the days of the Star Chamber, the Secretaries of State had exercised responsibility for arrest and punishment of the authors, printers and publishers of seditious libels. Under the Licensing Act 1662 14 Car II, c 33, the Secretaries of State were conferred express statutory power of search and seizure. Having probable reasons to suspect an offence, they were empowered to instruct the King's Messengers, taking a constable with them, to search premises and seize property 'for the better discovering of printers in corners without licence' (s 15).[25]

The process of issuing warrants against suspects worked in the following way. A warrant signed by a Secretary of State would be addressed to one or more of his Majesty's Messengers, who were usually acquainted with the printing shops and persons involved in the production of the seditious publication; indeed, the Messengers would often have been responsible for the intelligence on which the warrant was based. The Messenger was instructed to take named persons into custody (or in the case of 'general warrant' simply the authors, printers and distributers of a named publication) and bring them before the Secretary of State for examination together with their books and papers. The Secretary of State might also issue a warrant after, and occasionally before, examination directing a gaoler to commit the individual to prison. But practice varied, as did the regularity of the use of such warrants. From time to time, Secretaries of State had been subject to criticism for abusing the system and on occasion it was claimed that there was no authority for such powers as representing an illegitimate and unlawful interference with individual liberty.[26]

The latter argument had been advanced before the courts in *R v Kendal & Row*[27] in 1700 on a return to a writ of habeas corpus by two prisoners committed to Newgate Prison under the warrant of Secretary of State William Trumbull. The prisoners were alleged to have aided the escape of Sir James Montgomery, who was himself being held by a Messenger under warrant of commitment for treason. Several exceptions were made to the return,

---

[24] MA Thomson, *The Secretaries of State 1681–1782* (Oxford, Clarendon, 1932) 112–13.

[25] See Lord Camden's discussion in *Entick v Carrington* (n 12) 1052 and 1069–70. On the Secretaries of State's role in clamping down on seditious writing and the use of warrants, see generally Thomson (n 24) 114–26.

[26] Sir John Trenchard, Secretary of State for the Northern Department in 1693–95, who had been accustomed to sending Messengers with blank warrants for names to be filled in, came in for criticism of both sorts: Thomson (n 24) 116–18; Sir J Trenchard, *History of Parliament Online*, accessed 14 February 2014. In 1731–32 the *Gentleman's Magazine* (*GM*) carried a lively and well-informed debate on the power of Secretaries of State to commit and of the Messengers (vols I–II, 477–78, 914–15).

[27] *R v Kendal & Row* (1700) 1 Ld Raym 65; 91 ER 304; Skin 596; 90 ER 267; 12 Mod 82; 88 ER 1178; Comb 343; 90 ER 517; also *R v Yaxley* (1693) Comb 224; 90 ER 443; Carth 291; 90 ER 772; Skin 369; 90 ER 164, in which it was argued that the Secretary of State had no power to commit as he was not a Justice of the Peace. The objection was overruled but perhaps because of statutory authority (35 Eliz c 2) for the accused refusing to answer whether he was a Jesuit, seminary or massing priest.

including that the Secretary of State had no power to commit but only the Privy Council acting in aggregate. Counsel argued that the Secretaries of State had no power to administer oaths and could not therefore be justices of the peace with power to commit. There were, however, authorities from Elizabeth I's reign in which it had been accepted that committals by Sir Francis Walsingham, Principal Secretary to the Queen and Privy Counsellor, constituted a good return to a writ of habeas corpus.[28] In addition, in 1591 the judges had given an extra judicial opinion to Elizabeth I after the Queen had inquired into the circumstances in which a prisoner taken into custody at her command or that of her Privy Counsellors would not be released by the courts. The judges responded, ambiguously, that in the case of commitment for high treason by Her Majesty, the Privy Council or any one or two of the Counsellors, a person should not be released in the absence of acquittal at trial. This carried the suggestion that in other cases a person could be committed, but might be bailed.[29]

The King's Bench upheld the detention of Kendal and Row. Justice Rookby said that the Secretary of State was 'a centinel, who watches for the publick good, and of such authority that he was a conservator of the peace at common law'.[30] He considered that it had been settled in Elizabethan times that Secretaries of State had such power since, although no statute conferred the power, it was incident in the office of Secretary of State. Holt LCJ is reported to have said that it was 'clear law' and that in his memory he was aware of only one occasion the power had been doubted. He said that the power to commit was exercised at common law before there even were justices of the peace. Considerations of public interest were again central to the court's judgment, as well as usage and acceptance of the power.

Significant also was the court's rejection of the further exception taken to the return that Montgomery's own commitment had been unlawful and thus it had been no crime to help him escape. Dismissing the point, the court held that the Secretary of State had the authority to commit to a Messenger for examination or transfer to gaol.[31]

Two subsequent eighteenth-century cases, *R v Derby* and *R v Dr Earbury*, confirmed the authority of *Kendal & Row* as to the power of the Secretaries

---

[28] In *Hellyard's Case* (1887), a return by the Warden of the Fleet, to whom the Hellyard had been committed, was held to be insufficient as it did not show the cause of the commitment. But the power to commit was not doubted, nor was it suggested (although the report is scant) that the commitment had to have been qua Privy Counsellor, and the Warden was given an opportunity to amend his return. In *Howel's case* (1587) 1 Leonard 70; 74 ER 65, it was held that a return to a commitment by a single Privy Counsellor had to specify the cause of the commitment as well as the fact of it.

[29] 1 Anderson 297; 123 ER 482 (34 Eliz I); *Entick v Carrington* (n 12) 1054–55.

[30] *R v Kendal & Row* (n 27) Skin 596, 598–99.

[31] One exception was allowed: that the warrant should have specified the treason Montgomery was charged with, since assisting him to escape fixed the offender with the same offence. However, the prisoners were bailed rather than discharged.

of State to arrest, and in *R v Derby*, this was expressly applied in a case of seditious libel. These cases are central to unpicking the holding in *Entick v Carrington* and therefore require further elaboration. A third case, *R v Erbury*, also referred to the King's Bench having bailed a person arrested for seditious libel and is a further record of that court accepting the legality of the power.[32]

In *Derby's case*, a warrant issued by the Secretary of State in the court vacation authorised a Messenger to make a search for Derby the printer and 'to seize and secure him for publishing and vending a scandalous and seditious libel called the Observator, No 74, and to bring him before me to examine the premises, and to be dealt with father according to law'. Derby appeared before the Lord Chief Justice and entered a recognisance to appear on the first day of Michaelmas Term 1711. He continued to be held by the Messenger and appears not to have been examined by the Secretary of State, as one of the exceptions raised, unsuccessfully, by his counsel on the return date was that the warrant was permitted at the Secretary of State's pleasure for an indefinite period and it should have been limited in time.[33] Counsel for Derby also argued that the Secretary of State had no power at all to commit a person other than for treason or felony, or at least no power before the person had been examined on oath. This was unanimously rejected. Parker LCJ held that the Secretary of State must have a power to seize a person, the implication being that otherwise the power to commit would be worthless since a person must be seized in order to be committed.

As to the question whether the Secretary of State could seize a person for the purposes of examination, both Parker LCJ and Powys J expressed the view that this was 'a privilege, and for the benefit of the innocent man'. Although it is not immediately apparent how the power could be said to *benefit* individuals, since it was used to hold people for days on end and pressure them to enter recognisances, there was also a logic in this point. Since a person would need to be seized before he could be committed to prison, a power to instruct a Messenger or other person to arrest a suspect is certainly a logical extension of, if not actually entailed in, the power to commit. And since it must be preferable that a person is given an opportunity to account for himself before being committed to prison, such a power was thought to mitigate rather than exacerbate the intrusion into individual

---

[32] *R v Erbury* (1722) 8 Mod 177; 88 ER 130, which referred to the fact that the defendant had been arrested for seditious libel under warrant of the Secretary of State and bailed by the King's Bench.

[33] Rejecting this submission, Parker LCJ held that specifying the time a person could be held was 'never done in this world' and he suggested that it would not be in the interests of suspects, who would be held to the last day of any specified period. This reasoning was no doubt even more unconvincing to a man who was being indefinitely detained under such power than it is today. He also rejected the contention that the warrant had to set out the facts; it only had to set out the species of crime.

liberty. The problem is that recognising such a power also afforded the Secretary of State a means of intimidating suspects and of forcing them to enter recognisances and bind themselves to keep the peace under threat of commitment. In practice, as we shall see, the power to arrest for examination was open to abuse and was a great weapon in the hands of the Secretaries of State. The third member of the court, Justice Eyre, thought the matter clear and stated simply that the issue had been settled by *Kendal & Row* and the Elizabethan authorities, which was a reasonable view of those cases.[34]

In *R v Dr Earbury*, the Duke of Newcastle had issued a warrant for seizure of the papers of Dr Earbury, for him and the papers to be brought before him on suspicion of authoring a treasonable paper, the Royal Oak Journal. Dr Earbury was brought before the Secretary of State's secretary, a justice of the peace, who, despite having failed to obtain a confession or examine any other witnesses, gave him a choice between entering a recognisance in the sum of £100 and an undertaking to appear before the King's Bench on an appointed day, or be committed to gaol. Unsurprisingly, Dr Earbury entered the recognisance. He then issued a motion for it to be discharged. Rejecting the motion, the Lord Chief Justice[35] stated that *Kendal & Row* 'settled upon solemn debate, 'that a Secretary of State might issue out his warrant to apprehend the person of any man on suspicion of treasonable practices'.

Objection was also taken to the seizure of Dr Earbury's papers, which his counsel noted raised an issue that 'never was yet resolved'. But on this point the court expressed no opinion 'whether it was legal, or not', as the point was not before it on the motion.[36] There is no record of any subsequent action in trespass and this issue lay dormant until it was finally argued out in *Entick v Carrington*.

These cases show that well before the events giving rise to *Entick v Carrington*, the authority for the Secretaries of States to issue warrants of arrest for seditious libel was established. The King's Bench had upheld the legality of warrants of arrest for treasonable writings and for seditious libel, and affirmed that this followed in principle from the recognition in *Kendal & Row* of the power of the Secretaries of State to commit for political crimes. The basic principle driving the cases was that a power of arrest was a logical and sensible corollary of a power to commit, as well as being an important tool for enabling Secretaries of State to keep peace and order in society. By placing these cases alongside those relating to the substantive law of seditious libel, the cases are seen to be reflective of a more general judicial tendency in the eighteenth century and before to mould the law of seditious libel into an effective tool in tackling anti-government writings. Moreover, the courts

---

[34] *R v Derby* (1711) Fort 140; 92 ER 794.
[35] Probably Raymond LCJ (the date of the case is unclear).
[36] *R v Earbury* (1733) 2 Barn KB 293; 94 ER 509; 2 Barn KB 346; 94 ER 544.

showed no concern for, or appreciation of, the improper or excessive use of the power to arrest and eschewed attempts to confine its use.

It can also be seen that the one point that the courts had not considered was the legality of searches and seizures of papers conducted under such warrants. Yet the fact that there was no authority approving such practices does not mean that they were not legal; it was simply that no one had ever challenged them in appropriate proceedings. The very same considerations that led the courts to uphold the power of committal and arrest applied to the case of seizure. It was a power exercised pursuant to the responsibilities of the Secretaries of State as 'centinels of the publick good' for preventing the dissemination of subversive writings. It was a power that was of obvious utility in identifying and successfully prosecuting seditious libels (possibly more so even than the ability to examine suspects since it would identify actual seditious writings or documentary evidence of involvement in the possession of suspects). And it was also a long-established practice the legality of which had never been doubted by any court. There was also a further point. If the mere writing and possession of a seditious libel was an offence because, as Holt CJ had held in *Bear's case*, it was dangerous to the state for libels to be collected or kept, and if seditious libels had to be turned-over to a magistrate, it is hard to deny a power for the Government to search for and seize those that it discovered. We therefore find that directly analogous considerations, relating to custom and usage, public interest and principled extension of existing authorities relating to powers of committal and arrest, also supported a power of search and seizure of personal property. The Government could therefore have expected with some considerable justification that if the legality of the power of search and seizure ever fell to be decided by the courts, it would be affirmed, just as the powers to arrest and commit had been.

III. THE PRELUDE TO *ENTICK V CARRINGTON*

A. Action Taken against *The Monitor* and *The North Briton* on Allegations of Seditious Libel

Let us now consider how the law of seditious libel came to be used in events that form the immediate context of *Entick v Carrington*.

By 1762, there were a multiplicity of different forms of printed papers in circulation: newspapers, magazines, regular essay papers, occasional pamphlets and one sheet handbills. *The Monitor* was a political paper published every Saturday for almost a decade between 1755 and 1765. It took the form of a single six-page essay, usually in the form of a letter. Such essay papers are often regarded as forerunners to the modern editorial. *The Monitor* was financed by Lord Beckford, a radical whose family wealth came from West Indies sugar plantations. He had strong connections to the

City, which provided the main audience for *The Monitor*. The main editors and writers were the lawyer Arthur Beardmore and the schoolmaster and writer John Entick.

Upon becoming Prime Minister in May 1762, John Stuart, 3rd Earl of Bute, King George III's former tutor, was sufficiently concerned by the influence of *The Monitor* and the incessant criticism of the government in its pages that he immediately set up a competing paper called *The Briton*. In its first edition published on 29 May 1762, it described its purpose as to 'oppose and expose and depose The Monitor', which was described as 'incendiary' and libellous against the King and the government.[37]

But the establishment of *The Briton* was ill advised and ill fated. It provoked an immediate response from the radical Member of Parliament John Wilkes and his sponsor Lord Temple. Both were supporters of Pitt (Temple was Pitt's brother-in-law) and opposed Lord Bute and his agenda of peace with France. Wilkes had been a contributor to *The Monitor* and is believed to have authored seven of the essays in 1762 and others before. He probably wrote two of the editions cited in the warrants at issue in *Entick v Carrington*, but since the authors were anonymous, we cannot be sure.[38] With the publication of *The Briton*, Wilkes saw an opportunity, and eight days after *The Briton* was first published, *The North Briton* appeared in the coffee shops, taverns and clubs of London. Written by Wilkes and the poet Charles Churchill and funded by Lord Temple, *The North Briton* gave Wilkes a platform for audacious attacks on the Ministry of Lord Bute, provoking a political crisis and legal firestorm that has left an indelible mark on the history of the country.[39]

The King's Chief Messenger, Nathan Carrington, and three others arrived at John Entick's house on 11 November 1762 at 11 o'clock in the morning. Entick's door was open. Entering the house and finding Entick there, the Messengers took him into custody and searched the house for all of his books and papers, including by rifling through a bureau, a writing desk and several drawers. They took up books and papers, perused and read others, and continued to do so for four hours. The search was carried out pursuant to a warrant issued on 6 November 1762 by Lord Halifax, Secretary of State for the South. It was addressed to the Messengers and purported to:

> [A]uthorize and require you, taking a constable to your assistance, to make strict and diligent search for John Entick, the author, or one concerned in writing of several weekly very seditious papers, intitled the Monitor, or British Freeholder, No. 357, 358, 360, 373, 376, 378, 379, and 380, printed for J. Wilson and J. Fell

---

[37] RD Spector, *Political Controversy—A Study in Eighteenth-Century Propaganda* (London, Greenwood Press, 1992) 35.

[38] ibid 35; Cash (n 22) 88.

[39] The government published a second pamphlet, *The Auditor*, to counter *The North Briton*: 'There followed in these weeklies a lively controversy that spread to the newspapers': PDG Thomas, *John Wilkes: A Friend to Liberty* (Oxford, Clarendon, 1996) 19.

in Pater Noster Row, which contains gross and scandalous reflections and invectives upon his majesty's government, and upon both houses of parliament; and him, having [been] found you are to seize and apprehend, and to bring, together with his books and papers, in safe custody before me to be examined concerning the premisses and further dealt with according to law.[40]

Lord Halifax was identified as one of the Lords of His Majesty's Privy Council and principal Secretary of State.

The search of Entick's house was carried out without a constable present, as was required by the warrant (a stipulation carried over from the Licensing Acts regime). Entick was then taken together with his books and papers before Lovel Stanhope, law-clerk to the Secretaries of State and a justice of the peace, who was used by them to take depositions in cases involving the public.[41]

Halifax also issued three other warrants. One named Arthur Beardmore, another his law clerk, David Meredith. A fourth named the two publishers, Isaac Wilson and John Fell, as well as a printer John Medley and a former editor, Jonathan Scott. Scott may have been named as a formality, or possibly to permit his papers to be seized, since it was primarily upon his intelligence that the warrants had been made.[42]

Beardmore had been apprehended about an hour before Entick. The Messengers read his private correspondence back to 1752, examined books and ledgers. They required Beardmore to open locked drawers and bureaus, and read and seized a good deal of private and even legally privileged correspondence. Beardmore and Meredith were taken and imprisoned at the house of the Messenger Blackmore. There Beardmore was subject to 'close' confinement, and for two days he was denied use of pen, ink and paper or to see a client. He was unable to work on various legal cases that he had on. Wilkes went and sat with him for a day.

Entick, Beardmore and Meredith were granted bail by the King's Bench after six days, and the other men who had been detained under the warrants were bailed a few days later.[43] Entick, Beardmore, Meredith, Wilson and

---

[40] *Entick v Carrington* (n 12) 1034 (spelling as reproduced in St Tr).

[41] ibid 1035.

[42] On 11 October 1762, he had made a declaration before a Justice of the Peace at Westminster that attested to his own involvement in the establishment of *The Monitor* and to Entick and Beardmore's authorship. His declaration is set out in ibid 1033. Peters (later Professor and biographer of Pitt the Elder), '"The Monitor" 1755–1765: A Political Essay Paper and Popular London Opinion', a thesis presented for the Degree of Doctor of Philosophy in History (University of Canterbury, Christchurch, October 1974) states at 600 that Scott may have been named for appearances but also notes there is no evidence of him having been arrested. It is in fact difficult to see that Scott would have been named to prevent suspicion falling on him if, unlike the rest, he was not to be arrested but this may nevertheless be the explanation. (There is no complete account of the litigation arising from *The Monitor* and *The North Briton* affair and in piecing together the account here, I have been greatly helped by Peters' excellent account at Appendix IV of her thesis.)

[43] See *Beardmore v Carrington and others* (1764) 2 Wils KB 244; 95 ER 790; Annual Register (hereinafter AR) 1764, VII 73.

Fell were only released from their recognisances on 22 June 1763, over six months later, it being noted that no prosecutions had been brought against them.[44]

The government might have had second thoughts about prosecutions that would have been highly unpopular with the public, but it is more likely that prosecutions were never intended.[45] The action against *The Monitor* was part of a concerted effort to intimidate *The Monitor* and *The North Briton* and put them out of print, at least temporarily.[46] They were not intended to lay the basis for prosecutions. A warrant relating to Nos 1–25 of *The North Briton* was issued on 18 November 1762. No 25 had not even been published, and a second warrant, bearing the same date, refers to Nos 1–26.[47] The warrants were general warrants in that they referred to 'the Authors, Printers and Publishers of a seditious and scandalous weekly paper, entitled *The North Briton*', but did not identify any suspects by name.

The question why the warrant for *The North Briton* was not issued until 18 November and for its character as a general warrant might partly be answered by the absence of any evidence equivalent to Jonathan Scott's information in the case of *The North Briton*. Yet, as an explanation, this is incomplete as Scott named only Entick, Beardmore and Meredith and, as noted above, Halifax issued a fourth warrant naming others which was only indirectly supported by Scott's information. The probable reason for issuing a general warrant is that they gave much greater power to the Messengers to investigate and intimidate those suspected of involvement in a publication. General warrants provided authority for the Messengers to detain anyone they suspected of involvement. They thus placed the Messengers in the position of a justice of the peace or a Secretary of State by allowing them to assess the strength of the evidence against individuals and decide who to arrest. A general warrant was a frightening piece of paper in the hands of skilful Messenger. The general warrant issued against *The North Briton* was never served and no arrests were made; instead, it was used to intimidate those involved.

The Messengers showed the first warrant to a bookseller who had been vetting drafts for Wilkes for libellous passages. He quit. They showed it to the printer, William Richardson, who also quit. Wilkes appealed to his friend Dryden Leach (who had an important role in a later legal action),

---

[44] AR 1763, VI 82. Cash (n 22) 88 erroneously states that Beardmore was let off easy.

[45] Cash (n 22) 88–89; cf M Peters (n 42) 601–602.

[46] Peters says that copies of *The North Briton* and *The Monitor* had been presented to the law officers for their advice at the same time: Peters (n 42) 599–600. I have not been able to verify this. The request for advice relating to *The Monitor* on 3 November 1762 and the reply the following day can be found at BL Add MS 22131 f4-f22; see also *Cal HOP* (n 23) I 201. Advice was received on *The North Briton* Nos 6, 8, 9, 10, 11, 12, 14, 20 and 23 (only) on 16 November: *Cal HOP* (n 23) I 203.

[47] BL Add MS 22131 f29–f32.

who managed to get No 26 printed, but then Leach's journeyman printer, Peter Cook, was also nobbled by Messengers who produced the second warrant naming No 26. Wilkes wrote to Churchill: 'I have seen Leach, whose printer, Peter Cook, had the terrors of the Lord-of the Isle [ie, Lord Bute], so strong before him, that he has fallen ill to avoid printing the paper.'[48] As in the case of *The Monitor*, the warrants were used as a means of harassment and disruption rather than to lay the ground for prosecutions for seditious libel. In the case of *The North Briton*, no arrests were even made.

The timing of the action against *The North Briton* and *The Monitor* is explained by the fact that on 3 November 1762, preliminary peace terms had been agreed with France and fell to be debated in Parliament before the end of the year.[49] Both publications were stridently opposed to a peace treaty. *The Monitor*'s readership included merchants and City folk whose wealth was derived from colonial projects at the centre of the dispute with France and were especially opposed to concessions being made. The Bute ministry was attempting to silence the main opposition and ease the conclusion of the treaty.[50] But the attempt badly misfired. *The North Briton* managed to stay in print and *The Monitor* was back in print on 27 November 1762, having missed only two issues, immediately criticising the peace terms.[51] But, more significantly, Wilkes and Churchill were incited to ever-more virulent and skilful assaults on the Bute ministry and what it saw as attacks on press freedom and personal liberty.[52]

The events relating to *The Monitor* and *The North Briton* nonetheless demonstrate the manner in which the law of seditious libel could be used, and was at times used, as a means of disrupting and deterring the government's critics without any resort to actual prosecution. The government must have felt secure from adverse legal action. Although Wilkes sought to persuade

---

[48] 2 December 1762, BL Add MS 30878 f18. See further Thomas (n 39) 23 and Cash (n 22) 89.

[49] Indeed, *Cal HOP* (n 23) I 201 records Halifax's receipt of the provisional peace treaty immediately before his request for advice from the law officers on *The Monitor* on 3 November 1762. The connection was first suggested in *The North Briton* No 27, 4 December 1762, 170–71, and it is the explanation preferred by Thomas (n 39) 22–23; Cash (n 22) 88; Spector (n 37) 35–36. Peters (n 42) 599 has taken a slightly broader view: 'The warrants of 6 November 1762 certainly appear to be part of a tougher attitude of the government towards the press in response to the attacks on Bute and the controversy over the peace.'

[50] On 25 November 1762 Lord Bute was hissed and stoned by a mob outside the Houses of Parliament and troops had to be called. Lord Bute infamously bought the vote in the House of Commons, which voted 227 to 63 on 14 December 1762 in favour of the peace terms. John Almon described: 'A corruption of such notoriety and extent had never been seen before ... a shop was publicly opened at the Pay Office, whither members flocked' in exchange for their vote (cited in Cash (n 22) 91).

[51] The essay opens with the statement that 'Whole Publication on the 13th and 20th was prevented by the Confinement of the Gentlemen concerned in the Monitor, and of the Printer and Publishers, taken up by Virtue of a Warrant issued from one of His Majesty's principal Secretaries of State.' Its content was an attack on the peace terms.

[52] See, eg, Thomas (n 39) 24–26.

Beardmore to bring a claim for false imprisonment, he refused.[53] The fear of prosecution continued to hang over him and as a lawyer he must have doubted his chances of success. Of course, no claim could have been brought by Wilkes himself or those working for him on *The North Briton* as no one had actually been detained and no property had been seized. The basic legal preconditions for actions in trespass or false imprisonment were absent.

Peace with France was concluded in the spring of 1763, but it did not prevent the downfall of Lord Bute, who resigned on 8 April 1763, in part at least due to the unpopularity created by *The Monitor* and *The North Briton*.[54] Ironically this event led to the most famous of all the attacks on the government, No 45 of *The North Briton*. Written by Wilkes, No 45 was a sustained attack on the King's speech on the commencement of the new ministry. Wilkes adopted the device of attributing the content of the speech to the King's Ministers rather than to the King himself (to make a charge of treason more difficult to stick) and purported to question whether 'the imposition' of the speech was 'greater on the Sovereign, or on the nation'. But it was obvious that the King was the principal object of the attack, together with Lord Bute, who was now given the role of puppet-master. The King's reference to the need for 'that spirit of concord, and that obedience to the laws, which is essential to good order' provoked an impassioned rejoinder from Wilkes stating that the spirit of concord was not to be expected from persons whose private houses were now made liable to be entered and searched at pleasure. The 'spirit of liberty' of the people should, he wrote, arise in proportion to the 'weight of the grievance they feel'. The people too have prerogative, he said: 'Freedom is the English subject's Prerogative.' As George Nobbe has written, such passages 'stimulated the imaginations of men all over the world'.[55] But the King had had enough and considered the words treasonable.

On 26 April 1763, Lord Halifax issued another general warrant authorising his Messengers to search for the authors, printers and publishers of No 45 of *The North Briton*, which was described as a 'seditious and treasonable' paper. The inclusion of the word treasonable is notable, not only as an indication of the reaction of the government (which must have considered it justified) but also because it had the deliberate purpose of evading a defence of parliamentary privilege, which Wilkes was sure to raise. This time, it seems clear, the government intended to pursue Wilkes personally.[56]

---

[53] Peters (n 42) 602; Cash (n 22) 88.

[54] See, eg, Cash ibid 97.

[55] George Nobbe, *The North Briton: A Study in Political Propaganda* (New York, Columbia University Press, 1939) 213; for other discussion, see Spector (n 37) 153–56; Cash (n 22) 100.

[56] Reference to treason was included at the request of the Attorney General Charles Yorke. Cash (n 22) 101 gives an account of the suggestion being made by the retired Chancellor Lord Hardwicke, Charles Yorke's father, whom he had approached for advice. Another exception to privilege was breach of the peace, but notably this was not expressly alleged. The warrant can be found at BL Add MS 22131 f37.

However, the Messengers first made a serious mistake. They broke into the house of Dryden Leach, who on the basis of faulty intelligence was thought to have printed No 45.[57] They pulled Leach from his bed, seized papers and took him and his servants to be held under guard. They detained him for four days. This mistake left the government vulnerable to a legal challenge to the practice of issuing general warrants which, given Leach's undoubted innocence, was particularly strong.

Other Messengers broke into the house of George Kearsley, the only person whose name appeared in *The North Briton* itself. Under interrogation by Lord Halifax himself on 29 April 1763, Kearsley provided the names of the printer, Richard Balfe, Churchill and Wilkes (he had, he said, let it be known that he would do so if ever examined).[58] The net tightened. Balfe and his apprentice Charles Shaw were also detained and under examination provided further evidence of Wilkes' involvement.[59] Wilkes himself was detained on Saturday 30 April 1763. His house was searched and papers seized.[60] The events ignited an incendiary series of legal proceedings, the most extraordinary that there had ever been, and which there may ever have been, of which Lord Camden's judgment in *Entick v Carrington* formed the coup de grâce.

B. *The Monitor* and *The North Briton* Cases

Wilkes' lawyers immediately applied for a writ of habeas corpus, but did so, unusually, in the Court of Common Pleas, where Pratt CJ was considered less government-minded than Mansfield LCJ, who presided in the King's Bench. Pratt CJ's initial reaction to the general warrant produced was that it was 'most extraordinary' and he ordered the issue of a writ of habeas corpus at lunchtime on the Saturday.[61] But on this occasion the government was one step ahead of the game and Wilkes was committed to the Tower of London by a second warrant before the writ of habeas corpus had been served on the Messengers. Following the issue of a second writ on the Monday, Wilkes was finally brought before the court on 3 May 1763. The reporter noted that the court 'was crowded to such a degree as I never saw

---

[57] In fact, as we have seen, Leach printed only an earlier issue (he was in the process of printing a second). See *Leach v Money, Watson and Blackmore* (1765) 19 St Tr 1001, 1004.

[58] BL Add MS 22132 f35–f36.

[59] BL Add MS 22132 f39 f43.

[60] See further Cash (n 22) 102–09, which includes a hilarious account of the apprehension of Wilkes. Balfe's involvement appears to have come out during the course of cross-examination of Lord Halifax in *Wilkes v Wood* (1763) 19 St Tr 1153, 1160–61, where it was admitted that the warrant under which Wilkes was arrested had been made before they had evidence against him.

[61] *Wilkes' habeas case* (n 17), 982.

it before'.[62] Wilkes was allowed to give a speech to the assembled throng extolling the virtues of liberty, which, he said, were 'so sure of finding protection and support' in the court of Common Pleas. After an adjournment to 6 May and another speech by Wilkes to like effect, the court ordered Wilkes released, 'Whereupon there was a loud huzza in Westminster-hall'.

There was, however, no celebration about the contents of the judgment that Pratt CJ delivered on behalf of the court, which found for Wilkes only on the narrow ground of parliamentary privilege.[63] The court rejected arguments—albeit in line with prior authority[64]—that the warrant should have set out the evidential basis for the allegation and should also have set out the allegedly seditious words. This gave great latitude to the Secretaries of State (as well as justices of the peace) to issue warrants to detain undesirables without needing to identify the reasons for suspecting that a person was guilty of seditious libel or even identifying particular seditious words. Moreover, assuming the validity of general warrants—which Wilkes decided not to challenge—anyone suspected of involvement could be rounded up. The latitude given to the government and its officers was certainly clear to Pratt CJ. He reached the conclusion that a warrant did not have to set out the grounds or the evidential basis for the allegation with reluctance. He noted that it could be said that 'every man's liberty will be in the power of a justice of the peace' and he would have found it 'very weighty and alarming' had the issue not been resolved by previous authority.[65] But his appreciation of the scope of the power to issue warrants later proved influential in his judgment in *Entick v Carrington*.

---

[62] ibid 984.

[63] The government's approach to this issue is extremely puzzling. In the first place, the Crown allowed the point to be argued, although, having not issued any suit against Wilkes, he could not insist that it be determined at this stage. Then the Crown hardly pressed the point and refused to say that privilege could not be raised. This was despite the fact that reference to treason had been deliberately included in the writ by the Attorney General in order to preclude any issue of privilege arising (see n 56 above). Perhaps, on reflection and given the popular furore, the government was not prepared to allege treason. Interestingly, Cash recounts how after Pratt CJ had given judgment, Serjeant Nares, who had appeared for the King, jumped to his feet with a message that the Attorney General and the Solicitor General wished to be heard. It is interesting to speculate whether this belated intervention by the Attorney General was in order to raise treason as a bar to privilege. But whatever it was that they wished to say, Pratt CJ was having none of it. He said: 'It is too late': Cash (n 22) 116. Parliament later passed a resolution denying privilege for seditious libels, a point remarked upon by Lord Camden in *Entick v Caringon* (n 12) 1065. After Balfe and Kearsley were questioned on 9 May 1763, informations were entered against Kearsley and Wilkes, although that against Wilkes was later dropped. Wilkes was later prosecuted for republishing No 45.

[64] *Wilkes' habeas case* (n 17), 988; *R v Wyndham* 1 Str 3; 93 ER 347. The Court held that the species of the offence must be recorded, a proposition which itself may have gone further than the law required. *cf R v Despard* (1798) 7 Term Rep 736; 101 ER 1226.

[65] *Wilkes' habeas case* (n 17), 988 and 991 (the latter quote appears in an extract from 'A Digest of the Law of Libels' reproduced in State Trials). Pratt CJ appears to have had less sympathy with the argument that the warrant should set out the seditious words. He could not see the point since the court could not adjudge whether they constituted a sedition because innuendo may be necessary to make the whole out: at 989.

Before that case, however, Pratt CJ was to be provided with plenty more evidence of the breadth of the power to issue warrants and the scope for abuse. Wilkes was formally charged with seditious libel (not treason) in the hope that he would lose his parliamentary privilege by expulsion or resolution of Parliament, but following the aphorism that attack is the best form of defence, Wilkes issued several claims for false imprisonment and trespass against the Messengers, the Under-Secretary of State Robert Wood, the Treasury Solicitor Phillip Webb and Lord Halifax personally.[66] He also organised over a dozen printers and apprentices, who had also been rounded up under the general warrant, to bring claims. Such suits, brought by ordinary people, were 'unheard of' at the time: 'People of high station were shocked. People on the street were excited.'[67] There was widespread concern about the actions taken by the government under the general warrants.

The first trials came on in July 1763 before Pratt CJ. Two cases, one brought by William Huckell, a journeyman printer who had worked for Leach and been detained for six hours, were tried first. After a 12-hour hearing on 6 July 1763, the jury, after retiring for only a few minutes, returned a verdict of guilty and awarded Huckell £300 plus costs. The second claim by James Lindsay, another printer, the following day resulted in a judgment of £200. Following this, the Messengers agreed to verdicts in 12 other cases against printers for £200 each, subject to a motion for a new trial on the grounds that the level of damages was excessive.[68]

Indeed, the government, which was indemnifying all the defendants in these actions[69] and running their defences, was shocked by the level of the awards. On the motion for a new trial, it was objected that Huckell had worked for only a guinea a week and in custody had been treated very civilly and been given 'beef-steaks and beer, so that he suffered very little or no damage'. Pratt CJ held that the small injury done to Huckell and the 'inconsiderateness of his situation and rank in life did not appear to [the jury] in that striking light, in which the great point of law touching the liberty of the subject appeared to them at the trial'. He said that the jury had been struck by the Secretary of State 'exercising arbitrary power, violating Magna Carta, and attempting to destroy the liberty of the kingdom, by insisting upon the legality of this general warrant' and that the jury had been entitled to award exemplary damages.[70]

---

[66] Thomas (n 39) 32–33.

[67] Cash (n 22) 123.

[68] *Addenda to the cases concerning Mr Wilkes ('Addenda')* 19 St Tr 1381, 1404–05; also AR 1763 VI 88; AR 1764 VII 81. These sources are not entirely clear as to whether there were 12 or 13 such cases but a list of damages awards prepared on behalf of the Treasury Solicitor and held at the National Archives identifies 12: TNA TS 11/3237. I am grateful for David Feldman for identifying this useful source.

[69] *Addenda*, ibid 1406 and 1415.

[70] ibid 1405.

These claims led to great celebration amongst the ordinary folk in London; in the light of public sentiment, the government decided it safer not to pursue a bill of exceptions in the King's Bench.[71] The decision may also have been influenced by the fact that, despite Pratt CJ's clearly expressed views on the illegality of general warrants, the jury verdict had not established any proposition of law and their legality could be argued another day.

Actions by Entick, Beardmore, the clerk Meredith and the booksellers Wilson and Fell were notified to the government a few days after these awards, on 15 July 1763.[72] The timing is unlikely to be a coincidence: *The Monitor* claims may well have been encouraged by the awards made in those concerning *The North Briton*. However, it is also significant that, as we have seen, the recognisances binding the men had been lifted in June and it was only after this that they would have felt safe from prosecution and willing to risk an action challenging the government.

On 6 December 1763, a claim for trespass that Wilkes had issued against Robert Wood came for trial before Pratt CJ. This was an audacious claim. Wood was an Undersecretary of State who had attended Wilkes' house whilst papers were seized by the Messengers, but he had not himself seized the papers and was not named in the warrant. Wood's presence and seeming influence over events was the basis for Wilkes to claim that Wood was a joint tortfeasor. Like *Entick v Carrington*, the claim only related to trespass and not false imprisonment. Rather than demur to the defence and put the legality of the general warrant and the legality of search and seizure in issue, Wilkes' lawyers chose to join issue and put the facts and issues before the jury. This was part of a strategy of forcing the claims to be presented on the facts to be determined by juries, rather than by judges on points of law, which was a strategy pursued in all the suits.[73] Wilkes and his lawyers surely recognised that they would have better chances of success in front of juries than judges. But more importantly, jury trial meant that the facts would be established and this meant witness evidence on both sides of the case. This provided a stage on which to present to the public how the warrant system led to unjustifiable invasions of personal privacy and individual liberty. One consequence of this strategy in *Wilkes v Wood*, no doubt intended, was that both Wood and Lord Halifax himself had to give evidence and could be, and were, subject to cross-examination.

Wood entered a general plea of not guilty and also a special justification that he had been sent with a message and played no part in the arrest. A second factual point at issue was Wilkes' authorship of No 45, which Wood

---

[71] Cash (n 22) 133, note 33. A note in AR 1764 VII, 81 records final settlement on 21 June 1764 in 14 cases of £120 each and Huckell £175. In total, 26 claims resulting from the general warrants were commenced, although not all were determined: BL 41355 f1199.

[72] *Cal HOP* (n 23) I, 295. The claims were commenced on 2 September 1763: AR VI 1763 98; GM 1763 XXXIII 462.

[73] See the account in the Martin Papers vol X, BL Add MS 41355 f194–f195.

pleaded in justification. The government may have thought that a favourable ruling on this point would have been of assistance in the prosecution of Wilkes, and Pratt CJ warned the jury to be particularly careful in finding Wilkes to be author for this reason.[74]

The court heard evidence of how the Messengers executed the warrant against Wilkes by rummaging through all of his private papers that they could find and by piling them in a sack, without any kind of inventory being taken, and by the attendance of a smith to open bureaus and drawers that were locked. Under examination, Lord Halifax was forced to admit that he had issued the warrant three whole days before he had received any information at all against Wilkes and that the warrant 'lay dormant, whilst they were upon the hunt for intelligence'. Lord Halifax also resisted disclosing the evidence that had been obtained and upon which the arrest had been based, but upon being pressed by Pratt CJ, the statement of Walter Balfe (but not that of Kearsley) was produced.[75]

Serjeant Glynn for Wilkes argued that the use of general warrants was contrary to liberty and the constitution and urged the jury to award exemplary rather than trifling damages. The Solicitor General, appearing for the defence, said that he was at a loss to understand what Mr Wilkes meant by bringing an action against Wood, who neither issued the warrant nor executed it. He said that this was the first time he ever knew a private action represented as the cause of all good people of England. In his summing up to the jury, however, Pratt CJ made it clear that he regarded the general warrant as unlawful and that if Wood had been involved damages should be awarded, pointing out that it resulted in a 'discretionary power given to messengers to search wherever their suspicions may chance to fall'. This, he said, would affect the person and property of every man in the kingdom and would be 'totally subversive to the liberty of the subject'. The jury found Wood to have been involved and acquitted Wilkes of authorship of No 45 into the bargain (thus scuppering his prosecution). The substantial sum of £1,000 damages was awarded against Wood. A bill of exceptions was denied as being out of time and therefore the general warrant issue and the power of search and seizure were given no further consideration in the case.[76]

On 10 December 1763,[77] Dryden Leach's case against the Messenger Money for false imprisonment and trespass was heard, again presided over by Pratt CJ. The jury once again returned a verdict for the plaintiff, this time with £400 damages and costs. It was reported that the plaintiffs offered to

---

[74] *Wilkes v Wood* (n 60) 1168.
[75] ibid 1160–61.
[76] ibid 1154, 1159 and 1167.
[77] *Leach v Money, Watson and Blackmore* (n 57) 1006; AR 1764 VII 115. The case came back for judgment on 16 June 1674. The date of trial given in the report at 1 Blk W 555; 96 ER 320 seems to be wrong.

accept nominal damages—which carried an entitlement to cost—in this and the next five causes, which was 'readily acquiesced in by the counsel for the crown, commended by the court, and applauded by the whole audience'.[78]

A Bill of Exceptions *was* received in *Leach v Money,* and a number of other cases concerning printers detained under the general warrants, effectively maintaining that the claims were bad in law. *Leach's case* was treated as the test case and came before the King's Bench in 1765, shortly before *Entick v Carrington* was decided. Several important issues were raised, including the application of the Constables Protection Act 1750 (which was eventually determined in *Entick v Carrington*) and the legality of general warrants. The Solicitor General argued the case for the defence. On 18 June 1765, the matter was adjourned for further argument, but the court made comments which led to the appeal being dropped. Lord Mansfield expressed preliminary views on several aspects of the case, including that the protections of the Act could only apply to persons acting in obedience to the warrant. Most dramatically, he expressed the 'clear opinion'—in accordance with the approach of Pratt CJ in the trials—that general warrants were unlawful. He said that 'it is not fit, either upon reasons of policy or sound construction of law, that, where a man's being confined depends on an information given, it should be left to the officer to ascertain the person'.[79] As to the argument of long usage, he said this ordinarily has 'great weight', but 'will not hold against clear and solid principles of law, unless the inconvenience of overturning it will be of very ill consequence indeed'. The central objection was that general warrants placed Messengers in the position of justices of the peace (or Secretaries of State) as it fell to them to decide who to detain and on what evidence. Wilmot, Yates and Aston JJ expressed equally firm opinions.

When the matter came back to court on 8 November, the Attorney General himself appeared and stated that he had not been able to overcome the point that Leach, not having actually been a printer or publisher of the editions in question, could not have been seized within the terms of the warrant, which was only addressed to the printers etc., and therefore the Messengers had not been acting in obedience to it. He mentioned a case at Middlesex Sittings where a warrant requiring 'loose and disorderly persons' was held not to cover the taking up of a woman of character. This is puzzling since, while the point had been argued by the plaintiff, Lord Mansfield had previously seemed to indicate (at least as reported) that the Messengers had had probable cause for taking up Leach and this was sufficient. But Lord Mansfield recalled the case at Middlesex Sittings and agreed that it was conclusive of the matter.[80]

---

[78] AR 1763 VI 115; *Leach v Money, Watson and Blackmore* (n 57), 1006.

[79] 1 Blk W 555, 562; 96 ER 320, 323.

[80] *Leach v Money, Watson and Blackmore* (n 57), 1028; also 1 Blk W 555, 563; 96 ER 320, 324. Leach recovered £400 and in linked claims four servants appear to have recovered £5 each (Treasury Solicitor's list, n 68).

What was going on here is not easy to fathom. The Attorney General may have been seeking to keep the issue of general warrants alive, or perhaps avoid a more embarrassing or more wide-ranging judgment, such as that later given by Lord Camden in *Entick v Carrington*, and with the additional risk of it being in the King's Bench, which may not have felt so constrained to depart for previous King's Bench authority. Whether this was the case or not, general warrants could no longer safely be used and no more were ever issued.[81]

Whilst *Leach v Money* and the associated cases had been progressing through the courts, the actions brought by Entick, Beardmore and others relating to *The Monitor* had come on for trial. Arthur Beardmore's claim against Nathan Carrington and three other Messengers had come on for trial at the Guildhall on 5 May 1764, and again the trial was presided over by Pratt CJ. This case raised false imprisonment and seizure of papers and, in contrast with *The North Briton* cases, was not concerned with a general warrant. Pratt CJ was reported as having instructed the jury that both the detention of Beardmore and the seizure of his papers had been illegal, and that they had to assess damages on this basis, but he recommended moderation damages as the Messengers were only servants.[82] The jury nonetheless awarded Beardmore £1,000 (although he had asked, unrealistically, for £10,000). Beardmore offered to forgo the verdict if Lord Halifax would consent to have the claim against him determined (Halifax had delayed the claim against him personally and the trial date had been put off), but this was not forthcoming.[83]

The defence issued a motion for a new trial on the grounds of excessive damages and it was argued in Westminster Hall before all the judges of the Common Pleas. On 26 May 1764, the motion was rejected. In the court's judgment (presumably given by Pratt CJ), it is extremely forthright in making clear its view that the government's practices had been unconstitutional. It reasoned that since the liability was joint and several, the matter could properly be approached as if it were a judgment against Lord Halifax himself:

> [A]nd can we say that 1000l are monstrous damages as against him, who has granted an illegal warrant to a messenger who enters into a man's house, and prys into all his secret and private affairs, and carries him from his house and business, and imprisons him for six days. It is an unlawful power assumed by a great

---

[81] Thomson (n 24) 124, who also points out that the utility of the general warrant was undermined just as much by concession that a person who was not actually the printer or publisher (etc) could not be lawfully apprehended (and the officer would not benefit from statutory protection) since the utility of the general warrant lay in the ability to apprehend a number of suspects without firm evidence and cross-question them for information.

[82] AR 1764 VII 72–74; GM 1764 XXXIV 246; (1764) Wils Rep 244, 245; 95 ER 790, 791.

[83] AR 1764 VII 73; (1764) Wils Rep 244; 95 ER 790 (which appears to give an incorrect date of the trial).

minister of State. Can any body say that a guinea per diem is sufficient damages in this extraordinary case, which concerns the liberty of every one of the King's subjects?[84]

Since this was not a general warrant case, the court's certainty that the warrant was illegal, both in relation to the arrest and the seizure of papers, is striking, but the point was not put in issue by the defence and formed no part of motion for a new trial. The issue was not considered until *Entick v Carrington*.

By contrast with Beardmore, and although this is not entirely clear, Entick, Wilson and Fell appear to have brought claims against the King's Messengers in trespass only and not false imprisonment. Following a further trial on 21 June 1764, Wilson and Fell were awarded £600.[85] *Entick v Carrington* was heard in July 1764 and concerned search and seizure of Entick's property. The jury, exceptionally in all these cases, returning a verdict of not guilty but it was a special verdict setting out the facts and requesting the advice of the court as to whether the search and seizure was unlawful given the facts as they found them to be. In the event that the search and seizure was unlawful the jury assessed damages at £300. The matter rested until the following year.

Claims by Entick, Beardmore, Meredith, Fell and Wilson against Lord Halifax personally were tried on 11 and 12 December 1764. In those cases, which are not reported, the plaintiffs' lawyers chose not to challenge the legality of the warrants. In Beardmore's case, which was tried first, the case focused on the absence of evidence of probable cause, the fact that Lord Halifax's clerk, Lovell Stanhope detained him for six days before examining him, and the fact that he was not brought before Lord Halifax as the warrant had required.[86] Damages were awarded taking account of the recovery in previous actions. Beardmore was awarded £1,500 (this was intended to be inclusive of the previous £1,000),[87] Entick £20, Wilson £40 and Fell £10. Meredith (who may only have pursued this claim and therefore there was no reduction to prevent double recovery) was awarded £200. The fact that the

[84] ibid see also GM 1764 XXXIV 248.

[85] AR 1764 VII 80–81. This record of the case refers to the claim being in trespass but also refers to the detention of the men. False imprisonment claims were, however, brought against Lord Halifax as discussed in the main text.

[86] Accounts of the trials can be found at AR 1974 VII 112–13 and in the correspondence of the Duke of Newcastle BM Add MS 329 64 f273, f279, f281, f283, f289 and TNA TS 11/3237 Part 1. On 4 December 1764 William Samuel Powell wrote to Lord Newcastle that the jury's award reflected the fact that Lord Halifax had 'caused Beardmore to be taken into custody without proof or just suspicion of his guilt, to be confined an unreasonable time before examination, and then trusted the examination of him to a person who had no lawful authority. I hear the friends of Lord Halifax think the damages moderate, and given out, that there will be no farther contest in this cause'.

[87] See AR 1974 VII 112. Treasury Solicitor's list (n 68) is thus guilty of double counting as it lists these award cumulatively.

plaintiffs seem not to have challenged the legality of the warrants relating
to their detentions may highlight the difficulty of sustaining any judgment
on a bill of exceptions in the Court of King's Bench. It may also have been
considered unnecessary given that damages had been recovered against the
Messengers on this basis and it was certainly unnecessary given that there
were other flaws in the execution of the warrants which enabled damages
to be obtained against Lord Halifax. There was clearly canny litigation
strategy at play, which, particularly at the distance of 250 years, can only
be guessed at. It even puzzled onlookers at the time and the scant accounts
are confused as to what, if anything, the cases had to say about the legality
of the warrants.[88] It seems clear that the plaintiffs' lawyers in these cases,
as well as those against the Messengers, chose to focus on their strongest
points rather than the most constitutionally significant, as well as ensuring
that the cases were decided by jury trial. The objective was to inflict embarrassing and politically significant defeats on the government, not to obtain
reasoned judgments on lofty points of constitutional law.

This brings us, in our conclusion to this discussion of the litigation leading
up to the judgment in *Entick v Carrington*,[89] to remark upon two features of
the litigation which stand out. First, it is significant that there had not been
a single reasoned judgment on the legality of either general or ordinary warrants or as to their use given following full argument. Formally at least, even
the legality of general warrants remained open. Although the defendants and
the government had suffered heavy defeats, and indeed had failed to land a
single significant blow in all the litigation, their lawyers had at least managed
to avoid the infliction of a knockout blow by the courts. That is not to under-
estimate the importance of comments of the King's Bench in *Leach v Money*
in 1765 or of Camden CJ in *Wilkes v Wood* two years before on general
warrants. But these were not binding precedents. Despite the constitutional
importance of the series of cases following the action taken against *The Monitor* and *The North Briton*, there was no monument to the battles won in
the pages of the case reports in terms of a reasoned judgment of a court on a
point of law. But as we have seen, this was not the primary objective.

---

[88] See the correspondence at n 86 and Treasury Solicitor's notes, ibid. In general, the plaintiffs' lawyers picked their battles with care. The legality of general warrants was not challenged
in *Wilkes' habeas case*, for example, and the issue of the legality of warrants to arrest and
detain seems to have been deliberately avoided in both *The Monitor* and *The North Briton*
claims. Dryden Leach's case was presumably put forward as the test case on general warrants
because it was the strongest as Leach had been entirely innocent of involvement.

[89] It was only long after *Entick v Carrington* had been decided by the Common Pleas in
November 1769 that Wilkes' own action against Lord Halifax was tried, Lord Halifax having
long delayed it. Damages were awarded at £4,000, again much less than had been claimed
and so disappointed the crowd—'the jurymen were obliged to withdraw privately, for fear of
being insulted'—but a substantial sum nonetheless given the moderate injury. See *Addenda*
(n 68) 1406–07. The excessive amount of £20,000 had been claimed; Wilmot CJ had urged
moderation in his summing-up.

The legal monument resulting from these cases was eventually supplied by *Entick v Carrington*, but as we shall see this is in large part due to the fact that the court decided of its own initiative—and in contrast to the attitude of the King's Bench—that the constitutional nettles should be grasped in the wider public interest.

A second important facet of the litigation is that the government's use of warrants had been placed under the microscope and thoroughly discredited in a series of jury trials. The exorbitant nature of the power and the intrusion into the personal liberty of ordinary people had been exposed in open court in a number of cases, most of which had been presided over by Pratt CJ.

IV. LORD CAMDEN CJ'S JUDGMENT IN *ENTICK v CARRINGTON*

A. The Issue in *Entick v Carrington* and Lord Camden's Approach to it

Entick's case against the Messengers was a case in trespass for unlawful seizure of personal property. There was no element of false imprisonment in the suit. This was surely designed to test the issue left open by *Dr Earbury's case* whilst avoiding a direct assault on the power of the Secretary of States to issue warrants and the precedents of *Kendal & Row*, *R v Derby*, *R v Erbury* and *R v Dr Earbury*.[90]

The jury in *Entick v Carrington* had returned a special verdict that set out the facts as they had found them and asked for advice on whether the facts amounted to a trespass. In some of the previous cases the juries had declined judicial invitations to deliver special verdicts preferring to deliver general verdicts of guilty, thus making it more difficult for their views to be overturned by the judiciary.[91] In *Entick v Carrington* the jury, finding the defendants not guilty took the opposite course and this brought the legality of the action under the warrant squarely before the court for determination as a matter of law.

After hearing argument on the special verdict twice in Easter Term 1765—on 13 May and 18 June 1765 (the latter being the date *Leach v Money* was argued in the King's Bench and the ex tempore remarks of that court made, of course, just the other side of Westminster Hall)[92]—Lord Camden CJ

---

[90] Why Entick rather than Beardmore or Meredith's case was used as the test case is a mystery.

[91] WJ Smith (ed), *The Grenville Papers: being the correspondence of Richard Grenville, Earl Temple, K.G. and the Right Hon. George Grenville, their friends and contemporaries* 4 vols (London John Murray, 1852–1853) vol ii, 71–76, (Wilkes to Temple) 9 July 1763.

[92] AR 1765 VIII 88, 101; *Leach v Money, Watson and Blackmore* (n 57) 1012. The Court of Common Pleas and the Court of King's Bench both convened in Westminster Hall.

indicated that he considered the case of utmost importance to the public and made clear to counsel that he desired to give judgment on every point and that they were to be 'argued to the bottom'. There is here a striking contrast with the approach taken by the King's Bench in *Leach v Money*, which had shown no inclination to examine the points to their roots. The precipitous intervention of the King's Bench judges in that case led to its premature conclusion and raised the suspicion that the government had dodged the issue. Lord Camden's approach was conspicuously different and contains an implicit criticism of the approach that had been taken across Westminster Hall. Argument was heard on one further occasion in Michaelmas Term and judgment delivered on 27 November 1765. Lord Camden said that 'the public, as well as the parties, have a right to our opinion'.[93] His judgment could have rested on a narrow point—for example, that the Messengers had not acted in strict obedience to the warrants—but he chose to deal squarely with every question raised, as well as several others that were not.

B. Secretaries of State as Conservators of the Peace

The Messengers had claimed the protection of s 6 of the Constables Protection Act 1750 (24 Geo 2 c 44), which provides that no action shall be brought against any constable, headborough 'or other officer' for 'any thing done in obedience to any warrant under the hand or seal of any justice of the peace'.[94] The first question identified by Lord Camden was whether Secretaries of State were 'conservators of the peace'. A conservator of the peace is an ancient common law office referring to persons with special responsibility for keeping the peace. It pre-dates justices of the peace as judges of record appointed by the King. Had the Secretaries of State been conservators of the peace, they may have been within the equity of the statute, although they were not within its words.

In order to answer this first question, Lord Camden undertook a remarkable exercise in historical detective work, tracing the origin of the office of Secretary of State and of the practice of the Secretary of State to issue warrants for committal and arrest. The origin of the office of Secretary of State was found to lie in the role of the monarch's private secretary rather than in any position with responsibility for conserving the peace. The conservators of the peace in past ages had been recognised as including the King, the

---

[93] AR 1765 VIII 146; *Entick v Carrington* (n 12) 1045.

[94] Section 6 is still in force today. It affords protection even if the warrant is illegal: 'if the constable acts in obedience to the warrant, then, though the warrant be an unlawful warrant, he is protected by the Statute of 1750': *Horsfield v Brown* [1932] 1 KB 355 per Macnaghten J. Actions against Messengers could be brought, but only on certain conditions that had not been fulfilled. On the broad meaning of 'officer', see citations in *Tchenguiz v Director of the Serious Fraud Office* [2013] EWCA 1578 [12].

Chancellor, the Treasurer, the High Steward, the Chief Justice, the judges of the several courts, sheriffs, and high and petit constables and even coroners, but not Secretaries of State.[95] Lord Camden then succeeded in showing that the practice of issuing warrants originated in a special and particular delegations of power from the King (which had been condemned by the Petition of Right) and later in the fact that Secretaries of State were members of the Privy Council and issued warrants in this capacity, as well as later under the powers granted by Parliament under the Licensing Acts.[96] Thus, Secretaries of State were not to be treated as conservators of the peace.

Once Lord Camden had concluded that Secretaries of State could not be regarded as conservators of the peace, he needed to go no further. However, he chose to proceed to consider the authority of the Privy Counsellors to issue warrants of committal and to ask on what authority this was based. The reason that he gave for doing this was, he said, that he wanted to examine the foundation for Lord Holt's judgment in *Kendal & Row*. He said that he would set out 'all that I have been able to discover touching the matter' and then, after declaring his opinion, 'leave others to judge for themselves'.[97] What he meant, I suggest, is for others to judge for themselves whether *Kendal & Row* had been correctly decided.

Lord Camden traced the authority of the Privy Council to commit to the Statute of Westminster I, 1275 (3 Ed 1), under which such commitment was recognised as being by 'command of the King' within the terms of the statute. But early authority holding that a single Privy Counsellor had power to commit in cases of high treason was found to be based on a confusion of statutory powers granted in Edward VI's reign for common law power, which meant that the authority 'stands upon a very poor foundation, being in truth no more than a conjecture of law without authority to support it'.[98] The Elizabethan cases involving Sir Francis Walsingham compounded the mistake, he claimed, by accepting the power to commit, but they did not specify in what cause.[99] The opinion of all the judges in 1591 was found to be an example of studied obscurity reflecting the dangerous times, which (as well as being extra-judicial) actually left open every question other than a power in a single Privy Counsellor to commit for treason.[100] In the *Seven Bishops' case* in 1688, an objection had been taken to the warrant of commitment signed by 13 Privy Counsellors on the basis that it was not

[95] *Entick v Carrington* (n 12) 1046.
[96] ibid 1046–52. See on justices of the peace and conservators of the peace, R Burn, *The Justice of the Peace, and Parish Officer* (23rd edn by Sir G Chetwynd) vol III (London, Butterworths, 1820) 108–11 (also expressing the view that the status of conservator of the peace could be acquired by usage).
[97] *Entick v Carrington* (n 12) 1052.
[98] ibid 1053.
[99] ibid 1053–54.
[100] ibid 1054–55.

expressed to have been signed in Council. The objection was dismissed, the court presuming the warrant to have been executed in Council, but Lord Camden said that if any one of the Counsellors could have committed the bishops, 'that would have been a flat answer'.[101] Lord Camden concluded that the right of individual Privy Counsellors to commit in any case beyond treason had not been recognised. Therefore, he said, insofar as *Kendal & Row* recognised such a power beyond the case of treason, he would be 'forced to deny' Holt LCJ's opinion in that case 'to be law'.[102] *Kendal & Row* had gone further—it had held Secretaries of State to be conservators of the peace with powers both to arrest and commit, and, albeit only implicitly, this was not limited to cases of treason.

Lord Camden's judgment on the first issue, in many parts brilliant, is not convincing in every respect. On a fair reading of the Elizabethan authorities, a broader power vested in Privy Counsellors was implied. *Kendal & Row* had—perfectly reasonably—read the authorities in this way. *Kendal & Row* had also been based on other considerations, some of which had merit. In particular, regard was had to functions of the Secretaries of State not as the office had been hundreds of years before, but as it had evolved to be. The King's Bench expressly recognised the Secretaries of State functioned as conservators of the peace. The reasoning of the court in *Kendal & Row*, as opposed to the authorities preceding it, was subjected to little analysis by Lord Camden. Nor did he consider the cases in the King's Bench which had developed the line of jurisprudence further. In Lord Camden's view the reasoning in such cases was erroneous if not based on existing and sufficiently clear prior authority. As others have remarked, this view of the common law, which precludes its evolution, is unduly narrow. It is a view that diverged markedly from the approach taken by Holt LCJ.[103]

At this juncture, we must consider the analysis of Sir William Holdsworth. Holdsworth wrote that the most important question decided by *Entick v Carrington* had been 'the power to arrest possessed by a Secretary of State'. He concluded that: 'Lord Camden's judgment ... settled that the only power to arrest which [the Secretary of State] possessed was a power, as Privy Counsellor, to arrest in cases of high treason.' For this reason, he considered the judgment to be comparable in importance to the Act abolishing the Star Chamber and the Habeas Corpus Act 1679, 'because in all cases, except in the case of high treason, it prevented arrests from being made at

---

[101] ibid 1057.

[102] ibid 1053.

[103] See n 12 above and reference to *Ashby v White*. In *R v Despard* (1798) 7 TR 735, 742; 101 ER 1226, 1230, Lord Kenyon CJ stated: 'if that be true, farewell to the common law of the land'.

the discretion of the executive, and so gave abundant security that, if an arrest was made, it could only be made by regular judicial officers acting in accordance with known rules of law'. Holdsworth wrote that *Entick v Carrington* settled this issue as a matter of law.[104]

Frederick Siebert, probably following Holdsworth, in his famous study of the law of the period regulating the press, analysed the case in the same way,[105] and Lord Diplock in *Rossminster* held the same view.[106]

This analysis is not, however, accurate. Key to Holdsworth's analysis was the statement of Lord Camden that he was forced to deny the opinion in *Kendal & Row* to be law to the extent that it extended beyond committal for high treason.[107] There is no doubt that this statement does introduce a degree of opacity into Lord Camden's judgment, which is for the most part so admirably clear and incisive, but it did not determine that the power of Secretaries of State to arrest for seditious libel was unlawful.

It is important to recall that Lord Camden's analysis of the authority of the Secretaries of State to issue warrants was directed at answering what he presented as the 'first question', which was whether the Secretaries of State could be regarded as a conservator of the peace. What was relevant to this question was the *origin* of the power to commit and whether it revealed Secretaries of State to be conservators of the peace. The *extent* of the power to commit and arrest was not at issue and did not fall for determination. Indeed, Lord Camden went on to determine—the 'second question'—that even if Secretaries of State were to be regarded as conservators of the peace, they were not within the equity of the Constables Protection Act's protection of justices of the peace.[108] His remarks on *Kendal & Row* were therefore clearly *obiter dictum*.

Not only were the remarks *obiter dictum*, but in other parts of his judgment, Lord Camden made plain that he accepted that *Kendal & Row* and the later authorities of *R v Derby*, *R v Erbury* and *R v Dr Earbury* did provide lawful authority for the powers of Secretaries of State to arrest for seditious libel. Thus, he began his consideration of the first question by referring to the 'singular' power of Secretaries of State and stated that it was 'chiefly exerted against libelers, whom he binds in the first instance to their

---

[104] Sir WS Holdsworth, *A History of English Law* (London, Methuen & Co Ltd) vol X, 667 and 672.

[105] Siebert (n 7) 379-80.

[106] *Inland Revenue Commissioners v Rossminster* [1980] AC 952, 1009: 'a Secretary of State, it was held [in *Entick v Carrington*], did not have any power at common law or under the prerogative to order the arrest of any citizen or the seizure of any of his property for the purpose of discovering whether he was guilty of publishing a seditious libel'.

[107] Holdsworth (n 104) 666.

[108] *Entick v Carrington* (n 12) 1060–61.

good behaviour, which no other conservator ever attempted'. After noting the dark and obscure origins of this power, he stated:

> Whatever may have been the true source of this authority, it must be admitted, that at this day he is in the full legal exercise of it; because there has been not only a clear practice of it, at least since the Revolution, confirmed by a variety of precedents; but the authority has been recognized and confirmed by two cases[109] in the very point since that period: and therefore we have not a power to unsettle or contradict it now, even though we are persuaded that the commencement of it was erroneous.[110]

Here, at the very outset of his judgment, Lord Camden states expressly that Secretaries of State enjoyed the 'full legal exercise' of a power to commit and arrest for crimes which he says in terms include seditious libel. He even identified the lawful authority for this power as deriving from its long usage and instances of judicial recognition. He went on to state that his enquiry into the origins of the power 'cannot be attended with any consequence to the public', but was relevant to the question of whether Secretaries of State were conservators of the peace. In other words he was not expounding the law as it was but seeking to search-out its origins.

Later in his judgment in the section considering the status and powers of the Secretary of State qua Secretary of State, Lord Camden referred to *Kendal & Row*, *R v Derby* and *R v Dr Earbury* and said that he would take no other notice of them on the point because they 'afford no light in the present inquiry by shewing the ground of the officer's authority, though they are strong cases to affirm it'.[111] Lord Camden thus repeated that the power claimed by Secretaries of State was confirmed by those authorities, despite the fact that they might have been built on dubious foundations, and noted that their status was of no consequence to his inquiry into the origin of the power. Then, at the end of his consideration of the first question, he returned to the point for a third time. After concluding that the Secretaries of State had 'assumed' the power to commit as a transfer of royal authority to themselves ('I know not how'), he stated that:

> At the same time I declare, wherein all my brothers do all agree with me, that we are bound to adhere to the determination of the Queen against Derby, and to the King against Earbury; and I have no right to overturn those decisions, even though it should be admitted, that the practice, which has subsisted since the Revolution, had been erroneous in its commencement.[112]

---

[109] Lord Camden is probably referring to *R v Derby* and *R v Earbury* but he could be referring to *Kendall & Row* or *R v Erbury* as one of the cases. He refers to the first three at 1052 and to the first two at 1058.

[110] *Entick v Carrington* (n 12) 1046.

[111] ibid 1052.

[112] ibid 1058–59.

The consequence of these statements is that Lord Camden did not hold that the Secretaries of State had no power to arrest for examination or to commit for seditious libel; but rather he accepted this power had been accepted by the King's Bench.

Holdsworth made no attempt to explain these passages in Lord Camden's judgment. There is, however, possibly an explanation that is consistent with Holdsworth's view. *Kendal & Row*, at least on Lord Camden's analysis, had identified the power to commit as vesting in the office of Privy Counsellor. The passages referred to above might then be thought to mean no more than that subsequent authorities extended *Kendal & Row* in holding that the power vested in Secretaries of State by virtue of that office, and that Lord Camden meant no more than that he was bound by authority to recognise that the power to commit now vested in the office of Secretary of State qua Secretary of State and not that it extended beyond committal for treason. He did not mean to say, on this view of the case anyway, that he accepted that the power extended to arrest for seditious libel. This argument draws some support from the fact that Lord Camden stated that he was examining the foundations of *Kendal & Row* because later authority had rested almost entirely on the authority of this case and from his comments that *Kendal & Row* should be interpreted strictly, to that which it was necessary to decide in that case, ie the case of treason.[113] It suggests, perhaps, that if the authority of *Kendal & Row* was to be limited to the power to commit for treason, so should the later authorities that stood on its shoulders.

There are, however, real difficulties in reading the judgment in this way. First, Lord Camden expressly referred to arrest for seditious libel in the same passage as stating that the Secretaries of State were in the 'full legal exercise' of their asserted power. The power to which he was referring was therefore the power in its full breadth. It is notable that Wilson's report of the case supports this reading. It records Lord Camden as having stated that 'it must be admitted that he is in the full exercise of this power to commit, *for treason and seditious libels* against the Government, whatever was the original source of that power'.[114]

Second, there is the difficulty that Lord Camden said the court was bound by at least one case, *R v Derby*, that clearly recognised a power vested in the

---

[113] ibid 1052.

[114] *Entick v Carrington* (n 12) Wils Rep 288; 95 ER 807, 816, emphasis added. The State Trials report was based on Lord Camden's own notes of his judgment, although a copy of Lord Camden's originals. But it does not constitute an authoritative text and was never approved by Lord Camden. It may not be a completely accurate record of the terms in which judgment was delivered. Wilson's report may be more accurate on certain points and it provides an insight into the understanding of a contemporary lawyer present when judgment was delivered. Furthermore, Wilson's report is the only report that was available until the publication of the State Trials version in 1816 (although other private records no doubt existed: see eg TB Howell's comments, *Entick v Carrington* (n 12) 1029).

Secretaries of State to arrest for seditious libel.[115] It is not easy to reconcile Lord Camden's statement that he was bound by this case irrespective of the merits of its legal premise with the idea that he would depart from it (effectively overruling it) insofar as it extended beyond committal or arrest for treason. Indeed, to assert that the authority of the case, insofar as it related to arrest for seditious libel, had been undermined by Lord Camden's restrictive view of *Kendal & Row* would be illogical, since its authority as a case about the powers of the Secretaries of State qua Secretaries of State had also been exposed as equally infirm and yet, on this analysis, Lord Camden said he was bound to accept the extension. It is difficult to see why he should be bound by it in one respect to follow an infirm precedent, but not in the other. We also should not lose sight of the fact that Lord Camden's comments on these points were *obiter dictum* and therefore he could not alter the status of previous authority in any event.

It may be said that the fact that Lord Camden expressed himself bound by *Dr Earbury's case*, which was not a seditious libel case, suggests that he was indeed only referring to the fact that the cases had recognised a power vested in Secretaries of State as opposed to Privy Counsellors. There is some force in this point. However, it also raises its own difficulties because *Dr Earbury's case* did extend to arrest for examination, and yet if restricted to the same extent as Lord Camden would have restricted *Kendal & Row*, to committal for treason, *R v Dr Earbury* like *R v Derby* would have to be, in effect, partially overruled in respect of the extent of the power it recognised. Indeed, Holdsworth appears to have assumed that the power to arrest (as opposed to commit) for treason survived Lord Camden's judgment.[116]

So, try as we might, there is no satisfactory way to reconcile Holdsworth's view with Lord Camden's reasoning. The final but perhaps most compelling point is that had Lord Camden's judgment limited the power of Secretaries of State to the power of arrest for treason, as Holdsworth claimed, Lord Camden could not have dealt with the issue of whether Secretaries of State had power to seize papers on suspicion of seditious libel in the way that he did. There would have been nothing at all in the assertion that the Secretary of State had jurisdiction to seize papers on such a charge if the Secretary of State did not even possess the power to arrest for it. Lord Camden would surely have made this point even if he had gone on to consider the other arguments in favour of the power on their merits. Not only did he not make this point, his reasoning assumed the power to arrest for seditious libel.

[115] The view expressed in *The Oxford History of the Laws of England*, vol XI, 48 is that the Common Pleas was not strictly required to follow the King's Bench, but it was accepted convention that they would respect the decisions of the other benches.

[116] Holdsworth (n 104) also contended that Lord Camden rejected arguments for the asserted power based on practice and public policy in the final part of his judgment dealing with search and seizure (667). But see n 122 below.

The question remains as to what precisely Lord Camden meant in saying that he denied Lord Holt's opinion in *Kendal & Row* to be law insofar as it recognised the power of Privy Counsellors to commit beyond the case of high treason. There is no doubt that some of Lord Camden's recorded reasons are difficult to reconcile with his clearly expressed view that the King's Bench authorities were good law. One possibility is that the report is not entirely accurate, and it is notable that Wilson's report of the case does not record Lord Camden denying *Kendall & Row* to be law if extended beyond treason. If such words were said, most probably Lord Camden meant that Holt LCJ's opinion would not have represented a true statement of the law as it had then stood, and the purpose of Lord Camden's exegesis was to identify the legal missteps on which the weight of precedent rested, rather than to suggest that any King's Bench authority (especially important for our purposes, *R v Derby*, but also *R v Dr Earbury* and *R v Erbury*) did not represent the law and should not be followed.[117] In other words, Lord Camden was not expounding the law, but was revealing how successive court judgments had encroached on individual liberty without in his view having any proper legal foundation whether in prior authority or parliamentary sanction. He said that after he had declared his opinions on this issue, he would 'leave others to judge for themselves'.[118] Indeed, he said—disingenuously in fact—that the task before him of uncovering the origin of the power to commit was not an agreeable one because it may tend to 'create, in some minds a doubt upon a practice which has been quietly submitted to', but which, he said, if properly regulated by law could have no significance for individual liberty since, if so regulated, it mattered not whether it was a Secretary of State or magistrate who exercised the law.[119] These comments support the view that Lord Camden's opinion on *Kendal & Row* was not intended to have legal significance. His audience was the general public and Parliament rather than tenants of the Inns of Court.

On the basis of this analysis, we must conclude that Holdsworth's influential analysis of *Entick v Carrington* does not paint an accurate picture. Whilst Lord Camden's judgment is itself somewhat opaque on this issue, Holdsworth presented *Entick v Carrington* as a case that finally resolved whether Secretaries of State had the power to arrest and commit for seditious libel; he approached the case as if the issue was squarely raised; and he analysed it as if the point was a central issue in the case. But the point was not at issue. No complaint of false imprisonment was made in the suit and the issue of the power of Secretaries of State to arrest or commit for

---

[117] At *Entick v Carrington* (n 12) 1052, Lord Camden justified his examination into the power of a single privy counsellor to commit on the basis that 'lord chief justice Holt has built all his authority upon this ground' and subsequent cases 'all lean upon and support them selves by my lord chief justice Holt's opinion'.
[118] ibid.
[119] ibid 1046.

seditious libel was of only indirect relevance to the question whether the Messengers were within the equity of the Constables Protection Act. Far from overruling or departing from established precedents recognising such a power, the precedents, and the power to commit and arrest for seditious libel, were *affirmed* by Lord Camden.

Comfort for our analysis can also be taken from the fact that in subsequent decades, leading texts continued to recognise the power of Secretaries of State to arrest beyond cases of treason. Hawkins' *Pleas of the Crown* continued to state that a Secretary of State could lawfully commit persons for treason 'and for other offences against the state, as in all ages they have done'.[120] And Blackstone continued to rely upon the authority of *Kendal & Row* for the proposition that a warrant of arrest could be granted in extraordinary cases by Secretaries of State.[121]

Lord Camden's judgment was therefore less significant in its legal consequences than is sometimes thought. But Lord Camden's acceptance that he was bound by King's Bench authorities renders his exposure of the inadequacies of those authorities more remarkable. As has been shown, this is an area in which the courts had consciously sought to make the powers of the government fit for purpose as state security powers. Lord Camden's judgment was thus also strikingly reactionary when viewed from the perspective of the long-standing judicial approach to the law of seditious libel.

C. The Power to Search and Seize Personal Property

The section of Lord Camden's judgment addressing the asserted power of Secretaries of State to issue warrants for the search and seizure of property in cases of seditious libel (the 'fourth issue') is more eye-catchingly antigovernmental in its content. The defence submitted that, irrespective of the Constables Protection Act, the seizure of Entick's papers had been carried out under lawful warrant issued by the Secretary of State. It is in this section of his judgment that Lord Camden made his oft-cited Lockean appeal to individual liberty and the right to property. It is also here that Lord Camden denounced the government's appeals to state necessity in explicit and forthright terms. It was said that 'it is necessary for the end of government to lodge such a power which a state officer; and that it is better to prevent the

---

[120] W Hawkins, *A Treatise of the Pleas of the Crown*, 8th edn by J Curwood (London, S Sweet, 1824) 175, footnotes omitted. It was noted that in *Entick v Carrington*, Lord Camden had 'inquired very critically into the source of this power to commit for libels and other state crimes', accepting that Lord Camden had done no more.

[121] W Blackstone, *Commentaries on the Laws of England*, 1st edn (Oxford, Clarendon, 1769) bk IV, 287; and 16th edn (1825) 289. See also *Stephen's New Commentaries on the Laws of England*, 10th edn, vol IV (London, Butterworths, 1886) 351.

publication before than to punish the offender afterwards'. Lord Camden answered that, if the legislature were of that opinion, it 'will revive the Licensing Act'. And he also held that the common law did not recognise appeals to state necessity.[122]

These sentiments could not be more at odds with the authorities that had developed the law of seditious libel, in both its substantive aspect and in relation to the associated powers of the Secretaries of State. It was precisely the concern for state necessity which had driven the development of the law, as our discussion has shown.

As has been explained, the weight of authority pointed to the courts recognising the power to seize property, and this represented, on one view at least, a limited and principled extension of, first, the power to arrest and, second, the duty to hand over seditious writings to the authorities. The most remarkable feature of this part of Lord Camden's judgment is the clarity with which he appreciated and exposed the true breadth and dangers of the power claimed, which he described as 'exorbitant'. In this he was fortunate since, as we have seen, the manner in which the claimed power was actually exercised had been demonstrated time and again in the trials relating to *The Monitor* and *The North Briton* over which he had presided.

Thus, Lord Camden understood what was involved in a suspect's belongings being ordered to be brought before the Secretary of State to be examined. He explained that giving effect to such a warrant involved a search of the house, the breaking open of 'every room, box, or trunk' and the seizure of all papers and books without exception. Nothing, he said, is left to the discretion or humanity of the Messenger: 'His house is rifled; his most valuable secrets are taken out of his possession, before the paper for which he is charged is found to be criminal by any competent jurisdiction...'.[123] Lord Camden referred to evidence given by the Messengers in *Wilkes v Wood* to the effect that they felt compelled to take everything—'sweep all'—and he invoked the vivid image of Wilkes' private pocket book filling up 'the mouth of the sack'.[124] Had Lord Camden not seen such evidence first hand, it is hard to imagine that counsel for the plaintiffs could have made such an impact on the court through submissions alone on the facts of Entick's case.

Lord Camden did not stop there. He went on to explain how the power could be exercised against an innocent person on the basis of secret evidence

---

[122] *Entick v Carrington* (n 12) 1073. The defence had gone as far as to say that the power was 'essential to government, and the only means of quietening clamours and sedition' at 1064. Lord Camden also rejected the defence's appeal to long usage which, in the absence of any supporting authority, he found 'incredible' and incapable of establishing its legality (at 1068), citing the case of *Leach v Money*. Long usage and acceptance were, however, often accepted as part of a justification for recognising a power, as Lord Camden had himself done at 1046 (power of arrest and committal) and in *Wilkes' habeas case* (n 17) 991. See also *R v Despard* (1798) 7 Term Rep 736, 744; 101 ER 1226, 1231.

[123] *Entick v Carrington* (n 12) 1064.

[124] ibid 1065.

of undisclosed informers. This was in part a reference to Lord Camden's own previous judgment in *Wilkes' habeas case*, in which he had held that a warrant of arrest for seditious libel had to set out neither the libellous words nor the evidence on which it was premised. This gave great latitude to the government to issue warrants which would be good and valid, although the basis for them might not have been sufficient. Upholding the government's submissions in the former case had seemed a victory for the government, but now Lord Camden turned his judgment back on the Crown by limiting the authority to cases of committal and arrest.

Lord Camden identified other dangers and lack of safeguards. He explained how the Secretary of State had over time 'eased himself of every part' of his own responsibility for superintending the execution of the warrants, such that he had become used to doing nothing more than signing and sealing the warrant itself. The examination of suspects and their papers was left to his law clerks.[125] He explained how the search could be conducted without the presence of the suspect, a constable or any other witness as to what occurred on the premises and what was taken seized. He explained that the only witnesses would often be the Messengers themselves, which leaves the injured without proof. If, for example, a Messenger acted in excess of his authority, or stole a bank note, or ate a beefsteak, there would be nothing the individual could realistically do about it even if he suspected it had occurred.[126]

Lord Camden was able to see that if such powers were valid innocent persons were 'as destitute of a remedy as the guilty'.[127] Unlike in the case of general warrants (*pace* the concession in *Leach v Money*), if an individual named in a warrant was apprehended but was in fact innocent, as long as the warrant had been faithfully executed, there would be no redress for the individual. Moreover, if a warrant had not been obeyed or if it had no adequate evidential basis, Lord Camden recognised that it was hardly open to most people to challenge the exercise of the power. In response to the defendants' submission that the power to search and seize had never been challenged, which supported, it was claimed, its legality, Lord Camden stated evocatively that: 'I answer, there has been a submission of guilt and poverty to power and the terror of punishment.'[128] History had shown that the guilty and innocent alike did not challenge the wide powers asserted by Secretaries of State, whether out of fear or poverty, or both. Lord Camden would have appreciated that *The North Briton* claims had been subvented by *The North Briton*'s backer (Lord Temple), and perhaps also Entick's case, and that in the whole course of English legal history, cases such as

---

[125] ibid 1063.
[126] ibid 1065.
[127] ibid.
[128] ibid 1068.

these, brought against the King's officials by ordinary folk, had never been seen before.

Lord Camden was also concerned about the broad scope for the government to use the power of search and seizure given the expansive approach that had been taken to the law of seditious libel. Here again we see the influence of the wider context of the law of seditious libel in Lord Camden's judgment. In an important but rarely remarked upon part of his judgment, Lord Camden referred to the developments in the substantive law of seditious libel in cases such as *R v Bear*. He said that after that case, the mere possession of a libel, unpublished, in one's home was criminal. Likewise, any person who came into possession of a libel was required to disclose it. Lord Camden clearly disapproved of these developments, but said that he had no right to deny them as law in the case before him. He recognised and was troubled by the implications if a power of search and seizure was recognised on the basis of suspicion of guilt of an offence of seditious libel. He realised that given how widely framed the offence of seditious libel had become, including transcribing and failing to deliver-up seditious writings, 'whenever a favourite libel is published (and these compositions are apt to be favourites) the whole kingdom in a month or two becomes criminal'.[129] Lord Camden again chose to illustrate his point provocatively by saying that if a popular libel was put about the country, the whole kingdom would soon be liable to having government agents rifling through their homes and private affairs. The offence of seditious libel had been widely defined to include possession of written words critical of the government in a private home. Had the Court of Common Pleas in *Entick v Carrington* recognised a power in the government to search and seize evidence of seditious libels, the King's officials would have been able to exercise the power not only against printers, publishers and authors, but also against anyone believed to have a seditious publication in their house.

The force of Lord Camden's judgment on the issue of the power to search and seize therefore lies not in his florid homage to personal property or in his bravado rejection of the reliance on state necessity, or even in his black-letter refusal to extend the law beyond what is laid down in authority and statute (the three aspects of his judgment that are generally fixed upon). The force and brilliance of Lord Camden's judgment is in the detail and in his appreciation of how the claimed power—for which there was a strong legal case on paper—was dangerous and ill-used. He understood how the law operated in practice in an excessive manner, how widely the claimed power could be deployed and how few safeguards existed against abuse, including the limited effectiveness of recourse to the courts themselves. These points were more influential on Lord Camden's decision and are still

---

[129] ibid 1072.

more persuasive today than the parts of his judgment that one finds recited in textbooks: his philosophies of law, liberty and property.

V. CONCLUSION

This chapter has attempted to shed fresh light on *Entick v Carrington* for the modern reader by explaining how the development of the law of seditious libel and the exercise of powers relating to seditious libel as disclosed in previous cases were highly material to the decision of the Court of Common Pleas and illuminate key aspects of the reasoning of Lord Camden. The only issue that was open to the court to determine in *Entick v Carrinton*, both on the state of the authorities and given the scope of the suit, was the claimed power of search and seizure. But the court's reasoning ranged far and wide and in so doing exposed the degree to which the courts had developed government powers to tackle what were perceived to be threats to the government and the state without parliamentary sanction (although, we have seen how the case did not, as some have claimed, abolish the power to arrest for seditious libel). In doing so, as well as by refusing to endorse the power of search and seizure—despite a weight of reason and authority in favour of such a power—the case can be considered alongside other famous judicial stands against the encroachment of state security powers.[130]

---

[130] Such as Lord Atkin's subsequently endorsed dissent in *Liversidge v Anderson* [1942] AC 206 and more recently the judgments of the House of Lords in *A (No1) v Secretary of State for the Home Department* [2005] 1 AC 68 and *AF (No 3) v Secretary of State for the Home Department* [2010] 2 AC 269.

3

Entick and Carrington, *the Propaganda Wars and Liberty of the Press*

JACOB ROWBOTTOM*

I. INTRODUCTION

WHEN TEACHING CONSTITUTIONAL Law, Lord Camden's judgment in *Entick v Carrington* is often boiled down to a simple proposition: that government must have legal authority to interfere with the rights of an individual and cannot simply assert state necessity as a justification. This important point provides one of the foundations of the modern British constitution and protects a key aspect of the rule of law. In this chapter, I will look at *Entick v Carrington* from a different perspective: as a case concerned with press freedom. The principle stated by Lord Camden did not directly address liberty of the press, so the relevance of the case to this topic may not be obvious to a student of Constitutional Law. Dicey does, however, make a connection between the two. The principle in *Entick* is reflected in Dicey's view of the rule of law as the absence of arbitrary power: 'no man is punishable or can be made to suffer in body or goods except for a distinct breach of law established in the ordinary legal manner before the ordinary Courts of the land'.[1] Press freedom, in his view, was merely an application of this aspect of the rule of law.[2] Publishers and journalists were 'subject only to the ordinary law of the land'.[3] Under this approach, the press should not be subject to any system of prior restraint, such as licensing, as no breach of the ordinary law had been established in the usual manner by a court. For Dicey, this principle provided a reason why 'liberty of the press has been long reputed as a special feature of English institutions'.[4]

---

* With thanks to Leslie Mitchell for comments on an earlier draft.
[1] AV Dicey, *Introduction to the Study of the Law of the Constitution*, 8th edn (London, Macmillan, 1915) 110.
[2] ibid 153.
[3] ibid 155.
[4] ibid 152.

The shortcomings of Dicey's account of the rule of law in the light of the modern regulatory state are well known, and his account cannot easily accommodate practices such as broadcasting regulation. In any event, his view of press freedom is relatively minimal by today's standards. To connect *Entick* with press freedom, we can look beyond the principle of the case, to the events and actors that surrounded the decision in 1765. The decision was one of several political and legal skirmishes that occurred in a period that is regarded as crucial to the development of freedom of the press and the right to criticise government. At the centre of these skirmishes was a propaganda war involving, among others, John Wilkes. The events that followed were to turn Wilkes into a symbol for the cause of press freedom and liberty. His name is still invoked today in debates on press freedom, with several critics of the Leveson Report, for example, warning that all that Wilkes had fought for would be lost if the Report were implemented.[5] The name of John Wilkes is frequently used by commentators to embody press freedom, yet to most lawyers, *Entick v Carrington*—a case with which Wilkes was so closely linked—tends to be remembered for a single aspect of the rule of law. This chapter will tell the story of the events surrounding *Entick v Carrington* and of its connection with liberty of the press in the 1760s.

II. POLITICS AND THE PRESS IN THE 1760s

The events leading to *Entick v Carrington* are rooted in the political developments at the start of the decade. When George III acceded to the throne in 1760, the government was led by a coalition of William Pitt, as Secretary of State, and the Duke of Newcastle, as Prime Minister. The country was engaged in the Seven Years' War, with Pitt—the dominant figure in government—at the helm of war policy. That ministry, which formed in 1757, had initially enjoyed the support of George II's grandson and heir, Prince George.[6] However, tensions began to emerge. By the time of his accession, George III already harboured bad feelings towards Pitt due to disagreements on questions of patronage.[7] With the new monarch also came changes to the personnel and dynamics within the government. The young King sought to give his former tutor and close adviser John Stuart, the Earl of Bute, a place in government.[8] Bute, who had little political experience,

---

[5] L McKinstry, 'A Free Press is at the Very Heart of British Democracy' *Daily Express* (London, 29 November 2012); and see B Johnson, 'It's a Vigorous, Voracious Press That Keeps Our Country Honest' *Daily Telegraph* (London, 14 October 2013).

[6] P Langford, *A Polite and Commercial People* (Oxford, Oxford University Press, 1989) 333.

[7] J Brewer, *Party Ideology and Popular Politics at the Accession of George III* (Cambridge, Cambridge University Press, 1976) 101; Langford (n 6) 333.

[8] See J Black, *George III: America's Last King* (New Haven, Yale University Press, 2006) 54.

was first appointed to the Privy Council and then became Secretary of State for the Northern Department in March 1761, which gave him equal status to Pitt. In addition to his favour from the monarch, Bute also had his own power base with the 'command' of 45 Scottish MPs and 16 Scottish peers, as well as substantial wealth and powerful family connections.[9] The existing coalition, which already contained some personal strains among its members, now had to accommodate a new powerful actor.

Tensions also emerged in government over the conduct of the war. A number of ministers, including Bute, concerned about the cost of the conflict and impact on the national debt, were keen to reach a peace agreement with France. Pitt, by contrast, wanted to pursue the war to 'complete victory'.[10] The matter came to a head when the Cabinet refused to accept Pitt's stance on the immediate need to declare war on Spain. Pitt resigned in October 1761. In May 1762, Newcastle resigned due to a Cabinet disagreement over the subsidy to Prussia. Bute replaced Newcastle as First Lord of the Treasury. Pitt's departure and the collapse of the coalition ministry arose due to the various tensions in personality and policy. However, Pitt's supporters placed the blame squarely on Bute. While the reality was more complex, parts of the opposition press pushed a view of Bute as a sinister figure manipulating the King and agreeing to peace terms that betrayed the national interest.

By this time, the political culture recognised the liberty of the press, at least in the absence of prior restraints. Just before the turn of the eighteenth century, the Licensing Acts lapsed and publishers were free from that system of press licensing. Despite this milestone, the press was still subject to a number of other controls. Siebert notes that taxes on publications, subsidies to writers and publishers, and the criminal law continued to give government a way 'of keeping the press in line'.[11] Siebert further divides the legal controls into the following categories: (1) the law of treason; (2) parliamentary prosecutions for breach of privilege (including reporting parliamentary proceedings, as well as libel of a Member of Parliament (MP) or an obscene publication); (3) the use of general warrants (the name given to a warrant that does not specify the person to be arrested, place to be searched, or property to be seized);[12] and (4) the law of seditious libel.[13] While the various laws gave broad powers to government, Barker reminds

---

[9] S Watson, *The Reign of George III 1760–1815* (Oxford, Clarendon, 1960) 70.

[10] ibid 72. Black (n 8) 60 notes that Pitt became isolated in his own ministry as a result of this position.

[11] F Siebert, *Freedom of the Press in England, 1476–1776: The Rise and Decline of Government Control* (Urbana, University of Illinois Press, 1952) 4.

[12] See J Law and E Martin, *A Dictionary of Law*, 7th edn (Oxford, Oxford University Press, 2009).

[13] Siebert (n 11) ch 18.

us that the press was 'rarely subject to a system of organised government or legal repression and it certainly never experienced the kind of rigorous censorship which occurred in parts of continental Europe'.[14] Given the sheer number of publications, to enforce these laws rigorously 'became increasingly impractical'.[15] Even when the government did decide to invoke these laws, there were sometimes difficulties in securing a conviction and, as we shall see, the danger of public humiliation.

While the laws did not establish a system of complete governmental control, these powers were nonetheless powerful tools to curb critical commentary. Of these controls, the use of warrants had considerable power to harass and intimidate writers and publishers without having to bring a prosecution or go before a judge or jury. The warrants not only allowed officials to violently intrude into people's homes, seize property and detain people, but could also require people to make applications to the court for bail and for the return of property. As Harris notes, the harassment of and burden on publishers generated by such warrants created a level of inconvenience that gave a strong incentive to self-censor.[16]

Such controls had been invoked at various times earlier in the century, for example, to deal with the Jacobite threat. By the middle part of the eighteenth century, harassment of the press declined and liberty of the press was to some degree tolerated by those in power.[17] Yet this was to change in the 1760s and a number of factors came together to create a political environment that would test the boundaries of press freedom and state controls. These factors included the political instability following the end of a period of Whig dominance, the accession of a new monarch, an economic slump in the aftermath of the war, an increase in the number of publications and the presence of some skilled political organisers.[18] The government, feeling vulnerable as a result of these various factors, attempted to clamp down on its critics and revive control of the press through legal means.[19] This clampdown was met with resistance, and some of the legal controls were challenged in both the courts and in practice. *Entick v Carrington* was one episode in these struggles, an episode that concerned the lawfulness of the warrants used to search and seize persons and their papers for seditious material. These struggles by no means secured complete freedom, but did end one of the most blunt tools for curbing the press.

---

[14] H Barker, *Newspapers, Politics and English Society, 1695–1855* (Harlow, Longman, 2000) 68.

[15] ibid 68.

[16] B Harris, *Politics and the Rise of the Press: Britain and France 1620–1800* (London, Routledge, 1996) 36.

[17] ibid 35.

[18] Brewer (n 7) ch 1.

[19] See Harris (n 16) 36.

III. THE BATTLE IN THE WEEKLY PRESS AND
THE FIRST SET OF WARRANTS

The facts of *Entick v Carrington* concerned a weekly publication called *The Monitor or British Freeholder*. The newspaper was established in 1755, under the patronage first of Richard Beckford (who died in 1756) and then William Beckford.[20] William Beckford, an Alderman, MP and future Lord Mayor of London, was wealthy and had inherited a substantial commercial interest in sugar plantations in Jamaica.[21] He was one of Pitt's 'most stalwart political allies'.[22] The two main writers for the paper were Arthur Beardmore and John Entick.[23] Beardmore was Beckford's solicitor, active in London politics and enjoyed close links with another Pitt ally, Earl Temple.[24] John Entick had worked as a schoolmaster and writer. In his publications, Entick referred to himself as the 'Rev. John Entick MA', though it is not known whether he was ever awarded a degree.[25] Beardmore and Entick were not the sole authors of *The Monitor*. The newspaper also received contributions from John Wilkes, the MP for Aylesbury since 1757, who was also appointed Colonel in the Buckinghamshire militia in 1762. Wilkes was said to be a man of 'unbound wit' and 'overwhelming charm',[26] a skilled propagandist and writer, but also a libertine known for his debauched lifestyle, a politician who bribed voters to maintain his place in Parliament and, with his missing teeth and crossed eyes, was sometimes referred to as the ugliest man in England. Yet Wilkes proved to be a key person in the events leading to *Entick v Carrington* and his persecution turned him into an unlikely hero and symbol of liberty.

The Monitor became '"the mouthpiece" for Beckford's opinions'[27] and it is therefore unsurprising that the paper functioned as part of 'Pitt's popular support',[28] criticising the new ministry and, in particular, Bute.[29] For example, on 22 May 1762, No 357 of *The Monitor* included an essay on favourites, a thinly disguised attack on the King's favourite Bute, thought to be written by John Wilkes. The essay begins with a quote from Tacitus on Sejanus, which reminds the author of the dangers of a prince having a favourite, and warns that favourites work 'to keep out men of merit, to

---

[20] See M Peters, '*The Monitor 1755–1765*: A Political Essay Paper and Popular London Opinion' (PhD thesis, University of Canterbury, New Zealand, 1974) for a detailed history.

[21] For a recent biography, see P Gauci, *William Beckford: First Prime Minister of the London Empire* (New Haven, Yale University Press, 2013).

[22] Peters (n 20) 112.

[23] ibid 20–29.

[24] ibid.

[25] J Humphreys, 'Entick, John (c.1703–1773)' (rev P Wilson) in *Oxford Dictionary of National Biography* (Oxford, Oxford University Press, 2004).

[26] I Christie, *Wilkes, Wyvill and Reform* (London, Macmillan, 1962) 12.

[27] Gauci (n 21) 83.

[28] Peters (n 20) 113.

[29] Peters (n 20) 306.

degrade patriotism with a mortal hatred; to assist him in the sacrifice of public interest to his private views'. The week after this essay was published saw the launch of a pro-government weekly paper, *The Briton*, financed by Bute and edited by Tobias Smollett.[30] In response to Bute's effort, the following month saw the first publication of *The North Briton*, an anti-government paper written by John Wilkes and Charles Churchill, and published by George Kearsley. This paper was largely financed by Pitt's ally (and brother-in-law) Earl Temple, who had sat with him in government and resigned at the same time in 1761. In the same month, the pro-government *The Auditor* was launched and financed again by Bute. Just as *The Monitor* and *The North Briton* targeted Bute, *The Auditor* and *The Briton* took aim at the ministry's critics. For example, *The Auditor* published a humorous political dictionary that referred to Wilkes as 'Colonel Squintum' (playing on his appearance), Beckford as 'Alderman Sugarcane' (referring to his commercial interests) and Entick as the 'drunken parson'.[31] The summer of 1762 therefore saw a war of words with two rival sets of weekly publications trading arguments and insults.

The ministry's strategy to rely on its own propaganda against opposition attacks proved to be unsuccessful.[32] Towards the end of the year, the government feared it was losing the war of words and Parliament was soon to consider the peace proposals. Given the sensitivity of this issue, the government turned to its legal tools to deal with opposition voices.[33] Around this time, *The Monitor* lost its publisher Jonathan Scott, as a result of either government pressure or concerns about the severity of the attacks on Bute.[34] On 11 October 1762, Scott gave information to an assistant to the Secretary of State, Lord Halifax, naming Beardmore and Entick as the writers of *The Monitor*.[35] Acting upon this information, Lord Halifax signed a warrant on 6 November 1762 directing the King's messengers to search for and seize Charles Beardmore and John Entick, along with their books and papers. Both were named as authors of eight editions of *The Monitor* published that year, which contained, according to the warrant, 'gross and scandalous reflections and invectives, upon His Majesty's government, and upon both Houses of Parliament'. A further warrant was issued for Beardmore's clerk Meredith and a separate warrant included the names of the printers and publishers of *The Monitor*.[36]

---

[30] Bute had already made significant investments into pro-ministry propaganda: see Brewer (n 7) 221–27.

[31] *The Auditor* (26 August 1762).

[32] R Rea, *The English Press in Politics 1760–1774* (Lincoln, University of Nebraska Press, 1963) 33.

[33] Siebert (n 11) 377.

[34] Peters (n 20) 39–41. Scott went on to publish three editions of his own rival version of *The Monitor*.

[35] *Entick v Carrington* (1765) 19 Howell's State Trials 1029.

[36] Peters (n 20) 600.

Of the eight issues of *The Monitor* named in the warrant, three included essays attacking favourites, including No 357 discussed earlier.[37] Like that earlier issue, No 360 opened with a reference to Sejanus in the reign of Tiberius.[38] No 380 made an implied comparison between Bute and the influence of Robert de Vere and others over Richard II, a historical reference that carried the suggestion of a sexual relationship between the King and his adviser. Peters notes that the warrant could just as easily have included attacks on favourites carried in other editions of *The Monitor* at the same time.[39] For example, No 372 (not included in the warrant) discussed Edward II and his favourite Piers Gaveston, another comparison alluding to the possibility of a sexual relationship.[40] No 377 (also not included in the warrant) made an implied comparison between Bute and Roger Mortimer in the reign of Edward II, a comparison that carried a suggestion that Bute was having a relationship with George III's mother, the Princess Dowager.[41] While noting that the choice of editions of *The Monitor* named in the warrant was 'haphazard', Peters speculates that this may have been due to 'tact and sound sense about publicity'.[42]

Other editions of the *The Monitor* named in the warrant looked at the conduct of foreign policy. For example, No 358 discussed the publication of papers concerning relations with Spain, arguing that the government had held back papers vindicating Pitt's position on the need for war with Spain.[43] No 373 criticised of the terms of the peace, warning of the danger 'if England, once more becomes the dupe of her enemies, and the House of Hanover deliver her interest up to the dubious advice and conduct of a Stuart' (the latter also referring to Bute's surname). The essay contrasts such a danger to the time when Pitt was at the helm and the 'whole land was full of joy and mirth'. Further attacks on the peace were published in No 376 (2 October 1762), commenting on the treatment of the King of Prussia. In her study of *The Monitor*, Peters writes that these essays 'were probably no more virulent and certainly no more seditious than those of earlier periods of intense controversy';[44] what made the difference was the 'tougher attitude' on the part of the government while the terms of the peace were being negotiated.[45]

---

[37] While the warrant cites Nos 378 and 379, these are not to be confused with the rival editions of *The Monitor* of the same number published by Scott, but not authored by Entick and Beardmore.

[38] *The Monitor* No 360 (12 June 1762).

[39] Peters (n 20) 399.

[40] *The Monitor* No 372 (4 September 1762).

[41] *The Monitor* No 377 (9 October 1762).

[42] Peters (n 20) 399.

[43] *The Monitor* No 358 (29 May 1762).

[44] Peters (n 20) 599.

[45] ibid.

The warrants were executed on 11 November 1762. Four messengers— Nathan Carrington, James Watson, Thomas Ardran and Robert Blackmore—entered Entick's house, breaking open doors and searching each room. The messengers then ransacked the property, breaking open boxes belonging to Entick, searching a bureau and several drawers to look through Entick's private papers. They seized a large number of books and charts belonging to Entick, which were delivered to Lord Halifax's assistant Lovel Stanhope. The messengers spent four hours at Entick's home, after which he was taken into custody for six days and was granted bail on 17 November. Earlier the same day, Charles Beardmore was subject to similar treatment and was imprisoned for six days. His wife was permitted to be with him during this time, but he was not allowed to privately converse with a client or write a letter to Beckford.[46] The violent means used by the messengers and their ability to ransack a home and rifle through possessions illustrate how the warrant was not simply a means to collect evidence of seditious libel, but was a powerful tool to intimidate and harass newspapers and authors.

These actions had repercussions beyond *The Monitor*. On 18 November 1762, Lord Halifax signed a general warrant targeting the authors, printers and publishers of Nos 1–25 of *The North Briton*. While this warrant was never served, Nobbe writes that the printer of the paper at the time, William Richardson, 'must have been given a quick look at the warrant', as he soon refused to continue his role with the paper.[47] While it is not clear whether Richardson had been bribed or 'merely frightened' by the government, Nobbe suggests that the action against *The Monitor*'s authors 'had perhaps made it easier to suborn *The North Briton*'s printer'.[48] Wilkes and Temple soon found a new printer, Dryden Leach, but this arrangement did not last and Leach only printed one edition of *The North Briton*, No 26. It is likely that Leach was scared off by a second general warrant, which targeted Nos 1–26.[49] The troubles faced by *The North Briton* illustrate how the action against Beardmore and Entick sent a signal to other authors and publishers about the possible consequences of their actions.

Following their release, no actions for seditious libel were pursued against Beardmore and Entick.[50] The lack of subsequent action possibly supports the view that the ministry only intended to cause a temporary disruption

---

[46] *Beardmore v Carrington* (1764) 2 Wils KB 244.

[47] G Nobbe, *The North Briton: A Study in Political Propaganda* (New York, Columbia University Press, 1939) 133.

[48] ibid 130.

[49] Rea (n 32) 34–35. Richard Balfe then took over as printer of *The North Briton*.

[50] Rea (n 32) 64 notes that 'on June 22, 1763, they were discharged from their recognizances by the Court of King's Bench'.

to *The Monitor* while the peace terms were being debated.[51] If this was the government's purpose, the strategy had mixed results. The publication schedule was disrupted only briefly and an edition of *The Monitor* was published on 27 November discussing the terms of the peace.[52] However, Peters notes that these events may have chilled the authors, as *The Monitor* subsequently lost its 'shrill edge'.[53] *The Monitor* continued to be published until 1765, but after these events took a more restrained tone, turned its attention away from foreign policy and gradually suffered a 'loss of purpose and direction'.[54] Despite the government's fears, the preliminaries of the peace were approved by Parliament with relative ease.[55] Shortly after the peace treaty was signed in February 1763, *The Auditor* and *The Briton* ceased to be published.[56] Despite this parliamentary success, Bute resigned in April 1763, the strains of office having taken its toll, and George Grenville succeeded him as First Lord of the Treasury.[57]

IV. *THE NORTH BRITON* AND THE SECOND SET OF WARRANTS

While *The Monitor* may have been tamed by events, the same cannot be said for *The North Briton*, which continued its vigorous attacks on the ministry into 1763. Even after Bute had resigned in April of that year, Wilkes continued to attack him, arguing that he wielded influence behind the scenes. The most famous edition of *The North Briton*, No 45, criticised the King's speech at the close of the parliamentary session, attacking several policies of the ministry, including the terms of the peace with France and the new tax on cider. The criticism focused on Bute's influence rather taking direct aim at the monarch, lamenting 'that a prince of so many great and amiable qualities, whom England truly reveres, can be brought to give the sanction of his sacred name to the most odious measures, and to the most unjustifiable public declarations'. The essay went on that a 'despotic minister' could 'dazzle his prince', with the honour of the Crown being 'sunk even

---

[51] Nobbe (n 47) 139; and A Cash, *John Wilkes: The Scandalous Father of Civil Liberty* (New Haven, Yale University Press, 2006) 88. See also *The North Briton* No 27 (4 December 1762), which, after asking why an action was not brought against *The Monitor* earlier, argues that 'at this important and critical juncture, it might be of excellent use to stop the mouths of those who imagine it possible to love their country, although they exclaim against the minister; and who really sigh for a good peace, yet might be inclined to represent the false *preliminaries* handed about, as most infamous and injurious to England'.

[52] *The Monitor* No 382.

[53] Peters (n 20) 602.

[54] ibid 359.

[55] Rea (n 32).

[56] ibid 37.

[57] Bute continued to advise the King, but his influence disappeared by 1766. See Langford (n 6) 355; Black (n 8) 88.

to prostitution'. Suggesting that the King was just a mouthpiece of his advisors certainly gave an unflattering picture of the monarch, particularly of a monarch who claimed a degree of independence.[58] The essay also contained a call to resistance:

> A nation as sensible as the English, will see that a spirit of concord when they are oppressed, means a tame submission to injury, and that a spirit of liberty ought then to arise, and I am sure ever will, in proportion to the weight of the grievance they feel. Every legal attempt of a contrary tendency to the spirit of concord will be deemed a justifiable resistance, warranted by the spirit of the English constitution.

In his biography of Wilkes, Bleackley describes this as a 'trenchant denunciation' of the King's speech, but that it was 'no more vitriolic than many of its predecessors'.[59] Nonetheless, the new ministry under Grenville chose to take a harder line against such publications and issued another search and arrest warrant in relation to No 45.

While it was generally known that Wilkes stood behind *The North Briton*, there was no hard evidence before the government to prove his authorship. Consequently, when Lord Halifax issued a warrant in relation to No 45, it called for the search and seizure of the unnamed 'authors, printers, or publishers' of *The North Briton*. This was a true general warrant insofar as it named only the crime alleged to have been committed and made no mention of the persons suspected or the premises to be searched. The warrant therefore gave the messengers huge discretion about who to search and detain, and was broader than that issued in relation to *The Monitor*, which at least named Entick and Beardmore. It was also broader than *The Monitor* warrants, as it described No 45 not only as 'seditious' but also 'treasonable'.

On 29 April 1763, Dryden Leach, who had only been involved in the printing of issue 26 of *The North Briton*, was arrested and was released after four days in custody.[60] On the same day, the messengers arrested the bookseller and publisher of *The North Briton*, George Kearlsey, who then told the authorities the names of others involved.[61] In total, 48 people were arrested under the warrant.[62] On 30 April, Wilkes was arrested under the warrant and taken to Lord Halifax's house.[63] Temple's lawyer, Charles Beardmore, applied for a writ of habeas corpus to secure Wilkes' release. While such applications were normally made before the King's Bench, the applicant

---

[58] Cash (n 51) 100.
[59] H Bleackley, *Life of John Wilkes* (London, John Lane, 1917) 91.
[60] For an account of these events, see Nobbe (n 47) 214–15.
[61] PDG Thomas, *John Wilkes: A Friend to Liberty* (Oxford, Clarendon, 1996) 29.
[62] Siebert (n 11) 378.
[63] *The Case of John Wilkes on a Habeas Corpus* (1763) 19 Howell's State Trials 981. See also Cash (n 51) and Nobbe (n 47) 216–32 for accounts.

chose to go before the Court of Common Pleas in order to avoid Lord Mansfield and appear before the more sympathetic Chief Justice Charles Pratt.[64] Pratt was an old schoolfriend of Pitt's and his legal career owed much to that friendship.[65] He had served as Attorney General in the Pitt–Newcastle government, but resigned his seat in Parliament in order to take up the post at the Court of Common Pleas in January 1762. The strategy employed by Wilkes' lawyers worked and Pratt CJ granted habeas corpus.

This did not, however, secure Wilkes' release. Before the writ could be served, Halifax drew up another writ committing Wilkes to the Tower of London.[66] By the time the writ of habeas corpus was served, the messengers named in it no longer had custody of Wilkes and the writ had to be returned. As these events took place, Wilkes' home was searched and various items seized by Robert Wood, the Under-Secretary for the Northern Department. In the meantime, a further application for habeas corpus was heard before Pratt CJ and granted on the grounds that Wilkes was protected by parliamentary privilege. Privilege allowed all MPs to be free from arrest except in cases of treason, felony and breach of the peace. Pratt concluded that Wilkes was therefore protected from arrest for libel.

The harsh treatment of Wilkes generated public sympathy and support for him. The actions of the government only worked to give greater publicity to *The North Briton* and Wilkes.[67] For example, Wilkes published details of his arrest and detention in the *North Briton* episode to highlight the treatment he had suffered and to gain public approval.[68] While he was detained in the Tower, Wilkes' friends organised a parade on the Easter Sunday, including MPs and businessman, to show their support for him.[69] When Pratt granted the second habeas corpus writ, members of a crowded court room shouted 'Wilkes and Liberty'[70]—a new slogan that summed up Wilkes' status as a champion for civil liberties. During this period, Wilkes emerged as a popular hero.

But this was not the end of the matter. Both the government and the Wilkites used various legal tools to advance their cause. The printers, publishers and authors of *The Monitor* and *The North Briton* that had been searched, imprisoned and had items seized brought various actions for false imprisonment and trespass. At the same time, the government pursued Wilkes for seditious libel.

---

[64] Rea (n 32) 46; Bleackley (n 59) 104.
[65] P Brown, *The Chathamites* (London, Macmillan, 1967) 45.
[66] Cash (n 51) 107.
[67] Nobbe (n 47) 213.
[68] Brewer (n 7) 166. A letter to his daughter written from the Tower of London was sent out to a number of newspapers; see Bleackley (n 59) 104.
[69] Cash (n 51) 111.
[70] Bleackley (n 59) 107.

V. ACTIONS FOR TRESPASS AND FALSE IMPRISONMENT

The use of general warrants against the Jacobites had been largely accepted in the earlier part of the century as a way to combat the threat of a Stuart restoration.[71] By the 1760s, changes in the political climate allowed for a reassessment of such measures, and the actions of the government in relation to *The Monitor* and *The North Briton* provided an opportunity to challenge the use of those warrants in court.[72] A number of the publishers, printers and writers that had been arrested and searched brought actions against the messengers and, in some cases, the Secretary of State. Fourteen of those actions sought damages for wrongful arrest and imprisonment. The first decision came on 6 July 1763, when William Huckle, who worked as a printer for Dryden Leach, won his action for false imprisonment and was awarded £300 by the jury.[73] While Huckle had been well treated during his six hours in custody and suffered relatively little damage, Pratt CJ held that those damages were not excessive.[74] He found that the jury was right to award exemplary damages:

> To enter a man's house by virtue of a nameless warrant, in order to procure evidence, is worse than the Spanish Inquisition; a law under which no Englishman would wish to live an hour; it was a most daring public attack made upon the liberty of the subject.

On the 7 July 1763, another of Leach's printers, James Lindsay, won £200 in a similar action. After this, the government agreed to pay similar damages to 12 other plaintiffs.[75] These early rulings did not decide whether general warrants were legal, and the award of damages was based on the fact that the warrants had not been properly executed. Nonetheless, the defeat was embarrassing for the government, and the court cases helped to rally public support. Crowds cheered for Wilkes as he travelled to sit in on these trials, while the Attorney General was hissed as he left the court.[76]

The government was to suffer further defeats. Wilkes brought an action against Robert Wood for unlawful trespass and seizure of papers.[77] Wood pleaded not guilty and argued that in any event, the general warrant provided justification for his actions. Part of that defence depended on Wood

---

[71] Langford (n 6) 358 and 698. See also P. Fritz, 'The Anti-Jacobite Intelligence System of English Ministers, 1715–45' (1973) 16 *Historical Journal* 265, 266–67.

[72] See Harris (n 16) 35; Langford (n 6).

[73] Siebert (n 11) 378; Thomas (n 61) 35.

[74] *Huckle v Money* (1763) 95 Eng Rep 768.

[75] Thomas (n 61) 35; Nobbe (n 47) 237.

[76] Rea (n 32) 61; Cash (n 51) 133.

[77] In that action, the Solicitor General described No 45 as 'a libel on the three branches of the legislative body, King, Lords, and Commons', which 'had attacked private persons, persons in public stations, with their names written at full length' and 'had already produced bloodshed'. *Wilkes v Wood* (1763) 98 ER 489.

showing that Wilkes had been the author of No 45. In the Court of Common Pleas, the jury found that the defendants had failed to prove Wilkes' authorship. This finding posed a challenge for the government's prosecution of Wilkes for seditious libel—how could it prosecute him if it could not show that he was the author? More significantly, the Chief Justice went on to discuss the legality of the general warrants and warned the jury that if the Secretary of State had a power to issue nameless warrants allowing his agents to break into people's houses and seize belongings on a mere suspicion of libel, then it would be 'totally subversive of the liberty of the subject' and was 'contrary to the fundamental principles of the constitution'.[78] The jury found for Wilkes and awarded him £1,000 in damages.

A further attack on the use of warrants came with the decision in *Leach v Money*. Dryden Leach—the unfortunate printer of one edition of *The North Briton*—sought damages for his arrest made under the general warrant targeting No 45. The case was argued twice before the King's Bench on a bill of exceptions. In the earlier hearing, Lord Mansfield stated that the level of discretion that the general warrants gave to the officer was contrary to common law principles,[79] and rejected an argument that the lawfulness of such a warrant can be founded on past usage. However, at the later hearing, the decision in Leach's favour was based on the fact that the defendant accepted that the warrant had not been properly executed, given that Leach himself was not the author, publisher or printer of that particular issue. While the final decision was based on this narrower ground, the earlier ruling from Lord Mansfield struck another blow against the legality of general warrants.

Entick and Beardmore brought claims for the searches concerning the eight editions of *The Monitor*.[80] In May 1764, Beardmore was awarded £1,000 for trespass and false imprisonment, which was later upheld by the King's Bench.[81] John Entick brought a similar claim against Nathan Carrington and the three other messengers who had searched his house and detained him. While the warrant at least named Entick, it was still broad in that it did not specify the premises to be searched or papers to be seized. The warrant did not even require that the papers seized be libellous.

The final ruling in *Entick v Carrington* was given by Pratt, now made Lord Camden, in the Court of Common Pleas.[82] After rejecting a defence that the messengers were given statutory protection under the Constables Protection Act 1750, Camden considered the defendants' argument that the warrant was lawful and that they therefore had a common law defence to a

[78] *Wilkes v Wood* (1763) 19 St Tr 1153; (1763) 98 ER 489.

[79] *Money v Leach* (1765) 97 ER 1075, 1088.

[80] While Beardmore was detained by the messengers in 1762, Wilkes suggested the possibility of a legal action. Beardmore initially declined to follow this advice, but he changed his mind after seeing Wilkes' success in the courts. See Nobbe (n 47) 133.

[81] *Beardmore v Carrington* (1764) 2 Wils KB 244.

[82] (1765) 2 Wils KB 275 and (1765) 19 Howell's State Trials 1029.

trespass action. He rejected this argument on the grounds that the Secretary of State had no power to issue such a warrant under statute or common law. He noted how the breadth of the warrant left open the potential for abuse, as it allowed papers to be seized with no witnesses present. Consequently, there was nothing to stop him taking away 'all papers, bank bills, or any other valuable papers'.

Lord Camden found that even if there had been a practice of using such warrants which had gone unchallenged in previous years, this was not sufficient to make the practice lawful. The lack of a legal challenge in earlier cases was more a sign of the poverty and fear of certain booksellers than evidence of legality. He noted how the Secretary of State previously had a power to issue some search warrants under the Star Chamber powers and then under the Licensing Act, which had lapsed. The only authority for a common law power to search for libellous material was a non-binding opinion of 12 judges in the reign of Charles II, which claimed a power to license the press under prerogative.[83] Lord Camden noted that Lord Chief Justice Scroggs had relied upon that opinion in the trial of Henry Carr for seditious libel (which was prosecuted by the future Judge Jeffries). In that reference, Camden connected the use of general warrants to two judges (Lord Chief Justice Scroggs and Judge Jeffries) that 'personified the arbitrariness of the administration of law under the Stuarts' in the eighteenth century.[84] By finding past usage to be rooted in the Star Chamber, the Licensing Acts and the views of a notorious judge, Lord Camden made a powerful point against the legality of the warrants.

Finally, Lord Camden then rejected the argument that the Secretary of State has the power as a matter of state necessity. The state necessity argument ran that it is better to prevent the publication of a libel and prevent any consequent harm than to simply impose a post-publication penalty. Camden saw how this justification would run counter to the absence of prior restraints that was central to the understanding of press freedom at the time. He stated that if such a power were necessary, Parliament would simply revive the Licensing Act. Similarly, the use of the warrants was not justified as a means of collecting evidence. This was especially true in the case of a libel, where the crime is 'committed in open daylight and in the face of the world'.

The Court of Common Pleas concluded that the Secretary of State lacked the power to issue a warrant to seize and carry away unspecified papers. The decision stands as a landmark, embodying a key part of the rule of law. Lord Camden emphasised the importance of the decision for liberty, noting that

---

[83] See P Hamburger, 'The Development of the Law of Seditious Libel and the Control of the Press' (1985) 37 *Stanford Law Review* 661.

[84] E Hellmuth, 'The Palladium of All Other English Liberties' in E Hellmuth (ed), *The Transformation of Political Culture* (Oxford, Oxford University Press, 1990) 490.

if he found the warrant to be lawful, 'the secret cabinets and bureaus of every subject in this kingdom will be thrown open to the search and inspection of a messenger, whenever the secretary of state shall think fit to charge, or even to suspect, a person to be the author, printer, or publisher of a seditious libel'. He also noted that a person's papers 'are his dearest property'. Given the high regard for property rights in eighteenth-century Britain, the connection between papers and a precious type of property provided powerful language in support of the protection of writers.[85] This reasoning has since been cited by courts to emphasis the sanctity of the home and respect for a person's private thoughts.[86]

In relation to press freedom, Lord Camden took what is, by today's standards, a very limited view. While he rejected the use of prior restraints, he concluded that his reasoning did not justify the publication of a libel:

> All civilized governments have punished calumny with severity; for these compositions debauch the manners of the people; they excite a spirit of disobedience, and enervate the authority of government; they provoke and excite the passions of the people against their rulers, and the rulers oftentimes against the people.

He then warned of the dangers of 'unjust acquittals' by juries:

> [F]or if kings and great men cannot obtain justice at their hands by the ordinary course of law, they may at last be provoked to restrain that press, which the juries of their country refuse to regulate. When licentiousness is tolerated, liberty is in the utmost danger; because tyranny, bad as it is, is better than anarchy; and the worst of governments is more tolerable than no government at all.

On this reasoning, libels go beyond the limits of press freedom, but the important point is for restraints to be imposed in accordance with the ordinary legal procedures. While on other occasions Lord Camden had advocated a broader protection for speech, his views on press freedom in *Entick* fit with the dominant view at the time.

While *Entick* and the related cases did not break new ground in the understanding of press freedom, they were nonetheless important victories that removed one of the tools used by the government to harass and intimidate the opposition press. The decisions also caused considerable embarrassment for the government, providing a reminder that attempts to clamp down on critics can backfire spectacularly. The cost to the ministry came not only in the legal defeat, but also in the publicity surrounding the trials. Wilkes was particularly skilled as a propagandist. Along with his supporters, he characterised the actions of the government as an attack on the liberty of

---

[85] W Blackstone, *Commentaries on the Laws of England, A Facsimile of the First Edition of 1765–1769* (Chicago, University of Chicago Press, 1979) 135: 'So great moreover is the regard of the law for private property, that it will not authorize the least violation of it; no, not even for the general good of the whole community.'

[86] See for example, *Lord Scarman in Morris v Beardmore* [1981] AC 446 at 464.

every subject.[87] The lawyers at the trials put this message forward, as did Wilkes in his speeches at the Court of Common Pleas. For example, in the hearing for the writ of habeas corpus, Wilkes told the courtroom that the issue before them was 'whether English liberty be a reality or a shadow' and described the actions of the ministry as 'star chamber tyranny'.[88] By framing the issue in this way, Wilkes was not seen as an attack dog of a particular political group, but as a champion of civil liberties.[89]

Freedom of the press was part and parcel of this popular cause. The government treatment of those involved in *The Monitor* and *The North Briton*, both in terms of the searches and some subsequent seditious libel actions, prompted the publication of essays and articles emphasising the importance of press freedom and raising the profile of that right. For example, in an essay discussing the government's actions against Beardmore and Entick, No 27 of *The North Briton* reminded readers that the 'liberty of the press, that bulwark of the liberties of the people, is so deservedly esteemed, that every attack made on it is productive of danger'.[90] A series of pamphlets debated press freedom and the actions of the government.[91] While many of the contributors on both sides of the debate agreed as to the prevailing view of press freedom, some authors sought to advocate broader protection. Notably, Father of Candor wrote a lengthy pamphlet condemning the use of the warrants and attacking the existing law of seditious libel.[92] He wrote that the 'liberty of exposing and opposing a bad administration by the pen' was 'the greatest benefit that can be derived from the liberty of the press'.[93] Yet that benefit was jeopardised by a law that punished even true libels, which made everyone 'afraid to utter what every body however could not help thinking'. Rea writes that Father of Candor 'most exactly and vigorously set forth the case for a free and untrammeled press in the early years of the reign of George III'.[94] Of course, the debate over press freedom was primarily a political rather than an intellectual exercise. Wilkes and his supporters invoked liberty of the press when criticising the ministry, while the government condemned licentiousness when it sought to curb the tide of criticism. The arguments made by the government's critics, however, underlined the importance of press freedom and in some instances advocated extending the scope of that liberty.

[87] J Brewer, 'The Wilkites and the Law' in J Brewer and J Styles (eds), *An Ungovernable People* (London, Rutgers University Press, 1980) 155.

[88] Cited in Cash (n 51) at 115–16. See also Bleackley (n 59) 105–06.

[89] See Brewer (n 87).

[90] 4 December 1762. Though Levy notes that Wilkes had relatively orthodox views on freedom of the press.

[91] See Rea (n 32) ch 7.

[92] See L Levy, *Emergence of a Free Press* (Oxford, Oxford University Press, 1985) 147–53.

[93] Father of Candor, *A letter concerning libels, warrants, and the seizure of papers; with a view to some late proceedings, and the defence of Them by the Majority* (London, 1764). The pamphlet was itself the subject of a prosecution; see *R v Almon* (1765) Wilmot 243.

[94] Rea (n 32) 111.

The final legal action following the searches was decided years later in *Wilkes v Halifax* in 1769, after Wilkes had returned from a period in France. By that time, it was clearly established that the general warrant used against Wilkes in 1763 was unlawful. In the Court of Common Pleas, with Wilmot CJ presiding, the jury awarded Wilkes £4,000 in damages. While this decision concluded the legal actions against the public officials, those actions were just one aspect of the aftermath of the war of words that had taken place in 1762. The government no longer had the broad warrants to use against Wilkes, but it did have a number of other legal tools at its disposal, in particular the law of seditious libel.

VI. SEDITIOUS LIBEL AND *THE NORTH BRITON*

While the actions against Entick and Beardmore were dropped, charges against Wilkes were pursued in both Parliament and the courts. In the House of Commons, a letter from the King was read out calling for the libel to be laid before the Chamber.[95] Under this unusual procedure, the House passed a motion that No 45 of *The North Briton* was 'a false, scandalous, and seditious libel'[96] and should be publicly burned by a hangman. This measure only fuelled public support for Wilkes. The hangman was met by a riotous crowd who attempted to stop him burning the paper, shouting 'Wilkes and Liberty', throwing mud, breaking the window of the sheriff's carriage and injuring the sheriff.[97] As part of the campaign against Wilkes, the Commons voted that the publication of seditious libel was not protected by parliamentary privilege.[98] In December 1763, Wilkes fled to France and would return four years later. In his absence, the Commons found him guilty of writing No 45 and consequently expelled him from the House of Commons in January 1764.

In separate proceedings, the House of Lords focused not on *The North Briton*, but on the *Essay on Woman*, a parody of Alexander Pope's *Essay on Man*, now thought to have been written by Thomas Potter, but with some additions made by Wilkes.[99] While Wilkes planned to print only 12 copies of this work from his house in Great George Street for private circulation,[100] the government got hold of a copy of some proofs by bribing one of Wilkes' employees.[101] In the Lords, Bishop Warburton, who published Pope's poem,

---

[95] See Cash (n 51) 150 and Nobbe (n 47) 245.

[96] Quoted in Nobbe (n 47) 245.

[97] Cash (n 51) 151; Nobbe (n 47) 252; Thomas (n 61) 45.

[98] Cash (n 51) 158–59, who notes that the House of Lords also agreed.

[99] R Postgate, *That Devil Wilkes*, revised edn (London, Dobson, 1956) 71.

[100] Cash (n 51) 130. The plan was not executed, and only small parts of the text were ever run off.

[101] Postgate (n 99) 66.

argued that the *Essay on Woman* libelled him and was a breach of privilege. The Lords voted that the *Essay* was a 'scandalous, obscene and impious libel', and then in January 1764, the House of Lords passed a motion of it 'appearing' that Wilkes was its author.[102]

Wilkes was also prosecuted for seditious libel in the courts. The government, however, faced a difficulty, as in *Wilkes v Wood* the defendants had failed to show that Wilkes was the author of No 45. As a result, he was not prosecuted for publication in *The North Briton*. Wilkes, however, had reprinted the essay in No 45 in a bound volume of the paper at his home in Great George Street. The reprinting of the essay then became the basis for the prosecution of Wilkes for seditious libel.[103] The government also brought a charge of obscene libel against him for publishing the *Essay on Woman*. He was convicted of both in 1764, with Lord Mansfield sitting as the judge. By this time, Wilkes had fled to France, as a result of which he was declared to be an outlaw in November 1764.[104]

Shortly after he returned to Britain in 1768, Wilkes was elected the MP for Middlesex in March, and a warrant for his arrest was issued in April. While Wilkes' outlawry was reversed on a technicality in June 1768, days later he was sentenced to two years in prison for the 1764 convictions by Sir Joseph Yates.[105] He was subsequently expelled from the Commons for having published libellous and obscene material (including *The North Briton* and the *Essay on Woman*). However, even while imprisoned, the constituency voted for Wilkes again as their MP in the subsequent election. The sequence was repeated until the Commons voted to give the seat to his distant runner-up, Henry Lowes Luttrell. While the ministry managed to keep Wilkes out for the life of the Parliament, the Middlesex elections were another episode that showed outside support for Wilkes and was a source of embarrassment for those in power. In the meantime, Wilkes had built up his power base in the City of London, where he became an alderman, and he was released from prison in April 1770.

VII. AFTER THE GENERAL WARRANTS

After the ruling in the general warrants cases and the fallout from the 1762 press war had died down, the ability of the government to use its remaining legal tools was tested in two further celebrated episodes in the late 1760s and

---

[102] Thomas (n 61) 50, who notes how Devonshire and Temple secured a change to the motion, which initially was to find that Wilkes was the author and order him to be taken into custody.

[103] Thomas (n 61) 46.

[104] Cash (n 51) 179.

[105] Thomas (n 61) 87.

early 1770s. The first of these episodes was the attempt by the government to use the law of seditious libel following the anonymous Junius Letters. The second episode, again involving John Wilkes, concerned attempts to restrict the publication of parliamentary proceedings.

A. Junius

While general warrants were no longer used following *Entick*, the law of seditious libel continued to provide a tool to restrict expression. The capacity of this tool to control political expression was tested with the publication of a series of anonymous essays, known as the Junius Letters, in *The Public Advertiser* from November 1768. What distinguished Junius' attacks on the ministry—now led by Grafton—was the 'sheer invective' he employed in his criticism of the government.[106] His powers as a writer excited much interest and may have kept potential litigants at bay, as 'the threat of that vitriolic pen sufficed to ward off private actions against his publisher'.[107] However, an attack on the King made in Letter 35 was seen by the government to have crossed the line and a prosecution for seditious libel was brought within days of its publication.[108]

The author remained anonymous, but six people connected with newspapers publishing the Letter were prosecuted, although not the anonymous author. While Lord Mansfield instructed the jury that its role was limited to deciding the fact of publication and meaning of the words,[109] the jury delivered not guilty verdicts for two of the publishers.[110] The cases against three other publishers were dropped. The only person convicted, John Almon, had been prosecuted for merely selling a copy of *The London Museum*, which had reprinted the Letter. The episode did not change the law of seditious libel. Lord Mansfield's direction on the limited role of the jury provoked debate and was opposed by Lord Camden, but remained the law until the enactment of Fox's Libel Act in 1792. The failure to convict in most of these cases gave a practical victory to the publishers and highlighted the hazards of prosecution. With much popular sympathy siding with the publisher, the government realised it would be difficult to convince a jury to convict for seditious libel.[111]

---

[106] Rea (n 32) 174.
[107] ibid 176.
[108] ibid 177.
[109] Though Siebert notes the ambiguity in Lord Mansfield's direction in the Miller and Baldwin cases: Siebert (n 11) 387.
[110] John Miller (*London Evening Post*) and Henry Baldwin (*St James Chronicle*).
[111] Siebert (n 11) 389.

B. Reporting Parliament

While reporting parliamentary proceedings was prohibited, a number of newspapers found ways around the law in the earlier part of the eighteenth century. Such techniques included publishing debates from an 'imaginary political club' (such as the 'Senate of Lilliput'), in which the names of members of the House of Commons were changed.[112] However, the various loopholes were closed by parliamentary enactments, so that such practices were largely dropped by 1757.[113] This issue flared up later in the century as some newspapers began reporting proceedings of Parliament openly. In 1771, two newspaper publishers, John Wheble and Roger Thompson, were called to the House of Commons after they published reports on parliamentary debates. When the two men failed to attend on several occasions, the House voted that they should be taken into custody for contempt[114] and requested that the King issue a royal proclamation for their arrest along with a £50 reward.[115] The House also ordered another publisher that had reported parliamentary proceedings, John Miller, to be taken into custody, after he too failed to attend the House following a request to do so.

John Wilkes orchestrated a plan to frustrate these attempts to enforce the ban on reporting parliamentary proceedings. As aldermen, Wilkes and two of his allies, Richard Oliver and Lord Mayor Brass Crosby, had the power to hear cases as magistrates. When publishers were arrested in accordance with the royal proclamation and decisions of the Commons, the three aldermen in the City of London found the arrests to be unlawful. The aldermen provoked further controversy by charging a messenger of the House of Commons with 'assault and false arrest'.[116] As a result, Oliver and Crosby were summoned to attend the House of Commons and were committed to the Tower of London.[117] Two people lost their liberty and the law prohibiting reporting Parliament remained in place. While this may not sound like much of a victory for press freedom, the practical result was very significant, as publishers could now report parliamentary proceedings without fear of punishment in the City of London. As Thomas notes, the actions taken by the Commons 'had completely failed to stamp out Parliamentary reporting' and even those publishers that stopped publishing debates during the confrontation were, by April, publishing reports 'as if there had never been any interruption'.[118]

---

[112] ibid 352.
[113] ibid 354.
[114] Thomas (n 61) 128.
[115] Rea (n 32) 204.
[116] Thomas (n 61) 132.
[117] ibid 138.
[118] ibid 139.

The episode shows that Wilkes, who had invoked the rule of law in the earlier battles over general warrants, was willing to use his own judicial functions to further his political goals. Nonetheless, the practical freedom to report on Parliament was an important constitutional development in allowing the public to know what was said and done in the legislature. It is said that the reports gave parliamentarians a presence 'in every coffee-house and in not a few homes' and the politicians adapted their style to appeal to this wider audience.[119] Harris writes that the effect was 'enormous' and that parliamentary reports became a 'staple element of the press' and made 'coverage of domestic politics more accessible'.[120] While it did not create democratic or accountable government, the change provided a necessary condition for such a system. As Wilkes stated, reporting the proceedings allowed the people to 'judge the conduct of their representatives'.[121]

VIII. CONCLUSION

Lord Camden's decision in *Entick v Carrington* is now primarily remembered by lawyers for upholding a key element of the rule of law. The events described in this chapter show how that case is also about the liberty of the press. During the 1760s and early 1770s, three key episodes in particular tested the boundaries of press freedom and the government's powers of control: (1) the press war of 1762 and its legal aftermath; (2) the Junius Letters; and (3) the reporting of parliamentary proceedings. The decision in *Entick* provided a legal conclusion to the first of these episodes. As Brewer has noted, the rule of law and freedom of the press were both central to the Wilkites as desirable features of the constitution and as means for making the government accountable.[122] The legal actions against the government officials brought accountability in the courts, while the press was used to expose abuses of power.[123]

This does not mean that we should uncritically buy into the mythology of these cases or see them as simple stories of heroes taking on an oppressive government. Not all of the tactics employed by Wilkes and his associates were consistent with the rule of law—at least by today's standards. For example, Lord Temple published an anonymous pamphlet, which Wilkes arranged to be sent to the jury sitting in his action against Wood.[124] Further pressure was placed on jurors by publishing their names and details in

---

[119] Langford (n 6) 705–06.
[120] Harris (n 16) 41.
[121] Cited in Hellmuth (n 84) 497.
[122] Brewer (n 87). *The North Briton* No 44 (2 April 1763) stated that: 'A minister is the servant of the public, and accountable to them.'
[123] Brewer (n 87) 142.
[124] Postgate (n 99) 62.

newspapers—though this practice was justified to ensure that the jury was not itself corrupted.[125] That the applications for habeas corpus were made in the Court of Common Pleas deliberately to reach a sympathetic judge is itself hardly a ringing endorsement of judicial impartiality. Furthermore, it is worth remembering the political connections of the judge in question. Pratt was an old friend and supporter of Pitt, while two other leading Pitt allies, William Beckford and Lord Temple, financed *The Monitor* and *The North Briton*, respectively. In a biography of Pratt, Eeles refutes any suggestion of partiality on the part of the judge and argues that he was a 'champion of the just and impartial administration of the law'.[126] Rea, however, argues that to have found in favour of the government would have been 'political and professional suicide', ending Pratt's chances of advancement under Pitt.[127] While it is unfair to judge eighteenth-century practices by twenty-first-century standards, there is an irony that the decision in *Entick*—which still stands as a beacon for the rule of law—is so closely bound up with the rough and tumble of eighteenth-century politics.

Similarly, when looking at press freedom, it is important to keep in mind the politics of the day. The press was not simply an instrument of opposition, but was also used by the government to defend its position and attack its critics. The different political factions had control of their own publications and employed their own writers. The two opposition newspapers in the warrants cases formed part of the infrastructure for factional propaganda and were bankrolled by wealthy members of a political elite. These wealthy patrons could provide support when those papers were under attack, through political connections and by financing the legal actions against the messengers. Such a power to mobilise against government restrictions would not have been enjoyed by all sections of the press.

Yet, while we should not idealise the press or romanticise the events, the significance of these cases should not be dismissed. An important issue was at stake in *Entick v Carrington*: the methods used by the government in its attempts to control and pressure certain parts of the press. The successes of Entick, Wilkes and Leach demonstrated that attempts to invoke draconian controls on the press could backfire and provided a warning to future governments. These changes did not, of course, make the press free. The government still had other tools at its disposal and would develop new mechanisms in the attempt to control publications.[128] It did, however, give the press a little more space in which to criticise the government, and removed some very blunt and oppressive tools for control.

---

[125] Brewer (n 87) 156.
[126] H Eeles, *Lord Chancellor Camden and His Family* (London, P Allan, 1934) 78.
[127] Rea (n 32) 69.
[128] See J Curran and J Seaton, *Power without Responsibility*, 7th edn (Oxford, Routledge, 2010) ch 2.

Beyond the immediate legal implications of *Entick*, the series of cases helped to shape attitudes to press freedom. Essays and pamphlets raised the profile of the issue. While many participants in the debate shared the same basic understanding of that right, some pamphlets argued for a broader definition. These debates also prompted a defence of a very specific vision of press freedom that reflected the political culture of the day, focusing on the dangers of corruption in office, abuse of power and threats to liberty. These concerns have a legacy in arguments sometimes advanced for press freedom today. More broadly, the events surrounding *Entick* provided a focus around which political organisers could rally public opinion, with cries of 'Wilkes and Liberty' and similar slogans. One historian of the press writes that this was 'the first significant occasion on which the press defined central issues on the political agenda in defiance of the elite consensus that ran Parliament'.[129] In so doing, it is often thought to signal the growth of extra-parliamentary politics, and a move towards popular sovereignty and accountable government.

These developments helped to shape the way the press were viewed and, around this time, arguments began to emerge that the press could play a constitutional role as a 'tribunal' of public opinion, a precursor to the Fourth Estate ideal.[130] Along these lines, De Lolme wrote that the people at large exercise 'censorial power'.[131] He accepted that the internal checks and balances in the constitution may not eradicate all evils, and that publicity in the press may compensate. As public officials know their actions will be 'exposed to public view', they will not 'dare' to engage in 'acts of partiality' or 'vexatious practices', which they might be tempted to undertake if away from the public eye. Consequently, De Lolme wrote that every subject has a right 'to lay his complaints and observations before the public, by means of an open press'. According to this view, the press now had a role to play in the system of constitutional checks and balances.

The story told here does not mean that press freedom was something 'won' by any particular individual or determined by a legal decision. Various social, political and economic factors help to explain the growth of the press and changes in its status. The events discussed here did, however, help to define the legal environment in which the press operated and provided a test of its boundaries. The discussion here merely seeks to show that the story of *Entick v Carrington* is as much about an ideal of press freedom as it is about the rule of law. While these events may be mythologised and idealised today, it is a story closely bound up with the often less than idealistic and murky world of factional politics in Georgian Britain.

---

[129] K Williams, *Read All about it: A History of the British Newspaper* (London, Routledge, 2009) 69.
[130] Hellmuth (n 84) 493–94; Barker (n 14) 15.
[131] JL de Lolme, *The Constitution of England* (London, Spilsbury and Kearsley, 1775).

4

Was Entick v Carrington
a Landmark?

TIMOTHY ENDICOTT

I. INTRODUCTION

A S THE SHIP approaches the continent from the open sea, it will be good if some feature on the coastline gives an indication of the lie of the land, and a guide for the journey. A landmark is a guide to a landscape.[1] The landscape that concerns us is English law in its diachronic aspect, and I will ask whether *Entick v Carrington* gives us a guide to that landscape. The decision came in a remarkable decade when Lord Mansfield, Lord Camden and Sir William Blackstone (in their different fashions) were each contributing to the articulation of the basis of public powers. We may well hope to find a guide in Lord Camden's most deliberate effort at accounting for public power and its limits.

A judicial decision will give a guide to the landscape if it changed the law, so that understanding the decision will help us to understand how the law developed. And it may also be a landmark if the court's explanation of the law influenced later decisions (or explanations of the law by scholars and historians), or simply by virtue of the usefulness of the report of the decision for explaining the law today. I think, in fact, that the decision is a landmark in each of these three senses.

To put first things first, *Entick v Carrington* made a significant change to the law. General warrants had already been held to be unlawful, so it may seem that the decision in *Entick* merely gave effect to precedents. But it is not so, and there is a reason for students today to learn about John Entick's case, although I wish they would also learn about the case of the historically much more important John Wilkes (and Lord Camden's rhetoric is just as high-flown in *Wilkes v Wood*[2] as in *Entick*). *Entick v Carrington*

---

[1] This usage seems to be a metaphor based on a landmark as a boundary stone: the King James Version translates Deuteronomy 27:17 as 'Cursed be he that removeth his neighbour's landmark.' See Oxford English Dictionary s v 'landmark'.

[2] *Wilkes v Wood* (1763) Lofft 1, 98 ER 489.

established that generality was not the real problem. The warrant to search John Entick's home and to seize his papers named him specifically.[3] The problem with the warrant was that the Secretary of State could not lawfully authorise by warrant the search and seizure of property on suspicion of seditious libel.

Entick is a landmark not only in the development of the law of the constitution, but also in the development of a distinctively English mixture of judicial restraint and judicial creativity. A judge in a healthy legal system sees *both* restraint and creativity as duties; Lord Camden's decision is a model of the common law method of devising new ways of controlling public powers, while disclaiming any power to legislate and, in fact, claiming to abide by the 'ancient venerable edifice' of the constitution. The result was a practical reform that protected civil liberties, on the basis of a very conservative understanding of the constitution, according to which public authorities are limited by law, but have powers that are not specified by law. I will defend that understanding against the twenty-first-century idea that public authorities may do nothing except what the law expressly or impliedly authorises.

II. LANDMARK DECISIONS

A decision is sometimes called a 'landmark' vaguely to indicate that it is an important case, and sometimes because it is a case that a student ought to know about. Perhaps we can give the term some precision if we remember that we are talking about the common law. It changes as the judges change their approach. It is changed overnight by an authoritative decision based on new grounds and it changes as the judges reinterpret old cases or re-discover new grounds in old cases. A landmark—for the purposes of understanding the development of the common law—is a case that had an important impact on the development of the law.

So it seems very attractive to think that the primary meaning of a 'landmark' must involve an important change in the law. I think there is something to this. Yet you never find the judges saying that 'the common law has always been in favour of the defendant in a case like this until now, but we hereby change it'. We can illustrate this familiar ambivalence about change in the common law by noting the cases that the justices of the UK Supreme Court have referred to as landmarks.

---

[3] Although the warrant was very general as to the class of belongings of that particular person might be seized. On ways in which laws and orders can be general, see T Endicott, 'The Generality of Law' in L Duarte Almeida, A Dolcett and J Edwards (eds), *Reading The Concept of Law* (Oxford, Oxford University Press, 2013).

A. Landmarks According to the UK Supreme Court

Six decisions have been referred to as 'landmarks' by the Justices of the Supreme Court since its inauguration,[4] and three are particularly interesting for our purposes.[5]

i. Conway v Rimmer[6]

This case is interesting because the House of Lords really did more or less say that they were changing the law as established in their decision on Crown privilege in *Duncan v Cammell Laird & Co Ltd*.[7] Thus, Lord Reid considered that the Law Lords should learn from '25 years' experience since *Duncan's* case' and concluded:

> [T]he House ought now to decide that courts have and are entitled to exercise a power and duty to hold a balance between the public interest, as expressed by a Minister, to withhold certain documents or other evidence, and the public interest in ensuring the proper administration of justice.[8]

Lord Morris agreed:

> Though precedent is an indispensable foundation upon which to decide what is the law, there may be times when a departure from precedent is in the interests of justice and the proper development of the law. I have come to the conclusion that it is now right to depart from the decision in *Duncan's* case.[9]

Lord Upjohn agreed, too:

> Times change ... the relation between Crown and subject becomes closer every day ... Then for 20 years the subject has been able to sue the Crown, and the increase in crime, motor accidents and the like have all led to a great increase in the number of cases where the Crown is asked to produce documents. So I think that in this field the courts are entitled from time to time to make a re-appraisal...[10]

It is interesting that the judges saw the change that they were making in the case as a rather specific overruling of a particular decision. They were candid about departing from a precedent of their court. Yet they rather

---

[4] To March 2015.
[5] The others are *St Helen's Smelting Co v Tipping* (1865) 11 HL Cas 642 (law of nuisance), referred to in *Coventry v Lawrence* [2014] UKSC 13; *Woolwich Equitable Building Society v Inland Revenue Commissioners* [1993] AC 70 (recovery of moneys paid under a mistake of law), referred to in *Test Claimants in the Franked Investment Income Group Litigation v Commissioners of Inland Revenue* [2012] UKSC 19, 142; and *Bankovic v UK* (2001) 11 BHRC 435 (the extent of application of the European Convention on Human Rights), referred to in *R (on the application of Smith) v Secretary of State for Defence* [2010] UKSC 29 [48].
[6] Referred to as a landmark in *In re A* [2012] UKSC 60 [16].
[7] *Duncan v Cammell Laird & Co Ltd* [1942] AC 624.
[8] *Conway v Rimmer* [1968] AC 910, 951–52.
[9] ibid 958.
[10] ibid 991–92.

downplayed the fact that they were departing not just from one decision, but also from a deeply entrenched practice of the common law, and they were ambivalent about departing from *the law* itself. Lord Morris called precedent an 'indispensable foundation upon which to decide what is the law', suggesting somehow that by reversing the decision in *Duncan*, they might not be changing the law.

This ambivalence notwithstanding, let's take *Conway v Rimmer* as our paradigm of a landmark: a decision in which the court of highest jurisdiction saw itself as changing *something* on important grounds of principle that changed the direction of the common law.

ii. Anisminic

The second case is *Anisminic Ltd v Foreign Compensation Commission*.[11] In *R (Lumba) v Secretary of State for the Home Department*[12] and *Eba v Advocate General for Scotland*,[13] the Justices of the Supreme Court referred with implicit approval to Lord Diplock's dictum in *In re Racal Communications Ltd*[14] that the decision in *Anisminic* was a 'legal landmark'.

Anisminic was an interesting and difficult case, in which no clear ratio emerges except that it is possible for an administrative tribunal to act without jurisdiction by virtue of a misinterpretation of the law.[15] Lord Reid made it clear in his leading speech in *Anisminic* that some mistakes of law *do* and some *do not* take an administrative body outside its jurisdiction. Lord Diplock, instead, treated the decision as if it had been that an administrative tribunal necessarily acts without jurisdiction if it bases its decision on an error of law:

> The break-through made by *Anisminic* [1969] 2 AC 147 was that, as respects administrative tribunals and authorities, the old distinction between errors of law that went to jurisdiction and errors of law that did not, was for practical purposes abolished. Any error of law that could be shown to have been made by them in the course of reaching their decision on matters of fact or of administrative policy would result in their having asked themselves the wrong question with the result that the decision they reached would be a nullity.[16]

Lord Diplock wanted to call *Anisminic* in aid as authority for a new general judicial authority to quash decisions for error of law, and calling *Anisminic* a 'landmark' was part of his claim that it had made a major change in the law.

---

[11] *Anisminic Ltd v Foreign Compensation Commission* [1969] 2 AC 147.
[12] *R (Lumba) v Secretary of State for the Home Department* [2011] UKSC 12 [304].
[13] *Eba v Advocate General for Scotland* [2011] UKSC 29 [34].
[14] *In re Racal Communications Ltd* [1981] AC 374, 382.
[15] For a discussion, see T Endicott, *Administrative Law*, 2nd edn (Oxford, Oxford University Press, 2011) 310–19.
[16] *In re Racal Communications Ltd* (n 14) 382.

iii. Home Office v Tariq

In *Home Office v Tariq*,[17] Lord Kerr, dissenting, called the decision of the majority in *the same case* a 'landmark':

> The withholding of information from a claimant which is then deployed to defeat his claim is, in my opinion, a breach of his fundamental common law right to a fair trial … This court's endorsement of a principle of non-disclosure … is a landmark decision, marking a departure from the common law's long established commitment to this basic procedural right. In my view, the removal of that right may only be achieved by legislation and only then by unambiguous language that clearly has that effect.[18]

Lord Kerr viewed the majority as making a significant and retrograde change in the law; calling the majority's decision a 'landmark' was a way of expressing his reason for dissenting.

These anecdotes about landmarks are reminders that: (1) judges do not generally set out to identify the decision they are making as a landmark; (2) calling a decision a landmark while it is being made can be derogatory; and (3) calling a decision of the past a landmark tends to be part of a claim that the decision changed the law in a wise direction. The ambivalence about change tends to fall away when people call a decision of the past a 'landmark'.

III. THE FAME OF *ENTICK v CARRINGTON*

Like the work of Sir William Blackstone, Lord Camden's decision in *Entick* has made more of a splash in the US than in the UK. Like habeas corpus, the doctrine in *Entick* was an element in the constitution that the American revolutionaries wanted to keep. In the first major case on the Fourth Amendment to the Constitution, the US Supreme Court justices presented *Entick* as the very model of a landmark:

> [H]is great judgment on that occasion is considered as one of the landmarks of English liberty. It was welcomed and applauded by the lovers of liberty in the colonies, as well as in the mother country. It is regarded as one of the permanent monuments of the British Constitution, and is quoted as such by the English authorities on that subject down to the present time.

> As every American statesmen, during our revolutionary and formative period as a nation, was undoubtedly familiar with this monument of English freedom, and considered it as the true and ultimate expression of constitutional law, it may be confidently asserted that its propositions were in the minds of those who framed the Fourth Amendment to the Constitution, and were considered as sufficiently explanatory of what was meant by unreasonable searches and seizures.[19]

---

[17] *Home Office v Tariq* [2011] UKSC 35.
[18] ibid [108].
[19] *Boyd v United States* 116 US 616 (1886).

In England, even though it is indeed a monument of the constitution, it is not evident that the decision in *Entick* had such a great impact. The damage awards in the other cases had already changed the political calculations, and in 1766, the House of Commons turned against the use of the warrants. I suppose that if *Entick* had been decided against the plaintiff, it would have become the *Darnel's* case of the eighteenth century and legislation would have had to follow.

I do not think that Lord Camden's decision played a very fertile role as a precedent for further judicial developments in the law either. In the eighteenth century, there are some rather incidental citations in *Brass Crosby's Case*,[20] *Cooper v Boot*[21] and *Warne v Varley*.[22] In subsequent decades, it was sometimes cited for its holding that it is the publishing of a libel, and not mere possession of a libel in a drawer in your home, that was a crime.[23] Or it is mentioned in discussions of the powers of secretaries of state, without really being needed,[24] or is referred to only to be distinguished.[25]

But by the first half of the twentieth century, *Entick* was taken for granted as a pillar of the constitution, eg, in Keir and Lawson's case book:

> The rules excluding the doctrine of State necessity and any appeal to the mere practice of a public authority played a very great part in *Entick v Carrington*, which is perhaps the central case in English constitutional law ... If *Entick v Carrington* has retained primary importance for the constitutional lawyer, it is because of the more general enunciations of principle which it contains.[26]

It took pride of place with Lord Denning, not only in his judgment in the *Rossminster* case,[27] but also as one of the landmark cases in a book he wrote late in his career, *Landmarks in the Law*, where he tells the story of *Entick* without adding much comment.[28]

---

[20] *Brass Crosby's Case* (1771) 2 Blackstone W 754; 96 ER 441.
[21] *Cooper v Boot* (1785) 4 Douglas 339; 99 ER 911.
[22] *Warne v Varley* (1795) 6 Term Reports 443; 101 ER 639.
[23] Eg, *R v Burdett* (1820) 3 B & A 717; 106 ER 823, 828.
[24] Eg, *Wilson v Reddall* (1819) Gow 161, 171 ER 870, *Harrison v Edwin Bush* (1855) 5 El & Bl 344; 119 ER 509.
[25] *R v Watts* (1830) 1 B & Ad 166; 109 ER 749.
[26] DL Keir and FH Lawson, *Cases in Constitutional Law*, 4th edn (Oxford, Oxford University Press, 1954) 170.
[27] *Inland Revenue Commissioners ex p Rossminster Ltd* [1980] AC 952. Where legislation provided for judicial warrants of search and seizure in tax fraud investigations, Lord Denning held that 'it is ... the duty of the courts so to construe the statute as to see that it encroaches as little as possible upon the liberties of the people of England'. The House of Lords overturned the decision, with Lord Wilberforce concluding that it is the duty of the courts to construe statutes according to their terms. Lord Denning invoked the spirit of John Wilkes and cited *Entick*, but, ironically, his approach was at odds with Lord Camden's view that: 'The best way to construe modern statutes is to follow the words thereof.'
[28] Lord Denning, *Landmarks in the Law* (London, Butterworths, 1984) 270–72.

I presume that the fame of *Entick* is partly due to Dicey, who used it in his explication of the rule of law. The first component of the rule of law, he said, is the principle that no is man punishable except for breach of the law established in the ordinary courts; the third is the principle that rights come from judicial decisions. The second is a version of the principle in *Entick*:

> We mean in the second place, when we speak of the 'rule of law' as a characteristic of our country, not only that with us no man is above the law, but (what is a different thing) that here every man, whatever be his rank or condition, is subject to the ordinary law of the realm and amenable to the jurisdiction of the ordinary tribunals ... The Reports abound with cases in which officials have been brought before the Courts and made in their personal capacity liable to punishment or to the payment of damages for acts done in their official character but in excess of their lawful authority. A colonial governor, a secretary of state, a military officer, and all subordinates, though carrying out the commands of their official superiors, are as responsible for any act which the law does not authorise as is any private and unofficial person.[29]

After 'a secretary of state', *Entick v Carrington* is footnoted. That is all the use that Dicey made of the case, and he did not quote Lord Camden. But this paragraph is the passage in Dicey that is actually read, and it has presented *Entick* to generations of lawyers as an exemplar of the rule of law.

Of course, others have used it as an exemplar. Before Dicey came along, *Entick* featured along with *Leach v Money* and *Wilkes v Wood* in EC Thomas' *Leading Cases in Constitutional Law*,[30] which would run for 70 years to an eighth edition under Owen Hood Phillips in 1947. And today, Harlow and Rawlings call the series of general warrants cases 'landmarks in the vindication of civil liberties'.[31] Perhaps because of these uses of the case in texts, the decision is cited quite often today.[32]

The citations tend to be rhetorical. *Entick* has been cited three times by the Justices of the UK Supreme Court since it was inaugurated in 2009.[33] *In re Guardian News and Media Ltd* illustrates the rhetorical kind of citation. *The Guardian* successfully sought the discharge of anonymity orders for

---

[29] AV Dicey *The Law of the Constitution*, JWF Allison (ed) (Oxford, Oxford University Press, 2013) 100.

[30] EC Thomas, *Leading Cases in Constitutional Law* (London, Stevens & Haynes, 1876).

[31] Carol Harlow and Richard Rawlings, *Law and Administration*, 3rd edn (Cambridge, Cambridge University Press, 2009) 750.

[32] Five times in the courts of England and Wales in 2013, and five times in 2014: *R (Youssef) v Secretary of State for Foreign and Commonwealth Affairs* [2013] EWCA Civ 1302 [25]; *Rani Poonam v Secretary of State for the Home Department* [2013] EWHC 2059 [42]; *Malik v Fassenfelt* [2013] EWCA Civ 798 [45]; *Smith v Ministry of Defence* [2013] UKSC 41 [90]; and *AKJ and others v Commissioner of Police of the Metropolis* [2013] EWHC 32 [71]; *Wiltshire v DPP* [2014] EWHC 4659 [8]; *R (Mills) v Sussex Police* [2014] EWHC 2523 [56]; *R (Allensway Recycling Ltd) v Environment Agency* [2014] EWHC 1638 [35]; *Commissioner of Police of the Metropolis v Bangs* [2014] EWHC 546 [40]; *R (Miranda) v Secretary of State for the Home Department* [2014] EWHC 255 [42].

[33] To March 2015.

terrorism suspects during proceedings in which the suspects were challenging their designation as suspects.[34] Lord Rodger said:

> Not E but Mr John Entick of Stepney has gone down in history as the plaintiff in the great case of *Entick v Carrington* (1765) 19 State Tr 1029.[35]

When the citations are not rhetorical, they sometimes treat *Entick* as a landmark that stands for more than it decided. In *Ahmed v Her Majesty's Treasury* and *Smith v Ministry of Defence*,[36] the Justices referred to principles purportedly established by *Entick*. In *Ahmed*, Lord Hope held that *Entick* supports the proposition that the claimant had a 'right to peaceful enjoyment of his property, which could only be interfered with by clear legislative words'.[37] This approach embellishes *Entick*, which said nothing about clear legislative words; in *Entick*, there was no general legislation of the kind that was at issue in *Ahmed* (in which the UK Supreme Court held that the United Nations Act 1946 section 1, authorising His Majesty 'to make such provision as appears to Him necessary or expedient' to apply decisions of the UN Security Council, did not authorise provisions that made no provision for procedural fairness).

In *Smith v Ministry of Defence*, Lord Hope endorsed the view of Elias J in the earlier case of *Bici v Ministry of Defence*, that 'combat immunity' from actions in tort

> ... is essentially an exception to the *Entick v Carrington* principle and as such should be narrowly construed. The courts recognise that very exceptionally the basic liberties of the citizen may have to give way to vital interests of state.[38]

What was the *Entick v Carrington* principle? In *Smith*, Lord Hope said that the principle established in *Entick* was 'that the executive cannot simply rely on the interests of the state as a justification for the commission of wrongs'.[39] *Entick* did indeed stand for *that*, but the effect of the decision is greatly embellished, if carelessness by commanders in overseas military operations is taken to be a civil wrong. Breaking into a person's house to take his belongings was a civil wrong in 1765, if the warrant of the Secretary of State did not authorise it; but it would never have occurred to Lord Camden that the Ministry of Defence could owe a duty of care in tort of the kind that was in issue in *Smith*, to British soldiers serving overseas. So there is no ground for saying that there would be 'an exception to the *Entick v Carrington* principle' if (contrary to the conclusion in *Smith*), the Ministry of Defence had no duty of care in negligence to soldiers engaged in overseas military operations.

---

[34] *In re Guardian News and Media Ltd* [2010] UKSC 1, [2010] 2 AC 697.
[35] [2010] UKSC 1, [67].
[36] *Ahmed v Her Majesty's Treasury* [2010] UKSC 2; and *Smith v Ministry of Defence* (n 32).
[37] ibid, *Ahmed* [75].
[38] *Bici v Ministry of Defence* [2004] EWHC 786 [90].
[39] ibid.

But where there *is* a civil wrong, *Entick* does at least stand for the proposition that the warrant of the Secretary of State does not legitimise it. It is, in fact, a principle that Lord Camden had established two years before *Entick* in *Wilkes v Wood*.[40] The only material differences I can see between the cases are that Wilkes had not been named in the warrant in his case and that Lord Camden was only instructing a jury as to the law in *Wilkes*, whereas in *Entick*, he gave judgment on the law after a special verdict. The arguments in Lord Camden's thrilling instruction to the jury in *Wilkes* are those of *Entick*, but with the addition of a flamboyant suggestion—which he can hardly have meant and which he could hardly have used as a basis for a judgment on the law if the issue had been before him—that an Act of Parliament could not authorise a departure from the spirit of the constitution:

> He then observed, that the present cause chiefly turned upon the general question, whether a Secretary of State has a power to force persons houses, break open their locks, seize their papers, &c. upon a bare suspicion of a libel by a general warrant, without name of the person charged. A strange question, to be agitated in these days, when the constitution is so well fixed ... No precedents, no legal determinations, not an Act of Parliament itself, is sufficient to warrant any proceeding contrary to the spirit of the constitution.

> ... He then congratulated the jury, that they had now in their power the present cause, which had been by so much art and chicanery so long postponed. Seventy years had now elapsed, since the Revolution, without any occasion to enquire into this power of the Secretary of State, and he made no doubt but the jury would effectually prevent the question from being ever revived again. He therefore recommends it to them to embrace this opportunity (lest another should not offer, in haste) of instructing those great officers in their duty, and that they (the jury) would now erect a great sea mark, by which our State pilots might avoid, for the future, those rocks upon which they now lay shipwrecked.[41]

So *Wilkes v Wood* was a sea mark and *Entick* was a landmark.

Entick established that a warrant specific as to the person fell within the rule that general warrants are unlawful. This change was important; it was a step in the imposition of the rule of law on the British Government. And the decision established the law on this point with an authoritative effect that *Huckle v Money* and *Wilkes v Wood* did not have, because of the special verdict in *Entick*: the judge directed the jury to decide the facts, and to assess damages in case the defendants were held liable, but reserved it for the full court to decide the law and its application to the facts. The process facilitated Lord Camden's direct attack on the legal issues.[42]

---

[40] *Wilkes v Wood* (1763) Lofft 1; 98 ER 489.
[41] ibid 3–4.
[42] See Hickman ch 2 in this volume for a nuanced account of the legal effect of the decision.

But the case's role as a landmark lies not only in that change. The decision has an important role in the wider development of the law. In fact, there are a variety of ways in which the case serves as a landmark. It is a landmark in advocacy. Notice that the key points in Lord Camden's speech had been put forward in the argument of counsel for the plaintiff:

> If any such power in a Secretary of State, or a Privy Counsellor, had ever existed, it would appear from our law-books; all the ancient books are silent on this head.[43]

> It is the publishing of a libel which is the crime, and not the having it locked up in a private drawer in a man's study.[44]

And if Lord Camden's grand rhetoric does much to explain the fame of the decision, we should give the plaintiff's counsel credit for the same bravura:

> [I]f they are held to be legal the liberty of this country is at an end ... this would be worse than the Spanish Inquisition; for ransacking a man's secret drawers and boxes to come at evidence against him, is like racking his body to come at his secret thoughts ... this would be monstrous indeed; and if it were lawful, no man could endure to live in this country.[45]

And there is conversely something poignant in the eloquence of the opening statement of counsel for the defendants:

> I am not at all alarmed, if this power is established to be in the secretaries of state.[46]

Here is the classic picture of the advocate as officer of the court: for him to say that *he* is not alarmed, as if it is something worth mentioning to the Court, is to presuppose that he is not a mere mouthpiece for the defendants, but someone who comes to sober judgment, independent of the judgment of his client, on the points of law on which he advises the Court. *Entick* is a landmark in the development of the complex role of the common law barrister as advocate, and yet as independent.

And within Lord Camden's reasoning, I think that *Entick* also stands as a landmark in the developing doctrine of statutory interpretation. Lord Camden had a pithy recommendation for statutory interpretation in the modern world:

> The best way to construe modern statutes is to follow the words thereof.[47]

Lord Camden was not being clever; he meant to propose his method of construction to be chosen over alternatives that might be chosen (and that might rightly have been chosen in respect of construction of more ancient statutes).[48]

---

[43] (1765) 2 Wils KB 275, 286.

[44] ibid 282.

[45] ibid 282–83.

[46] ibid 283.

[47] ibid 290.

[48] Counsel for the defendants put the alternative to him: 'Supposing there is a defect of jurisdiction in the Secretary of State, yet the defendants are within the stat. 24 Geo. 2, c. 44, and though not within the words, yet they are within the reason of it; that it is not unusual in Acts of Parliament to comprehend by construction a generality where express mention is made only of a particular': ibid 284.

I mention this just to point out the multifarious fruitfulness of Lord Camden's decision, but I will focus on the doctrine of the powers of public authorities, as it is of course the nub of the decision.

IV. THE POWERS OF PUBLIC AUTHORITIES AND THE ANCIENT VENERABLE EDIFICE

Where do public powers come from in the English constitution? It is not easy to find a source in the sense of a starting point. Even the Duke of Normandy claimed a lawful right of succession to the throne of England (allegedly promised to him by Edward the Confessor) when he invaded in 1066, conquered Harold II's army and killed him, laid waste to the north, and subjugated England. To a chaotic, decentralised country, French Vikings brought a simple administration and an effective military. They ruled on the basis of a continuity of royal authority, not much constrained by the rather indeterminate traditional role of assemblies of leading men under the Anglo-Saxons, but certainly constrained by understandings (doubtless under-theorised understandings) of responsibility to the people (or at least to the barons) and to God. The king's powers were closely constrained in some respects by feudal relations, but were not articulated in any act of constitution making, and the limits of those powers were not enforced by any separation of state powers. The king's power was far from absolute—no one imagined that he had authority to enslave his barons—but it was unspecific. He held his authority as a king to act for the good of the kingdom and as a ruler under God, and not for his own gratification. But there was no state apparatus, and no law, to secure the king's adherence to his duty to act for the good of the kingdom.

In order to secure revenue, the king needed to keep the barons relatively happy in general, and in particular he needed to consult them about taxes. Those needs evolved into duties, as kings promised the barons from time to time that they would do right,[49] and as the King's court developed specialisations that became courts of law and a specialisation that became Parliament, and as Parliament acquired a House of Commons and evolved into a constitutional legislative authority.[50] In addition to those duties, it had all along been the king's duty to administer justice.

The Plantagenet kings discharged their duty to legislate responsibly by legislating in Parliament, and they discharged their duty to administer justice by delegation to their judges. They sent out judges to administer justice according to law in the king's name; in a stroke of accidental genius, they did not tell the judges what the law was, but gave them authority to issue writs

[49] As in Henry I's coronation charter in 1100 or John's Great Charter.
[50] See JH Baker, *An Introduction to English Legal History*, 3rd edn (London, Butterworths, 1990) 234–39.

in the name of the king (a technique that had been missing in Normandy). The power to issue writs to sheriffs in the king's name gave the judges not merely a jurisdiction to resolve disputes, but a constitution-building authority that they used, eg, to construct *habeas corpus ad subjiciendum* as a control on arbitrary detention (at first, against local authorities including local courts). Legislative and judicial powers became separated gradually from the rest of the power of the king, until Sir Edward Coke was able to hold— as the king's judge, in the king's name—that the king could not decide judicial cases personally, but only through his judges,[51] and that the king had no authority to create offences or to change the common law without an act of Parliament.[52] These separations of legislative and judicial power from the king's own personal rule were not new with Coke; the two ideas, separating the legislative and the judicial power from the king's own rule, had both been asserted by John Fortescue in the 1460s, and were not new then.[53] But they were not fully established in Fortescue's time or in Coke's. That took major legislative acts of constitution building by Parliament, including the Habeas Corpus Act 1640, the Bill of Rights 1689 (protecting the privileges of Parliament and outlawing taxation without Parliament—though that had been widely viewed as constitutionally unacceptable since the reign of Edward III), and the Act of Settlement 1701 (protecting judicial independence by tenure in office that was secure against the Crown).

This constitution had not reached this point by defining three branches of government, but by defining the judicial and legislative roles, and creating new institutions for their discharge. Judicial and legislative institutions began as courts within the court of the king. They emerged as independent high courts with specified powers and were protected against interference from the Crown, with the judges acting in the name of the king, and the king legislating in Parliament. The royal power in general was undefined; the judicial and parliamentary powers came to be defined and to be established as exclusive to the judicial and parliamentary institutions.

Long before the Glorious Revolution and the Act of Settlement, the constitution had included the role of Parliament and the authority of the common

---

[51] *Prohibitions del Roy* (1607) 77 ER 1342; 12 Co Rep 64. 'His Majesty was not learned in the laws of his realm of England, and causes which concern the life, or inheritance, or goods, or fortunes of his subjects, are not to be decided by natural reason but by the artificial reason and judgment of law, which law is an act which requires long study and experience, before that a man can attain to the cognizance of it: that the law was the golden met-wand and measure to try the causes of the subjects; and which protected His Majesty in safety and peace: with which the King was greatly offended, and said, that then he should be under the law, which was treason to affirm, as he said; to which I said, that Bracton saith, *quod Rex non debet esse sub homine, sed sub Deo et lege* [That the King ought not to be under any man but under God and the law].'

[52] *Case of Proclamations* (1611) 77 ER 1352; 12 Co Rep 74.

[53] Sir John Fortescue, *De Laudibus Legum Angliae*, trans A Amos (London, Butterworth, 1825), available at http://archive.org/details/delaudibusleguma00fortuoft.

law courts. The constitution was dynamic, and had evolved and was evolving when *Entick v Carrington* was decided. As a constitution in recognisable form, to which Lord Camden could appeal for justification for his decision, it was perhaps 500 years old or so—its roots were certainly more distant from *Entick v Carrington* than *Entick v Carrington* is from us. It was, of course, roughly as old as the common law. Lord Camden relied on its antiquity:

> [T]he common law did not begin with the Revolution; the ancient constitution which had been almost overthrown and destroyed, was then repaired and revived; the Revolution added a new buttress to the ancient venerable edifice.[54]

Various further advances were being achieved at the time of *Entick* in the development of relations among the legislature, the judiciary and the executive; perhaps the most important in principle and in practice are the accountability of the ministers of the Crown to the House of Commons, and the convention that the monarch assents to legislation approved by both Houses, and acts on the advice of his or her ministers. More recent, and very important in principle, is the development of the judges' power to act in the name of the Queen to remedy and to prevent abuse of the prerogative by the Queen's ministers, developed in a series of cases centred on *R v Criminal Injuries Compensation Board ex p Lain*[55]—a decision that Lord Scarman called 'a landmark case comparable in its generation with the Case of Proclamations'.[56] These are significant changes, and yet the ancient venerable edifice is still recognisable in 2015. In 2015, the UK has the Plantagenet constitution, with various important amendments:

— It is now the constitution of the United Kingdom.
— The judges cannot be dismissed by the Crown.
— The Queen's ministers must have the confidence of the House of Commons.
— The Queen must act on the advice of her ministers and must assent to legislation approved by both Houses of Parliament.
— The Members of Parliament in the Commons are elected by universal suffrage, and all adult citizens are eligible for election to the House of Commons or appointment to the House of Lords.
— The Commons have achieved ascendancy over the Lords rather broadly by convention and have specific legal powers to legislate against the will of the Lords.

And there have been other amendments, of course. But in general terms, the source of public powers is the same in 2015 as it was 800 years ago.

What was the source of public powers in the ancient venerable edifice? The king had authority under God for the government of the realm. The

---

[54] (1765) 2 Wils KB 275, 292.
[55] *R v Criminal Injuries Compensation Board ex p Lain* [1967] 2 QB 864.
[56] *Council of Civil Service Unions v Minister for Civil Service* [1985] AC 374, 407.

extent of his authority was not defined, although many instances and aspects of it were perfectly well understood.[57] And he held his undefined authority not for his own pleasure, but in his responsibility for the peace, order and good government of the realm. He had what power was appropriate to the discharge of that responsibility, he discharged his responsibility to do justice according to law through his judges and he made laws for the realm in Parliament. His ministers, agents and servants had authority under him for pursuing the public purposes for which they were given authority, and had no authority to act contrary to statute or to the common law.

I will call this the 'positive conception' of the powers of public authorities. While it involves—needless to say—an extraordinarily simplistic truncation of the more sophisticated conclusions that we would draw from a proper understanding of more than 1,000 years[58] of constitutional history, I think it is roughly accurate. And I will defend it as a conception of the powers of public authorities that is potentially a part of a healthy, balanced constitution. You may say that it is a royalist view, suiting Blackstone and perhaps Mansfield, but at odds with the go-ahead attitudes of Lord Camden. I will argue to the contrary that it is the conception of public powers that informs *Entick v Carrington*. This is a surprisingly hard argument to make. The argument has to deal with the attractions of a different, negative conception.

A. The Negative Conception of Public Powers

The rule of law, according to Adam Tomkins:

> [P]rovides that *the executive may do nothing without clear legal authority first permitting its actions* ... Whereas the rule of law provides that the executive may do nothing without clear legal authority, individuals may conversely do anything unless expressly prohibited by law. Authority for these propositions is contained in the seminal common law case, *Entick v Carrington*.[59]

Tomkins has other leading lights of public law—in the academy and on the bench—on his side. In *R v Somerset County Council ex p Fewings*,[60] Lord

---

[57] Blackstone used the technique of explaining the prerogative by reference to examples, starting with 'the right of sending ambassadors, of creating peers, and of making war or peace' and proceeding with several others. Sir William Blackstone, *Commentaries on the Laws of England*, with notes by George Sharswood, Book I, Chapter VII (Philadelphia, JB Lippincott, 1893) 240.

[58] I say this because although there was a deep discontinuity in the exercise of public authority in 1066, there was not such a deep discontinuity in the principles on which the rulers based their justifications for its exercise. A good deep understanding of the English constitution in 1765 would involve an understanding of its roots before 1066.

[59] A Tomkins, *Public Law* (Oxford, Oxford University Press, 2003) 78.

[60] *R v Somerset County Council ex p Fewings* [1995] 3 All ER 20 at 25.

Justice Bingham had the following to say to a local authority in respect of its ownership of land:

> [I]t is not lawful for you to do anything save what the law expressly or impliedly authorises. You enjoy no unfettered discretions. There are legal limits to every power you have.

Mr Justice Laws had held at first instance that:

> For private persons, the rule is that you may do anything you choose which the law does not prohibit ... But for public bodies the rule is opposite, and so of another character altogether. It is that any action has to be taken must be justified by positive law.[61]

And Paul Craig is of a similar view:

> A core idea of the rule of law to which all would subscribe is that the government must be able to point to some basis for its action that is regarded as valid by the relevant legal system. Thus in the UK such action would commonly have its foundation in statute, the prerogative or in common law power ... If the government cannot provide a legal foundation for its action then the UK courts would regard this action as unlawful, since there would be no lawful authority for it.[62]

I will call this the 'negative conception' of public powers: no such powers exist unless they have been specifically conferred by law.

Contrast this negative conception with the positive conception: that public authorities have undefined, open-ended, inherent powers to carry out their own appropriate role for the public good unless such a power is specifically taken away by law.

I think we should prefer the positive view as an account of the sources of public power in 2015. My reasons for rejecting the negative view are not only that it is against the English genius—instanced in the common law—for dealing with matters as they arise, in a pragmatic fashion, rather than trying to give prior authorisation to everything that ought to be authorised. There are other reasons, which are as follows.

i. Entick *does not Support the Negative Conception*

Contrary to Tomkins' claim about *Entick*, there is no authority in Lord Camden's decision for the proposition that the executive may do nothing without clear legal authority. The decision is only authority for the proposition that the executive cannot assert a defence to a claim in trespass without

---

[61] The Council had banned hunting on its land on the ground that it was cruel to animals; Laws J held that they had based their decision on a consideration that was irrelevant to the proper exercise of their powers; the Court of Appeal upheld the ruling on the narrower ground that the Council had not considered its statutory duty promote the benefit of the area.

[62] Constitution Committee, *Relations between the Executive, the Judiciary and Parliament* (HL 2006–07, 151) 98.

clear legal authority. This is not pettifogging; it is absolutely essential to remember that in *Entick*, the defendants were liable in trespass unless the say-so of the Secretary of State lawfully authorised the entry into Entick's house and the taking of his property.

We should agree with Tomkins, on the other hand, that it would be a crude misunderstanding of *Entick* to think of it as based merely on a doctrine of protection of property. It is not that Lord Camden did not hold that the law protected Entick's real and personal property; he certainly did hold that. But his reasons for the protection of property very clearly concern a person's interests in privacy, and in liberty of thought and expression. There was, in particular, something special about papers:

> Papers are the owner's goods and chattels: they are his dearest property; and are so far from enduring a seizure, that they will hardly bear an inspection; and though the eye cannot by the laws of England be guilty of a trespass, yet where private papers are removed and carried away, the secret nature of those goods will be an aggravation of the trespass, and demand more considerable damages in that respect.[63]

So the case was not decided on an unreasoned preference for property owners. But it was most certainly not decided on the basis that a public authority can do nothing unless the thing is expressly or impliedly authorised by law. Lord Camden did not decide that state authorities can only do what the law authorises them to do; he decided that state authorities have no defence to the tort of trespass that the law does not give them.

> No man can set his foot upon my ground without my license, but he is liable to an action, though the damage be nothing ... If he admits the fact, he is bound to show by way of justification, that some positive law has empowered or excused him. The justification is submitted to the judges, who are to look into the books; and if such a justification can be maintained by the text of the statute law, or by the principles of common law. If no excuse can be found or produced, the silence of the books is an authority against the defendant, and the plaintiff must have judgment.[64]

The silence of the books does not mean that a secretary of state, or his henchmen, cannot do anything. The principle in *Entick* is not that the interests of the state cannot justify action by a public authority that has not been expressly or impliedly authorised by law. Instead, the principle is as Lord Hope put it in *Smith v Ministry of Defence*: that the interests of the state are not 'a justification for the commission of wrongs'.[65]

---

[63] (1765) 19 St Tr 1029, 1066.

[64] ibid. It is rather figurative to say that the silence of the books is an authority against the defendant; Lord Camden meant that if there is an entry to or taking of property without the consent of the owner, the entry or taking is *prima facie* a trespass, and will be conclusively held to be a trespass unless the defendant shows the lawfulness of the entry or taking.

[65] *Smith v Ministry of Defence* (n 32) [90].

Incidentally, it is not just that Lord Camden did not happen to say anything in support of the negative conception in *Entick*; he would have dissented from it, as Christopher Vincenzi showed:

> It remained unclear following *Entick v Carrington* whether acts of government which were not specifically authorised by common law were only unlawful if they interfered directly with an existing personal or proprietorial right. Lord Camden evidently thought so, for the following year he advised the government that it could, without legislation, prohibit the export of wheat by proclamation.[66]

So Lord Camden was against the negative conception. The negative conception may be sound, you will say, even if *Entick* is not authority for it, and even if Lord Camden did not share it. But there are other reasons against it.

ii. History is Against the Negative Conception

I do not see how to reconcile the negative conception with the Plantagenet constitution. So much the worse for Plantagenet constitutional law, you may say (and I suppose there are some people who would fall into the mistake of saying that there was no constitutional law under the Plantagenets). But now, if you suppose that the negative conception is a sound understanding of public powers in 1765 or 2015, there is a problem: when did the constitution switch polarity, from the positive conception under which the Crown (and, I think, other public authorities too) had unspecified powers that were limited by law, to the negative conception under which no state authority has the power to do anything unless it is specified by law? Under the Commonwealth perhaps? But if so, the polarity was reversed again 10 years later, when the Restoration proceeded on the ground that Charles II had been King since Charles I was beheaded. In the Glorious Revolution? But the Bill of Rights 1689 did not specify the powers of the executive. Its purpose was that the Lords and the Commons 'might not againe be in danger of being Subverted', and it was enacted 'for the Vindicating and Asserting their auntient Rights and Liberties'. It was, as Lord Camden described it, the addition of a buttress to the ancient venerable edifice. It specified things that the executive could not do, and it presupposed the executive's unspecified authority to act for the good of the kingdom. After all, they were declaring William to be a king:

> [T]o hold the Crowne and Royall Dignity of the said Kingdomes and Dominions ... And that the sole and full Exercise of the Regall Power be onely in and executed by the said Prince of Orange.

The real, material change in the constitution was not in 1689, but came only as the convention developed that the monarch had to act on the advice of ministers who could only hold office while they had the confidence of the

---

[66] C Vincenzi, *Crown Powers, Subjects and Citizens* (London, Pinter, 1998) 11–12.

House of Commons. Of course, the country was propelled into that trans-formation towards more responsible government by the fact of the Glorious Revolution. It was understood on all sides that the King was there because the parliamentarians wanted him there, and that the basis of his reign was to be different from what the Stuarts had envisaged. But the Glorious Revolution did not guarantee responsible government; this was accomplished in the day-to-day operation of government only over the following two centuries and more. At no point in that development do we have any reason to say that the basis of public power reversed its polarity. The negative conception of public powers is not something that can gradually evolve. Since 1689, the Crown has gradually become accountable to the representatives of the people for all aspects of the use of its powers, and to the courts for the lawfulness of its use of powers. New limits have been imposed on public powers, and new controls have been imposed on their exercise. But there was never a point at which it became the case that the law exhaustively specified the powers of the Crown, or the powers of other public authorities.

iii. The Negative Conception Would not Advance the Purpose of Securing Responsible Government

After the Civil War, the Instrument of Government of 1653, you might say, really did adopt the negative conception. It defined the executive power. The parliamentarians did not (at that point) want a king, so they made the Lord Protector 'chief magistrate', and stated that he would have authority over the exercise of administration of government.[67] The arrangement got them the chief executive whom they wanted. If the Instrument had been lawfully adopted, the Lord Protector would have had clear legal authority permitting his actions. But that would not have achieved the purpose of the negative conception of public power, which, as Tomkins points out, is to give substance to the rule of law. Express conferment of general executive power is no more specific than going on with a monarch with unspecified executive power.

The US, though, had a more gifted class of constitution framers. They did a better job of the specification, not simply providing (in Article II of their new Constitution) that 'the executive power shall be vested in a President of the United States of America', but listing the responsibilities of the President (basically, command of the military, general oversight of the executive departments of government, granting reprieves and pardons, making treaties by and with the advice and consent of the Senate, and nominating ambassadors, Supreme Court justices, and other officers of the US). But it may be

---

[67] Article II: 'the exercise of the chief magistracy and the administration of the government over the said countries and dominions, and the people thereof, shall be in the Lord Protector'.

no surprise to learn that, from Alexander Hamilton and James Madison to the Supreme Court Justices today,[68] Americans have argued both about the nature and extent of the enumerated powers, and about whether the vesting of the 'the executive power' involves general unspecific authority (with the enumerated powers as instances) or whether the enumerated powers are exclusive. Some have thought that the negative conception of public powers offers the best interpretation of their constitution, but the US Supreme Court has held that 'Article II grants to the President the executive power of the Government, i.e., the general administrative control of those executing the laws'.[69] The US Constitution did a much better job than the English Protectorate's Instrument of Government, both in specifying executive powers and in limiting them. But it would be rather meaningless to say that the US President may do nothing without clear legal authority first permitting his actions, because the unclarities are dramatic in the executive power of the government he leads.

I do not think that either the Instrument of Government or the US Constitution were defective, merely by virtue of the open-endedness of the executive powers they established, because it seems to me that the open-endedness is necessary in the public interest. If a constitution sets out to specify the powers of the executive, it must do so in wide open terms. Such a constitution might protect persons from the abuse of power (as the US Constitution does in various ways), but it would not be able to do so by setting out a specification of the powers of the executive, because it would not be possible to specify those purposes in a way that would constrain the officials while also enabling them to do what is worth doing in the public interest.

You may still think that the positive conception is medieval in the pejorative sense, is too cavalier, and is not conducive to limited government. The negative conception may seem to follow simply from the proposition that the king is under the law. But it does not. Blackstone went along with the traditional English view that: 'It is a maxim of the English law, as we have seen from Bracton, that *"rex debet esse sub lege, quia lex facit regem"*'.[70] But he was in favour of the positive conception of public powers. And he quoted Sir Henry Finch, writing at the time of Charles I's reign:

'The king hath a prerogative in all things, that are not injurious to the subject; for in them all it must be remembered, that the king's prerogative stretcheth not to the doing of any wrong.'

---

[68] For an overview, see the 'Annotated Constitution', prepared by the Congressional Research Service of the Library of Congress: www.law.cornell.edu/anncon/html/art2toc_user. html. The latest decision on the scope of the President's executive power is *National Labor Relations Board v Canning*, US Supreme Court, No 12-1281, 26 June 2014.

[69] *Myers v US* 272 US 52 (1926) 163–64.

[70] Blackstone, *Commentaries* (n 57) Book I, Chapter VII, 238.

On the positive conception, the king is under the law, and so: (1) the executive branch of government (like the other branches) may not act contrary to law; (2) Parliament may take executive powers away by law; and (3) disputes as to the nature and extent of executive powers, or complaints of abuse of those powers, may in a proper case be determined with binding effect by the courts. That is enough for the rule of law.

The negative conception may seem to be a constitutional essential, because without it, state necessity—or even just state interests—will be used as a pretext for irresponsible government. If public authorities have unspecified powers to pursue public goods, that seems to play right into the hands of counsel for the defendants in *Entick*, who argued that the Secretary of State had to be able to take on the power he claimed in order to protect the security of the state. But although they assumed the positive conception of public powers, Lord Camden and Sir William Blackstone both rejected the notion that state necessity justified uncontrolled executive powers—Lord Camden in *Entick* and Blackstone in his account of judicial review of administrative action in the Court of King's Bench. In his stirring account of the role of the King's Bench in restraining arbitrary use of power, Blackstone related that the Privy Council had ordered that no actions should be entertained in the courts against the Commissioners of Sewers:

> [I]n the reign of king James I, (8 Nov. 1616,) the privy counsel took upon them to order that no action or complaint should be prosecuted against the commissioners unless before that board; and committed several to prison, who had brought such actions at common law, till they should release the same: and one of the reasons for discharging Sir Edward Coke from his office of lord chief justice was for countenancing those legal proceedings. The pretence for which arbitrary measures was no other than the tyrant's plea of the necessity of unlimited powers in works of evident utility to the public, 'the supreme reason above all reasons, which is the salvation of the king's lands and people'. But now it is clearly held, that this (as well as all other inferior jurisdictions) is subject to the discretionary coercion of his majesty's court of king's bench.[71]

In the ancient venerable edifice, the king's ministers had an open-ended, discretionary jurisdiction to act for the protection and the good governance of the realm, subject to the constraints that the law imposed on them. And the courts had an open-ended, discretionary jurisdiction, in the name of the King, to stand against the arbitrary use of executive power. And it was and is contrary to the principles of the constitution to take that power away from the court.

There are the most pressing reasons to have a constitution that does what a constitution can to prevent abuse of power. There is no reason to have a constitution that says that executive officials have no powers that are not

---

[71] Blackstone, *Commentaries* (n 57), Book III, Chapter VI, 74.

bestowed on them by law. Paul Craig says that 'it is a core idea of the rule of law to which all would subscribe … that the government must be able to point to some basis for its action that is regarded as valid by the relevant legal system'; I think it is enough (for the rule of law in general and for the principle of *Entick*) if the government can show that the basis of its action is not regarded as unlawful by the relevant legal system.

Let me close with one irony concerning the negative conception: I think that it is alien to what Lord Camden called 'the spirit of the constitution' (*Wilkes v Wood*), because it sets up a distinct law for state authorities. Lord Camden treated the Secretary of State no differently from any private person who directs another to enter a home and seize papers. I suppose that on the negative conception of public powers, the seizure of Entick's papers by public servants was unlawful because no law clearly authorised it, whereas the seizure of his papers by a burglar acting in his private capacity would have been unlawful because there was a law prohibiting the trespass. As Mr Justice Laws put it, on the negative conception of public powers, 'for public bodies the rule is opposite, and so of another character altogether'. Lord Camden pointed out, just as he was coming to his conclusion in *Entick*, that:

> Serjeant Ashley was committed to the Tower in the 3d of Charles 1st, by the House of Lords only for asserting in argument, that there was a 'law of state' different from the common law.[72]

I am not proposing that any such measure ought to be taken against the scholars and judges who say that the legal position of public authorities is the opposite to that of natural persons (or, presumably, of private corporate bodies). But we should agree with Lord Camden that, even in 2015, there is no 'law of state' different from the common law that makes a private individual or corporation, and public authorities, liable in trespass.

---

[72] See A Thrush and JP Ferris (eds), *The History of Parliament: The House of Commons 1604–1629* (Cambridge, Cambridge University Press, 2010), s.v. Ashley, Francis: 'According to Sir Edward Coke, he presented "five damnable and desperate reasons" for rejecting the Commons' arguments, the gist of his case being that any constraints on royal power would result in anarchy. This extreme position offended both Commons and Lords, and he was censured and temporarily suspended from the Upper House until he acknowledged his offence at the bar.' I take it, incidentally, that there is an error in the Wilson report, which says: 'Sir Samuel Astry was committed to the Tower, for asserting there was a law of State distinct from the common law' (292). Perhaps there had been a typographical error, or perhaps Wilson did not know of Francis Ashley, and erred by attempting to make a correction: there was a Sir Samuel Astry (1632–1704) who was a clerk of the Privy Council under James II: Harriet Blodgett, 'Astry, Diana (bap. 1671, d. 1716)' in *Oxford Dictionary of National Biography* (Oxford, Oxford University Press, 2005). This form of allusion was a special trope of Lord Camden's: *cf* his statement in *Wilkes v Wood* (n 40) that 'Secretary Williamson, in Charles the Second's time, for backing an illegal warrant, was sent to the Tower by the House of Commons'.

V. CONCLUSION: CHANGE IN THE COMMON LAW

Did Lord Camden see himself as establishing a landmark? He must have: he had challenged the jury in *Wilkes* to establish a 'sea mark' to warn state officials away from the rocks; he knew, needless to say, that it was a big deal politically—'of the utmost consequence to the public'[73]—but also legally:

> I desire that every point of this case may be argued to the bottom; for I shall think myself bound, when I come to give judgment, to give my opinion upon every point in the case.[74]

But he was careful to present his decision as based on the ancient venerable edifice of the constitution, and not as new build. The genius of Lord Camden's judgment in *Entick* lies in his appeal to the ancient constitution as a justification for the undeniably new rule that the King's ministers could not lawfully authorise a search for evidence of seditious libel. His disregard of an established custom of arbitrary searches was artful:

> We shall now consider the usage of these warrants since the Revolution; if it began then, it is too modern to be law; the common law did not begin with the Revolution.[75]

And his assertion of judicial modesty was artful:

> If the king himself has no power to declare when the law ought to be violated for reason of state, I am sure we his judges have no such prerogative.[76]

The positive conception of public powers means that we need active, creative judges. But they can engage creatively in law making—and in constitution making—while seeking to give effect to ancient principles. There is a value in this approach, which is to temper the judges' potentially unruly or willful search for justice, with the continual discipline of searching for a rationale for what they seek to achieve, which is detached from their own impulses. It is a discipline that they can adopt without losing any of their independence.

The common law's specific mode of change involves a presupposition of continuity. So it may seem paradoxical, and yet I think that it is not surprising that in a great landmark case that is being cited by the highest court in this country and others 250 years after the decision, the reasons were ancient. That is, in fact, the distinctive way in which the common law changes.

---

[73] (1765) 2 Wils KB 275, 286.
[74] ibid.
[75] ibid 292.
[76] (1765) 19 St Tr 1029, 1073.

5

Entick v Carrington *and the Legal Protection of Property*

PAUL SCOTT

I. INTRODUCTION

*E*NTICK v CARRINGTON'S reputation as a seminal constitutional case risks obscuring the sense in which it is, in fact, a case about property. This chapter considers the place of property rights within the contested interpretive matrix of the case. It asks where the specific contribution which *Entick* makes to the common law protection of property rights stands in relation to the common law's historical and contemporary methods of protecting those rights, and identifies within *Entick* many of the key themes of the common law's attempts to protect property. It therefore suggests that even though the case has not usually been understood as laying down a rule which applies solely to property, and despite its traditional absence from the most prominent strands of common law thinking about property rights, *Entick v Carrington* is ready to be re-assimilated back into that body of common law thinking as the leading case on the right to property.

II. TWO INTERPRETATIONS OF *ENTICK*

Two plausible formulations of the legal rule laid down by the decision of Lord Camden CJ in *Entick v Carrington* exist in the imagination of the common lawyer. The first—the broad interpretation—would have it stand for the widest possible requirement of (bare) legality, such that every action by a public authority must be authorised by law either explicitly or by necessary implication. On this view, the case represents a significant advance on the struggles for legality of the seventeenth century, which attempted only to establish the subordination of the executive, and particularly the monarch, to human law—as opposed to the divine dictate which absolutists took to be the sole limit upon the sovereign's actions.[1] According to this reading of *Entick*, not only must public authorities obey the law, but they have no power to act at all except that which the law grants them, being not merely subjects of law but creatures of it.[2] This reading therefore reflects the logic of constituent power—the notion that public authorities, as with the state as a whole, should enjoy only those powers specifically assigned to them.[3] Moreover, it shows *Entick* in a light which would justify its reputation as a case of unsurpassed constitutional significance—regarded, the US Supreme Court once noted, as 'one of the permanent monuments of the British Constitution'[4]—and so render it deserving of the treatment that the present collection lavishes upon it. It is also, at least sometimes, the interpretation preferred in the modern literature, as when Adam Tomkins tells us that 'what Lord Camden meant was that for the executive to act it must have legal authority that permits its actions'.[5] If this broad interpretation—encapsulated by Tomkins' employment of the unqualified infinitive 'to act'—is accepted, it is difficult to imagine how, within a common law order lacking a codified constitutional document, any case might surpass *Entick* in its constitutional significance.

Implicit in this first interpretation of *Entick* is an ontological distinction between public and private actors, as made explicit by the dicta of Mr Justice Laws in *R v Somerset County Council ex p Fewings*.[6] Though 'nothing could be more elementary' than that the rule of law applies to both public and private actors, its application to private individuals (who 'may do anything [they] choose which the law does not prohibit') gives rise to consequences diametrically opposed to those arising from its application to public bodies: 'for public bodies the rule is opposite, and so of another character altogether. It is that any action to be taken must be justified by positive law'.[7] These remarks would seem consonant with the broadest possible interpretation of the decision in *Entick* (of which Laws J made no mention): that which denies the contingency of the requirement for legal authority, holding it to exist for all exercises of public power rather than merely those

---

[1] For a definition of absolutism capturing this point, see JP Sommerville, 'Absolutism and Royalism' in JH Burns and M Goldie (eds), *The Cambridge History of Political Thought 1450–1700* (Cambridge, Cambridge University Press, 1991) 348.

[2] In English law, the idea goes back at least as far as Bracton's maxim that 'The king must not be under man but under God and under the law, because the Law makes the king', later taken up by Coke in *Prohibitions del Roy* 12 Co Rep 64.

[3] On which see recently M Loughlin, 'The Concept of Constituent Power' (2014) 13 *European Journal of Political Theory* 218.

[4] *Boyd v US* 116 US 616 (1886) 625.

[5] A Tomkins, *Public Law* (Oxford, Oxford University Press, 2003) 79. See also, for example, P Cane, 'Prerogative Acts, Acts of State and Justiciability' (1980) 29 *International and Comparative Law Quarterly* 680, 686, which states that 'Entick v. Carrington rested on the principle that all governmental acts must be justified by reference to legal powers'.

[6] *R v Somerset County Council ex p Fewings* [1995] 1 All ER 513.

[7] ibid 524.

which infringe others' rights and are therefore prima facie unlawful. This position, whereby *Entick* lays down a rule which applies (indeed *can* apply) only to public bodies, has received some important endorsements, without ever achieving an unassailable priority.[8]

This interpretation of *Entick* is not unrivalled. A narrower variant considers it to stand for a more specific rule, whereby the requirement for public actors to show legal authority for their actions is not general or unqualified, but contingent upon the fact that the action in question represents a wrongful (tortious) interference with the legally protected interest of some person or persons. Where no such interference takes place, no authority must be identified. The case is, on this view, one of a number which which testify that 'the clearest authority must exist to justify any invasion of private rights or any interference with the liberty of the subject'.[9] Leaving aside the incautious reference to liberty, to which we will return, this reading—that lawful authority is required if and only if what is done constitutes an interference with a legally protected interest—is the version of *Entick* at work in the much-maligned decision as to the legality of phone-tapping in *Malone v Metropolitan Police Commissioner*.[10] Therein, Megarry V-C was at pains to emphasise that the case was not concerned with 'any form of tapping that involved electronic devices which make wireless transmissions, nor with any process whereby anyone trespasses on to the premises of the subscriber or anyone else to affix tapping devices or the like'.[11] This proved vital, for on Megarry's view, the reason that a search such as gave rise to *Entick* was unlawful was that 'it involves the tort of trespass to those premises: and any trespass, whether to land or goods or the person, that is made without legal authority is prima facie illegal. Telephone tapping by the Post Office, on the other hand, involves no act of trespass'.[12] Here there is no trespass and therefore no prima facie illegality. Because there is no prima facie illegality, there is no need to demonstrate the legal authority whose absence in John Entick's case saw those who had trespassed against him condemned in law.

Not only had no physical trespass taken place, but the submission that interference with Malone's privacy required legal authority also failed. It did so not because such interference could be executed without legal authority, nor because the common law could provide the requisite authority, but because the authorities could not sustain the existence of a 'right to telephonic privacy, sounding in tort'.[13] There was no need for legal

[8] Lester and Weait refer to it as the 'correct position' in explaining why the Ram doctrine is 'constitutionally illegitimate': A Lester and M Weait, 'The use of Ministerial Powers without Parliamentary Authority: the Ram Doctrine' [2003] *PL* 415, 422. On the Ram doctrine, see Adam Tomkins' contribution to this volume.
[9] *Clinch v Inland Revenue Commissioners* [1973] 1 All ER 977, 985 per Ackner J.
[10] *Malone v Metropolitan Police Commissioner* [1979] Ch 344.
[11] ibid 355–56.
[12] ibid 369.
[13] ibid 372–75.

authority: not because of the nature of the legally protected interest that had been interfered with, but because no such interest—neither property nor privacy—had been interfered with. The relevant property rights were not interfered with; privacy was not legally protected and so was not a right at all. The decision in *Malone* therefore turns on an implicit endorsement of a conception of the rule of law which discriminates neither between public and private actors nor between the different sorts of interests which the law protects: either type of actor can act without legal authority if there is no interference with a protected interest. It reflects the idea of legal equality which Dicey held to be a central feature of the rule of law: because 'every man, whatever his rank or condition, is subject to the ordinary law of the realm',[14] one's private law rights provide a simultaneous vertical protection.

The legacy of *Entick* is therefore a battleground upon which the dispute between these very different conceptions of the rule of law, and the distinction between private and public actors, is played out. The practical distinction between these conceptions is not, however, eternal. It may be reduced in one of two ways. The first involves an expansion of executive powers. So, for example, the bare requirement of general legality espoused by Laws J in *Fewings* loses some of its legal bite in the context of the powers possessed by the executive by virtue of the Crown's corporate status:[15] the burden of having to identify lawful authority is significantly lessened by the broad and amorphous nature of these powers, equivalent—it is sometimes said—to the 'legal capacities' of a natural person.[16]

A similar subversion of the distinction, though from the opposite direction, might be achieved via an expansion of the range of interests protected by law. Were it possible to arrive at the point that no action by the executive could be carried out without interfering with the legally protected interest of an individual, it would largely have ceased to matter which interpretation of *Entick v Carrington* was preferred. Even short of that, the incorporation of the European Convention on Human Rights (ECHR) into domestic law by the Human Rights Act (HRA) has gone some way to closing the gap between the broad interpretation of *Entick* and its narrow rival. The distinction between the two rests on the question of whether the need for legal authority is contingent upon the fact of interference with a legally protected interest. The rule, found in the HRA, that it is 'unlawful for a public

---

[14] AV Dicey, *Introduction to the Study of the Law of the Constitution*, 8th edn (Indianapolis, Liberty Fund, 1982) 114.

[15] On the question of what type of corporation the Crown is, see FW Maitland, 'The Crown as Corporation' (1901) 17 *LQR* 131.

[16] In *R v Secretary of State for Health ex p C* [2000] HRLR 400, 405, reference was made to *Halsbury's Laws*, which states that: 'At common law the Crown, as a corporation possessing legal personality, has the capacities of a natural person and thus the same liberties as the individual.'

authority to act in a way which is incompatible with a Convention right'[17] provides legal protection for a number of interests, not all of which were previously protected under domestic law, interference with which is either entirely forbidden or, where it is permitted, must be either 'in accordance with' or 'prescribed by' law. If the narrower reading of *Entick* is preferred, then the Human Rights Act can be seen to have significantly expanded the range of actions for which legal authority must be identified, albeit statutorily rather than by extension of the *Entick* rule to the Convention rights. As such, it is no longer possible for the state to interfere with one's right to a private and family life, say, or to free expression, if the law does not permit such interference; the tapping of Malone's phone could now take place only on the basis of statutory authority. The method by which this is achieved, however, usefully illustrates the duality of the rules which regulate the interaction of public and private actors.[18] The most straightforward way for the HRA to achieve the effect described would have been to explicitly grant to each individual the Convention rights. But the HRA does not do so, instead defining those Convention rights[19] and then providing that public authorities may not act incompatibly with them.[20] The result is that the interests protected under the HRA enjoy an intermediate status—they are actively defined and afforded to the individual as a matter of international law only; in domestic law, they exist in the first place as limits upon the executive, and only thereby, indirectly, are they constituted as protected interests of the individual.

III. PROPERTY AND THE DECISION IN *ENTICK*

These two readings of *Entick v Carrington* dominate. The case might, though, be understood as making a yet narrower contribution to the common law's regulation of the doings of public actors; one which speaks not to legally protected interests generally, but to property in particular. Several factors demand consideration of such a possibility. First, it must be remembered that, in returning the special verdict which brought the case before Lord Camden in the Court of King's Bench, the jury found the King's messengers not guilty of much of what was alleged: 'as to the coming with force and arms, and also the trespass in declaration ... the defendants are not guilty'.[21] It excepted from its verdict and 'pray[ed] for the advice of the Court' only on the more limited question of their guilt in 'breaking and

---

[17] HRA 1998, s 6(1).
[18] Such duality being merely a particular instantiation of the inherent duality of rights: W Hohfeld, 'Some Fundamental Legal Conceptions as Applied in Legal Reasoning' (1913) 23 *Yale Law Journal* 16.
[19] HRA 1998, s 1.
[20] ibid s 6(1).
[21] *Entick v Carrington* (1765) 19 St Tr 1029, 1032.

entering the house of the plaintiff' and searching and seizing his papers.[22] Read strictly, therefore, Camden's judgment does not relate to any of the other interferences with Entick's interests which did or might be argued to have taken place, but only to the narrower issue of the interference which has taken place with his property, both land and goods. In this sense, even if no other, *Entick* is a case about property.

The reading suggested by attention to the details of the special verdict is buttressed by a second factor: the specific language of Camden CJ, particularly in the passage which follows on from his famous declaration that: 'If it is law, it will be found in our books. If it is not to be found there, it is not law.'[23] In terms that we recognise as quite unambiguously Lockean, he asserts that 'The great end, for which men entered into society, was to secure their property' and that: 'That right is preserved sacred and incommunicable in all instances, where it has not been taken away or abridged by some public law for the good of the whole.'[24] As such, 'every invasion of private property, be it ever so minute, is a trespass' and anyone carrying out such interference is required to show that 'some positive law has empowered or excused him'.[25] If he cannot, he has by definition acted unlawfully.

Unlike in the reading which seems to prevail in *Malone*, within which no distinction is drawn between the legal interests against which public actors might trespass,[26] here the interests referred to are specifically those which are proprietary in nature. Whether or not Camden should be understood as suggesting that such rights are uniquely capable of prompting an enquiry into the legal basis of any interference, they are certainly singled out and prioritised over other interests that the law does or might protect—such priority perhaps explaining the rather ambitious submission in the *Malone* case which connected the requirement for legal authority to the 'interference' with Malone's supposed property right in the electrical impulses which carried his words through the phone lines.[27] From this perspective, then, *Entick* would be reconceptualised as contributing in the first place to the common law tradition which promotes and protects property rights against governmental intrusion, laying down the rule that such interference will rouse the courts to demand lawful justification—to show, in the contemporary language which the ECHR has given us, that an interference is not also a violation.

---

[22] ibid 1036.
[23] ibid 1066.
[24] ibid.
[25] ibid.
[26] *Malone v Metropolitan Police Commissioner* (n 10) 369: '*any trespass*, whether to land or goods or person ... is prima facie illegal'.
[27] ibid 357.

IV. PROPERTY RIGHTS IN CONTEXT

The language in which the decision in *Entick* is framed is not the only evidence of Lord Camden's predilection for Locke, nor of his concern for the protection of property rights. The question of the circumstances under which such rights could be legitimately interfered with was of considerable contemporary significance. The Stamp Act 1765, enacted in March of that year (six months before judgment was given in *Entick*), had imposed a series of taxes on the American colonies in order to meet 'the expenses necessary for the defence, protection, and security of the said colonies and plantations'.[28] When Lord Camden, who had previously sat in the Commons, returned to Parliament as a member of the House of Lords (having been ennobled in July 1765), the first speech he made was on the topic of the 'disturbances in America' which had followed that statute's enactment.[29] He spoke in support of the claim that, not having representatives in the Westminster Parliament, the colonists could not be taxed by it, for 'when the people consented to be taxed, they reserved to themselves a power of giving and granting by their representatives'.[30] Without representation, taxation was illegitimate, as the American patriot James Otis Jr (himself following Locke) had declared the previous year, noting the analogy with taxation via the prerogative: 'Are we not as really deprived of that right [to be taxed only by consent], by the parliament assessing us before we are represented in the house of commons, as if the King should do it by his prerogative?'[31] Later, debating the Declaratory Bill, which re-asserted the right of Parliament to legislate for the American colonies in face of protestations to the contrary and a boycott which forced Parliament to repeal the Stamp Act, Camden specifically invoked Locke to justify this connection between representation and taxation, quoting Locke's claim that 'the supreme power cannot take away from any man any part of his property without his own consent'.[32] Representation in Parliament was necessary to the granting of such consent; to tax without it was to reduce the colonists, Camden suggested, to a 'state of slavery'.[33]

---

[28] Stamp Act 1765, s 55.

[29] No constitutional objections to the taxing of the colonies seem to have been raised at the time of the Stamp Act's enactment: J Goldsworthy, *The Sovereignty of Parliament: History and Philosophy* (Oxford, Oxford University Press, 2001) 193.

[30] (1765) *Parliamentary History*, xvi, 168. His speech in this debate was so similar to that of Pitt, his friend from Eton turned political ally, that 'they were thought to have been prepared together beforehand'. PDG Thomas, *British Politics and the Stamp Act Crisis: The First Phase of the American Revolution 1763–1767* (Oxford, Clarendon, 1975) 186.

[31] J Otis, *The Rights of the British Colonies Asserted and Proved* [1764] in B Frohnen (ed), *The American Republic: Primary Sources* (Indianapolis, Liberty Fund, 2002) 132.

[32] (1765) *Parliamentary History*, xvi, 180. Referring to the response to his earlier speech, Camden claims to have been treated as 'the broacher of new-fangled doctrines, contrary to the laws of this kingdom, and subversive of the rights of parliament' (177). Pitt had earlier made much the same point ((1765) *Parliamentary History*, xvi, 108), though much of Pitt's rhetoric is based upon a dubious distinction between taxation and legislation (eg, 98).

[33] (1765) *Parliamentary History*, xvi, 180.

We might think of this question—whether Parliament enjoyed the right to tax the colonists—as relating to the terms on which the constitutional disputes of the previous century, to which Otis refers, had been settled. When ship-money was transformed from a well-established mechanism for ensuring adequate naval defences into a permanent tax of the sort that should not—according to the Petition of Right, purporting to re-assert a rule going back to the *Statutum de Tallagio non Concedendo* of 1297—have been levied without Parliament's agreement, the possibility of arbitrary monarchical rule was opened up.[34] The outcome of the Revolution of 1688 saw it re-affirmed that taxation under the prerogative, and therefore without parliamentary consent, was unlawful,[35] but the dispute regarding the Stamp Act suggests that the revolutionary settlement was underdetermined. If the requirement of parliamentary consent was intended only in order to curb the arbitrary power of the crown, then we gain no answer to the question of whether Parliament's right to tax extended to the colonies. If, however, the requirement for parliamentary consent stems from the Parliament's status as a proxy for the individual property owner—who, when Parliament consents to taxation, indirectly consents to his own taxation—then its right to tax the colonists must be doubted. Camden, consistently with his Lockean commitments, takes the latter view.[36] He also makes this link between taxation and consent in his judgment in *Entick*, listing taxes as one example of those situations in which 'every man by common consent gives up' his right to property 'for the sake of justice and the general good'.[37]

More than this, and seeming to go further than Locke, the earlier of Camden's speeches comes close to suggesting that property rights might constitute a stronger limit upon the legislative competence of Parliament—representation or no representation. He states that: 'The sovereign authority, the omnipotence of the legislature, my lords, is a favourite doctrine, but there are some things they cannot do ... They cannot take away any man's private property without making him a compensation.'[38] This extension of the underlying Lockean logic addresses in the first place the individualised nature of the deprivation of property, which the consent of the majority (not necessarily including the individual whose property is taken) does not so easily legitimate as it does the imposition of general taxation; as such, Camden suggests, compensation must be made. But this aspect of

---

[34] JR Tanner, *English Constitutional Conflicts of the Seventeenth Century: 1603–1689* (Cambridge, Cambridge University Press, 1928) 62–64, 76–77.

[35] Bill of Rights 1689, art 4.

[36] J Locke, *Two Treatises on Government* (Cambridge, Cambridge University Press, 1988) II, §140 'if anyone shall claim a power to lay and levy taxes on the people by his own authority, and without such consent of the people, he thereby invades the fundamental law of property, and subverts the end of government.'

[37] *Entick v Carrington* (n 21) 1066.

[38] (1765) *Parliamentary History*, xvi, 168.

Camden's thought brings his natural law worldview into conflict with the legal sovereignty of the Parliament in which he sat. Lord Mansfield, in the same debate, denied 'the proposition that parliament takes no man's property without his consent: it frequently takes private property without making what the owner thinks a compensation'.[39] This retort raises the issue of the adequacy of compensation, but does so in terms which suggest a more fundamental failure to clearly distinguish description of Parliament's actions from an account of the limits of its competence. It is conceivable and indeed likely that any dearth of examples of deprivation of property without compensation is explicable by reference not to the possibility in law of executing such interference, but to bare political reality. An elite group of property owners will not frequently be inclined to carry out such a deprivation, whether or not formally empowered to. In Camden's claim that proof of his proposition is to be found in 'the many private bills, as well as public, passed every session',[40] as well as in Mansfield's response, which contests it on the basis of a divergent description of past practice, we see how fine is this methodological line, which frequently confounds attempts to ascertain with precision the position of property vis-a-vis the state. Nevertheless, Camden's treatment of the matter confirms his as a world view that is persistently Lockean. His veneration of property rights in *Entick* is not solely a function of the limited question which the jury's special verdict had left for him to resolve, but is also a reflection of the special priority to which he, following Locke, consistently gave such rights. A decade later, in the debate on the New England Restraining Bill, which responded to burgeoning revolution in Massachusetts by seeking to limit New England to trading with the UK, Camden would again quote Locke—this time on the justice of resisting tyranny—and ask whether there was a 'country under heaven, breathing the last gasp of freedom, that will not resist such oppressions, and vindicate, on the oppressors' heads, such violations of justice'.[41]

V. THE PRIVILEGING OF PROPERTY IN *ENTICK*

Even those who interpret *Entick* narrowly do not generally suggest that its holding is limited to interferences with property.[42] Notwithstanding both the issue which arose for resolution and the terms in which Camden resolved it, the case has, where it is not claimed to ground a general requirement of legality, been consistently taken to require lawful authority not merely for interference with property, but for interference with any legally

---

[39] ibid xvi, 172.
[40] ibid xvi, 168.
[41] ibid xviii, 440–41.
[42] Though see KD Ewing, 'The Politics of the British Constitution' [2000] *PL* 405, 408.

protected interest. This is unsurprising, for *Entick* is easily and plausibly read as formulating a general rule whose application to property is one amongst many. Camden notes that 'every invasion of private property ... is a trespass', but not every trespass is an interference with property. Blackstone, writing almost contemporaneously, identified two distinct senses of 'trespass': the 'largest and most extensive sense' in which it 'signifies any transgression or offence against the law of nature, of society, or of the country in which we live, whether it relates to a man's person or his property' and 'the limited and confined sense ... [in which] it signifies no more than an entry on another man's ground without a lawful authority, and doing some damage, however inconsiderable, to his real property'.[43] Reference to law of nature aside, it seems that *Entick* applies to trespasses in this first, wider sense, rather than the latter, more specific, sense. If there was a time at which its legacy might have been tied to Blackstone's 'limited and confined' sense of the term, justified by the language of 'bruising the grass and ... treading upon the soil',[44] that time has passed. The contingencies of *Entick*'s posthistory should not, however, cause us to overlook that a special emphasis is here afforded to property rights. It is vital to explore the normative and practical foundations of that emphasis.

The reason offered by Camden CJ for singling out property rights is the role of property in prompting the move from state of nature into civil society. Just as the fact that in the state of nature one's natural rights to property are 'very unsafe, very unsecure'[45] had justified that move for Locke, as well as the rule (endorsed by Camden elsewhere and hinted at in *Entick*)[46] that the state cannot 'take from any man any part of his property without his own consent',[47] so too here does the pre-legal imperative to protect property justify a special legal status for those rights once established in law. But we should hesitate to endorse such logic, not least because it is not clear that the 'property' to which Camden appeals is the same as that which Locke had intended by the term; the latter was unambiguous in his use of the word to designate a wider set of interests than is directly at stake in *Entick*—men's 'lives, liberties and estates, which I call by the general name, property'.[48] By contrast, Camden specifies 'private property' which would seem (translated into Locke's terms) to refer not to this broader phenomenon, but to those material goods which, by virtue of the labour of the individual, have been removed from the stock of common property.[49]

[43] W Blackstone, *Commentaries on the Laws of England* [1765-69] (Chicago, University of Chicago Press, 1979) III, 208–09. The first book of the *Commentaries* was published in the same year as *Entick* was decided.
[44] *Entick v Carrington* (n 21) 1066.
[45] Locke, *Two Treatises*, II §123.
[46] *Entick v Carrington* (n 21) 1066.
[47] Locke, *Two Treatises*, II §138.
[48] ibid §123.
[49] ibid §27.

The fact that the circumstances of *Entick* require only a considera-tion of the specific issue of interferences with material property prevents us from knowing whether Camden's narrower conception of property is merely a consequence of the specific question which arises in the case or is indicative of an intentional departure from Locke which reflects Camden's own unquestionable commitment to property rights. If it is the latter, then an important, and unacknowledged, change has been made to the basic Lockean narrative. If Locke's 'life, liberty and estates' is the catalogue of interests which underpins the constitution of the social body, acting simulta-neously to justify its legal form and to limit its (legitimate) coercive capacity, Camden has effected a shift—perhaps a sleight of hand—in elevating one of the multiple aspects of this 'property' (albeit that most obviously associ-ated with the term) above the others and suggesting that it alone grounds the legitimacy of the state, and so is particular in its relationship to law. If property is being privileged on Lockean grounds, then Camden would seem to have unduly narrowed its scope, beyond even the small set of interests which Locke's modern heirs recognise it as the state's duty to protect.[50] As such, the preference for an interpretation of *Entick* which applies beyond the context of property is truer to the Lockean roots of Camden's argument than would have been one which accepted the narrower focus that Cam-den's specific wording gives it. For example, demanding legal authority for all trespasses (those against the person as much as those against property) protects the 'life' which Locke includes in his account of property in a man-ner which would be impossible were we to reify the terms of Camden's judg-ment. The normative basis of this privileging of property within *Entick* is thus dubious, and the manner in which the rule in *Entick* has been taken as applying beyond this context seems justifiable by reference to the normative origins of the position taken by Camden.

VI. THE INTERFERENCE WITH PROPERTY IN *ENTICK*

Even an interpretation of *Entick* which does not distinguish trespasses against material property from other trespasses nevertheless represents a narrower understanding of what should be protected than Locke had sug-gested; it leaves no room for Locke's 'liberties'. This narrowing of the rel-evant catalogue of interests between its initial formulation by Locke and invocation by Camden is best explained on pragmatic grounds. It reflects the distinction between those interests protected by law and to which the narrow interpretation of *Entick* will apply, and those which are not so

---

[50] Nozick's minimal state, for example, is 'limited to the functions of protecting its citizens against violence, theft and fraud, and to the enforcement of contracts'. R Nozick, *Anarchy, State and Utopia* (New York, Basic Books, 1974) 26.

protected, to which it cannot and so does not apply. The point can be made via consideration of the form of interference to which the specific interest at stake in *Entick*—a property right—has been subjected.

The interference with property evidenced by the search of John Entick's house by Nathan Carrington and the other of the King's messengers, and the seizure of papers they found there, falls within the weakest of any categories of interference we might construct. It is the weakest because such interference does not permanently modify the bundle of rights which make up the legal ownership by the owner of the property. Instead, it permits an interference with that property on the basis of a legal rule which is external to the legal being of the property—a rule which did not exist in the present case, but which, had it done so, would have presented no further legal or constitutional difficulty. Entick would have continued to own or occupy his house, and would have done so under the same general and ongoing conditions as prior to the interference. The interference, if lawful, would have been temporary, specific and exceptional, remaining outside of the property being interfered with rather than being written into it in order to re-define it. The narrower interpretation of the rule in *Entick*, that is, can be as it is because the decision in *Entick* is parasitic upon a body of private law rights which are not called into question by anything said or done therein.

This form of interference can be contrasted with interferences with interests such as privacy, which at common law are protected primarily according to the logic of 'residual' liberty. Residual liberty is an underexplored concept,[51] but can be seen to mean, first, that one was and is free to do, and free to be, that which it was not by law forbidden to do or to be, as Laws J described in *Fewings*.[52] But not all rights or liberties are primarily a question of what the individual may and may not do; many relate instead to what may or may not be done to the individual. And yet, formulated with reference to the state, the significance of saying that liberty is residual is less clear. If we say that the state may act except to the extent that it interferes with an established legal right, then the logic of residual liberty dissolves into something approaching absurdity—residual liberties are by definition the very opposite of established private law rights and so residual liberty is no liberty at all. Or, better, it is a liberty whose security (both horizontal and vertical) is co-extensive with one's private law rights;[53] beyond those, what

---

[51] See, though, the discussion in TRS Allan, *Law, Liberty, and Justice: The Legal Foundations of British Constitutionalism* (Oxford, Clarendon, 1994) 136–39 and 157–58.

[52] *R v Somerset County Council ex p Fewings* (n 6) 524.

[53] See, on this point, BV Harris, 'The "Third Source" of Authority for Government Action' (1992) 108 *LQR* 626, 631, referencing Lord Atkin's claim in *Eshugbayi Eleko v Government of Nigeria* [1931] AC 662, 670 that 'no member of the executive can interfere with the liberty or property of a British subject except on the condition that he can support the legality of his action before a court of justice'. Harris notes that it is unclear whether 'liberty' here refers only to 'that "liberty" protected by legal rights, or all liberty irrespective of whether it is protected by existing legal rights.' It is submitted that only the former reading is coherent.

liberty as exists is wholly contingent and is therefore liable to be denied the name liberty at all.[54] One's private law rights do not merely provide vertical protection against the state (as on Dicey's telling) but, in the absence of distinct positively defined public law rights, they establish the high water mark of such vertical freedom. The decision in *Malone* evidences this neatly and the broader reading of *Entick* is attractive in large part because it sidesteps this problem.

This residual status of most liberties at common law, as opposed to the legal protection traditionally afforded only to private law rights (including those relating to the person), is significant. Where an interest is protected only residually, the sort of interference evidenced by *Entick* cannot logically take place; there can never be an external interference with a legal interest which nevertheless persists unaltered. Instead, powers enjoyed by the state implicitly modify that interest. One does not enjoy a right to privacy with which the state is permitted to interfere, but where the state is permitted by law to act as it does (either because it has legal authority or because none is needed) there is, to that extent, no privacy: the (residual) legal existence of the interest is extinguished. There is no clash of rights, no prima facie trespass of the sort described by Lord Camden—the existence of the power to act mutes the liberty. We are reminded again of the inherent dualism of legal rules which this context makes plain: just as an individual 'right' can be indirectly implemented via an prohibition upon the state acting in certain ways, so too can a right be quashed, indirectly and implicitly, by permitting the state to do certain things.

The special status seemingly afforded to property by the judgment in *Entick* can therefore be seen to reflect, imperfectly but tellingly, a fundamental distinction between interests which are independently defined in law and so survive interference, and those which have no independent definition and so are re-defined where interference is lawful: not so much trespassed against by interference as extinguished. Property is not the only example of the former—amongst which also number those bodily rights also protected via the law of tort—but it is the most important one. Lord Camden, while appearing to single out property rights as uniquely or especially capable of triggering the requirement of legal authority, might instead be considered to have been simply butting his head against the limits of the framework within which he, as all English lawyers of the time, thought—and which still in part prevails at common law, despite the ever-increasing range of public law rights recognised by the courts. Locke's 'liberties' are excluded from consideration because, unless co-extant with some private law right, they usually had no legal existence which could prompt an enquiry of the sort Camden undertakes; having only a residual existence, they can be protected

---

[54] See, generally, P Pettit, *Republicanism: A Theory of Freedom and Government* (Oxford, Oxford University Press, 1997).

only by a general requirement of authority of the sort that the broad reading of *Entick* provides.

The relative slightness of the interference with property in *Entick* is also reflected in the thin formal/procedural requirements which Lord Camden imposes for any putative justification of it. Two features of these formal requirements are notable when contextualising the manner in which the law protects against such interferences in relation to the protection it provides as against other forms of interference with property. First, though the set of laws which can authorise the interference with property is restricted to those which are 'positive', these might be found in either 'text of the statute law, or ... the principles of common law'.[55] There is therefore no restriction to interferences which are authorised by statute and so no sense in which the interference is possible only as a corollary of the sovereignty of Parliament. It is true that Camden did not consider himself to have the power to recognise a common law rule which would authorise the interference in question if such a rule did not already exist ('we have no right, without an act of parliament to adopt a new practice in the criminal law, which was never yet allowed from all antiquity'),[56] but had there been better evidence of such a rule's existence than mere practice since the revolution, the prima facie trespass could have been justified by the common law.[57] Second, the rules which justify such interference need not be formulated according to any particular standard of clarity; it suffices that they be 'found in our books'.[58] As will be seen, elsewhere the common law sets a higher bar.

VII. DEPRIVATION OF PROPERTY

Despite, then, the factors which weight in favour of such a conclusion, *Entick* has not been treated as regulating interferences with property. Nor, indeed, has the case been incorporated into the wider body of law relating to interferences with property, many of them more severe than that at issue in *Entick*. The legally weakest form of interference, exemplified by *Entick*, leaves the bundle of rights of the property owner intact; at the opposite end of the spectrum, the most severe form of interference deprives the owner of the property altogether.[59] Though the protection which the rule in *Entick* provides against weak interference with property logically entails at least an equal degree of protection against stronger interference, the tendency of

---

[55] *Entick v Carrington* (n 21) 1066.
[56] ibid 1067.
[57] ibid 1067–68.
[58] ibid 1066.
[59] This form of interference is variously labelled deprivation, confiscation or, in certain circumstances, requisition.

the courts has been to treat these as separate phenomena, with more severe interferences addressed by a distinct and more specific line of authority and more onerous procedural rules. The breadth of the rule in *Entick*—its application beyond interferences with property—has in this sense seen it separated out from the treatment of property at common law, notwithstanding Camden's placing of emphasis there and the fact that key concepts of the relevant body of law are present in particularly acute form in *Entick*.

That expropriation is the most severe interference with private property imaginable is reflected in the distinction within Article 1 of Protocol 1 of the ECHR between the deprivation of possessions—which is prohibited except under the conditions laid down therein—and the 'control' of property, the right of the state to do which is expressly stated to not be 'impaired' by the rule against deprivation. However, this is no foreign novelty; domestic law has long set its stall against the taking of property by the state. In mapping the manner in which the law protects against such interference, it is necessary to distinguish between the taking of property under the prerogative and that authorised by statute.

A. Deprivation under the Prerogative

Where property is to be taken, parliamentary approval will usually be required. As noted above, one of the great constitutional outrages of the Stuart era was the Court of Exchequer Chamber's willingness to let the claim to necessity override the property rights of those being required to pay ship money,[60] while taxation by prerogative was explicitly condemned by the Bill of Rights 1689.[61] Nevertheless, until the twentieth century, it was understood that the prerogative could be used to take property or to take possession of it where the defence of the realm required it, even outside of those situations of impending invasion which had traditionally been held to justify such taking.[62] In such cases, no compensation was payable at law—'The municipal law of this country does not give compensation to a subject whose land or goods are requisitioned by the Crown'[63]—but the historical record suggests that compensation was usually paid,[64] and in 1920 Lord

---

[60] *R v Hampden* (1637) 3 St Tr 825.

[61] Article 4.

[62] eg, *The King's Prerogative in Saltpetre* (1606) 12 Co Rep 12; *In re A Petition of Right* [1915] 3 KB 649.

[63] *The Zamora* [1916] 2 AC 77, 100 per Lord Parker of Waddington.

[64] Where Fortescue notes the right of the King to take 'necessaries for his household', it is on the proviso that the taking be compensated, for the King 'cannot despoil any of his subjects of their goods without due satisfaction for them'. Sir J Fortescue, 'In Praise of the Laws of England' in S Lockwood (ed), *On the Laws and Governance of England* (Cambridge, Cambridge University Press, 1997) ch XXXVI.

Atkinson felt able to state that 'it does not appear that the Crown has ever taken for [the defence of the realm] the land of the subject without paying for it, and that there is no trace of the Crown having, even in the times of the Stuarts, exercised or asserted the power or right to do so by virtue of the Royal Prerogative'.[65] Regardless of the position under the prerogative, various nineteenth-century statutes permitted the requisition of property, though with compensation payable.[66] The House of Lords had in 1916 been ready to hold that compensation was similarly payable (at least in some cases) under the prerogative; on receiving an intimation to that effect, the Crown withdrew its appeal[67] and lived to fight the point another day.[68] It is therefore not surprising that the Law Lords later held that where, as here, a statutory power and a prerogative power co-exist, the executive will be required to make use of the former, for: 'What use would there be in imposing limitations, if the Crown could at its pleasure disregard them and fall back on prerogative?'[69] A fundamental principle regarding the relationship between statutory and prerogative powers was thus established specifically in order to prevent the exploitation of this lacuna in the protection of property left by the prerogative. There is now, however, less of a gap to exploit, the decision in the *Burmah Oil* case having established that the prerogative required the payment of compensation for the taking or destruction of property; only damage carried out in the actual conduct of war was exempt.[70] All of Camden's fears—the interference with property on the basis of poorly attested authority and its confiscation without the consent, via representation in the legislature, of those whose property is being taken—are encapsulated by the use of the prerogative to justify interference with property and deprivation of property in particular. Yet, while the prerogative remains capable of overriding established private property rights, the trajectory of the law's development in this area has been unambiguously in the direction of diminishing that capability, ensuring that the deprivation of property is limited to genuinely exceptional circumstances by these means, and the bulk of the fears voiced by Camden have in this way been addressed.[71] Though

---

[65] *Attorney General v De Keyser's Royal Hotel* [1920] AC 508, 539 per Lord Atkinson. See also the US case *Vanhorne's Lessee v Dorrance* (1795) 2 Dall 304, per Patterson J.

[66] The most important example being the Defence Act 1842.

[67] From *In re A Petition of Right* (n 62).

[68] GR Rubin, *Private Property, Government Requisition and the Constitution, 1914–1927* (London, Hambledon Press, 1994) 52–53.

[69] *De Keyser's Royal Hotel, Limited v The King* [1919] 2 Ch 197, 216 per Swinfen Eady MR, quoted in *Attorney General v De Keyser's Royal Hotel* (n 65) 526 by Lord Dunedin.

[70] *Burmah Oil Co v Lord Advocate* [1965] AC 75. The decision was immediately nullified by the War Damages Act 1965, confirming that whatever limits might exist on the prerogative, statute could evade.

[71] In *Youssef v Secretary of State for Foreign and Commonwealth Affairs* [2013] EWCA Civ 1302, an asset-freezing case, Laws LJ accepted that the power to 'bar the appellant from access to funds or other economic resources' could not be found in the prerogative: [25]–[26].

far removed from it in many ways, the Lockean themes of *Entick* are no less evident in this area of law: the common factor—property—works to bridge a seemingly significant gap.

B. Deprivation of Property via Statute

Expropriation on the basis of statutory authority has a long and distinguished history.[72] It evades the very fundamental democratic criticisms to which the prerogative power, when not partially shielded by necessity, is subject. More specifically, it potentially accords with the Lockean injunction against the taking of property without consent (which of course post-dates the origins of statutory expropriation) which we have already encountered in Camden's treatment of the rights of Parliament to tax colonies, but which was understood by those same colonists as applying equally to expropriation.[73] That the possibility of statutorily authorised deprivation is at odds with the more extreme position hinted at by Camden in the debate on the disturbances in America—whereby property rights are constituted as a hard limit upon parliamentary sovereignty—is merely the inevitable consequence of that position's incompatibility with parliamentary sovereignty. If Parliament can make or unmake any law whatsoever, then it can make laws either taking property or authorising others to do so.[74]

The claim that legislative authorisation amounts to consent in the Lockean sense is assisted by the historical practice of making each act of expropriation the subject of fresh statutory authority.[75] The common law does not, though, surrender in the face of such authority, remaining zealous in its protection of property rights against statutory interference—often in ways which make the more general rule in *Entick*, which applies to interferences with property which do not threaten ownership, seem of minimal importance. Where property is taken for purposes other than defence of the realm, not only must the authority for doing so be found in statute, but the authority in question must be explicit in its authorisation of the deprivation, providing a procedural protection commensurate with the greater

[72] FA Mann identifies as the first instance of compulsory purchase via statute an Act of 1541 (33 Hen 8 c 35) permitting the City of Gloucester to secure its water supply: FA Mann, 'Outlines of a History of Expropriation' (1959) 75 *LQR* 188, 194. Stoebuck, alternatively, dates the process to 1427: WB Stoebuck, 'A General Theory of Eminent Domain' (1972) 47 *Washington Law Review* 553, 565. On the need for parliamentary authority, see also the decision of Coke in *The Case of the Isle of Ely* (1609) 10 Co Rep 141a.

[73] Stoebuck (n 72) 567.

[74] See on this point Goldsworthy (n 29) 69–70.

[75] The practice of producing an ad hoc scheme each time expropriation was to be authorised was superseded only in 1845 with the Land Clauses (Consolidation) Act, which standardised the schemes by providing a series of clauses which could be adopted wholesale by statutes authorising expropriation for particular purposes.

extent of the relevant interference.[76] According to *Entick*, interference with a standing property right may be authorised either by the common law or statute—it suffices that the authority is 'found in our books'. Interference at this opposite end of the spectrum must be founded upon unequivocal statutory language. This rule, an instantiation of a broader interpretative presumption against doubtful penalisation,[77] provides an extra layer of protection than would the mere requirement of statutory authorisation, but can nevertheless be understood as reflecting the same logic as motivates the decision in *Entick*.

C. Compensation

Alongside the interpretive presumption against deprivation, there stands an equally important presumption against such taking being uncompensated.[78] One should not therefore construe a statue as 'interfering with or injuring persons' rights without compensation unless one is obliged so to construe it'.[79] This is not of course compensation as received by John Entick following the finding for him by Lord Camden—a remedy for interference held tortious due to the absence of legal authority—but compensation which the courts assume to be a requirement of lawful interference; compensation which renders legal rather than providing recompense for an illegal act. This is in keeping with what has been said about the nature of interference in *Entick*: being temporary and exceptional, it does not affect ownership or the bundle of rights which make up ownership (and which influence the value of property). Interferences which do are presumed to make good that loss of value. This second presumption of interpretation provides an additional layer of defence against this most intrusive form of interference with property: unless the contrary intention is signalled with appropriate clarity, the owner is to be deprived of his specific property, but left with the equivalent in value. Its importance derives from the fact that there is no right to compensation at common law.[80] Again, the common law simultaneously recognises the ultimate superiority of Parliament and demands that Parliament, in employing its supremacy in a manner which permanently interferes with property rights, does so with sufficient clarity. The claim

---

[76] Any number of authorities might be cited here. See, for example, those listed by Mann (n 72) 199, note 54.

[77] This is how it is regarded by Bennion: O Jones, *Bennion on Statutory Interpretation*, 6th edn (London, Butterworths Law, 2013) pt XVII.

[78] See, eg, *London & North Western Railway Company v Evans* [1893] 1 Ch 16, 28 per Bowen LJ; *Attorney General v De Keyser's Royal Hotel* (n 65) 542 per Lord Atkinson; *Burmah Oil Co v Lord Advocate* (n 70) 167 per Lord Upjohn.

[79] *Attorney General v Horner* (1884) 14 QBD 245, 257 per Brett MR.

[80] T Allen, *The Right to Property in Commonwealth Constitutions* (Cambridge, Cambridge University Press, 2000) 17.

that the presumption therefore amounts to 'a rule of constitutional law'[81] is of primarily rhetorical significance, but captures the special and consistent priority given to property rights by the common law. It comes as close as is logically possible to vindicating Lord Camden's suggestion that Parliament 'cannot take away any man's private property without making him a compensation'[82] without putting itself at odds with the fundamental constitutional rule. Property is treated, in short, as though its preservation were the 'great end' for which man entered society.

So, while expropriation outside of defence contexts may happen (but only on the basis of statutory authority), the common law has even there developed a dual-pronged method of mitigating the impact of this particular instantiation of Parliament's sovereignty. The nature of these presumptions of interpretation, as well as the forms of interference which they help to obstruct, means that the rule in *Entick* will, as far as the protection of property is concerned, often be left in the shadows. This is despite the fact that, as a matter of empirical reality, *Entick*-style interferences with property are likely to be significantly more frequent than is full-blown expropriation. We should not be fooled by the priority given to these presumptions of interpretation, however, for they do not supplant but rather augment the rule in *Entick*; where the point at issue is the clarity of the rule which authorises interferences, we have taken for granted that such a rule exists at all. The rule in *Entick*, or an analogue thereof, is therefore presumed by everything said about the particular circumstances under which deprivation can take place. That it is not always named merely confirms its axiomatic status.

VIII. RECONFIGURATION OF PROPERTY

A third form of interference with property must be considered, for it is possible to interfere with a person's property in a permanent fashion without taking that property from the person; without extinguishing in its entirety the bundle of rights which make up the notion of ownership. Instead, this bundle might be modified in a fashion disadvantageous to the person recognised as the owner. This need not necessarily be done by directly diminishing the bundle of rights enjoyed by the owner, as when, for example, more onerous requirements of planning permission are imposed. It might equally happen by the granting of another sort of right to someone who is not an owner, which has the indirect effect of diminishing that bundle of rights, as when, for example, rights of occupation are granted to a non-owner. In each case, there has been interference, for the modification of legal rules changes what it means for one to own land or own a home, but in neither case has

---

[81] Mann (n 72) 199.
[82] (1765) *Parliamentary History*, xvi, 168.

the interference called into question the fact that one owns the thing in question. Unlike in the first category, which comprises the events in *Entick*, the interference does not exist elsewhere in the law; it is neither temporary, nor intermittent, nor exceptional. It does not leave the property as it was. Instead, the interference is written into the bundle of rights which together make up property on a permanent basis. One still owns one's property, but the significance of that statement is not what it previously was. Some such interferences are in this sense analogous to those interferences described above with liberties that are only protected residually: the fact that the law permits an individual to do something implicitly re-defines the rights of another individual. Here, however, there is a positively defined right at stake and so the approach of the courts to such implicit re-definitions of property rights is distinct from the less procedurally onerous approaches evidenced, in divergent ways, by the decisions in *Entick* and *Malone*.

At common law, this sort of interference short of deprivation is addressed by the same interpretive presumptions as counter (uncompensated) taking. In a case which turned on the question of whether a power to make an order 'regulating the exercise by either spouse of the right to occupy the dwelling-house' included the power to make an order prohibiting such exercise, it was noted by Lord Pearson that such an interpretation:

> [M]akes a very drastic inroad into the common law rights of the property-owning spouse. According to a well-established principle of construction, an interpretation which has this effect ought not to be adopted unless the enactment plainly bears that meaning.[83]

Elsewhere, Lord Reid confirmed that the presumption against taking property without compensation applies as much to 'control' of property as to any confiscation of it:

> It would be possible to distinguish this statement of the principle on the ground that planning legislation does not take away private rights of property: it merely prevents them from being exercised if planning permission is refused. But that would, in my view, be too meticulous a distinction. Even in such a case I think we must be sure that it was intended that this should be done without compensation.[84]

These principles of construction, then, extend far beyond actual deprivation so as to be engaged by any attempt to diminish the rights enjoyed by the owner of property. They 'bite' most clearly in cases where the interference with property is the result of the contingent mode of exercise of a statutory power; where a statute permits the doing of a thing, but does not mandate it, the statute cannot be held up as a defence to any interference with private

---

[83] *Tarr v Tarr* [1973] AC 254, 264.
[84] *Westminster Bank Ltd v Minister of Housing and Local Government* [1971] AC 508, 529. See also *London & North Western Railway Company v Evans* (n 78) 27.

rights unless the power is such as to make the interference inevitable.[85] Where, instead, the power inevitably constitutes a re-definition of property rights because it cannot be exercised in a non-interfering fashion, the common law will not protect against this partial 'taking'. And there is no right to compensation unless the statute provides for it—the impossibility of exercising the relevant statutory power in a non-interfering fashion is understood as having authorised the diminution of some person's property right. The most important example is *Hammersmith and City Railway Company v Brand*,[86] in which the House of Lords held that even where the value of property was reduced by the construction of a railway (authorised by a private Act of Parliament), the property's owner was not owed the compensation which would have been owed to a landowner whose property was taken; any action in nuisance was superseded by the statute. As Mr Justice Blackburn explained it:

> [I]f the Legislature authorizes the doing of an act (which if unauthorized would be a wrong and a cause of action) no action can be maintained for that act, on the plain ground that no Court can treat that as a wrong which the Legislature has authorized, and consequently the person who has sustained a loss by the doing of that act is without remedy, unless in so far as the Legislature has thought it proper to provide for compensation to him ... He suffers a private loss for the public benefit.[87]

Here the possession of which the plaintiff was deprived was, in the first place, the action in nuisance rather than the overall property right and even then only indirectly—as the corollary of the permission granted to a person against whom such action could otherwise have been brought. Nevertheless, the action in nuisance had been part of the bundle of rights which previously made up ownership and so there had been an interference with property—a permanent one which had significantly diminished the value of the property. The principle is therefore well established that 'where Parliament by express direction or by necessary implication has authorised the construction and use of an undertaking or works, that carries with it an authority to do what is authorised with immunity from any action based on nuisance. The right of action is taken away'.[88] The Janus-faced nature of legal rights means that the courts will not need to insist upon sufficient clarity in the interference with property itself, for a suitably clear statutory permission will produce the same result. There is therefore a lesser degree of protection than is provided against outright expropriation, for it is clear that such expropriation could never be effected merely by granting suitably clear permission

---

[85] *Metropolitan Asylum District v Hill* (1881) App Cas 193.
[86] *Hammersmith and City Railway Company v Brand* (1869–70) LR 4 HL 171.
[87] ibid 195.
[88] *Allen v Gulf Oil Refining Ltd* [1981] AC 1001, 1011.

to a third party to act in a certain way. The decision in *Hammersmith* suggests, therefore, that these intermediate interferences with property rights are analogous in the first place to the interference in *Entick*, in that the identification of lawful authority provides a defence to otherwise tortious conduct. But in *Entick*, the interference was specific, temporary and exceptional; here it is permanent, and so the stronger analogy is interferences with liberties which were traditionally protected only residually at common law. Just as the grant or recognition of new powers to the state can amount to a re-definition of an individual's interests which are protected only residually, so too can the recognition of a power to act—by either state or private actor—re-define one's private law rights. Regardless, however, of how we conceptualise such controls on property, the fundamental requirement of authority is a component of the legal response.

If interferences at one end of the spectrum can be authorised by either common law or statute, while those at the other end require (explicit) statutory authority, then where do these intermediate interferences fall? The answer is twofold. In one sense, the common law cannot justify these sorts of interferences, for the rules of common law are already by definition built into the bundle of rights which make up ownership—if that bundle includes a duty to allow others to act in a certain way, then there is no interference with one's rights when they do so. On the other hand, the processes of common law decision-making admit the possibility that the judgment of a court will introduce or alter general rules relating to the rights/liabilities/duties of property owners or some subset thereof, thereby effectively re-defining their property. The decision of a court can therefore effect an interference with or control the rights of property owners where it has the effect of altering the content of the common law, even though the common law would not recognise to any actor the power to carry out such general interference with property rights.

IX. PRESUMPTIONS OF STATUTORY INTERPRETATION AND THE PRINCIPLE OF LEGALITY

This review of the different forms that interference with property rights might take and how the common law deals with them shows that while the decision in *Entick* provides a basic form of protection to property rights, amongst others, it deals directly with a relatively weak form of interference and sets a relatively low procedural bar for the formalities which any legal authorisation for such interference with property must demonstrate. The interference with protected interests might be based on a rule of statute or of the common law, while what matters is not the precision with which it is formulated, but merely whether the rule in question is 'found in our books'. If *Entick* may be taken to represent a procedural or formal conception of the rule of law,[89] that conception is a very generous one; limited not merely in the requirement it imposes, but also (on the dominant interpretation) in its suggestion that these requirements apply only where there is an interference with those substantive interests protected by law. Elsewhere in the common law, as we have seen, that bare formalism is augmented, commensurately with the extent of the interference being thus effected, by a presumption against the deprivation of property, for which clear words are required, and a similar presumption against deprivation of property without compensation for those thereby deprived. In this line of case law, *Entick* plays almost no role. Notwithstanding the evocative terms of Camden's judgment, the case does not emerge, as might be expected, as the keystone of the common law's protection of property, as the signifier of the constitutional priority given to that legal institution. On the one hand, the rule is therefore a victim of its own axiomatic status: anywhere a higher degree of protection is implemented, the rule in *Entick* is implicitly applied, but not necessarily named. But it is not only this status which sees the case overlooked within the jurisprudence on the right to property. The form of interference at stake in *Entick* as well, perhaps, as the motive for which such interference will normally be executed—loosely, questions of law and order—similarly work to isolate the case from the bulk of common law jurisprudence on the protection of property rights against the state, where the interferences in question are more drastic and the motives for their execution potentially less palatable.

Given the traditional absence of *Entick* from the main body of case law on the protection of property via principles of statutory interpretation, however, it is notable that a recent invocation of the case by the Supreme Court finds it not only associated with property in general but also exemplifying the principle of legality; as testifying to, Lord Hope suggests, 'the right to peaceful enjoyment of [one's] property, which could only be interfered with by clear legislative words'.[90] In the aftermath of the principle of legality's now-classic formulation in *Simms*,[91] the identity of these two approaches—the principle of legality and the presumption against doubtful penalisation—was not at first secure. In one early post-*Simms* case, it was argued that the principle of legality was something beyond a rule of statutory interpretation[92]—that it was in fact what has been described as

---

[89] P Craig, 'Formal and Substantive Conceptions of the Rule of Law: An Analytical Framework' [1997] *PL* 467.

[90] *Her Majesty's Treasury v Ahmed* [2010] UKSC 2 [75]. See also *Youssef v Secretary of State for Foreign and Commonwealth Affairs* [2013] EWCA Civ 1302 [25] per Laws LJ.

[91] *R v Secretary of State for the Home Department ex p Simms* [1999] UKHL 33, [2000] 2 AC 115. For the origins of the phrase, see *R v Secretary of State for the Home Department ex p Pierson* [1998] AC 539, 587.

[92] *R v Worcester CC ex p SW* [2000] HRLR 702.

a 'principle of substantive law that limited the exercise of non-statutory powers'.[93] An acceptance of this interpretation would have undermined the relative procedural generosity of the rule in *Entick* by requiring the courts to read down alleged non-statutory powers to interfere with protected interests; the space left open by Camden for interferences with private law rights founded upon the common law would have been closed off. In rejecting it, the Queen's Bench was implicitly aligning itself with the European Court of Human Rights, which in a seminal case made clear that the common law was capable of grounding a justified interference with one of the qualified Convention rights. To deny that possibility would 'deprive a common-law State which is Party to the Convention of the protection of [the qualification] and strike at the very roots of that State's legal system'.[94]

Alternatively, the two approaches might have been distinguished on the basis of the sorts of rights to which each of the two rules of construction relates. In *Simms*, Lord Hoffmann refers to the impossibility of using general or ambiguous words to override 'fundamental rights'. To invoke *Entick* as an illustration of the principle of legality might therefore be taken to elide any implicit distinction between such fundamental rights as are now recognised by the common law[95] (and so no longer protected merely residually) and the 'ordinary' private law rights at stake in *Entick*; that case has in this way been retrospectively reconceptualised as an instantiation of a public law right to property rather than as a simple corollary of the fact that private law rights apply equally against the state. This reconceptualisation also seems to rule out the possibility of discrimination in terms of the level of procedural protection offered to public and private law rights; in each case, the principle of legality applies. To the bare 'found in our law' standard applied by Camden has, it seems, been added a consideration—which *Entick* did not originally demand—of the clarity of the provision allegedly authorising interference. This linking of *Entick* to the case law on deprivation confirms the manner in which the question of how the principle of legality relates to older rules of statutory interpretation has been answered—the formulation of the principle of legality is novel, but we should not be thereby misled as to the novelty of its substance, which is well known to the common law.[96]

This invocation of *Entick* as evidence of the principle of legality's application to property is therefore revealing. It indicates a conflation both of

---

[93] M Cohen, 'Medieval Chains, Invisible Inks: On Non-statutory Powers of the Executive' (2005) 25 *OJLS* 97, 115.

[94] *The Sunday Times v UK* Series A No 30 (1979–80) 2 EHRR 245, 270.

[95] An exhaustive catalogue of which is, almost by definition, impossible. The Court of Appeal has listed some of the relevant rights in respect of which the principle of legality has been adopted, noting that all are 'detailed and specific rights'. *R (Nicklinson) v Ministry of Justice* [2013] EWCA Civ 961 [65].

[96] A fact acknowledged by Lord Hoffmann himself in *R (Morgan Grenfell & Co Ltd) v Special Commissioner of Income Tax* [2003] 1 AC 563, 607: 'the wider principle itself is hardly new. It can be traced back at least to *Stradling v Morgan* (1560) 1 Pl 199'.

the different types of interference which might be carried out with one's property—there is no need to separate out, as above, the different forms such interference might take, for each reflects the same general principle—and a simultaneous conflation of the different means by which the common law works to ensure that such interferences happen only with the clear consent of the legislature. It would also seem to imply that the lower level of procedural protection afforded against the sorts of interferences with property evidenced by *Entick* has been supplanted by the higher form of protection which the common law provides against interferences with property of a more fundamental nature; that all such interferences now require lawful authority that does not merely exist but is sufficiently explicit. Though this does not yet exclude interferences on the basis of common law authority, the direction of travel in this area of law is certainly such as to minimise such interferences, the only common law power of warrantless entry preserved by the Police and Criminal Evidence Act reforms being that to deal with or prevent a breach of the peace.[97] Having achieved priority as a case of more general constitutional significance, *Entick* has begun to move back into place as the keystone of the system by which the common law protects property rights.

X. *ENTICK*, PROPERTY AND THE PUBLIC INTEREST

Another aspect of Camden's paean to property provides connects *Entick* to the body of common law dicta on property: the claim that the right to property is 'sacred and incommunicable' except where 'taken away or abridged by some public law for the good of the whole'.[98] This last qualification raises the spectre of a substantive limitation on any interference with property, focused upon the motive for such interference. Such a rule would preclude deprivations or controls on property not calculated to promote the public interest, but instead to advance some private end. In *Entick*, the good of the whole is promoted (or might plausibly be said to be promoted) by the existence of a system for the protection of law and order of which search and seizure, where legally authorised, is a necessary part. Similarly, the prerogative power to take property is so closely associated with the defence of the realm and is (now) so tightly tied to that motive that, where it is exercised in accordance with the normal public law standards, its contribution to the public good will normally be beyond challenge. Elsewhere, the question of whether such relatively drastic interferences with property are

---

[97] Police and Criminal Evidence Act 1984, s 17(6).
[98] *Entick v Carrington* (n 21) 1066. Salmon LJ, commenting in the late 1960s on the idea as to the appropriate balance between public good and private right implicit in these dicta, suggested that these remarks 'had an odd ring—both archaic and incongruous'. *Chic Fashions (West Wales) Ltd v Jones* [1969] 2 QB 299, 319.

executed 'for the good of the whole' is a more controversial one, reflecting quite fundamental disagreement as to the legitimate role of the state and the fact that many of its potential ends cannot be achieved through transient and temporary interference, but only where property is diminished or taken. This difference of purpose again contributes to a plausible explanation of the detachment of *Entick* from the line of authority which addresses interferences with property of a more drastic nature.

Here, however, the prospects for *Entick*'s accommodation within a single body of law relating to property, and the limitation of interferences with it to circumstances in which the public good is thereby promoted, are less promising. A formalisation of such a limit as a legal rule is, like the notion that uncompensated taking might be legally impermissible, of course incompatible with Parliament's sovereignty. It would be wrong to suggest, however, that the absence of a legally enforceable rule to that effect excludes considerations of the public interest from the question of whether interferences with property can lawfully take place. The political aspects of the constitution, amongst them the need to secure parliamentary backing (and perhaps that of the wider public) for legislative proposals, provide some minimum guarantee that the expropriation permitted by the statute will be in keeping with the public interest. We see this attested to as far back as Blackstone, who starts from the proposition that the individual's private interest should not be made to yield to the public interest, 'for it would be dangerous to allow any private man, or even a public tribunal, to be the judge of the common good, and to decide whether it be expedient or no'. What neither a court nor a private person can do, however, is within the power of Parliament: 'the legislature alone can, and frequently does, interpose, and compel the individual to acquiesce'.[99] To require interferences with property to have a statutory basis, therefore, does not merely provide a more or less convincing basis for saying that the requirement of consent has been met, but amounts to a legal mechanism for ensuring that the public interest (or something which might plausibly be labelled as such) has been considered and found to be in favour of interfering, or permitting interference, with private property. Here, as elsewhere, legal rules secure the functioning of the political constitution; where the outcomes are undesirable, the fault often lies with politics and not law. Again, this narrative is challenged by the willingness of Lord Camden to countenance a justification for the trespass against John Entick's property based upon a common law rule, for in situations where the justification for interference exists at common law, it is difficult to see from where derives the certainty that the sanctity of property has been abridged 'for the good of the whole'.[100] Where, however, as in the context of deprivation of

---

[99] Blackstone (n 43) I, 135.
[100] *Entick v Carrington* (n 21) 1066.

property, more procedurally demanding accounts of the rule of law preclude justification by the common law, they work to ensure that the public interest is protected even without its explicit invocation as a criterion of legitimate interference with private rights.

The need to ensure that interferences with property promote the public good applies more forcefully where the deprivation is being carried out by a private actor. As such, in the case of the private Acts used to carry out much of the expropriation necessary for projects such as the expansion of the railroad system in the nineteenth century, the relevant private bill procedures were such as to ensure 'that a public case had to be made out before a Parliamentary Committee justifying the bestowal of those powers [of expropriation] ... in the public interest'.[101] Moreover, the courts at times indicated a willingness to interpret bylaws made by railway companies and other private companies more restrictively than those made by democratically elected local authorities, whose rules should be 'supported if possible ... [and] "benevolently" interpreted', with credit given 'to those who have to administer them that they will be reasonably administered'.[102] It could not be said, then, that the courts were wholly unaware either of the dangers of granting rule-making powers (including the power to make rules interfering with property) to private actors or of the public interest considerations which might provide public bodies with greater latitude in interfering with private rights.

Though it is incapable of founding a substantive limitation upon Parliament, the claim that interferences with property should be tied to the motive for which the interference is carried out finds strong support within the case law. On the basis of a review of a range of Commonwealth authorities Michael Taggart felt able to conclude that there exists 'a constitutional principle that private property should only be taken for public purposes'.[103] Such a principle would be in keeping with the idea of property (and legitimate interference with it) advanced in *Entick*, but—as with the suggestion that there is a constitutional rule against taking without compensation—it is not clear what legal status this 'principle' might have. Taggart refers to its expression in 'administrative law doctrine and the law and techniques of statutory interpretation',[104] some of which have been canvassed above. While undoubtedly true, these expressions of the principle do not assist

---

[101] M Taggart, 'Expropriation, Public Purpose and the Constitution' in C Forsyth and I Hare (eds), *The Golden Metwand and the Crooked Cord: Essays in Honour of Sir William Wade QC* (Oxford, Clarendon, 1998) 103. But compare RW Kostal, *Law and English Railway Capitalism 1825–1875* (Oxford, Clarendon, 1994) 131.

[102] *Kruse v Johnson* [1898] 2 QB 91, 98–99 per Lord Russell CJ, quoted in Michael Taggart, *Private Property and Abuse of Rights in Victorian England: The Story of Edward Pickles and the Bradford Water Supply* (Oxford, Oxford University Press, 2002) 102.

[103] Taggart (n 101) 112.

[104] ibid 112.

it in overcoming its incompatibility with the fundamental rule of English constitutional law.

To constitute Taggart's 'principle' as a legal limitation enforced by the courts would surpass even the aggressive role of the courts in narrowly interpreting statutes alleged to justify interference with property. To render it instead a political norm would be ambiguous as between its inductive and deductive function. It was noted above that part of the divergence in views between Camden and Mansfield seemed to result from the mixed normative and descriptive elements of their assessments of Parliament's role in relation to property. The same might be said here: it is unlikely that Parliament has in the past been frequently minded to grant power to deprive for an explicitly non-public purpose—using Taggart's standard of taking land from one person 'in order to confer a benefit upon another without any substantial countervailing public benefit'[105]—and it seems no more likely to employ its legislative omnicompetence to do so in future. Even the private Acts of Parliament which come closest to exemplifying expropriation for non-public purposes are easily and not unconvincingly translated into public interest terms.[106] As such, Taggart's ostensibly normative 'constitutional principle' is as much a description of political practice as it is the practice of the courts on those rare occasions where Parliament's statutory outputs might be plausibly interpreted as permitting interference in contravention of Taggart's principle. We would be wise, however, to be sceptical of making such a leap, not least because the fact that Parliament legislated to promote certain private interests would be strong prima facie grounds for holding the promotion of that private interest to be in wider public interest. That is, it would indicate that the 'substantial countervailing public benefit' to which Taggart refers exists even if it is not immediately apparent—we may disagree with this verdict, but such disagreement is of course exactly the reason we make decisions via democratic mechanisms rather than entrusting them to the courts. Once again, we see that to read *Entick* as a case about property, is to find in microcosm all of the key themes of the common law protection of property rights; the question of the public interest is merely one more example of this.

XI. CONCLUSION

As a part of the political sideshow to the legal fallout from the attempted suppression of John Wilkes' writings on contestable legal grounds, the House of Commons debated the legality of general warrants on several

---

[105] ibid 105.
[106] See, eg, *Hammersmith and City Railway Company v Brand* (n 86) 190 per Baron Bramwell.

occasions. The combined effect of these joint processes has been described as conforming to the 'prime directive' of the English law of search and seizure: 'even promiscuously general searches did not violate the liberty of the subject or infringe the maxim about a man's home so long as Parliament had laid down the law'.[107] When called upon to identify how property is protected at common law (and, conversely, how it might be legitimately interfered with), we arrive at a similar conclusion. The common law has evolved a series of rules which prevent deprivation and uncompensated deprivation without clear legal authority. Amongst these must be numbered the rule laid down by *Entick* whereby minor and transient interferences require justification by law, but that such justification might be found in the common law; more severe interferences require clear statutory authority. Though these latter rules incorporate a requirement of legality such as that implemented by *Entick*, this aspect is often taken for granted, with attention being focused instead on the more limited question of whether the authorisation is suitably explicit. If deprivation is to be uncompensated, that too must be made unambiguous. Only the residual and now heavily circumscribed prerogative powers relating to confiscation in wartime stand as an exception to this. *Entick v Carrington* does not lay down a rule which protects property specifically, but captures many of the most important themes of the common law's commitment to protecting property rights, and this particular facet of the decision becomes more prominent with the passage of time.

We therefore arrive at the final question. As a matter of domestic law, what is it that protects property against interference up to and including expropriation? If all that the law has to offer is a requirement of legality (as in *Entick*) augmented by the principle of legality (as we would now call the canon of construction which protects property against uncompensated deprivation on the basis of general language), then the answer must surely be that it is the political process which ultimately undergirds the protection of property and the willingness of those involved—either as electors or formal participants in the legislative process—to see property interfered with or confiscated which either sees it happen or (more often) ensures that it does not. This fact captures many of the most vital themes of Lord Camden's concern with property rights, as attested to in *Entick* and elsewhere. First, it gives interferences with property rights by public authorities the legal basis they require. Second, the existence of legislation permitting interference permits the construction of a narrative whereby those whose property rights are opened up to interference have consented, indirectly, to that interference. Third, the need to navigate the political process requires that the

---

[107] LW Levy, *Origins of the Bill of Rights* (New Haven, Yale University Press, 1999) 163.

justification for interference be formulated in a manner which at least purports to represent the public interest. This is as it should be. The legal rules require the expression of political will via certain channels without placing (as would in the end be fruitless) limits upon its substantive content. Where, then, we find that property is too poorly protected against interference or (perhaps more realistically) too often treated as sacrosanct, it is not in most cases the law on which we should seek to place the blame, but the political process which produces, or fails to produce, the statutory rules in question.

6

The Authority of Entick v Carrington

ADAM TOMKINS

I. INTRODUCTION

T
WO HUNDRED AND fifty years on from the great case of *Entick v Carrington* and we are still unsure of its legacy. We know that the case is remembered, but we do not always know why. Was it a great case because of what it said about general warrants, because of what it said about search and seizure, and because of what it said about the protection of private property? Or is it that, while it said true and important things about all these matters, at the same time it tapped into a much broader and richer seam of thinking, teaching us not only something of particular powers and their lawful limits, but also of power itself and of the way the law should approach it? I have always thought so.

Constitutional lawyers remember *Entick v Carrington* because—or so we have liked to tell ourselves—it is among the leading authorities on the rule of law. In 2003 I was bold enough to write the following:

> [I]n English public law the rule of law has at its core a single, simple, and clear meaning. It is a rule that concerns the power of the executive, of government ... and it governs the relationship of the executive to the law. The rule of law provides that the executive may do nothing without clear legal authority first permitting its actions ... For the executive to act it must have legal authority that permits its actions. If no such authority can be found, the executive may not so act.[1]

As sole authority for these propositions, I cited *Entick v Carrington*. In their contributions to this book, Timothy Endicott and Paul Scott each argue that to read propositions of law as broadly crafted as these into the fine-print of *Entick v Carrington* is, at best, a stretch. Perhaps they are correct. However, this chapter argues that, if they are correct, something of value will have been lost.

---

[1] A Tomkins, *Public Law* (Oxford, Oxford University Press, 2003) 78–79.

Rather a lot of the literature on the rule of law omits consideration of *Entick v Carrington* entirely. Lord Bingham finds no room for it, for example, in his late masterwork, *The Rule of Law*.[2] David Dyzenhaus considers *Liversidge v Anderson*[3] at length in both *Hard Cases in Wicked Legal Systems* and *The Constitution of Law*, but *Entick* is cited in neither.[4] David Beatty goes further, citing case law from 18 jurisdictions—but not from England and Wales—in his *The Ultimate Rule of Law*.[5] Brian Tamanaha is kinder to England, saying that, while she has 'no written constitution, no explicit bill of individual rights … and no judicial review', she is 'the acknowledged birthplace of liberalism and the bastion of the rule of law'. In the paragraphs that follow, Tamanaha cites Hobbes, Locke, Dicey, Magna Carta, habeas corpus and Sir Edward Coke in support of these claims—but not *Entick v Carrington*.[6]

Lord Bingham opens his book by noting that 'credit for coining the expression "the rule of law" is usually given to' Dicey (whilst recording that, even if he popularised the phrase, he certainly did not invent the idea lying behind it).[7] In Dicey's account of the rule of law, *Entick v Carrington* appears, but only as a footnote and, even then, only to support an illustration of a principle rather than as authority for anything grander. No sense that *Entick v Carrington* is a great case (or a 'landmark')[8] could be gleaned from reading Dicey on the rule of law.[9] We shall return to Dicey and his footnote later.

That *Entick* is a great case and, specifically, that it is a great constitutional case about the rule of law may be a twentieth-century notion. Nowhere do its praises appear to have been more enthusiastically sung than in the works of Keir and Lawson and Heuston. Keir and Lawson produced their *Cases in Constitutional Law* (first edition 1928) in order to aid the teaching of constitutional law: 'knowledge of the legal principles on which the English constitution rests … can best be acquired by a study of leading cases', they wrote.[10] Their book considered legislation and the sovereignty of Parliament, subordinate legislation, prerogative powers, parliamentary privilege

[2] T Bingham, *The Rule of Law* (London, Allen Lane, 2010).
[3] *Liversidge v Anderson* [1942] AC 206.
[4] D Dyzenhaus, *Hard Cases in Wicked Legal Systems: Pathologies of Legality*, 2nd edn (Oxford, Oxford University Press, 2010) and *The Constitution of Law: Legality in a Time of Emergency* (Cambridge, Cambridge University Press, 2006).
[5] D Beatty, *The Ultimate Rule of Law* (Oxford, Oxford University Press, 2004).
[6] B Tamanaha, *On the Rule of Law: History, Politics, Theory* (Cambridge, Cambridge University Press, 2004) 56–57.
[7] Bingham (n 2) 3.
[8] See Endicott, ch 4 in this volume.
[9] Although, as Bradley and Ewing put it, 'the spirit of *Entick v Carrington* seems to run through Dicey's arguments': A Bradley and K Ewing, *Constitutional and Administrative Law*, 15th edn (Harlow, Pearson, 2011) 92.
[10] D Keir and F Lawson, *Cases in Constitutional Law* (Oxford, Oxford University Press, 1928) v.

and taxation before it reached 'judicial control of public authorities', but the first case extracted under that heading was *Entick v Carrington*. In their notes introducing the heading, Keir and Lawson wrote as follows:

> In England, any person—whether he be a private individual or a public officer makes no difference—who interferes with the private rights of the subject renders himself liable to an action in tort, unless he can justify his act by putting forward a defence recognised by law ... It was settled once and for all in the great constitutional struggle of the seventeenth century ... that the mere plea of act of State is not a legal defence to an action in tort. In other words, it is not open to any public officer to defend himself by alleging generally that he has acted in the public interest. He must point to some specific authorisation either at common law or by statute.

These were the propositions of law which Keir and Lawson considered *Entick v Carrington* to represent.[11]

Heuston's *Essays in Constitutional Law* (first published in 1961) commenced with an essay on sovereignty. The second essay was on the rule of law. Heuston started this essay with Coke and Bracton before moving swiftly on to Dicey. He summarised Dicey's account of the rule of law and then wrote: 'Let us be concrete. Here are two great cases. The first is *Entick v Carrington*. If one case had to be chosen to illustrate more than any other the fundamental principles of English constitutional law, it would be this one. It is, as Professor Lawson has remarked, the case to take to a desert island.'[12]

Modern textbooks continue to feature *Entick v Carrington* prominently in their treatment of the rule of law. Bradley and Ewing, for example, under a heading 'Government according to law', state that:

> [T]he principle of legality requires that the organs of the state operate through law. If the police need to detain a citizen or if taxes are levied, the officials concerned must be able to show legal authority for their actions. In Britain, their authority may be challenged before a court of law, as was done in *Entick v Carrington* ... It is because of the principle of legality that legislation must be passed through Parliament ... The rule of law serves as a buttress for democracy, since new powers of government may be conferred only by Parliament.[13]

Elliott and Thomas describe *Entick v Carrington* as a 'celebrated case', as do Le Sueur, Sunkin and Murkens.[14] Le Sueur, Sunkin and Murkens, and

---

[11] D Keir and F Lawson, *Cases in Constitutional Law*, 2nd edn (Oxford, Oxford University Press, 1933) 124.

[12] R Heuston, *Essays in Constitutional Law*, 2nd edn (London, Stevens, 1964) 35. Heuston's second 'great case' was the *Case of Wolfe Tone* (1798) 27 St Tr 614, which, as far as I can see, has now been entirely forgotten by constitutional lawyers.

[13] Bradley and Ewing (n 9) 96.

[14] M Elliott and R Thomas, *Public Law*, 2nd edn (Oxford, Oxford University Press, 2014) 68; and A Le Sueur, M Sunkin and J Murkens, *Public Law: Text, Cases and Materials*, 2nd edn (Oxford, Oxford University Press, 2012) 90.

Turpin and Tomkins all provide extracts from the judgment.[15] Twenty-first-century law students in the UK, it seems, are still expected to know about *Entick v Carrington*.

II. THE RULE OF LAW

All of the books referred to in the preceding paragraph inform their readers that there are many meanings attached to the phrase 'the rule of law'. Indeed, so many meanings are ascribed to it that we are not always sure what it means. The former President of the UK Supreme Court, Lord Phillips, said in evidence to a parliamentary committee in July 2014 that: 'The rule of law is not readily defined or readily understood. You ingest it, if you are a lawyer, as part of your upbringing and your practice. Belief in the rule of law is almost like a religion: it is crucial; it governs the way you behave.'[16] If even a President of the UK's top court cannot define the rule of law, perhaps Sidney Low was right when he observed of our constitution that: 'We live under a system of tacit understandings. But the understandings themselves are not always understood.'[17]

There have been as many attempts to offer clarity about the rule of law as there are competing interpretations of it. Some of these attempts have been more helpful than others. In my view, it is hard to improve upon the following statement, written by Professor Paul Craig:

> A core idea of the rule of law to which all would subscribe is that the government must be able to point to some basis for its action that is regarded as valid by the relevant legal system. Thus in the UK such action would commonly have its foundation in statute, the prerogative or in common law power ... If the government cannot provide a legal foundation for its action then the UK courts would regard the action as unlawful, since there would be no lawful authority for it.[18]

A particularly clear and striking example of this principle in action is the well-known case of *Fewings*.[19] Somerset County Council passed a resolution banning deer hunting on land it owned. The applicants, representing

---

[15] C Turpin and A Tomkins, *British Government and the Constitution: Text, Cases and Materials*, 7th edn (Cambridge, Cambridge University Press, 2011) 99.

[16] Lord Phillips, *Evidence to the House of Lords Constitution Committee*, 23 July 2014, Q19.

[17] S Low, *The Governance of England* (London, Fisher Unwin, 1904) 12.

[18] P Craig, 'The Rule of Law', written evidence to the House of Lords Constitution Committee, 2006: see House of Lords Constitution Committee, *Relations between the Executive, the Judiciary and Parliament* (HL 2006–07, 151) 98. Craig went on in his analysis to explain what various commentators have added to this core meaning of the rule of law. His own view is that the core meaning is necessary but not sufficient. For the present purposes, it is unnecessary to move beyond the core meaning.

[19] *R v Somerset County Council ex p Fewings* [1995] 1 All ER 513.

Quantock Staghounds, sought judicial review of the lawfulness of the council's decision. The power under which the Council purported to act was section 120(1) of the Local Government Act 1972, which provided that a local authority such as Somerset County Council may act for the 'benefit, improvement or development' of the land. The judge, Laws J, found that Somerset County Council's decision had been taken because of certain councillors' moral objections to hunting and that the words of section 120(1) were not broad enough to allow a local authority to decide that persons acting lawfully on its land should be prohibited from so acting because councillors found their behaviour to be morally repulsive. Laws J's decision was subsequently upheld, albeit on other grounds, by the Court of Appeal.[20] In his judgment Laws J said the following: 'a public body, such as a local authority, enjoys no such thing as an unfettered discretion. This is a sinew of the rule of law'.[21] In support of this dictum, Laws J cited Sir William Wade's authoritative text on *Administrative Law*, in which he observed that:

> The powers of public authorities are ... essentially different from those of private persons. A man making his will may, subject to any rights of his dependants, dispose of his property just as he may wish. He may act out of malice or a spirit of revenge, but in law this does not affect his exercise of his power. In the same way a private person has an absolute power to allow whom he likes to use his land ... regardless of his motives. This is unfettered discretion. But a public authority may do none of these things unless it acts reasonably and in good faith and upon lawful and relevant grounds of public interest.[22]

Laws J continued as follows:

> Public bodies and private persons are both subject to the rule of law ... But the principles which govern their relationships with the law are wholly different. For private persons, the rule is that you may do anything you choose which the law does not prohibit ... But for public bodies the rule is opposite, and so of another character altogether. It is that any action to be taken must be justified by positive law. A public body has no heritage of legal rights which it enjoys for its own sake; at every turn, all of its dealings constitute the fulfilment of duties which it owes to others; indeed, it exists for no other purpose.[23]

These remarks were uttered in the context of a case concerning a local authority (as opposed to a minister). The reason why this is important will become apparent below. Having noted this, however, we should also note that Laws J closed this passage of his judgment in *Fewings* by stating that 'under our law', the difference between a private person and a public body

---

[20] [1995] 1 WLR 1037.

[21] *R v Somerset County Council ex p Fewings* (n 19) 524.

[22] See now Sir William Wade and C Forsyth, *Administrative Law*, 11th edn (Oxford, Oxford University Press, 2014) 296.

[23] *R v Somerset County Council ex p Fewings* (n 19) 524.

'is true of every public body. The rule is necessary in order to protect the people from arbitrary interference by those set in power over them'.[24] Laws J then went on to further illustrate his point by reference to *Padfield*,[25] which was a case concerning not a local authority, but a Minister of the Crown.

Fewings may be contrasted with *Malone v Metropolitan Police Commissioner*.[26] Here the question was whether the police had the legal authority to tap the claimant's telephone. The police had acted under a warrant issued by the Secretary of State. Megarry V-C ruled that the police had not acted unlawfully, despite the fact that their action was not authorised by statute. He gave two reasons. First, Malone had no legal right or interest which could form the basis of any claim. At the time, English law knew no general right of privacy. Nor could it be said that Malone had any property right in words transmitted over the telephone. And nor could he rely on any contractual right of confidentiality. Second, Megarry V-C said that, given this, as 'the tapping of telephones ... can be carried out without any breach of the law, it does not require any statutory or common law power to justify it; it can lawfully be done simply because there is nothing to make it unlawful'.[27] 'England', said the judge, 'is not a country where everything is forbidden except what is expressly permitted.'[28]

This is not merely different from what Laws J said in *Fewings*, it is its direct opposite. Megarry V-C was able to arrive at his conclusion only by denying that there is any juridical difference between a public body such as the Metropolitan Police and a private person. He tested his conclusion that 'England is not a country where everything is forbidden except what is expressly permitted' with the example of smoking. There is no positive law permitting people to smoke, but it does not follow that smoking is therefore impermissible. Ergo, the absence of a law permitting telephone tapping does not mean that the practice of telephone tapping is unlawful. Laws J's answer to this in *Fewings* would be to insist that the analogy is both false and misleading. Smoking is an activity carried on by private persons, but Malone's telephone was not tapped by a private person; it was tapped in order to assist the police in the detection of crime. That is the public function of a public body, not the leisure activity of a private citizen. A common lawyer, on Laws J's reasoning, cannot analogise from the legal situation governing a private person's behaviour to determine the limits of a public body's lawful powers because, he says, the two are 'wholly different'.

---

[24] ibid.
[25] *Padfield v Minister of Agriculture, Fisheries and Food* [1968] AC 997.
[26] *Malone v Metropolitan Police Commissioner* [1979] Ch 344.
[27] ibid 367.
[28] ibid 366.

Malone took his case to the European Court of Human Rights, where he was successful.[29] Phone tapping engages the Article 8(1) right to respect for private and family life, home and correspondence. Under Article 8(2), an interference with this right will be lawful only if it is in accordance with the law, necessary in a democratic society and for a certain legitimate aim. The Strasbourg Court found that the first of these requirements was not met. In order to be 'in accordance with the law', there must be 'a measure of legal protection in domestic law against arbitrary interferences by public authorities with the rights safeguarded' by Article 8(1).[30] Further, 'the law must be sufficiently clear in its terms to give citizens an adequate indication as to the circumstances in which and the conditions on which public authorities are empowered to resort to' telephone tapping.[31] In short, 'a law which confers a discretion must indicate the scope of that discretion', otherwise the matter would be 'contrary to the rule of law'.[32] In the judgment of the European Court of Human Rights, the law governing telephone tapping as it was applied in Malone's case failed these tests. For this reason, the Court was unanimous in finding a breach of Article 8.[33]

Fewings and *Malone* represent two quite different views of what the rule of law requires. Does it mean that public bodies such as the government 'may do nothing without clear legal authority first permitting its actions' and that 'for the executive to act it must have legal authority that permits its actions'?[34] Or does it mean less than this: does it mean only that for public bodies such as the government to act *in a manner that interferes with our identifiable rights* requires positive justification in law—that *coercive* government action is unlawful unless it can be shown to be justified in positive law, but that, in other respects, the government is as free to carry on its business as ordinary private individuals are?

Dicey's formulation of the rule of law does not altogether answer the matter, but may favour Megarry V-C's judgment in *Malone* more than that of Laws J in *Fewings*. He wrote that in England the rule of law means not only that 'no man is above the law, but (what is a different thing) that here every man, whatever be his rank or condition, is subject to the ordinary law of the realm and amenable to the jurisdiction of the ordinary tribunals'.[35] He called this the idea of legal equality: 'the universal subjection of all classes to one law administered by the ordinary courts' in which 'every official … is

[29] *Malone v UK* (1985) 7 EHRR 14.
[30] ibid [67].
[31] ibid.
[32] ibid [68].
[33] The consequence is that since 1985, telephone tapping has been regulated in the UK by statute, first by the Interception of Communications Act 1985 and now by the Regulation of Investigatory Powers Act 2000.
[34] Tomkins (n 1).
[35] AV Dicey, *Introduction to the Study of the Law of the Constitution*, 8th edn (London, Macmillan, 1915) 193.

under the same responsibility for every act done without legal justification as any other citizen'.[36] A Secretary of State, he added, is 'as responsible for any act which the law does not authorise as is any private and unofficial person'.[37] It was this proposition in respect of which Dicey cited *Entick v Carrington* as authority.

Dicey recognised that officials may be 'subject to laws which do not affect the rest' of us, but insisted that this 'is in no way inconsistent with the principle that all men are in England subject to the law of the realm'. Laws to which officials may be additionally subject may increase their legal liabilities, but do not allow them to escape from the 'duties of an ordinary citizen'.[38]

Sir Ivor Jennings was as critical of this aspect of Dicey's argument as he was his entire account of the rule of law: 'all public officials', Jennings wrote, 'especially public authorities, have powers and therefore rights which are not possessed by other persons'.[39] Jennings saw that Dicey was considering in this aspect of his account of the rule of law not what we would now call public or administrative law, but the law of tort. Dicey's point was simply—and only—that 'if a public officer commits a tort he will be liable for it in the ordinary civil courts'.[40] If this is all the rule of law means, we can see how Megarry V-C's decision in *Malone* may be compatible with it: given the underdeveloped state of the law of privacy in the 1970s, it was at the time no tort for the police to authorise the Post Office to tap a telephone conversation. As it was no tort, there was no liability.

But this is precisely why public lawyers as diverse as Sir Ivor Jennings and Sir John Laws have insisted that this cannot be all that is demanded of the rule of law. The rule of law pertains to government and public authorities generally. Such bodies are no mere private persons. They have greater powers—and more power—than ordinary persons. It follows that we need more than 'the ordinary law' (as Dicey put it) effectively to regulate them. We need public law. This is the force of Laws J's judgment in *Fewings* and this is what Megarry V-C overlooked in *Malone*. This is a tension that cuts to the core of controversies in UK public law about the meaning of the rule of law. Is it a principle of ordinary law, which says that the government is subject to the ordinary law of the land just like everybody else? Or is it a special principle of public law, pertaining only to government and other public bodies—and not to private persons—as Laws J would have it

[36] ibid.
[37] ibid 193–94.
[38] ibid 194.
[39] Sir Ivor Jennings, *The Law and the Constitution*, 5th edn (London, University of London Press, 1959) 312.
[40] ibid. As Jennings noted, even this was not wholly true, given the Crown's immunity from tort at common law—a matter that had to be amended by legislation (Crown Proceedings Act 1947, s 2).

in *Fewings?* Perhaps the best view is that is should mean both. On the one hand, government ministers and other public bodies should be liable in tort and contract in the ordinary way, but, on the other hand, it should also be the case that (unlike for private persons) the actions of ministers and other public bodies require to be authorised by positive law.

In the final section of this chapter, I consider what *Entick v Carrington* tells us about these two accounts of the rule of law. First, I explore them a little further with reference to recent developments in British constitutional practice. I start with a story from the House of Lords Constitution Committee.

III. PRE-EMPTION AND RAM

According to its terms of reference, the House of Lords Constitution Committee examines the constitutional implications of public bills coming before the House and keeps under review the operation of the constitution.[41] In the course of its legislative scrutiny function in 2010–12, the Committee encountered several examples of what it called the 'pre-emption of Parliament'; that is to say, instances where the government had taken action preparing for the implementation of a bill before that bill had been passed by Parliament. In one or two cases, so advanced were the government's preparations that the House of Lords was told that it could not amend the legislation in question, for to do so would leave the law in limbo. This was said, for example, with regard to the re-organisation of the health service in England under what became the Health and Social Care Act 2012. It was also the case with regard to the so-called 'bonfire of the quangos' under what became the Public Bodies Act 2011.[42] Neither the Committee nor the House of Lords was happy about this. When it comes to law-making, it is the constitutional function of the Upper House to act as a revising chamber, scrutinising and, where necessary, re-considering proposals which have been passed by the House of Commons (oftentimes with little and sometimes even with no debate in that House). This constitutional function cannot be performed effectively if their Lordships are being told that it is all too late, as ministers have started to take steps towards implementing their proposals even before they have been enacted. Effective parliamentary scrutiny is a

---

[41] I have served as one of the Committee's legal advisers since 2009. This chapter is written purely in a personal capacity and relies solely on the public record: nothing I write here should be taken as representing the view of any member, committee or official of the House of Lords. For an assessment of the Committee's work, see A Le Sueur and J Simson Caird, 'The House of Lords Select Committee on the Constitution' in A Horne, G Drewry and D Oliver (eds), *Parliament and the Law* (Oxford, Hart Publishing, 2013) ch 11.

[42] See House of Lords Constitution Committee, *The Pre-emption of Parliament* (HL 2012–13, 165) [1]–[2].

vital constitutional principle in a parliamentary democracy; departures from it should be contemplated only where clearly necessary (as where legislation is required to be fast-tracked, for example).

Its concerns led the Constitution Committee to undertake an inquiry into the 'pre-emption of Parliament'. Its report on the matter was published in May 2013.[43] The Committee recognised that, as well as the principle of effective parliamentary scrutiny, the constitutional principle of the rule of law was also highly material to the inquiry. As the Committee put it, 'the exercise of state power requires legal authority'.[44] What legal authority empowers the government to implement statutory provisions which have yet to be passed into law by Parliament? Three sources of domestic law confer powers on ministers: legislation, the royal prerogative and the common law. Of these, it is the third which is least understood and it was ministers' common law powers that became central to the Committee's inquiry, as we shall see.

In early 2013, HM Treasury stated, in its written evidence to the Committee, that: 'Ministers may do anything a natural person can do.' In Whitehall this is known as the 'Ram doctrine', named after a memorandum written in 1945 by Granville Ram, First Parliamentary Counsel. Ram's memorandum was written in the context of the passage of the Ministers of the Crown (Transfer of Functions) Act 1946, legislation that provided for Orders in Council to be made by which the functions of ministers could be generally re-distributed. (It is worth noting that the view must have been taken in government that primary legislation was required in order to achieve the re-distribution of ministerial functions; that is to say, that absent primary legislation, there would have been no power to do so.)

The memorandum was not published until 2003.[45] A researcher working for the Liberal Democrat peer and human rights lawyer Lord Lester of Herne Hill attended a seminar at which government lawyers were speaking about a 'Ram doctrine' which, they said, meant that ministers could do anything a natural person could do. Lord Lester put down a long series of parliamentary questions about this, which were answered by Baroness Scotland of Asthal[46] and which accompanied the publication of Ram's memorandum.[47]

Ram's legal analysis was as follows. First, he distinguished Ministers of the Crown from other public bodies (which he called 'statutory corporations'). Second, he stated that, whereas a public body is 'entirely a creature of statute and has no powers except those conferred upon it by or under

---

[43] ibid.
[44] ibid [4].
[45] See A Lester and M Weait, 'The Use of Ministerial Powers without Parliamentary Authority: The Ram Doctrine' [2003] *PL* 415.
[46] At the time a junior minister in the House of Lords and later Attorney General (2007–10).
[47] See Lester and Weait (n 45).

statute', a minister is not a creature of statute and 'may, as an agent of the Crown, exercise any powers which the Crown has power to exercise, except so far as he is precluded from doing so by statute'. Third, he glossed this statement by adding that 'in other words, in the case of a Government Department, one must look at the statutes to see what it may not do, not as in the case of a [public body] to see what it may do'. Fourth, he stated that 'it is sometimes thought that a Minister's functions are limited to those for which he has been expressly authorised by statute to incur expenditure. This is an inversion of the true position which is that although a Minister may do anything which he is not precluded from doing, he will only be able to pay for what he does if Parliament votes him the money'.

It is clear from the terms of his memorandum that Ram's analysis was focused on the question of whether legislation is necessary or appropriate to authorise government actions. Ram was not purporting to and did not lay down any more general principle of constitutional law. Rather, he offered an answer to a particular question: namely, 'when is legislation required to authorise an extension of Government powers?' In their written evidence to the Constitution Committee in 2013, HM Treasury relied on the Ram doctrine as authority for the proposition that departments may 'use their inherent power, relying on the fact that Ministers may do anything a natural person can do, unless limited by legislation'. As examples, HM Treasury stated that 'it is not necessary for legislation to provide for Departments to pay rents, salaries, or acquire the goods and services they need for their administrative functions'. Sir Stephen Laws QC[48] supported this, telling the Committee that, under the Ram doctrine: 'Ministers have the power to do anything a natural person may do provided they have the funds to do it.'[49] It should be noted, however, that the claims made by HM Treasury and by Sir Stephen Laws in the name of the Ram doctrine are not actually made in Ram's memorandum. Ram did not say that ministers may exercise any powers that natural persons may exercise; on the contrary, he said that ministers may exercise any powers which *the Crown* has the power to exercise.[50]

The House of Lords Constitution Committee was concerned about this and took evidence on it from a range of leading public lawyers, including Lord Brown,[51] Professor Sir Jeffrey Jowell,[52] Lord Lester,[53] Sir Stephen Sedley[54] and (a week later) the incumbent Attorney General, Dominic Grieve MP. Sir Jeffrey Jowell and Sir Stephen Sedley told the Committee that

---

[48] First Parliamentary Counsel, 2006–12.

[49] Sir Stephen Laws, written evidence to the House of Lords Constitution Committee, 2013.

[50] Lester and Weait ((n 45) 421) have made the same point, pointing out that Ram 'did not claim that a government department can do anything that a natural person can do'.

[51] Lord of Appeal in Ordinary and Justice of the Supreme Court, 2004–12.

[52] Director of the Bingham Centre for the Rule of Law.

[53] Liberal Democrat peer, leading human rights QC and co-author of Lester and Weait (n 45).

[54] Lord Justice of Appeal, 1999–2011.

the first they had heard about the Ram doctrine was when Lord Lester and Matthew Weait published their article on it in *Public Law* in 2003. Lord Brown said that the first he had heard of it was when the Committee asked him to give evidence on it; this despite the fact that he had been Treasury Counsel from 1979 to 1984 and a judge for 27 years thereafter. Sir Stephen Sedley said as follows:

> What appears to be being made in Whitehall, out of Ram, is a fabrication. Ram never said what is attributed to him. His proposition that government can do anything reasonably ancillary to its explicit functions is completely unobjectionable, but it is nowhere near the proposition that appears to have been derived from it in Whitehall that government can do anything that a private individual can do. The converse is the case.[55]

Other witnesses agreed. Lord Lester said that Whitehall's Ram doctrine was 'an extraordinarily presumptuous statement' and was 'clearly unlawful'. Sir Jeffrey Jowell concurred, describing it as 'a constitutional heresy'.[56]

When the Attorney General came to the Committee a week later to give his evidence, he appeared to agree with the criticisms voiced of the Ram doctrine. He said that in the exercise of their powers, ministers and the Crown are 'circumscribed by public law; by propriety; by human rights … I do not think that Whitehall thinks the Government can do everything a private individual can do, because it is circumscribed by those very things I have just listed'.[57]

The Committee's verdict was clear: 'the description of the scope of Government power denoted by the term the "Ram doctrine" is unhelpful and inaccurate' because it 'creates an impression that ministers possess greater legal authority than is' truly the case.[58] In the Committee's view, the very phrase the 'Ram doctrine' should no longer be used.[59] The government 'agreed in principle' with the Committee's advice. While the government maintains that the principle described in the Ram memorandum is valid, it has re-stated it in the following terms: 'the Crown has common law powers which may be exercised subject to overarching legal constraints'.[60] In a short debate on the Committee's report, the Commercial Secretary to the Treasury, speaking on behalf of the government, stated that the government had removed references to the Ram doctrine from its publications and internal guidance, and accepted 'absolutely' that 'the actions of a Minister are constrained by public law [and] human rights'.[61]

[55] Evidence to the House of Lords Constitution Committee, 27 February 2013, Q67.
[56] ibid.
[57] Evidence to the House of Lords Constitution Committee, 6 March 2013, Q57.
[58] House of Lords Constitution Committee (n 42) [59].
[59] ibid [60].
[60] HM Government, *Response to the House of Lords Constitution Committee Report on the Pre-emption of Parliament*, 2014.
[61] HL Deb 6 February 2014, col GC157 (Lord Deighton).

IV. THE POWERS OF MINISTERS

This is welcome. To state that the Crown (and, by implication, Ministers of the Crown) have common law powers is consistent with what Sir Granville Ram wrote 70 years ago. To state that ministers may do anything a natural person may do is to make an altogether different point, and one for which there is no support in Ram's memorandum. Whitehall's mistake has been to merge these two statements, as if the latter is but an innocent re-casting of the former.

But we should pause. There is more we need to know. We need to understand not only that it is not the case that ministers may do anything a natural person may do, but also what ministers *may* do. In particular, we need to understand what the common law powers of the Crown may enable or empower ministers to do.

Let us accept, for the purposes of the argument, that ministers enjoy three sorts of powers: statutory powers, prerogative powers and the common law powers of the Crown. By 'prerogative powers' I mean the prerogative as Blackstone understood it: ie, those powers *unique to the Crown* which the common law recognises as being part of the Crown's lawful authority. By 'the common law powers of the Crown' I mean what others have dubbed the 'third source' of authority: the power ministers have that derive neither from statute nor from the prerogative.[62]

Disputes about statutory powers are the bread and butter of our public law. Most often the claim is that a statutory power has been exercised for an improper purpose,[63] unreasonably[64] or unfairly.[65] More rarely, the dispute concerns not the exercise of a power, but its extent. Thus, for example, in *R v Secretary of State for Health ex p Keen*, the court had to rule on whether or not the National Health Service Act 1977 authorised the Secretary of State to take steps in preparation for the establishment of hospital trusts when the legislation that would allow for the establishment of such trusts remained before Parliament.[66] The court ruled that the 1977 Act did authorise the Secretary of State to take such preparatory steps.

---

[62] The leading academic authority is Professor Brian Harris. See his three *LQR* articles: 'The "Third Source" of Authority for Government Action' (1992) 108 *LQR* 626; 'The "Third Source" of Authority for Government Action Revisited' (2007) 123 *LQR* 225; and 'Government "Third Source" Action and Common Law Constitutionalism' (2010) 126 *LQR* 373; see also Margit Cohn, 'Medieval Chains, Invisible Inks: On Non-statutory Powers of the Executive' (2005) 25 *OJLS* 97.

[63] *Padfield v Minister of Agriculture, Fisheries and Food* [1968] AC 997.

[64] *Associated Provincial Picture Houses v Wednesbury Corp* [1948] 1 KB 223; *R v Ministry of Defence ex p Smith* [1996] QB 517; *R (Wagstaff) v Secretary of State for Health* [2001] 1 WLR 292.

[65] *Cooper v Wandsworth Board of Works* (1863) 14 CBNS 180; *R v Secretary of State for the Home Department ex p Doody* [1994] 1 AC 531; *R (Osborn) v Parole Board* [2013] UKSC 61, [2014] AC 1115.

[66] *R v Secretary of State for Health ex p Keen* (1990) 3 Admin LR 180.

From time to time, there is uncertainty about the extent of prerogative powers. In *BBC v Johns*,[67] a case in which the BBC (established under Royal Charter) argued that the Crown's immunity from general taxation applied to it, Diplock LJ famously stated that it is '350 years and a civil war too late for the Queen's courts to broaden the prerogative. The limits within which the executive government may impose obligations or restraints on citizens of the United Kingdom without any statutory authority are now well settled and incapable of extension'.[68] Yet, some have argued that this is precisely what the Queen's courts did in *R v Secretary of State for the Home Department ex p Northumbria Police Authority*.[69] A police authority challenged the lawfulness of a decision made by the Home Secretary to allow police chief constables access to CS gas and to plastic baton rounds in some cases without the consent and despite the objections of the local police authority. The High Court and the Court of Appeal found that the Home Secretary's decision was lawful under the prerogative, despite the fact that authority was sparse (to say the least) to show that there had previously existed a prerogative power to keep the peace within the realm.

Concerns about the prerogative and its impact on the rule of law are diminishing. Happily, cases such as *Northumbria Police Authority* are rare.[70] Moreover, the extent of the prerogative is lessening, as the reach of legislation grows. The civil service was put onto a statutory footing by the Constitutional Reform and Governance Act 2010. The Fixed-term Parliaments Act 2011 significantly curtailed prerogative powers to dissolve Parliament. The *Cabinet Manual* has codified, albeit informally and not as a matter of enforceable law, the rules pertaining to the appointment of the Prime Minister in the event of a hung Parliament.[71] Concerns about the uncertain extent of ministerial prerogative powers, as expressed for example in 2003–04 by the House of Commons Select Committee on Public Administration,[72] have dissipated following the publication in 2009 by the Ministry of Justice of what appears to be a comprehensive (and, assuming Diplock LJ was correct in *BBC v Johns*, a closed) list of such powers.[73]

---

[67] *BBC v Johns* [1965] Ch 32.

[68] ibid 79.

[69] *R v Secretary of State for the Home Department ex p Northumbria Police Authority* [1989] QB 26.

[70] More recent cases concerning the prerogative have tended to be about the exercise (or non-exercise) of prerogative powers rather than their extent: see, for example, *R (Abbasi) v Secretary of State for Foreign and Commonwealth Affairs* [2002] EWCA Civ 1598, [2003] UKHRR 76 and *R (Sandiford) v Secretary of State for Foreign and Commonwealth Affairs* [2014] UKSC 44, [2014] 1 WLR 2697.

[71] HM Government, *Cabinet Manual* (2011).

[72] House of Commons Select Committee on Public Administration, *Taming the Prerogative* (HC 2003–04, 422).

[73] Ministry of Justice, *Review of the Executive Royal Prerogative Powers: Final Report*, 2009.

Recent years have seen greater difficulties arise in relation to ministers' common law powers. In *R v Secretary of State for Health ex p C*,[74] the issue was whether it was lawful for the Secretary of State to maintain a list of persons unsuitable to work with children. There was no express statutory authority for the list to be maintained and nor is there a prerogative power to maintain such a list. Hale LJ, for a unanimous Court of Appeal whose other members were Lord Woolf MR and Mustill LJ, cited the following statement contained in *Halsbury's Laws of England*: 'At common law the Crown, as a corporation possessing legal personality, has the capacities of a natural person and thus the same liberties as the individual.' Hale LJ also cited with approval a passage from Wade and Forsyth's *Administrative Law*, which observed that the Crown's common law powers include the power to make contracts, employ civil servants and convey land.[75] Hale LJ ruled that private persons could have maintained a list such as that maintained by the Secretary of State and that therefore the Secretary of State was acting lawfully. Maintenance of the list did not of itself interfere with the rights of others (there is no right to be provided with a job, the court observed). On this basis, *Entick v Carrington* was distinguished and *Malone* was followed. Hale LJ said that *Entick* was 'perhaps the best known example' of the principle that 'neither the Crown nor a private individual may exercise their freedoms in such a way as to interfere in the rights of other without lawful authority'.[76] Here, as there was no interference in the rights of others, the principle in *Entick* did not apply.

The scope of ministers' common law powers was re-visited by the Court of Appeal in *Shrewsbury and Atcham Borough Council v Secretary of State for Communities and Local Government*,[77] in which Carnwath and Richards LJJ expressed divergent views on the matter. The court accepted that it was bound by the decision in *ex p C*. Carnwath LJ expressed a number of reservations about that decision. Richards LJ stated that he did not share these reservations and that, in his judgment, *ex p C* was correctly decided.[78] At issue in *Shrewsbury and Atcham* was whether the Secretary of

---

[74] *R v Secretary of State for Health ex p C* [2000] HRLR 400.

[75] See now Sir William Wade and C Forsyth, *Administrative Law*, 11th edn (Oxford, Oxford University Press, 2014) 180, which reads as follows: 'the Crown as a corporation sole has all the powers of a natural person and may enter into contracts and own and convey land and do all the many other things its subject may do ... These are considerable powers in many circumstances and they are generally exercised by ministers on behalf of the Crown'. Wade and Forsyth go on to note that in the exercise of these powers, ministers are responsible to Parliament and, when appropriate, subject to judicial review; they state further that such common law powers cannot be exercised inconsistently with a statute and, citing the House of Lords Constitution Committee (above), that their exercise is circumscribed by public law.

[76] *R v Secretary of State for Health ex p C* (n 74) 405.

[77] *Shrewsbury and Atcham Borough Council v Secretary of State for Communities and Local Government* [2008] EWCA Civ 148; [2008] 3 All ER 548.

[78] ibid [72].

State had acted lawfully in embarking on an exercise of local government re-organisation before the relevant statutory powers had been enacted. The Court of Appeal held unanimously that the Secretary of State had acted lawfully.[79]

On the issue of the scope of ministers' common law powers, Carnwath LJ said the following: first, he noted that it was a matter of 'continuing academic controversy', but that, as a matter of the law of precedent, the decision in *ex p C* was binding on the Court of Appeal in *Shrewsbury and Atcham*. *Ex p C*, in Carnwath LJ's words, 'confirms that the powers of the Secretary of State are not confined to those conferred by statute or prerogative, but extend, subject to any relevant statutory or public law constraints, and to the competing rights of other parties, to anything which could be done by a natural person'.[80]

Second, he expressed 'some sympathy' with the approach of counsel for the local authority in the case that the clock should be re-wound 'to a time when the accepted wisdom was that ministers had only two sources of power: statute or prerogative'.[81] Third, he noted that the passage from Wade and Forsyth's *Administrative Law* which Hale LJ had cited with approval in *ex p C* was 'of limited assistance'. For Carnwath LJ, powers to make contracts, employ civil servants and convey land are 'in the nature of ancillary powers, necessary for the carrying out of any substantive ... function'.[82] His Lordship added that: 'The obvious need for such powers to my mind throws no light on what, if any, non-statutory substantive functions the Crown retains.'[83] Carnwath LJ stated that 'analogies with the powers of natural persons seem to me unhelpful ... The Crown is not a creature of statute. As a matter of capacity, no doubt, it has power to do whatever a private person can do. But as an organ of government, it can only exercise those powers for the public benefit, and for identifiably "governmental" purposes within the limits set by the law'.[84] He cited with approval the following statement found in *De Smith's Judicial Review*: 'The extension of the Ram doctrine beyond its modest initial purpose of achieving incidental powers should be resisted in the interest of the rule of law.'[85] He concluded, however, that as the court was bound by *ex p C*, further debate was not useful at the Court of Appeal level.

---

[79] The discussion in the case on the scope of the ministers' common law powers was obiter. As Carnwath LJ noted, 'no-one is suggesting that local government reorganisation as such falls within any residual non-statutory central government power. It is accepted on all sides that legislation is needed to give effect to the present proposals': ibid [49].

[80] ibid [44].

[81] ibid [45].

[82] ibid.

[83] ibid.

[84] ibid [48].

[85] ibid.

Richards LJ disagreed with a number of Carnwath LJ's observations. He said this: 'the process of government includes a vast amount of work in relation to the formulation of policy, drafting new legislation and preparing for its implementation', but that it is 'necessary to explain the basis on which that ordinary business of government is conducted'.[86] The 'simple and satisfactory' explanation, in his view, is that:

> [I]t depends heavily on the 'third source' of powers, i.e. powers that have not been conferred by statute and are not prerogative powers in the narrow sense but are the normal powers (or capacities and freedoms) of a corporation with legal personality ... I accept, of course, that such powers cannot override the rights of others and, when exercised by government, are subject to judicial review ... But I think it unnecessary and unwise to introduce qualifications along the lines of those suggested by Carnwath LJ to the effect that they can only be exercised 'for the public benefit' or for 'identifiably governmental purposes'.[87]

Waller LJ, for his part, doubted whether anything he said would influence any future debate and stated that, since *ex p C* was in any event binding on the court, it was not appropriate for him to add very much. He indicated, however, that 'instinctively' he favoured 'some constraint on the power by reference to the duty to act only for the public benefit'.[88]

The UK Supreme Court has now considered the matter, although whether the constitutional issues are any clearer or have been taken any further forward may be open to doubt. *R (New London College) v Secretary of State for the Home Department*[89] concerned the Immigration Rules (made pursuant to the Immigration Act 1971) and official guidance issued by the Home Office as to the application of certain of the Immigration Rules. The Immigration Rules, whilst they are made by the executive branch, are required to be formally laid before Parliament before they come into force;[90] Home Office guidance, by contrast, is not. International (ie, non-European Economic Area) students may come to the UK to study at universities and colleges of further education. In order to do so, they require an entry visa. Such a visa will ordinarily be issued where the student is sponsored by a licensed university or further education college. New London College had its license revoked, meaning that the number of international students it could accept on its courses was very substantially reduced.

---

[86] ibid [73].

[87] ibid [73]–[74].

[88] ibid [80]–[81]. Commentary on *Shrewsbury and Atcham* is as divided as the Court of Appeal was in that case. For an analysis sympathetic to Richards LJ, see R McManus, 'The Crown's Common Law Powers' [2010] *Judicial Review* 27; for an analysis more sympathetic to Carnwath LJ, see J Howell, 'What the Crown May Do' [2010] *Judicial Review* 36.

[89] *R (New London College) v Secretary of State for the Home Department* [2013] UKSC 51; [2013] 1 WLR 2358.

[90] Immigration Act 1971, s 3(2).

The College sought judicial review of the decision to revoke its licence. Among other arguments, it contended that the decision had been made without lawful authority. Case law has established that 'any requirement which a migrant must satisfy as a condition of being given leave to enter or remain' in the UK is a 'rule' which, to be lawfully valid, must be contained in the Immigration Rules (or in primary legislation).[91] The conditions required to be satisfied by universities and colleges in order for them to be licensed as sponsors of international students were not contained in the Immigration Rules, but only in the guidance issued by the Home Office. The College argued that the fact that these conditions had not been laid before Parliament meant they lacked statutory authority and were, as a result, unlawful. The Supreme Court was unanimous in dismissing this claim. Lord Sumption (with whom Lords Hope, Clarke and Reed agreed) said that rules with which *migrants* must comply must be laid before Parliament as Immigration Rules, but that the licensing conditions were rules with which *universities and colleges* must comply. There was no requirement in the Immigration Act 1971 for such requirements to be laid before Parliament in order for their breach to attract legal sanction.

In his judgment, Lord Sumption briefly considered the nature of the powers of the Crown. He stated that 'it has long been recognised that the Crown possesses some general administrative powers to carry on the ordinary business of government which are not exercises of the royal prerogative and do not require statutory authority'.[92] He then noted that 'the extent of these powers and their exact juridical basis are controversial'.[93] He cited *ex p C* and *Shrewsbury and Atcham* and said that the Court of Appeal in those cases had held that the basis of the power was the Crown's status as a common law corporation sole, 'with all the capacities and powers of a natural person subject only to such particular limitations as were imposed by law'.[94] However, he then said that 'it is open to question whether the analogy with a natural person is really apt in the case of public or governmental action, as opposed to purely managerial acts of a kind that any natural person could do, such as making contracts, acquiring or disposing of property, hiring and firing staff and the like'.[95]

But the question, Lord Sumption concluded, did not need to be resolved on the appeal before him. This was because 'the statutory power of the Secretary of State to administer the system of immigration control must necessarily extend to a range of ancillary and incidental administrative powers

---

[91] See *R (Alvi) v Secretary of State for the Home Department* [2012] UKSC 33; [2012] 1 WLR 2208 [94].
[92] *New London College* (n 89) 28.
[93] ibid.
[94] ibid.
[95] ibid.

not expressly spelt out in the Act, including the vetting of sponsors'.[96] In other words, 'if the Secretary of State is entitled (as she plainly is) to pre-scribe and lay before Parliament rules for the grant of leave to enter or remain in the United Kingdom which depend upon the migrant having a suitable sponsor, then she must also be entitled to take administrative meas-ures for identifying sponsors who are and remain suitable'.[97] This right, he said, 'is not of course unlimited. The Secretary of State cannot adopt measures for identifying suitable sponsors which are inconsistent with the Act or the Immigration Rules. Without specific statutory authority, she can-not adopt measures which are coercive; or which infringe the legal rights of others…; or which are irrational or unfair'.[98] The licensing of sponsors was not, however, coercive; it was a scheme under which licensed universities and colleges could benefit substantially. No university or college was com-pelled or obliged to participate in the scheme (it was simply a consequence of not participating in the scheme that a university or college would be able to accept only vastly reduced numbers of international students).

Lord Carnwath (who, as Carnwath LJ, was one of the judges in *Shrewsbury and Atcham*) agreed with Lord Sumption that the College's claims should be dismissed, but gave an alternative reason. He said that the system of licensing sponsors was an 'adjunct' of the 'specific function of providing for entry for study' under section 1 of the Immigration Act 1971; ie, that it was a power ancillary or incidental to that particular power of the Secretary of State rather than a power ancillary to the more general powers of the Secretary of State to make rules concerning leave to enter and remain in the UK.[99]

The decision of the Supreme Court in the *New London College* case does not resolve the disagreement in *Shrewsbury and Atcham* between Carnwath and Richards LJJ, but, rather like the Constitution Committee's report on *The Pre-emption of Parliament*, it does cast doubt on the appropriateness of determining the scope of the government's power by analogising with those of a natural person.

To conclude, all the sources are agreed that ministers—as Ministers of the Crown—may exercise the common law powers of the Crown. But the sources do not speak with one voice as to the extent or nature of these powers. One view is that, because the Crown is a corporation sole, it has (and therefore ministers have) the capacities of a natural person and the same liberties as the individual; see the passage from *Halsbury's Laws of England* cited by Hale LJ in *ex p C.* A second view is that the common

---

[96] ibid.
[97] ibid [29].
[98] ibid.
[99] ibid [36]–[37].

law confers upon the Crown (and therefore upon ministers) only the ancillary powers necessary for carrying out substantive functions (which must be conferred by statute or the royal prerogative). There seems to be no definitive list of what these ancillary powers may be, but the making of contracts, the employment (and firing) of staff, and the ownership and conveyance of property are cited as examples. A third view, offered by Carnwath LJ in *Shrewsbury and Atcham* but rejected by others, is that ministers may exercise common law powers only for the public benefit and for identifiably governmental purposes. All the sources accept that neither the Crown nor ministers may exercise common law powers coercively or to interfere with the legal rights of others.

Even after *New London College*, the question remains open as to whether these common law powers extend beyond what Lord Sumption described in that case as 'general administrative powers to carry on the ordinary business of government'. The power at issue in *New London College* (ie, the power to revoke a college's licence as a sponsor) was held not to be a common law power, but one necessarily implied into the Immigration Act. We are left in that case with the suggestion—but it is no more than a suggestion—that ministers' common law powers are purely 'managerial' and do not empower 'public or governmental action', being confined to such matters as making contracts, acquiring or disposing of property, and hiring and firing staff.[100]

V. *ENTICK v CARRINGTON*

Where does *Entick v Carrington* sit among the lines of authority discussed in the preceding sections of this chapter?

Lord Camden's analysis of the issue is reported in *State Trials* as the 'fourth and last question' his judgment deals with.[101] Before he gets to it, the judgment addresses, first, whether the Secretary of State is a conservator of the peace; second, whether the Secretary of State fell within the scope of a statutory provision rendering justices of the peace safer in the execution

---

[100] I noted above Professor Harris' analysis of the 'third source' of authority for government (n 62). It is notable that Professor Harris recognises several limits to the Crown's common law powers. Thus, he writes that 'the government's freedom to do that which is not prohibited does not extend to law-making. The government can only make laws affecting the rights of others, that is delegated legislation, if expressly or impliedly authorised by Parliament to do so' ((1992) 108 *LQR* 626, 634). And he adds: 'the government has great resources at its disposal which allow it the potential to reach into the lives of every person in the country. Unregulated government activity is therefore a far greater, and quite different threat to the community than the unregulated activities of natural or juristic persons' (635). In his conclusions, he remarks as follows: 'government action authorised by this third source is incapable of affecting those interests of legal persons which are protected by legal rights' (650–51).

[101] The report of the case at 2 Wils KB 275 does not include the detail found in the passages considered here: what we have in that report is a much shorter summary at 291.

of their warrants; and, third, whether the defendants acted in obedience to the warrant. The fourth and last question was whether the warrant was lawful.

Lord Camden's analysis of this matter may be divided into five steps. First, he considered the justifications offered, in the absence of authority, that the warrant is lawful; ie, that 'such warrants have been issued frequently since the Revolution' and that 'this power is essential to government' and is the only means available for 'quieting clamours and sedition'.[102] Second, he outlined the breadth and nature of the power that was claimed as lawful, noting that: 'it is executed against the party before he is heard or even summoned',[103] that 'it is executed by messengers with or without a constable ... in the presence or absence of the party as the messengers shall think fit, and without a witness',[104] that an innocent person is 'as destitute of remedy as the guilty'[105] and that it extends to the seizure of all papers, whether or not they are said to be libellous. Given the scope of the power, Lord Camden stated that 'the law to warrant it should be clear in proportion as the power is exorbitant'.[106] This was the context in which the famous line is recorded: 'If it is law, it will be found in our books. If it is not to be found there, it is not law.'[107] To a twenty-first-century public lawyer, this is striking. We have become accustomed to proportionality analysis being attached to the extent of an interference with an individual's rights (is the interference necessary in a democratic society etc). Here, by contrast, Lord Camden talks of proportionality in the context of the nature of the power that the government was seeking to exercise. That power is so exorbitant, he rules, that the law authorising it must be both clear and clearly stated in our books. All of this is true, it seems, even before we get to the point about how the exercise of the power had an impact on the individual.

Only in the third step did Lord Camden turn to the nature of Entick's interest that was interfered with. This interest is framed in the language of property and, of this interest, Lord Camden stated that 'every invasion of private property, be it ever so minute, is a trespass'.[108] Lord Camden then noted that trespass is committed, even if there is no damage to property, if the 'invasion' has no 'justification'. Justification can be demonstrated only if 'some positive law has empowered or excused' the invader.[109] Whether there is justification is a question of law for the judges, 'who are to look into the books ... [to see] if such a justification can be maintained by the text of

---

[102] (1765) 19 St Tr 1029, 1064.
[103] ibid.
[104] ibid 1064–65.
[105] ibid 1065.
[106] ibid 1066.
[107] ibid.
[108] ibid.
[109] ibid.

the statute law, or by the principles of common law'.[110] If no such justification can be produced, 'the silence of the books is an authority against the defendant'.[111] Fourth, Lord Camden made plain that the burden of proof as to this matter is on the defendant. It is not that the claimant must prove that the trespass was unlawful: 'it is now incumbent upon the defendants to show the law, by which this seizure is warranted. If that cannot be done, it is a trespass'.[112] Finally, he insisted that the justification shown must be well established at law and that the courts must take care not to create new justifications: 'What would Parliament say, if the judges should take it upon themselves to mould an unlawful power into a convenient authority, by new restrictions? That would be, not judgment, but legislation.'[113]

As far as the rule of law and the modern cases considered in this chapter are concerned, what then is the authority of *Entick v Carrington*? Does *Entick v Carrington* lend more support to the *Malone* and *ex p C* line of authority or to *Fewings*? On one view, the matter is inconclusive and depends on whether one takes the core of Lord Camden's reasoning to be his second or his third step. Was it the *nature of the power* that the government claimed for itself which really animated his conclusions or was it *the nature of Entick's interest* (the right to property) with which the exercise of the power interfered that drove him to his conclusions? Put another way, what was the question which he was really asking himself: was it 'given the exorbitant nature of the power the Government are claiming, it requires clear legal authority' or was it 'given the common law's protection of private property, any interference with private property requires clear legal authority'? The former question gives priority to the second step in Lord Camden's analysis; the latter gives priority to the third step. The former would suggest that the rule in *Entick v Carrington*—the proposition of law for which it is authority—is broader, while the latter would suggest that it is narrower.

Can we know which is correct (or which is better)? It may be that some assistance may be derived from the way in which Entick's case was put by counsel. On this matter, the two published reports of the case are at one.[114] What shines out is that the case was not argued on the basis of a violation of property rights. It was argued on the basis, first, that the powers of a Secretary of State were not to be confused with those of a Justice of the Peace and, second, that the power claimed by the defendants was 'contrary to the genius of the law of England' on grounds of that law's protection of *liberty* (not property). If the power to seize papers were as suggested by the defendants, 'the liberty of this country is at an end', for 'it is the publishing

---

[110] ibid.
[111] ibid.
[112] ibid.
[113] ibid 1067.
[114] *cf* (1765) 19 St Tr 1029, 1038 with 2 Wils KB, 282–83.

of a libel which is the crime, and not the having it locked up in a *private* drawer in a man's study'.[115] The word private is repeated a few sentences further on: 'Has a Secretary of State a right to see all a man's private letters of correspondence, family concerns, trade and business? This would be monstrous indeed!'[116]

Confining the rule in *Entick* to the protection of private property would be the narrowest interpretation of the case. I do not find this to be an attractive interpretation, not least because this appears to be rather starkly at odds with the way in which Entick's case was presented by his lawyers. I do not take Lord Camden to be saying that justification by positive law to be found in the books is required only in cases of trespass. To read the judgment in this way would be to do as if only the third step in his analysis carried any weight and would overlook the importance to his reasoning and approach of the second step.

A second interpretation would be to say that the rule in *Entick* applies wherever the executive is seeking to exercise coercive powers. (On this view, the error in the judgment in *Malone* was less that the government did not need clear and positive legal authority for phone tapping and more that the practice of phone tapping was seen as somehow other than coercive.) In *ex p C*, Hale LJ was at pains to underscore that the maintenance of the list was of itself not a coercive act; inclusion on the list did not (for example) deprive anyone of a qualification or of a licence. It may well lead to a person not being able to obtain the job of his choice, but, as Hale LJ said, 'no one has a right to be provided with a job'. Hale LJ cited *Entick v Carrington* as authority for the principle that: 'Neither the Crown nor a private individual may exercise their freedoms in such a way as to interfere with the rights of others without lawful authority.' The importance of powers not being coercive was also noted by the Supreme Court in *New London College*: specific statutory authority would be required, said Lord Sumption, for the Secretary of State lawfully to adopt measures that are 'coercive' or that 'infringe the legal rights of others'.

A third interpretation—the broadest—would be that the rule in *Entick* applies irrespective of the nature of the power in question and irrespective of the nature of the right or interest with which exercise of the power interferes. On this view, all government powers (of whatever description) need positive legal authority: the government may do nothing without prior legal authority. This is how I described the rule in 2003.[117] But, if this is correct, both *Malone* and *ex p C* were wrongly decided. So be it; I think they were. Moreover, I think *Entick v Carrington* shows us where the judges went

---

[115] (1765) 19 St Tr 1029, 1038. Emphasis added.
[116] ibid.
[117] Tomkins (n 1) 78–79.

wrong in those cases. For, as Lord Camden noted, what matters is not only how powers impact on the rights and interests of the individual; what matters, in addition to this, is that we understand the nature of government power itself. Such power may be great—exorbitant, even. The common law shows no preference in favour of small or weak government. But it does insist that the government's powers find their authority in law.

Putting together these various strands of authority, it seems that the legal position may be summarised as follows:

(a)   Whereas, under the common law, individuals are free to do anything which is not prohibited, all government actions require legal authority.
(b)   For statutory bodies (including local government), this means their actions must be authorised by statute.
(c)   For Ministers of the Crown, this means that their actions must be authorised by statute, under the prerogative or under the common law powers of the Crown.
(d)   Where there is an overlap between these sources of ministerial power, statute prevails; it is unlawful for ministers to pre-empt or frustrate their statutory powers by seeking to rely on overlapping prerogative or common law powers.
(e)   The prerogative powers of the Crown (including those exercised by ministers) may not be broadened.

To these propositions I would add the following:

(a)   The common law powers of the Crown are ancillary or incidental only.
(b)   They extend only to such matters as entering into contracts, paying rents or salaries, and conveying property.
(c)   They must be understood to operate subject to the rule of law; they are not an exception to the rule of law, which requires that government action is authorised by prior law.

7

Law, Liberty and
Entick v Carrington

DENIS BARANGER

> It has always been one of the pillars of freedom, one of the principles
> of liberty for which on recent authority we are now fighting, that the
> judges are no respecters of persons and stand between the subject
> and any attempted encroachments on his liberty by the executive,
> alert to see that any coercive action is justified in law.[1]

I. INTRODUCTION

ENTICK v CARRINGTON is generally known for a set of legal propositions for which it stands as authority, notably that 'express legal
authority must be shown for interferences with individual rights'.[2]
The judgment, we are told, 'has assumed an importance which is in many
ways comparable with the 1789 (French) *déclaration*' of the rights of man
and citizens.[3] A few lines from Camden's opinion are piously quoted in
every textbook, especially those establishing a common law right of property rooted in natural law:

> The great end for which men entered into society, was to secure their property.
> That right is preserved sacred and incommunicable in all instances where it has
> not been taken away or abridged by some public law.

Yet this brief justification in terms which were indeed familiar to the natural law thinking of the age should be approached carefully. It appears
under the pen of a member of the bench whose penchant to use natural

---

[1] *Liversidge v Anderson* [1941] UKHL 1; [1942] AC 206, 244 per Lord Atkin.
[2] C Turpin and A Tomkins, *British Government and the Constitution: Text and Materials*,
7th edn (Cambridge, Cambridge University Press) 101. See also D Feldman (ed), *English Public
Law* (Oxford, Oxford University Press, 2004) 502.
[3] Lord Irvine of Lairg, *Human Rights, Constitutional Law and the Development of the
English Legal System* (Oxford, Hart Publishing, 2003) 278.

law arguments was most probably much more moderate than that of other famous contemporaries, first among whom stood Lord Mansfield. David Lieberman has related the way in which those two 'rivals' (Camden and Mansfield) had, a few years after *Entick v Carrington*, expressed vastly diverging understandings of the role of natural law in the English legal system. In the celebrated copyright law case of *Millar v Taylor*,[4] Mansfield had asserted in the King's Bench that the common law drew from such sources as 'the principles of Right and wrong, the fitness of things, convenience, and policy'.[5] Camden retorted somewhat abruptly in the House of Lords that, far from relying on such uncertain resources, judges should in fact 'never pretend to decide upon a claim of property without attending to the old black letter of our law, without founding their judgment upon some solid written authority, preserved in their books or in judicial records'.[6] Such a statement falls very well in line with what Camden had already said in *Entick v Carrington*. And with regard to that latter case, one is tempted to observe that the legal reasoning in Camden's opinion would work perfectly well, or maybe even better, without this natural law *cameo*. Remove the celebrated paragraph on natural law and most of the reasoning in *Entick v Carrington* remains intact. The logical structure of the case does not depend on it.

In this chapter, I would like to suggest that the value of Camden's opinion does not in the main reside in this somewhat rhetorical—but rhetoric is of course a significant part of judicial argumentation—incrustation of a natural law argument. Rather, I would like to draw attention to two other dimensions of the case. The first such dimension is the way in which Camden has grounded these general principles and lofty words in a realistic approach to power and liberty. This will be the focus of the next two sections of the chapter. Section II will be devoted to a brief analysis of the common law approach to liberty, of which *Entick v Carrington* appears as a fine example. Section III will attempt to show how the case reads, in Camden's own terms, as an 'inquiry into authority' which aims at removing all semblance of legitimacy to the abuses of power committed at Entick's house. The other dimension I would like to draw attention to in section IV is the fact that in many regards, *Entick v Carrington* paves the way for many legal features of the modern state, notably a rationalised system of legal sources and the principle of parliamentary sovereignty. It deserves to be remembered as a move in the direction of the positivist legal approach to the state.

---

[4] *Millar v Taylor* (1769) 4 Burr 2303; 98 ER 201.
[5] ibid.
[6] D Lieberman, *The Province of Legislation Determined: Legal Theory in Eighteenth-Century Britain* (Cambridge, Cambridge University Press, 1989) 96–98.

II. THE SYLLOGISM OF LIBERTY

The Fourth Amendment to the US Constitution has stated in a concise manner a constitutional prohibition of 'unreasonable' searches and seizures. It is often said that this was 'mainly based on the English cases on general warrants, especially *Entick v Carrington*'.[7]

Be that as it may, the language of the Fourth Amendment differs significantly from that of *Entick v Carrington*. In the US Constitution, the rule has been expressed in absolute terms:

> The right of the people to be secure in their persons, houses, papers, and effects, against unreasonable searches and seizures, shall not be violated, and no warrants shall issue, but upon probable cause, supported by oath or affirmation, and particularly describing the place to be searched, and the persons or things to be seized.

The structure of the rule in the Fourth Amendment is more or less the following:

— a constitutional right is asserted;
— its violation is prohibited (although the sanctions and/or remedies are not stated in the amendment);
— however, there is no illegal infringement of the right if a certain process of law (stated in the amendment) is followed.

A similar structure appears, although in an even more concise statement, in section 8 of the Canadian Charter of Rights and Freedom (Part one of the Constitution Act 1982):

> Everyone has the right to be secure against unreasonable search and seizure.

This is not the way in which the classical (to make it simple, prior to the nineteenth century) British common law used to approach liberty. The 'bias of the common law in favour of liberty' (Heuston) refers generally to a certain tendency of common law rules and procedures to favour the liberty of the individual subject. But this tendency itself not only consists in certain substantive legal rules, it also points to a structure of argumentation which appears both in the great declarations of rights (the 1215 Magna Carta, the 1628 Petition of Right, the 1689 Bill of Rights etc) and in landmark cases such as *Entick v Carrington*.

This logical structure could be summarised in this way: a wrongful infringement of liberty has taken place; this calls for the affirmation (or re-affirmation) of certain propositions of law which have been violated; finally, a remedy is granted. The wrong/remedy connection is well known and, in

---

[7] *Halsbury's Laws of England*, 4th edn, vol 8 (London, Butterworth, 1974) 557, para 843. See Megarry VC in *Malone v Commissionner of Police of the Metropolis* [1979] Ch 344, 369.

the context of statutory interpretation, has often been summed up in the 'Heydon rule':

> [F]or the sure and true interpretation of all statutes in general ... four things are to be discerned and considered:
>
> 1st. What was the common law before the making of the Act.
>
> 2nd. What was the mischief and defect for which the common law did not provide.
>
> 3rd. What remedy the Parliament hath resolved and appointed to cure the disease of the commonwealth.
>
> And, 4th. The true reason of the remedy; and then the office of all the Judges is always to make such construction as shall suppress the mischief, and advance the remedy, and to suppress subtle inventions and evasions for continuance of the mischief, and pro privato commodo, and to add force and life to the cure and remedy, according to the true intent of the makers of the Act, pro bono publico.[8]

This conceptual connection between mischief and remedy is also to be observed in the context of the common law approach to liberty. Yet in the case of the great declarations or common law cases regarding liberty, the formula is a little bit more complex than a mere association between a wrong and a remedy. First, it requires a *fact pattern*; that is, a certain grievance is formulated (declarations) or a certain 'wrong' or 'mischief', sometimes in the form of an abuse of power (common law cases) is described. Lawyers have an ingrained tendency to focus on the proposition(s) of law. But it is remarkable that lengthy statements of facts—in our case the governmental wrongdoing and its damageable effect on liberty—should appear in both the great declarations of the rights of Englishmen and in the landmark cases in the development of civil liberties. It is also remarkable that this statement of the fact pattern should have disappeared where written constitutions and 'rights-based' constitutional cultures have thrust their roots, as in the case of the US Bill of Rights. There are, however, some reminiscences of this factual dimension in certain legal texts, such as Justice Jackson's opinion in the *Steel Seizure* case:

> The example of such unlimited executive power [as implied by the Solicitor General's interpretation of the executive article of the constitution] that must have most impressed the forefathers was the prerogative exercised by George III, and the description of its evils in the Declaration of Independence leads me to doubt that they were creating their new Executive in his image.[9]

Second, in response to this wrongdoing or abusive behaviour, a *principle of law* is formulated. It can take the form of a liberty or (in the words of Dicey) of a 'right to a liberty'. But it can take many other legal forms. At this

---

[8] *Heydon's Case* (1584) 3 Co Rep 7a; 76 ER 637.
[9] *Youngstown Sheet & Tube Co v Sawyer* 343 US 579 (1952), 641.

stage, the infringement of liberty can also be justified by certain other rules: not every deprivation of liberty is a legal wrongdoing against which redress can be obtained. A person can be rightfully imprisoned because he or she has been properly accused of some criminal offence, a person of unsound mind can be detained in a psychatric facility etc. It is not rare, however, that the right and the legal justifications for evading it should be formulated together.

But if no such legal excuse can be put forward, the third element of the formula is that a *remedy* is provided: either in general terms (as in the 1689 Bill of Rights: 'full redress and remedy', 'effectual provisions for the settlement of' grievances etc) or in more specific terms. There are many such remedies: a legal appeal, a civil action for damages and a writ of habeas corpus, for example.

Entick is a fine example of how this syllogistic reasoning is put to work. I am fully aware that this is not a logical syllogism *stricto sensu*. However, I use that term in order to point to the way in which particular facts are subsumed under a general formula of law in order to deduce a legal consequence in the form of a remedy. As for the legal proposition, *Entick*'s status as a landmark case relies on the way Camden has formulated simultaneously:

— the principle that public authorities have to provide the legal authority permitting their action;
— the available legal 'pedigrees' for such an action (either a statute or a common law power);
— the fact that the right of property was a part of the common law.

The legal propositions I have just stated are scattered throughout the decision instead of being expressed in a self-contained paragraph which legal commentators can easily cut and paste. Indeed, more modern precedents are sometimes more straightforward in the way they express the legal principle. One could compare the style of Camden's opinion with, for instance, Lord Denning's language in *DPP v Head*:

> No one in this country can be detained against his will except under the warrant of lawful authority; and when that warrant is required by law to be in writing, it must be produced on demand to the person detained, and to any other person properly concerned to challenge the detention. When the legality of the detention has to be proved in a court of law, the document itself must be produced. It is the best evidence and nothing else will do.[10]

Entick is also authority for the proposition that a remedy should be available when an official has acted without clear legal authority. In his discussion of

---

[10] *DPP v Head* [1959] AC 83, 106.

the rule of law in *Law of the Constitution*, Dicey refers to the case in order to insist on this:

> With us, every official, from the Prime Minister down to a constable or a collector of taxes is under the same responsibility for every act done without legal justification as any other citizen. The reports abound with cases in which officials have been brought before the courts and made, in their personal capacity, liable to punishment, or the payment of damages.[11]

But, interestingly, a significant part of Camden's opinion is devoted to the fact pattern, the misdeeds of which *Entick* has been the victim. The syllogism of liberty in *Entick* incorporates a 'factual' premise which is decisive in order to give shape and authority to the legal propositions which ensue. A rule protecting the subject's liberty is expressed in contrast with a manifest abuse of power. The meaning of the legal principle can only be grasped with reference to these facts. One of the great merits of the case resides in the way in which this 'factual' premise is expressed. I speak of a 'factual' premise, but, as we shall see, this part of the argument is replete with legal erudition. Yet all this erudition amounts to showing that no legal authority whatsoever could have permitted the actions of the perpetrators. What is left is 'mere' arbitrary power; it is 'power' in the Hobbesian sense of a natural faculty, a return to this state of nature to which Camden alludes by saying that men have left it in order to 'enter into society' with a view to 'secur[ing] their property'.

This laying bare of the arbitrary and therefore non-legal (one could say *extra-legal* even before it can be held to be *illegal*) nature of the power exercised against *Entick* occupies a very important portion of Camden's opinion; nearly all of it, in fact. I shall now turn to this aspect of the case.

III. AN 'INQUIRY INTO AUTHORITY'

Even before it is a case about liberty and the rule of law, *Entick v Carrington* is a case about power. This is why the doctrinal formulations of the rule in *Entick* are Janus-faced: either they insist on the protection of individual liberty (*Entick* establishes a 'right' against illegal searches and seisures or papers, a legal protection against general warrants etc) or they emphasise

---

[11] AV Dicey, *Introduction to the Study of the Law of the Constitution*, 8th edn (Indianapolis, Liberty Fund, 1982) 114. The issue of damages, however, is more conspicuous in other contemporary cases related to the Wilkes scandal and involving the same administrative personnel. See, eg, *Beardmore v Carrington* (1764) 19 St Tr 1405; 95 ER 790, in which Camden upheld a 'hefty punitive-damage' (Akhil Reed Amar) against Carrington for granting an illegal warrant: 'Can we say that 1000 pounds are monstrous damages as against him, who has granted an illegal warrant to a messenger who enters into a man's house, and pries into all his secret and private affairs...?' See AR Amar, *America's Unwritten Constitution: the Precedents and Principles We Live by* (New York, Basic Books, 2012) 128n.

the 'public law' restraint on officials ('the executive may do nothing without clear legal authority first permitting its actions').[12]

If *Entick v Carrington* is an important moment in the history of the rule of law, it seems to be in the sense that it establishes that the law must rule not in the abstract, but over concrete expressions of governmental power. Camden's opinion reads as a minute examination of power and its diverse manifestations, at least those manifestations of which the law is able to take cognisance.

A. The Laying Bare of Arbitrary Power

In the US Fourth Amendment case of *Boyd v US* (1886), after citing (and praising) Camden's opinion in *Entick v Carrington*, Justice Bradley said:

> It is not the breaking of (a man's) doors and the rummaging of his drawers that constitutes the essence of the offense; but it is the invasion of his indefeasible right of personal security, personal liberty, and private property ... it is the invasion of this sacred right which underlies and constitutes the essence of Lord Camden's judgment.[13]

This interpretation can be grounded in Camden's famous words at the end of his opinion:

> The great end for which men entered into society, was to secure their property. That right is preserved sacred and incommunicable in all instances where it has not been taken away or abridged by some public law.[14]

But this 'Lockean' paragraph only comes at the conclusion of a lengthy opinion which recites the misdeeds of the King's messengers as well as of the Secretary of State. The conclusion may be in terms of abstract rights closely resembling the 'self-evident' rights of the American constitutional tradition. This resemblance, however, may be misleading. The 1765 English case firmly anchors this 'natural law' conclusion in a 'realistic' analysis of power. The right to property plays a role in the case, but most of the reasoning is about a very concrete practical guarantee against breaking into houses and seizing papers.

Camden is aware of the potentially disruptive, not to say revolutionary, nature of his 'inquiry into authority':

> This is no very agreeable task, since it may possibly tend to create, in some minds, a doubt upon a practice that has been quietly submitted to, and which is of no moment to the liberty of the subject: for so long as the proceeedings under this

---

[12] A Tomkins, *Public Law* (Oxford, Oxford University Press, 2003) 78.
[13] *Boyd v US* 116 US 616 (1886), 630.
[14] *Entick v Carrington* (1765) 19 St Tr 1029, 1066.

warrant are properly regulated by law, the public is very little concerned in the choice of that person by whom they are issued.[15]

But he nevertheless embarks on this task with impressive energy. He aims at systematically removing the appearances of legality in order to uncover what really happened and how the people involved should really be called:

> Before I argue (on) the question, whether the Secretary of State be within [24. Geo 2. c 44] *we must know what he is.*[16]

This is a *leitmotiv*: the court will not be satisfied with appearances. The word 'power' is not central to Camden's vocabulary, but one should be attentive to the fact that all the other possible denominations prove to be inadequate. In general, the vocabulary with which the ancient constitution used to handle power is methodically laid to rest: 'rights' of public authorities, 'privileges', 'magistrates' etc.

This 'inquiry into the authority' of the Secretary of State and his accessories could read as a direct rejoinder to the submissive attitude of many members of the bench in the seventeenth century. Camden's opinion contrasts sharply with, say, Lord Chief Justice Hyde's judgment in the *Five Knights' case*.[17] Every line of Hyde's (short) judgment smacked of an overly deferent attitude to royal authority. Conversely, Camden is careful to reject any hint of an 'argument from authority'. Magic solving legal standards such as that of 'matters of state' and imprisonment 'per speciale mandatum regis' cannot prevent a judicial inquiry into the justifications of an infringement of the subject's liberty anymore.[18]

The defendants argued that they were acting as 'officers' within the meaning of several Acts of Parliament, notably 24. Geo 2. c 44. Their argument was also relative to the Secretary of State. As the officer of the Crown under whose authority the search had taken place, the Secretary of State could fall under several legal descriptions, all of which would have provided him with a legal justification to issue the warrant, as well as his servants who operated the search. This forces Camden to what he himself calls 'an inquiry into the authority of that minister', viz the Secretary of State. A great part of the case then reads as a survey of the law of public offices: their names, their history and the scope of their powers. Most of these offices had been created when the king was literally, and not only nominally, a fountain of justice. His officers were his instruments in order to despatch this general function of rendering justice to his subjects. This is the field of what lawyers, in England as well as in the rest of Europe, called 'jurisdiction'.

---

[15] ibid 1046.
[16] ibid. Emphasis added.
[17] *R v Darnel* (1627) 3 St Tr 1.
[18] F Cohen, 'Transcendental Nonsense and the Functional Approach' (1935) 35 *Columbia Law Review* 809 at 820.

What results from Camden's 'inquiry into the authority' of Lord Halifax is that it does not appear to be an authority at all. This is where the archaic language of the statutes meets the contemporary practice of government. No legal denomination seems to fit the power which has been used in the facts of the case. The many such denominations put forward by Carrington's counsels are methodically set aside. This is the negative input of the case. Yet the very same reasoning can be shown to have had a positive effect. Camden has contributed to the legal recognition of some new mechanisms of power for which the remedies available at common law were not adjusted. In the case of *Entick*, a *quo warranto* or a habeas corpus would not do. They were applicable to traditional scenarios, while the kind of governmental arbitrary power which had been witnessed in the facts of *Entick* called for new remedies based on a modernised vision of the activity of state bodies. This is where *Entick* differs from otherwise analogous seventeenth-century cases such as *Hampden* or the case of the *Seven Bishops*.[19]

The importance of *Entick v Carrington* lies not only in the legal propositions for which it stands as authority. Unlike the fourth amendment or of section 8 of the Canadian Charter, these propositions are not self-contained. The constitutional importance of *Entick* relies on a certain approach to administrative power and also (as we shall see) to government. I suggest calling this approach a 'realistic' one. And if the the value of Camden's 'realistic' approach to power is not fully appreciated, it may well be that the lesson from *Entick* has not been fully learned. One is sometimes tempted to wonder whether certain important cases such as *Entick* do not operate the way in which 'screen-memories' are held to operate according to psychoanalysts. They stand out as very important expressions of major principles of the law. Yet these pious principles are often disregarded or their ambit is restricted by exceptions. Not only that, but they can also disappear entirely, for no clear reason. With very analogous (although distinguishable) facts of the case, the principle expressed in *Entick* can be referred to or it can be entirely set aside through asserting a contrary principle, such as that underlying Sir Robert Megarry VC's opinion in *Malone v Commissionner of Police of the Metropolis* (anything which is not forbidden by law is lawful and, in this regard, agents of the state are in the same position as ordinary citizens).[20]

Malone v Commissionner of Police of the Metropolis, in which wire tapping was held to be no trespass, is evidence that *Entick* can be fairly easily distinguished if needs be. There are now so many statutes in the statute book that it is not difficult to find an empowering clause in one of them. And this

<hr/>

[19] *R v Hampden* (1637) 3 St Tr 825; *Trial of the Seven Bishops* (1688) 12 St Tr 183.

[20] That officials should be subjects to the *Entick* principle while ordinary citizens could rely on the *Malone* principle was later settled by Sir John Laws in *R v Somerset County Council ex p Fewings* [1995] 1 All ER 513.

was already the case at the time of *Entick*, or at least some of Camden's contemporaries thought so. In 1756, Lord Hardwicke had complained that 'our statute books have of late years increased to such an enormous size, that no lawyer ... can pretend to be master of all the statutes'.[21] Moreover, *Entick* was only one step—an important but at the same time somewhat imperfect one—in the direction of building an adequate system of judicial review of administrative action. For a long time, before the *GCHQ* case[22] and other contemporary developments in the judicial review of administrative action, courts have allowed ministers and other public authorities unfettered discretion where statutes were granting them blank cheque powers. *Entick* did not prevent this and may even have encouraged it. The realism of *Entick* is limited by its legalism, namely what one would be tempted to call the 'can you please show some ID?' approach to the legality of administrative action. The law is expected to provide a pedigree establishing the existence of power, but nothing more. The test in *Entick* was a formal one: was there or not an authorisation in the law books for a given power? Yet the fact that the law should authorise a certain power in this way did not mean that the said power had been justly or reasonably exercised.

B. The Invention of the Executive

In his dissenting opinion in the *Liversidge* case, Lord Atkins noted that:

> [T]he power to make orders ... necessary for the defence of the realm [which was used in the case, belonged to] an executive minister and not ... any kind of judicial officer.

Despite the progress of the modern notion of separation of powers after the Glorious Revolution, this clear-cut distinction between executive action and judicial function was not fully in place in the 1760s. It may well be that the distinction has never been fully made, as is shown by Lord Blackburn's observation in *Coomber v Berkshire Justices* that:

> [T]he administration of justice ... and the preservation of order and prevention of crime by means of what is now called police are among the most important functions of government [and] by the constitution of this country these functions do of common right belong to the Crown.[23]

Yet Camden goes some way towards making such a distinction more effective, as he purports to show that the actions of the King's messengers at *Entick*'s house cannot be described as operations of law enforcement.

---

[21] Speech to the House of Lords, cited in Lieberman (n 5) 14.

[22] *Council of Civil Service Union v Minister for the Civil Service* [1985] AC 374.

[23] *Coomber v Berkshire Justices* (1883) 9 App Cas 61, 71, quoted in G Marshall, *Police and Government: The Status and Accountability of the English Constable* (London, Methuen, 1965) 37.

Entick is one of the many episodes through which the word 'executive' has decisively moved from its original meaning towards its current one: that of the 'executive power' in the modern sense of a governmental power that can exist despite the absence of any act of law enforcement.

This part of the case reads as a short treatise on law enforcement in the middle of the eighteenth century. Camden emphatically uses a fairly quaint vocabulary, as when he speaks of 'the great executive hand of criminal justice'.[24] This is reminiscent of the fact that, before referring to a branch of government, the word 'executive' appeared in the context of criminal law and especially of local law enforcement, as when Selden spoke in 1649 of 'the executive power of the Law (which) rested much in the Nobility'.[25] In the eighteenth century, 'executive justice' referred commonly to what we call today 'criminal justice'.[26]

The defendants referred to several Acts of Parliament, notably 24. Geo 2. c 44, in order to justify their claim that the Secretary of State and themselves had acted as 'conservators of the peace', or possibly as 'justices of the peace' or constables. But these official denominations did not fit the reality of governmental action in the 1760s. After the Glorious Revolution, the constitutional landscape was now settled once and for all. England had become a constitutional monarchy and, more specifically, a parliamentary government in which ministers were at the same time more powerful and more responsible. Camden's opinion reflects this state of things and comes up with a new image of government. The constitutional context of the 1760s, and more largely of the post-1689 era, is very much in the background of the case.

The opinion shows that none of these descriptions will fit the action of the Secretary of State and his accessories. Some offices, such as that of 'conservator of the peace', are simply obsolete. One should turn to 'magistrates of known authority and daily employment' and not 'antiquated powers and persons known to have existed by historical tradition only'.[27]

The reference to other well-known offices does not prove more helpful. For instance, the analogy with the office of a constable is rejected: the power of the Secretary of State is at the same time too widespread ('so extensive that it spreads throughout the realm') and too narrow ('its object is so confined that [he] does not pretend to the authority of a constable') to be assimilated to that of a constable. Lord Halifax purported to do nothing of the kind. What he undertook was closer to what Frenchmen call 'haute police' or 'police politique' (issuing warrants against political libellers), while the constable is rather an officer of ordinary, local 'basse police'.

---

[24] *Entick v Carrington* (n 14) 1064.
[25] I draw this quotation from the entry 'Executive' in the *Oxford English Dictionary* (in which it is cited to as: SELDEN *Laws Eng.* I. xvi. 29 (1649)). This is the oldest reference to the word 'executive' in this sense to be quoted in the *OED*.
[26] See, eg, Martin Madan's pamphlet *Thoughts on Executive Justice* (London, 1785).
[27] *Entick v Carrington* (n 14) 1061.

The defendants go to great lengths in order to suggest that they and the Secretary of State have acted within the four corners of the 'jurisdictio', the function of enforcing the law with normal, adequate means. But this is done to no avail. In fact, as Camden notes, constables have such judicial powers as to 'administer an oath' or to 'take bail'. But Camden makes it clear that what was done in the case of *Entick* was concerned with government and, even more precisely, with the political rather than merely administrative nature of 'government'. However, the reference to the medieval notion of 'gubernaculum' is not adequate either, exactly because of the legal propositions for which *Entick v Carrington* stands as authority. Camden's opinion seals the fate of the distinction made in earlier cases (notably *Bates' Case*) between ordinary and absolute royal power. In *Bates*, it was said that:

> The King's power is double, ordinary and absolute … the ordinary is for the benefit of particular subjects, for the execution of civil justice, the determining of *meum*; and this is exercised by equitie (sic) and justice in ordinary courts, and … is nominated … Common Law … The absolute power of the king is not that which is converted or executed to private use, to the benefit of any particular person, but is only that which is applied to the general benefit of the people … and this power is [not] guided by the rules, which direct only at the Common Law, and is most properly named policy and government.[28]

Modern government cannot be held to be absolute as it ought to be accountable to Parliament insofar as policy is concerned and to the courts of law as regards its legality. In requiring legal authority for every executive action, *Entick* is one of the foundations of modern judicial review.

A fine example of the inadequacy of the old vocabulary, as well as of the move from the idea of 'jurisdiction' (enforcing the law in order to maintain peace and justice) to that of executive government is the discussion about the Privy Council. Camden notes that the type of warrants issued in the case of *Entick* cannot rely on the 'right' or 'privilege' of the privy councillors acting 'in common' to issue such warrants and commit to custody. This may have been a practice, but Camden shows that it was obsolete as early as the reign of Charles I:

> In the great debate in the third of king Charles the first … no privy councillor's warrant does occur; but instead therefore you will find the secretary of state dealing forth the king's royal mandate, and the privy councillor's authority at rest.[29]

---

[28] *Bates' Case* (1606) 2 St Tr 371. See contra DL Keir and FH Lawson, *Cases in Constitutional Law*, 4th edn (Oxford, Clarendon, 1954) 69: 'We no longer speak of ordinary or absolute power, but we have the distinction none the less.' I would beg to differ, precisely because the concept of government has radically evolved since, at least, 1689. This is all the more true since the developments of the judicial review of executive action in Britain, and especially since the GCHQ case (*Council of Civil Service Union v Minister for the Civil Service* (n 20)). The greater the perimeter of prerogative powers that are 'amenable to judicial review' (to quote from Lord Roskill's opinion in this case), the more outdated this distinction between an ordinary and an absolute sphere of governmental powers appears to be.

[29] *Entick v Carrington* (n 14) 1055.

'These warrants', Camden concludes, 'were then deceased and gone.'[30]

The reference to the Privy Council was unhelpful because, in political terms, it had been for a long time a merely formal body of the king's advisors. The reality of power lay elsewhere, although it took a certain time for the constitutional conventions of cabinet government to be properly established. What was certain was that ministers were sworn in as members of the Privy Council, but also that only a handful of privy councillors were members of the king's executive cabinet and were called upon to transact the business of the state. The title of 'minister' was unknown to the law in the eighteenth century.

This is another aspect of Camden's realism in his opinion. Not only does he investigate into the legal authorities, but he also looks into the history of government. What makes Camden's opinion fascinating is the way in which it intertwines a legal inquiry and a political history of government.

As for the Secretary of State:

> [I]t is not difficult to account for the growth of this minister's importance. He became naturally significant from the the time that all the courts of Europe began to admit ambassadors, from upon the establishment of this policy, that whole foreign correspondence passed through the secretary's hands.[31]

As a result, 'no part of [the employment of the Secretary of State] requires the authority of a magistrate'.[32]

Entick reads as an attempt to make some room for the notion that the Secretary of State was neither a mere instrument of the Crown (the reference to a possible prerogative power is quickly set aside) nor an ordinary lower judicial officer (a conservator of the peace or a justice of the peace). Although the maxim that the king can do no wrong does not appear in the case, it can be said to be there implicitly in the background. Something illegal has been done and, because of the maxim, it cannot be ascribed to the Crown. It has to be imputed to one of the monarch's 'counsellors', namely one of his 'principal secretaries of state'.

The solution in *Entick* would probably have been the same if there had not been a political element to the case and if the official who issued the illegal warrant had not been a Secretary of State. Yet the presence of this political dimension in the case is not accidental either. The breaking into *Entick*'s house and the seizing of his papers could not be regarded as an act of law enforcement as those who were involved in it, namely the Secretary of State and his accessories, had no jurisdiction. What they did was not 'executive' in the ancient sense of giving effect to the law in keeping with the law's own substantive and procedural requirements, but it was 'executive' in the modern sense of the word: it was related to governmental power.

[30] ibid 1056.
[31] ibid 1047.
[32] ibid.

Entick expresses the concern that this 'new' governmental power should not be a foreign territory for the common law. What Camden's lengthy inquiry into authority comes down to is that, inasmuch as it can be distinguished from 'mere' enforcement of the law, governmental action does not for that reason stand outside the perimeters of the law. The traditional immunities which could have covered the political activity of the state are systematically rejected: 'matters of state', 'prerogative' (as there was no prerogative power of the Crown to issue this kind of warrants),[33] common utility etc. What makes the case so modern is that there had to be a legal framework for something which was not an enforcement of existing law, but was nevertheless an expression of political power by one of the highest authorities in the state. The law did not know of 'ministers', but they had become important in despatching the business of the state. There had to be a point at which the courts of common law would have to take their existence into account. Otherwise, some of the most important officers of the Crown could have infringed the liberties of the subjects in a very damaging way:

> If this point (whether the warrant is lawful) should be determined in favor of the jurisdiction, the secret cabinets and bureaus of every subject in this kingdom will be thrown open to the search and inspection of a messenger, whenever the Secretary of State shall think fit to charge, or even to suspect, a person ... of a seditious libel.[34]

This is why Camden insists on the applicability of the 'ordinary course of law' to the case. The facts of the case stood at the crossroads between property, private life, the intimacy of the house and the (increasingly) normal activity of citizens engaged in political opposition. *Entick* is a case about the normalisation of political opposition, however virulent or distateful. It is not set in the earlier context of the seventeenth-century civil wars or in the later context of the upheaval generated in England by the French Revolution or in the American colonies by the War of Independence. In its modern sense, government does not mean 'extraordinary' government. The power exercised by Carrington and the other King's messengers was an ordinary, albeit illegal, exercise of governmental activity. The arbitrariness of the wrongdoing was rooted in the very banality of the evil committed in the name of the King's government. It could not be justified or ennobled by a reference to an extraordinary 'reason of state' or to high treason. There was nothing so 'special' about the case that it should have justified a 'special' warrant (which, in that case, as well as in the case of the arrest warrant against Wilkes,[35] meant a warrant drafted in general terms). The ordinary course of law ought to match the ordinary course of government.

---

[33] Feldman (n 2) 12.
[34] *Entick v Carrington* (n 14) 1063.
[35] *R. v Wilkes* (1763) 2 Wils 151, quoted by Feldman (n 2) 13.

IV. *ENTICK*, THE LAW AND THE MODERN STATE

The positive contribution of *Entick* does not end there. The requirement that public authorities should bear the burden of establishing that they had authority to act as they did is not only a negative requirement, a check on official maladministration. There is also a positive contribution to the case, in the sense that it points to the ways in which the modern state should be structured. The case also brings with it many changes in the approach to the legal system and eventually to the fabrication of a 'state' in British law. I would point to three such contributions: to the system of legal sources; to parliamentary sovereignty; and to the concept of a state.

A. Positive Law and Legal Sources

To the historian of legal ideas, reading *Entick v Carrington* is a bit like biting into a poisonous apple. The case is replete with invitations to connect the legal principles expressed in the case with philosophical references. This is of course the case of the famous statement that:

> [T]he great end, for which men entered into society, was to secure their property. That right is preserved sacred and incommunicable in all instances, where is has not been taken away by some public law for the good of the whole.[36]

This sounds like a clear foundation in natural law for 'the importance attached by the common law to the relative inviolability of a dwelling house' as well as a serious invitation to place *Entick v Carrington* next to Blackstone's *Commentaries* or some of Mansfield's opinions as evidence that the mid-eighteenth century witnessed the high tide of natural law thinking in the history of the common law.

Yet this natural law cameo comes very late in the course of Camden's opinion and is not a central element in his reasoning. What matters is not that property is a natural right or indeed any statement about the nature of property, but that any infringement on it must be based on positive law. A lawyer of the positivist school could very well point to *Entick* as evidence for his or her view of the law as consisting only of positive enactments and precedents to be found in the lawbooks. The 'importance attached by the common law to the privacy of the home' as expressed in *Entick*[37] refers explicitly to positive law and works very well without any reference whatsoever to natural law:

> No man can set his foot upon my ground without my licence, but he is liable to an action, though the damage be nothing ... If he admits the fact, he is bound to show by way of justification, that *some positive law* has empowered or excused him.[38]

---

[36] *Entick v Carrington* (n 14) 1066.
[37] See *Morris v Beardmore* [1981] AC 446, 464.
[38] *Entick v Carrington* (n 14) 1066, emphasis added.

Entick can thus serve as the formulation of a larger principle of legality:

> [T]he idea that the citizen enjoys the freedom to do as he or she pleases and that any interference with individual liberties must be justified by law.[39]

There is an underlying theory of legal sources in *Entick v Carrington*. This theory is deeply connected with a larger understanding of the way in which law should act as a bulwark of liberty. Or, to put it another way, the underlying theory of liberty in *Entick* requires a specific theory of legal sources. This theory is expressed in Camden's famous words:

> If it is law, it will be found in our lawbooks. If it is not to be found there, it is not law.[40]

The reference to the 'lawbooks' is not a call for a greater use of the historical method and of antiquarianism in the law. To be properly understood, it should be combined with Camden's taste for clarity (as more conducive to liberty and absence of arbitrariness) and his distaste for the 'dark and obscure' authorities of the law. This is a way for Camden to entrench his opinion into normality and reject any reference to reason of state and other ways of setting aside the ordinary law of the land:

> Ad ea, quoe frequenter accidunt, jura adaptantur.[41]

The common law is the ordinary law of the land. What is ordinary is well known and should not be drawn from the 'dark' corners of the law. This strategy is remarkable in the sense that it is exactly the reverse of that used by many seventeenth-century lawyers in order to justify their claims for liberty. Coke's ordinary strategy in such cases was to immerse himself in the archives in the Tower of London in order to uncover an adequate, generally unheard-of precedent which he would then throw at his adversaries in the House of Commons or in court. Camden's strategy regarding legal sources is the exact opposite. What is too old, too rare, is not conducive to liberty. This strategy somewhat anticipates the way in which Dicey in 1885 would reject 'discussions of antiquaries' as the foundation of constitutional law.[42]

In fact there is no magic to the words Camden uses. He is very clear about what he means by 'the whole body of the law'. This 'whole body of the law' is showed to break into two main parts: statute law and the common law. This distinction is the key to the whole case: it is in accordance with it that Camden structures his promenade into the variety of possible legal justifications for issuing the warrant and breaking forcibly into *Entick*'s house. Is there a statute warranting the power exercised by the King's messengers? If not, is this a common law power?

---

[39] Lord Irvine of Lairg, 'Sovereignty in Comparative Perspective: Constitutionalism in Britain and America' (2001) 76(1) *New York University Law Review* 1.

[40] *Entick v Carrington* (n 14) 1066.

[41] ibid 1061.

[42] Edmund Burke, *Select Works of Edmund Burke* (Indianapolis, Liberty Fund, 1999).

Camden is therefore one of the authorities one can turn to when it comes to the widespread notion that 'statute law and common law ... constitute a single, coherent integral body of law'.[43] *Entick* appears as a move towards an early variety of positivism, one which had faith in the notion that there could be some ascertainable legal sources for the exercise of powers, or the absence thereof. 'How, Ronald Dworkin asks in the first page of *Law's Empire*, can the law command when the law books are silent or unclear or ambiguous?'[44] The answer in *Entick* seems to be that: (a) if the lawbooks are silent, there is no power; and (b) if the lawbooks speak, they speak decisively (with no penumbra or grey area left) to the question of the legality of administrative action. The case is a moment in the historical development of what Dworkin calls the 'plain fact view of the grounds of law', namely that 'questions of law can always be answered by looking in the books where the records of institutional decisions are kept'.[45]

B. Parliamentary Sovereignty

'Such is the power', says Camden, 'and one would naturally expect the law to warrant it.' But what kind of law should it be? *Entick* has established the principle that only the common law or a statute could authorise executive action. Camden's rejection of 'state necessity' and 'matters of state' as justifications meant that only the ordinary law of the land could provide such authority. No 'reason of state' stood above the law of the land as expressed in statutes and common law precedents. This falls into line with the 'rationalisation' of the system of sources that is apparent in the case:

> [W]ith respect to the argument of state necessity ... the common law does not understand that kind of reasoning, nor do our books take notice of any such distinctions.[46]

The only available justification for an act of 'executive' power, then, was a statute or a common law rule. In the absence of a common law rule expressed by the courts, only an Act of Parliament will confer appropriate authority. Nothing less than a statute will do. This idea is expressed fairly clearly when Camden examines the power of searching and seizing supposedly libellous papers:

> It is then said that it is necessary for the ends of government to lodge such a power with a state officer; and that it is better to prevent the publication before than to punish the offenders afterwards. *I answer, if the legislature be of that opinion,*

---

[43] P Atiyah, 'Common law and Statute law' (1985) 48 *MLR* 1.
[44] R Dworkin, *Law's Empire* (Oxford, Hart Publishing, 1998).
[45] ibid 7.
[46] *Entick v Carrington* (n 14) 1073.

they will revive the Licensing Act. But if they have not done that I conceive they are not of that opinion.[47]

As a result, Camden was pointing in the direction of establishing Parliament as the only possible authority in the state which can empower administrative and executive authorities. In other words, *Entick v Carrington* would deserve a more conspicuous place in the line of cases that have established the principle of parliamentary sovereignty. Dicey wrote that 'the maintenance of rigid legality ... was the certain road to parliamentary sovereignty'.[48] Certainly, *Entick* was an important step in establishing this spirit of 'rigid legality'.

As a matter of fact:

[H]ad Parliament in 1760 passed a statute authorizing the Home Secretary to seize people's papers whenever he thought such action desirable, Carrington's 'trespass' would have been lawful, and *Entick*'s suit would have failed ... Parliament might impinge upon property rights and personal liberties whenever and however it thought fit. After *Entick*, Parliament could if it had wished have passed legislation affording 'general warrants' an entirely lawful status.[49]

Parliament had done so through 'Licensing Acts' regulating the press in the seventeenth century. They were held to authorise general warrants which could be issued without naming any persons in particular. But these acts had expired in 1694. Analogous enabling legislation also existed in relation to the American colonies.[50]

In fact, there is a common legal ground between *Entick* and the cases which have affirmed the supremacy of statutory legislation in British law. Let me take the example of *Stockdale v Hansard*. When Lord Denman affirmed that a resolution of the House of Commons could not be authority for the seizure of some allegedly libellous papers, he said that:

It is a claim for an arbitrary power to authorise the commission of any act whatever, on behalf of a body which in the same argument is admitted not to be the supreme power of the state.[51]

In the eyes of the law, the House of Commons alone, without the concurrence of the Crown and the House of Lords, is deprived of the authority to allow the publishing of libellous papers. It cannot from its own authority allow an otherwise illegal action. The facts of the case are exactly the reverse of those in *Entick* (the House had authorised the publishing of libellous papers

---

[47] ibid, emphasis added.

[48] Although when he wrote of 'rigid legality', he was putting the emphasis on habeas corpus rather than the rule against illegal searches and seizures as the main instrument for the judicial supervision of 'the whole administrative action of the government'. Dicey (n 11) 139.

[49] I Loveland, *Constitutional Law, Administrative Law, and Human Rights* (Oxford, Oxford University Press, 2012) 54.

[50] See *Boyd v US* (n 13) 623.

[51] *Stockdale v Hansard* (1839) 9 Ad & El 1, 107–08.

rather than ordering their seizure and the publisher was a private person, not a public authority). But the legal principle is analogous: only an Act of Parliament could be the legal justification for such an action. Accordingly, the defendant (Hansard) had failed to establish that he had published the libel under authority of Parliament. After *Entick v Carrington* was decided, the condemnation of general warrants was re-affirmed by resolutions of the House of Commons, but these resolutions failed to be converted into a declaratory Act, as the House of Lords refused to give its consent to such a measure.[52] *Entick* reads as a spur to legislative action. It is an invitation to future parliaments to enact the kind of legislation that empowers public authorities to act in such situations. And, indeed, modern parliaments have been very keen to defer to that invitation.

C. The State

ECS Wade has written that:

> *Entick v Carrington* ... set at rest, though not so conclusively as has sometimes been asserted, the claim of the Executive, already curtailed in many directions, to justify arbitrary interference with personal liberty or private property under cover of the plea of public interest or matter of state.[53]

Yet the traditional distaste of the common law for matters of state does not exhaust the role of the state in British law. Nor does it make the concept of state useless when it comes to interpreting *Entick v Carrington*. In fact, *Entick* is very much a case about the state: one that contributes to the building of a conceptual framework in British law that can be summed up under the notion of a state. As we saw, the case proceeds by removing certain appearances of legality and showing an underlying reality of arbitrary power. Had there been a proper legal authority on which to base the warrants, however, liberty and property would not have been at risk. The case reads as a critique of the post-feudal administrative machinery. Because of the disorderly nature of these institutional arrangements, many authorities could pretend that they had the power to do certain things that were damageable to the liberty and property of the subject. For instance, based on unclear precedents and obscure authority, the Privy Council could claim a dubious 'right' or 'privilege' to issue general warrants without showing cause. Many authorities could claim to be empowered to act, while their title to do so was unclear. The legal regime of warrants was far from clear. The coordination between those entities was also imperfect: did the smaller

---

[52] See Sir JAR Marriott, *The Mechanism of the Modern State* (Oxford, Clarendon, 1927) vol II, 257.

[53] ECS Wade, 'Act of State in English Law: Its Relations with International Law' (1934) 15 *British Year Book of International Law* 98, 98.

officers who penetrated into Mr Entick's house and seized his papers act upon the authority of the Secretary of State? Did the Secretary of State act as an officer of the King and under the banner of prerogative? What was exactly the scope of the Privy Council's powers? *Entick*'s sub-text seems to be that there was not enough of a state in 1765.

Entick would be an excellent test ground for Kelsen's theory of the state. Two important statements by Kelsen are of interest in this context: (1) the state, says Kelsen, is only another name for a relatively centralised legal order; (2) 'power is not a kind of substance which lingers behind social order. Political power is the efficacy of an order of constraint which is recognized by law'.[54] Both ideas are intertwined: that the state is only another name given to the legal order means that acts of power that can be observed in social life are only of interest to the legal science if they are grounded in a legal habilitation. From such a point of view, power is not distinct from law: 'the dualism of law and power is a superfluous splitting in two of the object of our knowledge'.[55] To sum up Kelsen's position, 'the power of the state is the power organized by positive law'.[56]

Despite the obvious anachronism that accompanies this thought experiment, it may not be amiss to imagine how Camden could have reacted to this approach. Had Camden read Kelsen, he might have said something along these lines:

> [A]s far as the activity of the public authorities in this country is concerned, our legal order as it now stands is a mess. Not only is this causing a threat to liberty. But furthermore, this is evidence that ill-intentioned (or ill-advised) people can claim (or think) that they act in the name of the state while in fact they are self-empowered, which amounts to not being empowered at all. Take the pseudo-norms enacted by the Secretary of State in the case of *Entick v Carrington*. Where is the superior norm which has authorized the issuing of this warrant? Nowhere. But we, common law judges, are going to change this. The common law, supplemented by the statute book, is a relatively centralized legal order which is in good working order. From now on, we, members of the bench, will demand that every public authority should show the legal basis for the power it claims to use. We will make sure that every act of power will be authorized by a corresponding legal rule, otherwise we will declare this act 'illegal and void'. Therefore, as we have the common law and a sovereign parliament, we also have a state.

This thought experiment, for all its faults, may have the virtue of showing how the state developed in Britain through a process of rationalising the relationship between law and power. *Entick v Carrington* is certainly an important moment in such a process. Yet neither this case nor any other gave way to an entire re-kindling of the legal system of the kind that took

---

[54] I quote here from the French translation: Hans Kelsen, *Théorie Générale du Droit et de l'Etat*, trans B Laroche and V Faure (Paris, Bruylant-LGDJ, 1998) 245.

[55] ibid 244.

[56] ibid 243–44.

place in other countries. What did not emerge was an all-encompassing legal entity—in the French legal parlance, a *personne morale*—called 'the state'. British public law has never given birth to such a creature. However, the absence of a state structure of the continental type also came with some disadvantages. One of them, emphatically, was the fuzziness of the institutional theory. This lack of clarity of the overall institutional architecture of the state is such that if there was a state at all in Britain, it had to be a complex set of public authorities and 'officials'. What unified these authorities was not a French or German state or even, as in the US, a written constitution which operated, in the words of Justice Blair in the case of *Chisholm v Georgia*, as 'the only fountain from which I shall draw',[57] ie, the only source from which power could flow. In Britain, the 'fountains' were the common law and the statutes enacted by a sovereign parliament. *Entick v Carrington* was very much in the background when Dicey wrote that 'the principles of private law have with us been by the action of the Courts and parliament so extended as to determine the position of the Crown and of its servants; thus the constitution is the result of the ordinary law of the land'.[58] If there is a theory of the state in *Entick v Carrington*, it is one which revolves around the common law and the common law courts.

---

[57] *Chisholm v Georgia* 2 US 419 (1793).
[58] Dicey (n 11) 121.

8

Entick v Carrington
in Scots Law

TOM MULLEN

I. INTRODUCTION

THIS CHAPTER CONSIDERS the significance of the landmark case of *Entick v Carrington*[1] for Scots law and for Scots lawyers, and others in Scotland interested in constitutional matters. How far, if at all, has it been influential and in what ways? In order to pursue this question, it is necessary to consider the different aspects of the case, ie, the varying propositions of law or constitutional principle for which it is thought to stand. It can be understood in at least four ways. First, it can be seen as a case about the law of search warrants. It supports the proposition that a search warrant must be specific and that a general warrant is not a lawful means of authorising a search of private premises. Second, it can be understood as a case affirming the importance of property rights in English law.[2] Third, it has been seen as an important illustration of the role of the courts in protecting liberty or fundamental rights generally.[3] Fourth, it has also been taken to support the much broader proposition of constitutional law that executive government must always be able to show legal authority for its actions (either in the common law or statute) and that there is no general justification for executive action by reference to public interest or state necessity.[4] This principle is often referred to as an aspect of the rule of law.

Although it is Dicey's exposition of the rule of law which has been most discussed, and *Entick v Carrington* is routinely cited in textbook discussions of the rule of law, Dicey relegates the case to a footnote. It is cited as

---

[1] (1765) 19 *Howell's State Trials* 1029.
[2] KD Ewing, 'The Politics of the British Constitution' [2000] *PL* 405, 408.
[3] W Holdsworth, *A History of English Law* (London, Methuen/Sweet & Maxwell, 1938) xol X, 515, 658–72.
[4] DL Keir and FH Lawson, *Cases in Constitutional Law*, 5th edn (Oxford, Clarendon, 1967) 101, 307; RVF Heuston, *Essays in Constitutional Law* (London, Stevens, 1964) 35–36; ECS Wade and AW Bradley, *Constitutional and Administrative Law*, 15th edn (London, Longman, 2011) 92.

an example of the application of his second meaning of the rule of law, the principle of equality before the law, which meant that public officials could be sued in the ordinary courts for legal wrongs committed in the same way as a private citizen.[5] This ability to sue officials is a specific application of each of the four propositions mentioned above.

In this chapter, I will consider the influences that *Entick v Carrington* has had in Scotland in relation to the law of warrants and searches, the protection of liberty and fundamental rights, and the principle of executive government being subject to law. I will not consider its influence (if any) on Scots property law. I will deal first with the law of warrants and searches, and then the broader principles of constitutional law.

II. SEARCH WARRANTS AND THE CRIMINAL PROCESS

The earliest reference to *Entick v Carrington* I have identified in a Scottish law report appears, not surprisingly, in *Bell v Black and Morrison*,[6] the first of three reported cases arising out of an illegal search. Before discussing the details of those cases, it is helpful to put them into the context of the Scots law on warrants as it was before they were decided.

A. The Law before the Scottish General Warrant Cases

The law on search warrants is discussed by, amongst others, Hume and Alison, who are both regarded as institutional writers on Scots criminal law. Hume sets out the law on warrants in his *Commentaries*.[7] He does not identify search warrants as a distinct category, but does comment on searches in his discussion of arrest warrants. He describes the degree of specification required in a warrant as follows:

> In like manner, though it is certainly the better and more equitable course, to express the special cause for which a warrant is given; yet I do not know that the officer be justified if he refuse to execute, or the party if he resist, a more general warrant, which orders him to answer to such matters as shall, on examination before the magistrate, be laid his charge. But it is a different, and a far more exceptionable sort of warrant, which is general as to the person charged, and commands the bearer to apprehend all persons suspected of the matters there set

---

[5] AV Dicey, *Introduction to the Study of the Law of the Constitution*, 8th edn (Indianapolis, Liberty Fund, 1982) 114.

[6] *Bell v Black and Morrison* (1867) 5 Irv 57.

[7] D Hume, *Commentaries on the Law of Scotland Respecting Crimes* (Edinburgh, Law Society of Scotland, 1986 reprint) ii, 78.

forth, or to make search every where for stolen goods or the like. For, under a writ of this shape, every thing is committed to the judgment and discretion of the officer; which is very dangerous, and may prove the occasion of great abuses. Nay, more, though there have been no purpose to grant a general warrant, yet still if it so happen, *per incuriam*, that the writing omits, either *in gremio*, or by some plain and intelligible reference, to specify the person against whom it issues, it seems not to be a safe or lawful ground for taking anyone.[8]

As in a number of other instances, Hume draws a comparison with English law. At the end of the first sentence quoted above, there is a footnote stating:

Generally speaking, the law of England is more scrupulous in such matters than ours; yet Hale, (vol. ii. P.111); and Hawkins, (b. 2, c. 13, No. 10. No. 25) are of the opinion, that this holds in their practice too.[9]

Alison does treat search warrants as a distinct category.[10] He states that a search warrant must be specific:

The search warrant must be special as to the goods intended to be searched for, or at least the felony which it is intended to elucidate, and bring to punishment by the warrant craved for; but it does not appear to be indispensable that it should set forth the particular house meant to be searched for these goods, any more than the particular place where the criminal is suspected to be concealed. It seems in short to be a sufficient authority to search for the goods specified, taken on the felonious occasion charged, everywhere, in the same manner as it is sufficient warrant to search for the individual suspected wherever he is to be found.[11]

He then echoes Hume's comment about the law of England, saying that:

The English law, at the same time, is much more scrupulous in this matter of warrants than our practice [citing, inter alia, Hawkins and Hale]. Beyond all question a warrant is illegal which should authorise officers to search everywhere for stolen goods generally, without specifying either the goods sought for, or the houses suspected. If the former is not known and specified, the latter must be enumerated by place and name.[12]

It is interesting to compare the Scots position as set out by Hume and Alison with that set out in *Entick v Carrington* and the other cases on general warrants. Both Hume and Alison agree that a warrant to search everywhere for stolen goods would be invalid. Alison, however, does not seem to regard it as necessary that a search warrant specify the particular house to be searched for stolen goods, provided that the warrant specifies the goods which have

---

[8] ibid.
[9] ibid.
[10] Of course, a power to arrest and a power to search could be included in the same warrant.
[11] A Alison, *Practice of the Criminal Law of Scotland* (Edinburgh, W Blackwood, 1833) 146–47.
[12] ibid 147.

been stolen and the occasion on which they were taken. Similarly, a warrant to search a named house is valid even though the goods to be searched for are not specified in the warrant. It is not clear whether Hume believes similar latitude is allowed. The equivalent passage may be read either as saying that a warrant that failure to specify the place(s) to be searched is in itself enough to make the warrant invalid or that the combination of a failure to specify the person charged and a failure to specify the place(s) to be searched makes the warrant invalid.

Both in Scots and English law, a warrant which merely specified the crime(s) alleged to have been committed but not the person(s) to be arrested would have been regarded as illegal.[13] However, Alison's view certainly seems to give the investigating authorities more latitude in search warrants than did English law. Hale thought that a search warrant should specify the places to be searched[14] and, although none of the group of general warrant cases of which *Entick v Carrington* is one dealt with such a warrant, it can be assumed that judges in those cases took for granted that a warrant which failed to specify the places to be searched was invalid.

B. The Scottish General Warrant Cases

As noted above, the earliest Scottish case referring to *Entick v Carrington* is *Bell v Black and Morrison*,[15] the first of three reported cases arising out of the same set of facts. It is also the nearest equivalent Scottish case on its facts to the warrant in question purported to authorise an unlimited search for papers relevant to an offence. However, the first of the Scottish general warrant cases was decided a few years earlier.

In *Webster v Bethune*,[16] following an allegation that furniture and other effects had been stolen from a house, a warrant was granted to 'search, and detain, and inventory the said articles, and carry away the same to a place of security; and, if necessary, to break and force open all shut and lockfast places'. The warrant did not specify the person accused of the theft, the time when the offence had been committed or the particular place to be searched. On the strength of this warrant, Webster's house was searched three times. The headnote states that it was suspended as being an illegal general warrant. The summary of the argument in the report notes that counsel for the respondent admitted that he could not maintain the legality

---

[13] See Hume, passage quoted above; *Leach v Money, Watson and Blackmore* (1763) 19 ST 1001.

[14] Sir M Hale, *The History of the Pleas of the Crown*, vol II (London, Nutt and Gosling, 1736) 111.

[15] *Bell v Black and Morrison* (n 6).

[16] *Webster v Bethune* (1857) 2 Irv 596.

of such a general warrant. The very brief judgment given by Lord Justice-Clerk Hope states:

> [T]his party is entitled to get rid of this warrant, which is admitted to be indefensible. If we refuse to suspend he might suffer considerable damage. I never saw or heard of such a proceeding as this.[17]

The case does not state what the minimum requirements of a valid search warrant are, probably because the warrant and its execution were so obviously irregular.

In *Bell v Black and Morrison*, Bell brought a bill of suspension of a warrant granted by the Sheriff-Substitute of Fifeshire (sic). The case was heard by the High Court of Justiciary. The petition on which the warrant was based stated that the joint procurator-fiscals for the county were taking a precognition against one James Pringle, then in custody, who was accused along with other persons unknown of conspiring to kill or injure the Reverend James Edgar and John Ballingall, a farmer, and to set fire to their houses, and of sending them threatening letters. It also narrated their suspicion that Bell and four others were involved in the conspiracy and that they were informed and had reason to believe that written documents connected to the conspiracy and threatening letters were in Bell's possession. The petition asked the Sheriff-Substitute to grant warrant to officers of court to search Bell's house for 'the said written documents, and all other articles tending to establish guilt, or participation in said crimes, and to take possession thereof'. The warrant was granted as requested. It was executed and various writings, books and documents, including private letters, were removed.

Although suspected, Bell was not accused of any offence at that stage, so this was a warrant issued to find evidence against persons who were not only not charged but whose identities were unknown, and to seek that evidence in the house of another person who had not yet been charged. The Second Division with a single opinion delivered by Lord Justice-Clerk Inglis suspended the warrant. The petitioner's argument was framed in terms of Scots law, but he did refer to a warrant of this kind having been held to be illegal in England in *Entick v Carrington*. *Entick* is not, however, referred to in the judgment—nor indeed are any other authorities.

The court noted three peculiarities in the petition and warrant:

— It was granted against five different people, none of whom was charged with any crime.
— There was no limitation as to the kind of papers sought to be obtained other than that they related to the alleged conspiracy.
— The execution of the warrant was entrusted absolutely and without control to ordinary sheriff officers and their assistants.

---

[17] ibid 598.

It appeared to be the combination of circumstances which made the warrant illegal. The court did not make a specific statement as to the minimum requirements for the validity of a search warrant and did not state that any one of the three peculiarities was by itself fatal to the validity of the warrant.

Although the background to the case lacks the high political drama of the English general warrant cases, the court clearly thought it was dealing with a constitutional case:

> It involves considerations of such high constitutional principle, that if we had felt any hesitation as to the judgment we should pronounce, we should have asked the assistance and advice of the other Judges of this court. But entertaining no doubt at all, we consider it our duty at once to pronounce this warrant to be illegal.[18]

There are close parallels to Lord Camden's judgment in *Entick*. Some of the language is similar; Lord Inglis says: 'But the seizure of papers made in the circumstances with which we have to deal is a proceeding quite unknown to the law of Scotland.'[19] He also rejects the argument from practice in much the same manner as Lord Camden did, saying:

> We think it right to say that no mere official practice would, in our eyes, justify such a warrant. Nothing short of an Act of Parliament, or a rule of the common law founded on a usage known to and recognised by the Court, would at all affect our judgment on this question. If any such practice really exists, which we do not believe, the sooner it is put an end to the better.[20]

Lord Inglis expressed himself even more trenchantly in the first of two subsequent actions for damages based on the illegality of the warrant. As civil cases, these were brought in the Court of Session. Bell and his wife brought an action also reported under the name *Bell v Black and Morrison*.[21] The defenders argued that they would only be liable in case of malice and want of probable cause. Lord Inglis responded to this argument by saying:

> I can conceive nothing more startling or unconstitutional, than that the defence put forward in this action should be sustained.
>
> ...
>
> [A] more illegal proceeding it never was my duty as a judge to consider. It is as illegal as if it had been a warrant to bring up a party for examination under torture, and therefore the sense in which the warrant is illegal is the highest in which that word can be used.[22]

---

[18] *Bell v Black and Morrison* (n 6) 64.
[19] ibid.
[20] ibid.
[21] *Bell v Black and Morrison* (1865) 3 M 1026.
[22] ibid 1029.

In the same case, Lord Neaves said:

> If these pleas were to be sustained, it would make a most serious alteration in our
> constitutional law.
>
> ...
>
> It seems to me to be one of the most illegal warrants I ever heard of. Some of us
> can remember a time when, if such a warrant had been obtained in connection
> with a political offence, the dissatisfaction that would have been excited would
> not have been appeased by a mere claim of damages against a procurator fiscal.[23]

The other case, *Nelson v Black and Morrison*,[24] was brought by a man
who thought he had been defamed by being named in the petition for the
warrant. This case came before the First Division rather than the Second
Division. All four of the judges were different from those who heard the
civil action brought by Bell and his wife. However, one of the four judges,
Lord Ardmillan, had participated in the justiciary proceedings which had
declared the warrant illegal.

In *Nelson*, Lord President McNeill, with whom the other judges concurred, drew a distinction between two different types of illegality. If the
search was 'out of all law and reason', that was one kind of illegality which
he described as relating to 'the substance of the proceedings'. If, on the other
hand, the objection was 'merely that the premises ought not to have been
searched in this particular form', that was another matter.[25]

In the case of a substantive illegality, the pursuer need not prove malice
and want of probable cause. In the case of formal illegality, it was necessary
to show that the defender's statements were made maliciously and without
probable cause. Lord McNeill thought that the case fell into the latter category. A legal warrant could have been granted on the basis of the petition.
If the Sheriff had limited the search to particular documents or required it to
be carried out under his supervision, it would not have been illegal.

Lord Deas agreed that a warrant in the terms asked for would have been
legal if the Sheriff required it to be executed under his supervision. Lord
Ardmillan remained of the view that the warrant granted to search Bell's
house had been illegal. Nonetheless, although he emphasised that:

> ... a general warrant for a sweeping and indefinite search in the dwelling-house of a
> person not put under charge, for written documents ... which must be read before
> it can be seen what they instruct ... is a very strong and startling procedure...[26]

---

[23] ibid 1031. It is not clear what past political controversies Lord Neaves is referring to here.
[24] *Nelson v Black and Morrison* (1866) 4 M 328.
[25] ibid 330–31.
[26] ibid 332.

He also suggested that such a warrant would be legal 'if accompanied by proper securities against oppressive execution' such as supervision of its execution by the sheriff. 'The illegality of the warrant lay in the absence of such securities.'[27]

Was the approach taken by the court in *Nelson* consistent with that taken in the other two cases? Certainly, the courts were addressing different questions. As Lord Deas noted, the cases are distinguishable because Bell's action for damages was based on an actual search of Bell's house, whereas Nelson against whom the warrant had not been executed was suing for defamation. Also, both Lords McNeill and Deas thought that the cause of action was a judicial slander and there was authority that a prosecutor was not liable for slander unless he had acted maliciously and without probable cause.[28]

As far as criminal procedure goes, the cases can be reconciled on the basis that the judgment of the court in the first case can be read as holding that the warrant was illegal because a lack of limitation as to the papers to be searched was combined with the absence of judicial supervision of its execution. Based on these authorities, the minimum requirements of a search warrant in Scots law appear to be that the premises to be searched are specified and that *either* the papers or articles to be searched for are specified or, if they are not, that the execution of the warrant is judicially supervised. It is not clear if by this time a Scottish court would have endorsed Alison's suggestion that the particular house to be searched need not be specified. However, as a practical matter, it is unlikely that a sheriff or justice of the peace would have asked for such a warrant. Nonetheless, although the cases can be reconciled in this way, Lord McNeill's categorisation of the defect in the warrant as a 'want of formality' or 'want of caution' in execution rather than a defect of substance suggests a more relaxed attitude to the legality of warrants than is held by Lord Inglis.

However, as a matter of private law, ie, liability in damages, there is a clear inconsistency between the decision in the second *Bell v Black and Morrison* case and the decision in *Nelson*. In the first case, all four judges were agreed that proof of malice and want of probable cause were not required in the case of this warrant as it was wholly illegal and ultra vires. This was plainly inconsistent with the view taken in *Nelson* that the pursuer did need to prove malice and want of probable cause in respect of the same warrant!

So, viewed in isolation, *Bell v Black and Morrison* may seem to be a Scottish equivalent of *Entick v Carrington*. Viewed in the context of the related litigation, this interpretation seems less compelling. However, if we take a longer-term view, it is clear that the stricter attitude of Lord Inglis has prevailed. *Webster*, *Bell* and *Nelson* continue to be cited as the primary authorities for the proposition that general warrants are illegal and for the degree of

---

[27] ibid.
[28] ibid 331–33.

specificity required in warrants,[29] and it is assumed, contrary to what Alison states, that a search warrant must specify the premises to be searched.[30] It is also clear that *Bell v Black and Morrison* did not subsequently catch the imagination of lawyers in the way that *Entick v Carrington* has and never achieved the same iconic status.

Interestingly, and as a warning against complacency, Scottish prosecutors did apply for a general warrant as recently as 1987 in the Zircon affair. The BBC had made a series of television programmes on secrecy. One programme mentioned the existence of a secret spy satellite programme (Zircon). The government thought that there might have been breaches of section 2 of the Official Secrets Act 1911. A sheriff granted a warrant that authorised police to search the premises and if necessary any person found there for 'any sketch, plan, model, article, note or document or anything of a like nature including in particular any film which is evidence of an offence under said Act [the Official Secrets Act]'. This warrant was successfully challenged as it failed to specify the offence that had been or was about to be committed.[31] The warrant made no reference to any section of the Act, even though there were many different offences under it.[32]

C. Did *Entick v Carrington* Influence the Decision in the Scottish General Warrant Cases?

The obvious question is whether *Entick v Carrington* influenced the decision in the *Bell* litigation. Certainly, the nature of the warrant in *Bell* was similar to that in *Entick*, the latter was referred to by counsel in argument, the case was perceived by Lord Inglis to be of constitutional importance and the judgment includes rhetorical flourishes reminiscent of those in Lord Camden's judgment. However, these circumstances only make it plausible that *Entick* was influential. The terms of the judgment are equally compatible with the decision being grounded in Scots law. Counsel's argument referred to several Scots authorities—Hume, Alison and Hutcheson's *Treatise on the Offices of Justice of the Peace*—as well as *Entick*. There is no evidence within the judgment itself of influences as no authorities of any kind are cited, no doubt because, as Lord Inglis says, the illegality was particularly blatant.

---

[29] See, eg, RW Renton and HH Brown, *Criminal Procedure According to the Law of Scotland*, 6th edn (Edinburgh, W Green, 1996) pt II, 5–09 and 5–10; CN Stoddart, *Criminal Warrants*, 2nd edn (Edinburgh, Butterworths, 1999) 1.19, 5.05.

[30] See Stoddart (n 29) 1.19, who cites Hume, Alison, *Nelson* and *Webster* to support this proposition.

[31] *BBC v Jessop* (February 1987, unreported, High Court of Justiciary).

[32] A subsequent application for a more narrowly drawn warrant relating to suspected offences under s 2 of the Act was granted.

Subsequent developments suggest that *Entick v Carrington* was not a major influence on Scots law with regard to search warrants. The Scottish courts applied similar principles, but the case is not referred to in subsequent cases on warrants or in textbooks on the criminal process. Instead, the Scottish authorities are relied on.

That *Entick v Carrington* has not had a major influence on the law on searches is not surprising in view of the separate development of Scots criminal law, criminal procedure and policing, and the absence of any strong pressure for convergence between Scotland and England in criminal matters.[33] The fact that the law on search warrants came to be very similar in the two jurisdictions is more likely to be a case of parallel evolution.

D. Search Without a Warrant

Lord Camden's judgment in *Entick v Carrington* was broadly enough expressed to make it possible to use it as authority on searches without a warrant given its emphasis on the inviolability of property rights. It is in this context that the only recent reference to it in a Scottish criminal case occurs. That case is *Gillies v Ralph*.[34] Although it does not concern a search warrant, it does concern entry to premises by the police for the purposes of investigating crime. Section 14 of the Criminal Procedure (Scotland) Act 1995[35] allowed the police to detain a person reasonably suspected of having committed an offence punishable by imprisonment for up to six hours at a time without arrest or charge (later increased to 12 hours). In this case, the police went to the flat of which Gillies was the householder to try and find out the whereabouts of a man, James Scott, believed to be her boyfriend, in connection with an act of vandalism of which he was suspected. Gillies told them that Scott was not there and refused permission to search her flat. Then officers saw Scott in the hallway. One officer cautioned him and told him he was being detained under section 14 of the 1995 Act. He moved briskly up the hallway away from the officers and Gillies tried to close the front door. The police forced their way in and removed Scott from the flat. Gillies, the householder, was then charged and convicted of obstructing police officers in the execution of their duty under section 41 of the Police (Scotland) Act 1967.

On appeal, Gillies argued that the police had acted unlawfully in entering her house without consent or a warrant. The High Court of Justiciary allowed the appeal. The police had had no lawful authority to enter the

---

[33] There are some exceptions, eg, legislation on traffic offences, controlled drugs and national security issues.

[34] *Gillies v Ralph* 2008 SLT 978.

[35] Since repealed and replaced by the Criminal Justice (Scotland) Act 2014, sched 1, para 27(a).

house and Gillies was entitled to close her door to prevent their entry. The court accepted that there were some circumstances in which police officers were entitled to enter private property without consent or a warrant, but they declined to develop the common law further to authorise entry to private property in order to detain a person. Lord Reed, giving the opinion of the court, stated:

> If a police officer enters private property without permission to do so, he is (unless authorised by common law or statute) acting unlawfully under the civil law: *a fortiori*, if force is used without lawful justification. As Brennan J observed in *Halliday v Nevill* (para 4):
>
> > A police officer who enters or remains on private property without the leave and licence of the person in possession or entitled to possession commits a trespass and acts outside the course of his duty unless his entering or remaining on the premises is authorised or excused by law.
>
> That principle is, in Brennan J's words, 'of ancient origin but of enduring importance', and forms part of the common heritage of the legal systems of the United Kingdom and the wider common law world (cf. *Entick v Carrington*; *Great Central Rly v Bates*; *Eccles v Bourque*; *Kuru v State of New South Wales*).

Whilst it is interesting to see *Entick v Carrington* used in this way, it does not suggest that it has been a strong influence in itself; rather, it provides an example of parallel development. In fact, *Entick v Carrington* seems to have been more influential for the broader propositions of constitutional law for which it is thought to stand. It is to these which I now turn.

III. FUNDAMENTAL RIGHTS AND THE CONSTITUTIONAL LIMITS OF EXECUTIVE POWER

A. Cases Citing *Entick v Carrington*

The influence in Scotland of *Entick v Carrington* in relation to these broader propositions is to be found in the literature of constitutional law rather than in the cases. I have found only one case in which it is discussed, *Davidson v Scottish Ministers (No 2)*.[36] In two other cases there are passing references, but nothing substantive.[37] In *Davidson*, the House of Lords had to decide

---

[36] *Davidson v Scottish Ministers (No 2)* [2005] UKHL 74; 2006 SC (HL) 41.

[37] In *Dalziel School Board v Scotch Education Department* 1914 2 SLT 449, a dispute over the dismissal of a teacher, *Entick v Carrington* was apparently referred to in argument, but not in any of the judgments. More recently, in *Sovereign Dimensional Survey Ltd v Cooper* 2009 SC 382, in which the Court of Session had made an order equivalent to an Anton Piller order, the court merely quoted a passage from Lord Denning's judgment in *Anton Piller* which itself referred to *Entick v Carrington*, but the Inner House makes no comment on *Entick v Carrington*.

whether the apparent exclusion of coercive remedies against the Crown in section 21 of the Crown Proceedings Act 1947 prevented interdict and specific performance being granted against the Crown in judicial review proceedings in Scotland. Lord Rodger made these comments on the historical importance of the law of tort or delict as a way of vindicating the subject's rights and freedoms:

> Reform of the private law and its procedures in respect of the Crown was no insignificant matter. By concentrating on judicial review, lawyers and judges today may tend to forget the historical importance of the law of tort or delict as a way of vindicating the subject's rights and freedoms. To take only the most obvious example, *Entick v Carrington* was an action of trespass for breaking and entering the plaintiff's house and seizing his papers. As Weir puts it in his peerless *Casebook on Tort* (p 18), in addition to providing compensation, the other function of the law of tort is 'to vindicate the rights of the citizen and to sanction their infringement. In this respect the flagship of the fleet is not negligence but trespass, protecting as it does the rights of freedom of movement, physical integrity, and the land and goods in one's possession'. So, if pushed too far, the doctrine that the Crown can do no wrong and so cannot be liable in tort could have been an engine of tyranny. But actions against officers of the Crown (such as Carrington, a King's messenger) as individuals meant that the law of tort could be used to protect the liberties and property of the subject.[38]

He ends that paragraph by commenting:

> Indeed Dicey's second meaning of the 'rule of law' as a characteristic of England was 'that here every man, whatever be his rank or condition, is subject to the ordinary law of the realm and amenable to the jurisdiction of the ordinary tribunals' (*Introduction to the Law of the Constitution*, p 193). The same applied in Scotland (*McDonald v Secretary of State for Scotland*[39] is indeed a more recent case in point).

The suggestion that Scots and English law both satisfied Dicey's second meaning of the rule of law was uncontroversial. Having considered the case law, I now move on to the literature.

B. Books and Articles on Constitutional Law

Although *Entick v Carrington* has not been cited in works on the criminal process, it has been regularly cited in books on constitutional law to illustrate both the role of the courts and common law in protecting liberty or fundamental rights and the general proposition that executive government must always be able to show legal authority for its actions (the principle of executive legality).

[38] *Davidson v Scottish Ministers (No 2)* [2005] UKHL 74 [73].
[39] *McDonald v Secretary of State for Scotland* 1994 SC 234.

The earliest reference that I have found in a work written by a Scots lawyer is in the *Source Book of Constitutional History from 1660*[40] by D Oswald Dykes, Professor of Constitutional Law and Constitutional History in the University of Edinburgh. Dykes reproduces a substantial except from the State Trials report in chapter XI, which is entitled 'Personal Liberty and Habeas Corpus', along with *Leach v Money* and *Wilkes v Wood*, and includes a paragraph on the general warrants cases in his introduction.[41] It is not clear to what extent Dykes' source book was read by lawyers. The preface makes clear that it was aimed principally at advanced students in history (ie, those studying for the honours degree). In any event, it does not claim to be a book on Scots law or to provide a Scottish perspective on the constitution. The preface refers to the constitutional history of 'this country' and the introduction refers to changes in the governmental machinery of 'this country'. This country is plainly the UK even though the book includes a substantial period before the Acts of Union (1660–1706).

A few years later, WIR Fraser, Advocate and Lecturer in Constitutional Law at the University of Edinburgh[42] and who later became Lord Fraser of Tullybelton, published a book which was aimed at lawyers, *An Outline of Constitutional Law* (1938).[43] The preface states that it was written at the suggestion of the General Council of the Law Society of Scotland and was intended primarily for candidates for professional examinations, although the author hoped that it would also prove to be useful to university students, particularly as there was no other book 'dealing with constitutional law from the point of view of the Scottish lawyer', with the exception of Dykes and Philip's *Chapters in Constitutional Law*.

Fraser does not cite *Entick v Carrington* in the context of search warrants. He discusses search warrants in his chapter on 'The Right to Freedom of the Person', where he says: 'the warrant must specify the premises to be searched and the articles to be seized. A general search warrant is illegal'.[44] There follows a summary of *Bell v Black and Morrison*. However, he does refer to *Entick v Carrington* in his chapter on the rule of law, specifically in his discussion of Dicey's second meaning of the rule of law, namely that of equality before the law. Having made the point that public officials are subject to the law in the same way as private individuals and can be sued for a legally wrongful act, he says that it is no defence that an action was necessary in the public interest and that this point was decided in *Entick v Carrington*, quoting the relevant passage from Lord Camden's judgment.[45]

[40] DO Dykes and JR Philip, *Source Book of Constitutional History from 1660* (London, Longmans, Green & Co, 1930).
[41] ibid 56–57.
[42] Fraser had previously been Lecturer in Constitutional Law at the University of Glasgow.
[43] WIR Fraser, *An Outline of Constitutional Law* (London, William Hodge & Co, 1938).
[44] ibid 191–92.
[45] ibid 17–18, quoting the passage at (1765) 19 *Howell's State Trials* 1029, 1073.

The next comprehensive account of Scots constitutional law was published in 1964, JDB Mitchell's *Constitutional Law*.[46] Mitchell cites *Entick v Carrington* in a footnote at p 144 and in in the text at p 180 in the course of a discussion of the prerogative, citing the passage from Camden's judgment on state necessity at the latter page. He also refers to it at p 334, in the chapter on fundamental rights, in the course of a discussion of freedom of property. He discusses the requirement for a warrant to enter property to be specific, which he notes was established in England in *Wilkes v Wood* and *Entick v Carrington*, and comments that similar principles were affirmed in Scotland in *Bell v Black and Morrison*.

After this, references to *Entick v Carrington* become commonplace. It is typically referred to on the context of discussion of the rule of law, particularly to support the proposition that executive government has no inherent powers and must always be able to show legal authority for its actions. Thus, for example, Clyde and Edwards refer to it in their textbook *Judicial Review*,[47] quoting the relevant passage from Lord Camden's' judgment. Similar use is made of the case by Ashton and Finch,[48] Munro[49] and Himsworth and O'Neill.[50]

Through these, and also through constitutional law texts written from an English perspective but widely read in Scotland, *Entick v Carrington* has become familiar to generations on Scots lawyers, but it is also worth examining whether it has become more widely known.

C. Publications for a Lay Readership

I have not conducted an exhaustive search of newspaper and periodical literature, but have identified several references to *Entick v Carrington* in Scottish publications aimed at the general reading public as opposed to lawyers or historians. The earliest reference I have found is in a lengthy article on the Aliens Acts 1793, which appeared in the *Edinburgh Review* for April 1825.[51] The article concerned the right of the Crown to exclude or dismiss an alien from the realm at pleasure. In analysing the reasons that had been given in the past to support the existence of such a prerogative, the author states:

---

[46] JDB Mitchell, *Constitutional Law* (Edinburgh, W Green, 1964; 2nd edn, 1968).

[47] Rt Hon Lord Clyde and DJ Edwards (Edinburgh, W Green, 2000) 4.14.

[48] C Ashton and V Finch, *Constitutional Law in Scotland* (Edinburgh, W Green, 2000) 63, 18.05.

[49] J Munro, *Public Law*, 2nd edn (Edinburgh, W Green, 2004).

[50] C Himsworth and C O'Neill, *Scotland's Constitution: Law and Practice*, 2nd edn (Haywards Heath, Bloomsbury Professional, 2009).

[51] 'Art IV. On the Alien Bill' *Edinburgh Review* (April 1825), 99–174. The article bears to have been written 'By an Alien'. The use of pseudonyms was not uncommon at the time. The content and forms of expression used suggest that the author was not in fact an alien.

In the most important judgment, which determined, that a warrant to search for, and seize the papers of the accused, in the case of a seditious libel is contrary to law, Lord Camden said, (*Entick v Carrington* 19 St. Tr. 1067) 'The judges must look into their books. If it is law, it will be found in our books. If it is not to be found there, it is not law.'

Here, the case is being used to support the principle of executive legality. In a sense this is a passing reference, but the description of the case as 'most important' seems noteworthy. What is also striking about the piece is the particularly detailed historical and legal analysis; the piece presupposed a highly educated and engaged readership.

Another reference appears in the *Glasgow Herald* of 3 January 1868. This article is a reproduction of an item from *The Times* of the previous day (something the *Glasgow Herald* regularly did at that time), under the title 'The Irish Fenian Press'.[52] *The Times* had been publishing extracts from Irish newspapers which the author regarded as seditious and the purpose of the article had been to explain the law of sedition to *The Times*' readers and to call for the law to be enforced against Irish nationalists. The author quotes a passage from Lord Camden's judgment in which he explains the reasons for punishing seditious libel. This is therefore an aspect of the case which is less resonant today and perhaps we should not read too much into it, as the piece was originally written for an English audience.

Rather more recently, a reference to *Entick v Carrington* appears in a book review in *The Scotsman* of 10 January 1924. The book in question was *The Principal Secretary of State: A Survey of the Office from 1558 to 1680* by FM Grier Evans.[53] The reviewer comments:

> The great battle fought over his right of commitment and of seizure of papers *receives adequate treatment* (my italics)., 'The author examines the conclusions reached in the various eighteenth century trials, especially *Entick v Carrington* and then illustrates by a brief survey of the records what in fact was the seventeenth century procedure. She shows that secretarial commitments upon warrants in which the cause of commitment was not shown were common. The abuse of this practice, *as is well known*, led to the passing of the Habeas Corpus Act. (Emphasis added)

This passage suggests both that the writer of the review was familiar with the general warrant cases and that the readers of *The Scotsman* were expected to have some idea of the eighteenth-century constitutional struggles.

Although this has been a highly selective survey, it suggests that the perception of *Entick v Carrington* as a key constitutional case was neither restricted to England nor to lawyers.

---

[52] *Glasgow Herald*, 3 January 1869. The author of the item in *The Times* was described as 'Scaevola'.

[53] FM Grier Evans, *The Principal Secretary of State: A Survey of the Office from 1558 to 1680* (London, Longmans, 1923).

D. The Influence of *Entick v Carrington* in Scots Constitutional Law

Having reviewed a number of sources referring to *Entick v Carrington*, I will now consider how significant it has been as a point of reference in Scots constitutional law and history. The references above show that in both the nineteenth and twentieth centuries, *Entick v Carrington* has been taken to illustrate principles common to Scots and English law.

As noted above, it does not seem that it has had much influence on the development of the law of search warrants. However, the broader significance of *Entick v Carrington*, whether as an exemplar of the importance with which the right of property was regarded, of the principle of executive legality or of the protection of liberty more generally, was clearly appreciated in Scotland. This is not surprising. From the mid eighteenth to the mid-twentieth centuries, political and legal thought was dominated by a unionist perspective.[54] There was widespread acceptance of the union and of Scotland's place within it. Whilst it was very important that major institutional differences had been preserved (the established church, education, the courts and Scots law), there was also a strong tendency to treat much of the pre-union English constitutional history as part of a constitutional inheritance common to Great Britain. More generally, there was a tendency not to distinguish clearly between terms like England/English, Scotland/Scots and Britain/British, or the precise political communities to which these terms referred.

More generally, broadening the focus beyond constitutional law, during the eighteenth century, there seems not to have been great enthusiasm for preserving some of the distinctive features of Scots law (eg, the continued importance of feudal principle) or great concern about the influence of English law and legal forms. The primary concern was with improvement in the law and the legal system to meet the needs of a developing society[55] and, in the nineteenth century, there was considerable support for the assimilation of Scots to English law, particularly in the field of commercial law.[56]

We can see the assumption of a common constitutional inheritance at work in Fraser's account of constitutional doctrine which displays impeccably Diceyan orthodoxy. Whilst discussing a number of areas where Scots law was different, he treats the basic doctrines of the constitution (eg, the rule of law and the sovereignty of Parliament) as British with no distinct Scottish dimension. There is no hint of the distinct perspective that emerged in the celebrated case of *MacCormick v Lord Advocate*[57] a mere 15 years

---

[54] C Kidd, *Union and Unionisms: Political Thought in Scotland 1500–2000* (Cambridge, Cambridge University Press, 2008).
[55] ibid 178–90.
[56] ibid 190–98.
[57] *MacCormick v Lord Advocate* 1953 SC 396.

later. Similarly, we have Dykes' omission of any national qualifier in the title of his work on constitutional history and his referring to 'this country' without saying which country he means.

We can also see the same assumption in works aimed at a lay audience. The article on the Aliens Act in the *Edinburgh Review* discussed above refers on the first page to 'an outrage on the ancient policy of England',[58] then on the second to the Alien Act being 'no standing part of the constitution of Britain'.[59] There follow numerous references to 'England', 'the Crown' and the 'English constitution'. The article ends with a plea to repeal 'this odious enactment' so that 'as Englishmen we shall not need to blush in the presence of these strangers'.[60] Whilst this might be read as indicating that the author was: (a) English; and (b) insensitive to the Scottish dimension of the UK, it was clearly thought that the readership would find this article relevant to them and, as we have seen, even Scots lawyers such as Dykes were prone to the tendency to elide the distinctions between England, Scotland and Britain.

Legal nationalism did not arise as a significant phenomenon until the mid-twentieth century,[61] but it did little to shake perceptions of a common constitutional inheritance. The reasons for this included that several of its exponents were unionist in their politics and that much of the emphasis was on private law rather than public law. One outstanding exception was the debate over the status of the Treaty of Union as fundamental law stimulated by Lord Cooper's remarks in *MacCormick v Lord Advocate*,[62] but although those remarks suggested that the two legal systems might rest on different basic foundational norms, that did not lead legal nationalists to suggest that there were other major differences of constitutional principle between Scots and English law. Even the devolution settlement which creates greater scope for divergence in substantive law including much of the law relating to Scottish government is built on essentially UK foundations; devolved government follows the Westminster system with relatively modest alterations, and the areas of law most affected by the broader propositions for which *Entick v Carrington* is today cited—judicial review and the law of government liability—are very close in Scotland and England and seem to have converged further in recent decades.

---

[58] 'On the Alien Bill' (n 51) 99.

[59] ibid 100.

[60] ibid 173.

[61] ID Willock, 'The Scottish Legal Heritage Revisited' in J Grant (ed), *Independence and Devolution: The Legal Implications for Scotland* (Edinburgh, W Green, 1976); Kidd (n 54) 198–210; L Farmer, 'Under the Shadow of Parliament House' in L Farmer and S Veitch (eds), *The State of Scots Law: Law and Government after the Devolution Settlement* (Edinburgh, Butterworths, 2001).

[62] See, eg, TB Smith, 'The Union of 1707 as Fundamental Law' [1957] *PL* 99; N MacCormick, 'Does the United Kingdom have a Constitution?' (1978) 29 *Northern Ireland Law Quarterly* 1.

IV. CONCLUSIONS

To return to the question with which I began—how far, if at all, *Entick v Carrington* has been influential in Scots law—as far as the law on search warrants goes, it seems not to have been a major influence, although the Scottish courts applied similar principles. As discussed above, this is not surprising in view of the separate development of Scots criminal law, criminal procedure and policing.

As to the broader significance of *Entick v Carrington*, the general ideas about the source and nature of the powers of executive government and the role of the courts in protecting individual liberty and controlling government power seem to have been pretty much the same in Scotland and England in the 250 years since it was decided, and the case itself is routinely referred to by textbook writers. These aspects of the concept of the rule of law are conceived of in the same way by Scots lawyers as they are by English lawyers.

Appendix

Entick v Carrington (1765) 19 State Trials 1029

The Case of Seizure of Papers, being an Action of Trespass by JOHN ENTICK, Clerk, against NATHAN CARRINGTON and three other Messengers in ordinary to the King, Court of Common-Pleas, Mich. Term: 6 GEORGE III A. D. 1765

[This Case is given with the above-mentioned title; because the chief point adjudged was, That a warrant to search for and seize the papers of the accused, in the case of a seditious libel, is contrary to law. But this was not the only question in the Case. All the other interesting subjects, which were discussed in the immediately preceding Case, except the question of General Warrants, were also argued in the following one; and most of them seem to have received a judicial opinion from the Court.

The state of the case, with the arguments of the counsel, is taken from Mr. Serjeant Wilson's Reports, 2 Wils. 275. But instead of his short note of the Judgment of the Court, the Editor has the pleasing satisfaction to present to the reader the Judgment itself at length, as delivered by the Lord Chief Justice of the Common-Pleas from written notes. It was not without some difficulty, that the copy of this Judgment was obtained by the Editor. He has reason to believe, that the original, most excellent and most valuable as its contents are, was not deemed worthy of preservation by its author, but was actually committed to the flames. Fortunately, the Editor remembered to have formerly seen a copy of the Judgment in the hands of a friend; and upon application to him, it was immediately obtained, with liberty to the Editor to make use of it at his discretion. Before, however, he presumed to consult his own wishes in the use, the Editor took care to convince himself, both that the copy was authentic, and that the introduction of it into this Collection would not give offence. Indeed, as to the authenticity of the Judgment, except in some trifling inaccuracies, the probable effect of careless transcribing, a first reading left the Editor's mind without a doubt on the subject. But it was a respectful delicacy due to the noble lord by whom the Judgment was delivered, not to publish it, without first endeavouring to know, whether such a step was likely to be displeasing [1030] to his lordship; and though from the want of any authority from him, the Editor exposes himself to some risk of disapprobation, yet his precautions to guard against it, with the disinterestedness of his motives, will, he is confident, if ever it should become necessary to explain the circumstances to his lordship, be received as a very adequate apology for the liberty thus hazarded. Hargrave.]

In trespass; the plaintiff declares that the defendants on the 11th day of November in the year of our Lord 1762, at Westminster in Middlesex, with force and arms broke and entered the dwelling-house of the plaintiff in the parish of St. Dunstan, Stepney, and continued there four hours without his consent and against his will, and all that time disturbed him in the peaceable possession thereof, and broke open the doors to the rooms, the locks, iron bars, &c. thereto affixed, and broke open the boxes, chests, drawers, &c. of the plaintiff in his house, and broke the locks thereto affixed, and searched and examined all the rooms, &c., in his dwelling-house, and all the boxes, &c., so broke open, and read over, pried into and examined all the private papers, books, &c. of the plaintiff there found, whereby the secret affairs, &c. of the plaintiff became wrongfully discovered and made public; and took and carried away 100 printed charts, 100 printed pamphlets, &c. &c. of the plaintiff there found, and other 100 charts &c. &c. took and carried away, to the damage of the plaintiff 2,000*l.*

The defendants plead 1st, not guilty to the whole declaration, whereupon issue is joined. 2dly, as to the breaking and entering the dwelling-house, and continuing four hours, and all that time disturbing him in the possession thereof, and breaking open the doors to the rooms, and breaking open the boxes, chests, drawers, &c. of the plaintiff in his house, and the searching and examining all the rooms, &c. in his dwelling-house, and all the boxes, &c. so broke open, and reading over, prying into, and examining the private papers, books, &c. of the plaintiff there found, and taking and carrying away the goods and chattels in the declaration first mentioned there found, and also as to taking and carrying away the goods and chattels in the declaration last mentioned, the defendants say, the plaintiff ought not to have his action against them, because they say, that before the supposed trespass, [1031] on the 6th of November 1762, and before, until, and all the time of the supposed trespass, the earl of Halifax was, and yet is one of the lords of the king's privy council, and one of his principal secretaries of state, and that the earl before the trespass on the 6th of November 1762, made his warrant under his hand and seal directed to the defendants, by which the earl did in the king's name authorize and require the defendants, taking a constable to their assistance, to make strict and diligent search for the plaintiff, mentioned in the said warrant to be the author, or one concerned in the writing of several weekly very seditious papers, intitled, 'The Monitor or British Freeholder, N° 357, 358. 360. 373. 376. 378. and 380, London, printed for J. Wilson and J. Fell in Paternoster-row,' containing gross and scandalous reflections and invectives upon his majesty's government, and upon both Houses of Parliament, and him the plaintiff having found, to seize and apprehend and bring together with his books and papers in safe custody before the earl of Halifax to be examined concerning the premises, and further dealt with according to law; in the due execution whereof all mayors, sheriffs, justices of the peace, constables, and all other his majesty's officers civil and military, and loving subjects, whom it might concern, were to be aiding and assisting to them the defendants, as there should be occasion. And the defendants further say, that afterwards and before the trespass on the same day and year, the warrant was delivered to them to be executed, and thereupon they on the same day and year in the declaration, in the day time about eleven o'clock, being the said time when, &c. by virtue and for the execution of the said warrant, entered the plaintiff's dwelling-house, the outer door thereof being then open, to search for and seize the plaintiff and his books and papers in order to bring him and them before the earl of Halifax, according to the warrant; and the defendants did then and there find the plaintiff, and seized and apprehended him, and did search for his books and papers in his house, and did necessarily search and examine the rooms therein, and also his boxes, chests, &c. there, in order to find and seize his books and papers, and to bring them along with the plaintiff before the said earl, according to the warrant; and upon the said search did then in the said house find and seize the goods and chattels of the plaintiff in the declaration, and on the same day did carry the said books and papers to a house at Westminster, where the said earl then and long before transacted the business of his office, and delivered the same to Lovel Stanhope, esq. who then was and yet is an assistant to the earl in his office of secretary of state, to be examined, and who was then authorized to receive the same from them for that purpose, as it was lawful for them to do; and the plaintiff afterwards (to wit) on the 17th of November in the said year was discharged out of their custody; and in searching for the books and papers of the plaintiff the defendants [1032] did necessarily read over, pry into, and examine the said private papers, books &c. of the plaintiff in the declaration mentioned then found in his house; and because at the said time when, &c. the said doors in the said house leading to the rooms therein, and the said boxes, chests, &c. were shut and fastened so that the defendants could not search and examine the said rooms, boxes, chests, &c. they, for the necessary searching and examining the same, did then necessarily break and force open the said doors, boxes, chests, &c. as it was lawful for them to do; and on the said occasion the defendants necessarily stayed in the house of the plaintiff for the said four hours, and unavoidably during that time disturbed him in the possession thereof, they the defendants doing as little damage to the plaintiff as they possibly could, which are the same breaking and entering the house of the plaintiff, &c. (and so repeat the trespass covered by this plea) whereof the plaintiff above complains; and this, &c. and wherefore they pray judgment, &c.

The plaintiff replies to the plea of justification above, that (as to the trespass thereby covered) he by any thing alledged by the defendants therein ought not to be barred from having his action against them, because he says, that the defendants at the parish of Stepney, of their own wrong, and without the cause by them in that plea alledged, broke and entered the house of the plaintiff, &c. &c. in manner and form as the plaintiff hath complained above; and this he prays may be inquired of by the country; and the defendants do so likewise.–There is another plea of justification like the first, with this difference only; that in the last plea it is alledged, the plaintiff and his papers, &c. were carried before lord Halifax, but in the first, it is before Lovel Stanhope, his assistant or law clerk; and the like replication of 'de injuria sua propria absq; tali causa,' whereupon a third issue is joined.

This cause was tried at Westminster-hall before the lord chief justice, when the jury found a Special Verdict to the following purport.

"The jurors upon their oath say, as to the issue first joined (upon the plea not guilty to the whole trespass in the declaration) that as to the coming with force and arms, and also the trespass in declaration, except the breaking and entering the dwelling-house of the plaintiff, and continuing therein for the space of four hours, and all that time disturbing him in the possession thereof, and searching several rooms therein, and in one bureau, one writing desk, and several drawers of the plaintiff in his house, and reading over and examining several of his papers there, and seizing, taking and carrying away some of his books and papers there found, in the declaration complained of, the said defendants are not guilty. As to breaking and entering the dwelling-house, &c. (above excepted) the jurors on their oath say, that at the time of making the following information, [1033] and before and until and at the time of granting the warrant hereafter mentioned, and from thence hitherto, the earl of Halifax was, and still is one of the lords of the king's privy council, and one of his principal secretaries of state, and that before the time in the declaration, viz. on the 11th of October 1762, at St. James's Westminster, one Jonathan Scott of London, bookseller and publisher, came before Edward Weston, esq. an assistant to the said earl, and a justice of peace for the city and liberty of Westminster, and there made and gave information in writing to and before the said Edward Weston against the said John Entick and others, the tenor of which information now produced and given in evidence to the jurors followeth in these words and figures, to wit, 'The voluntary information of J. Scott. In the year 1755, I proposed setting up a paper, and mentioned it to Dr. Shebbeare, and in a few days one Arthur Beardmore an attorney at law sent for me, hearing of my intention, and desired I would mention it to Dr. Shebbeare, that he Beardmore and some others of his friends had an intention of setting up a paper in the city. Shebbeare met Beardmore, and myself and Entick (the plaintiff) at the Horn tavern, and agreed upon the setting up the paper by the name of the Monitor, and that Dr. Shebbeare and Mr. Entick should have 200*l*. a year each. Dr. Shebbeare put into Beardmore's and Entick's hands some papers, but before the papers appeared Beardmore sent them back to me (Scott). Shebbeare insisted on having the proportion of his salary paid him; he had 50*l*. which I (Scott) fetched from Vere and Asgill's by their note, which Beardmore gave him; Dr. Shebbeare upon this was quite left out, and the monies have been continued to Beardmore and Entick ever since, by subscription, as I supposed, raised I know not by whom: it has been continued in these hands ever since. Shebbeare, Beardmore and Entick all told me that the late alderman Beckford countenanced the paper: they agreed with me that the profits of the paper, paying all charges belonging to it, should be allowed me. In the paper of the 22d May, called Sejanus, I apprehend the character of Sejanus meant lord Bute: the original manuscript was in the handwriting of David Meredith, Mr. Beardmore's clerk. I before received the manuscript for several years till very lately from the said hands, and do believe that they continue still to write it. Jona. Scott, St. James's 11th October 1762.'

'The above information was given voluntarily before me, and signed in my presence by Jona. Scott.   J. Weston'

"And the jurors further say, that on the 6th of November 1762, the said information was shewn to the earl of H. and thereupon the earl did then make and issue his warrant directed to the defendants, then and still being [1034] the king's messengers, and duly sworn to that office, for apprehending the plaintiff, &c. the tenor of which warrant produced in evidence to the jurors, follows in these words and figures: 'George Montagu Dunk, earl of Halifax, viscount Sunbury, and baron Halifax, one of the lords of his majesty's honourable privy council, lieutenant general of his majesty's forces, lord lieutenant general and general governor of the kingdom of Ireland, and principal secretary of state, &c. these are in his majesty's name to authorize and require you, taking a constable to your assistance, to make strict and diligent search for John Entick, the author, or one concerned in writing of several weekly very seditious papers, intitled the Monitor, or British Freeholder, Nº 357, 358, 360, 373, 376, 378, 379, and 380, London, printed for J. Wilson and J. Fell in Pater Noster Row, which contain gross and scandalous reflections and invectives upon his majesty's government, and upon both houses of parliament; and him, having found you are to seize and apprehend, and to bring, together with his books and papers, in safe custody before me to be examined concerning the premises, and further dealt with according to law; in the due execution whereof all mayors, sheriffs, justices of the peace, constables, and other his majesty's officers civil and military, and loving subjects whom it may concern, are to be aiding and assisting to you as there shall be occasion; and for so doing this shall be your warrant. Given at St. James's the 6th day of November 1762, in the third year of his majesty's reign, Dunk Halifax. To Nathan Carrington, James Watson, Thomas Ardran, and Robert Blackmore, four of the majesty's messengers in ordinary."

And the jurors further say, the earl caused this warrant to be delivered to the defendants to be executed. And that the defendants afterwards on the 11th of November 1762, at 11 o'clock in the day time, by virtue and for execution of the warrant, but without any constable taken by them to their assistance, entered the house of the plaintiff, the outer door thereof being open, and the plaintiff being therein, to search for and seize the plaintiff and his books and papers, in order to bring him and them before the earl, according to the warrant; and the defendants did then find the plaintiff there, and did seize and apprehend him, and did there search for his books and papers in several rooms and in the house, and in one bureau, one writing desk, and several drawers of the plaintiff there in order to find and seize the same, and bring them along within the plaintiff before the earl according to the warrant, and did then find and seize there some of the books and papers of the plaintiff, and perused and read over several other of his papers which they found in the house, and chose to read, [1035] and that they necessarily continued there in the execution of the warrant four hours, and disturbed the plaintiff in his house, and then took him and his said books and papers from thence, and forthwith gave notice at the office of the said secretary of state in Westminster unto Lovel Stanhope, esq. then before, and still being an assistant to the earl in the examination of persons, books, and papers seized by virtue of warrants issued by secretaries of state, and also then and still being a justice of peace for the city and liberty of Westminster and county of Middlesex, of their having seized the plaintiff, his books and papers, and of their having them ready to be examined, and they then and there at the instance of Lovel Stanhope delivered the said books and papers to him. And the jurors further say, that, on the 13th of April in the first year of the king, his majesty, by his letters patent under the great seal, gave and granted to the said Lovel Stanhope the office of law-clerk to the secretaries of state. And the king did thereby ordain, constitute, and appoint the law-clerk to attend the offices of his secretaries of state, in order to take the depositions of all such persons whom it may be necessary to examine upon affairs which might concern the public, &c. (and then the verdict sets out the letters patent to the law-clerk in *hæc verba*) as by the letters patent produced in evidence to the jurors appears. And the jurors further say, that Lovel Stanhope, by virtue of the said letters patent long before the time when, &c. on the 13th of April in the first year of the king was, and ever since hath been and still is law-clerk to the king's secretaries of state, and hath executed that office all the time. And the jurors further say, that at different times from the time of the Revolution to this present time, the like warrants with that issued against the plaintiff, have been frequently granted by the secretaries of state, and executed by the messengers in ordinary for the time being, and that each of the defendants did respectively take at the time of being appointed messengers, the usual oath, that he would be a true servant to the king, &c. in the place of a messenger in ordinary, &c. And the jurors further say, that no demand was ever made or left at the usual place of abode of the defendants, or any of them, by the plaintiff, or his attorney or agent in writing of the perusal and copy of the said warrant, so issued against the plaintiff as aforesaid, neither did the plaintiff commence or bring his said action against the defendants, or any of them, within six calendar months next after the several acts aforesaid, and each of them were and was done and committed by them as aforesaid; but whether, upon the whole matter as aforesaid by the jurors found, the defendants are guilty of the trespass [1036] herein before particularly specified in breaking and entering the house of the plaintiff in the declaration mentioned, and continuing there for four hours, and all that time disturbing the plaintiff in the possession thereof, and searching several rooms therein, and one bureau, one writing desk, and several drawers of the plaintiff in his house, and reading over and examining several of his papers there, and seizing, taking and carrying away some of his books and papers there found; or the said plaintiff ought to maintain his said action against them; the jurors are altogether ignorant, and pray the advice of the Court thereupon. And, if upon the whole matter aforesaid by the jurors found, it shall seem to the Court that the defendants are guilty of the said trespass, and that the plaintiff ought to maintain his action against them, the jurors say upon their said oath, that the defendants are guilty of the said trespass in manner and form as the plaintiff hath thereof complained against them; and they assess the damages of the plaintiff by occasion thereof, besides his costs and charges by him about his suit in this behalf laid out to 300*l.* and for those costs and charges, to 40*s*. But if upon the whole matter by the jurors found, it shall seem to the Court that the said defendants are not guilty of the said trespass; or that the plaintiff ought not to maintain his action against them; then the jurors do say upon their oath that the defendants are not guilty of the trespass in manner and form as the plaintiff hath thereof complained against them.

"And as to the last issue on the second special justification, the jury found for the plaintiff, that the defendants in their own wrong broke and entered, and did the trespass, as the plaintiff in his replication has alleged."

This Special Verdict was twice solemnly argued at the bar; in Easter Term last by serjeant Leigh for the plaintiff, and Burland, one of the king's serjeants, for the defendants; and in this present term by serjeant Glynn for the plaintiff, and Nares, one of the king's serjeants, for the defendants.

Easter Term, 5 Geo. 3.

Counsel for the Plaintiff. At the trial of this cause the defendants relied upon two defences; 1st, That a secretary of state as a justice or conservator of the peace, and these messengers acting under his warrant, are within the statute of the 24th of Geo. 2, c. 44, which enacts (among other things) that 'no action shall be brought against any constable or other officer, or any person acting by his order and in his aid, for any thing done in obedience to the warrant of a justice, until demand hath been made or left at the usual place of his abode by the party, or by his attorney in writing signed by the party, demanding the same, or the perusal and copy of such warrant, and the same hath been refused or neglected for six days after [1037] such demand,' and that no demand was ever made by the plaintiff of a perusal or copy of the warrant in this case, according to that statute, and therefore he shall not have this action against the defendants, who are merely ministerial officers acting under the secretary of state, who is a justice and conservator of the peace. 2dly, That the warrant under which the defendants acted, is a legal warrant, and that they well can justify what they have done by virtue thereof, for that at many different times from the time of the Revolution till this time, the like warrants with that issued against the plaintiff in this case have been granted by secretaries of state, and executed by the messengers in ordinary for the time being.

As to the first. It is most clear and manifest upon this verdict, that the earl of Halifax acted as secretary of state when he granted the warrant, and not merely as a justice of the peace, and therefore cannot be within the statute 24 Geo. 2, c.44, neither would he be within the statute if he was a conservator of the peace, such person not being once named therein; and there is no book in the law whatever, that ranks a secretary of state *quasi* secretary, among the conservators of the peace. Lambert, Coke, Hawkins, lord Hale &c. &c., none of them take any notice of a secretary of state being a conservator of the peace, and until of late days he was no more indeed than a mere clerk. A conservator of the peace had no more power than a constable has now, who is a conservator of the peace at common law. At the time of making this statute, a justice of peace, constable, headborough and other officers of the peace, borsholders and tithingmen, as well as secretary of state, conservator of the peace, and messenger in ordinary, were all very well known; and if it had been the intent of the statute, that a secretary of state, conservator of the peace, and messenger in ordinary, should have been within the statute, it would have mentioned all or some of them; and it not having done so, they cannot be within it. A messenger certainly cannot be within it, who is nothing more than a mere porter, and lord Halifax's footmen might as well be said to be officers within the statute as these defendants. Besides, the verdict finds that these defendants executed the warrant without taking a constable to their assistance. This disobedience will not only take them out of the protection of the statute, (if they had been within it), but will also disable them to justify what they have done, by any plea whatever. The office of these defendants is a place of considerable profit, and as unlike that of a constable and tithingman as can be, which is an office of burthen and expence, and which he is bound to execute in person, and cannot substitute another in his room, though he may call persons to assist him. 1 Hale's P. C. 581. This warrant is more like a warrant to search for stolen goods and to seize them, than any other kind of warrant, which ought to be directed to constables [1038] and other public officers which the law takes notice of. (4 Inst. 176.) 2 Hale's P. C. 149, 150. How much more necessary in the present case was it to take a constable to the defendants' assistance. The defendants have also disobeyed the warrant in another matter: being commanded to bring the plaintiff, and his books and papers before lord Halifax, they carried him and them before Lovel Stanhope, the law-clerk; and though he is a justice of the peace, that avails nothing; for no single justice of peace ever claimed a right to issue such a warrant as this, nor did he act therein as a justice of peace, but as the law-clerk to lord Halifax. The information was made before justice Weston. The secretary of state in this case never saw the accuser or accused. It seems to have been below his dignity. The names of the officers introduced here are not to be found in the law-books, from the first yearbook to the present time.

As to the second. A power to issue such a warrant as this is contrary to the genius of the law of England; and even if they had found what they searched for, they could not have justified under it. But they did not find what they searched for, nor does it appear that the plaintiff was the author of any of the supposed seditious papers mentioned in the warrant; so that it now appears that this enormous trespass and violent proceeding has been done upon mere surmise. But the verdict says, such warrants have been granted by secretaries of state ever since the Revolution. If they have, it is high time to put an end to them; for if they are held to be legal, the liberty of this country is at an end. It is the publishing of a libel which is the crime, and not the having it locked up in a private drawer in a man's study. But if having it in one's custody was the crime, no power can lawfully break into a man's house and study to search for evidence against him. This would be worse than the Spanish inquisition; for ransacking a man's secret drawers and boxes, to come at evidence against him, is like racking his body to come at his secret thoughts. The warrant is to seize all the plaintiff's books and papers without exception, and carry them before lord Halifax. What? Has a secretary of state a right to see all a man's private letters of correspondence, family concerns, trade and business?[1] This would be monstrous indeed! and if it were lawful, no man could endure to live in this country. In [1039] the case of a search-warrant for stolen goods, it is never granted, but upon the strongest evidence that a felony has been committed, and that the goods are secreted in such a house; and it is to seize such goods as were stolen, not all the goods in the house; but if stolen goods are not found there, all who entered with the warrant are trespassers. However frequently these warrants have been granted since the Revolution, that will not make them lawful; for if they were unreasonable or unlawful when first granted, no usage or continuance can make them good. Even customs, which have been used time out of mind, have been often adjudged void, as being unreasonable,

[1] Mr. Burke in his Short Account of a late short Administration, (this administration came into employment under the mediation of the duke of Cumberland, son to George the second, in July 1765, and was removed in July 1766: during its continuance in office the marquis of Rockingham was First Lord of the Treasury, and Mr. Dowdeswell Chancellor of the Exchequer) says, 'The lawful secrets of business and friendship were rendered inviolable by the Resolution for condemning the seizure of papers.' See New Parl. Hist. vol. 16, p.207.

contrary to common right, or purely against law, if upon considering their nature and quality they shall be found injurious to a multitude, and prejudicial to the commonwealth, and to have their commencement (for the most part) through the oppression and extortion of lords and great men. Davis 32 b. These warrants are not by custom; they go no farther back than eighty years; and most amazing it is they have never before this time been opposed or controverted, considering the great men that have presided in the King's-bench since that time. But it was reserved for the honour of this Court, which has ever been the protector of the liberty and property of the subject, to demolish this monster of oppression, and to tear into rags this remnant of Star-chamber tyranny.

Counsel for the Defendants. I am not at all alarmed, if this power is established to be in the secretaries of state. It has been used in the best of times, often since the Revolution. I shall argue, first, that the secretary of state has power to grant these warrants; and if I cannot maintain this, I must, secondly, shew that by the statute 24 Geo. 2 c. 24, this action does not lie against the defendants the messengers.

1. A secretary of state has the same power to commit for treason as a justice of peace. Kendall and Roe,[2] Skin. 596. 1 Salk. 346, S.C. 1 lord Raym. 65. 5 Mod. 78, S.C. Sir William Wyndham was committed by James Stanhope, secretary of state, to the Tower, for high treason the 7th of October, 1715. See the case 1 Stra. 2. And serjeant Hawkins says, it is certain, that the privy council, or any one or two of them, or a secretary of state, may lawfully commit[3] persons for treason, and for other [1040] offences against the state, as in all ages they have done. 2 Hawk. P. C. 117, sect. 4. 1 Leon: 70, 71. Carth. 291. 2 Leon. 175. If it is clear that a secretary of state may commit for treason and other offences against the state, he certainly may commit for a seditious libel against the government; for there can hardly be a greater offence against the state, except actual treason. A secretary of state is within the Habeas Corpus Act. But a power to commit without a power to issue his warrant to seize the offender and the libel would be nothing; so it must be concluded that he has the same power upon information to issue a warrant to search for and seize a seditious libel, and its author and publisher, as a justice of peace has for

---

[2] See this Case, in vol. 12, p. 1299.

[3] With respect to the power of a secretary of state to commit, see the Cases of Wilkes, p. 982, of this volume, and of Leech against Money and others, p. 1002 of this volume.

"If we are to learn from the records in courts of justice, and from the received practice at all times what is the law of the land, I have no difficulty in saying that the secretaries of state have the right to commit. This right was not even doubted by lord Camden, who expressed as great anxiety for the liberty of the subject as any man; indeed it has been thought by some persons eminent in our possession, who have considered the point since, that he rather overstepped the line of the law in the case of R. v. Wilkes, and certainly if that judgment can be supported, many other cases that have been solemnly determined, cannot be reconciled with it." Per lord Kenyon, C.J. in the Case of the King against Despard, 7 T. Rep. 742.

granting a warrant to search for stolen goods, upon an information that a theft has been committed, and that the goods are concealed in such a place; in which case the constables and officers assisting him in the search, may break open doors, boxes, &c. to come at such stolen goods. Supposing the practice of granting warrants to search for libels against the state be admitted to be an evil in particular cases, yet to let such libellers escape, who endeavor to raise rebellion, is a greater evil, and may be compared to the reason of Mr. Justice Foster in the Case of Pressing, [Vol. 18, p. 1323.] where he says, 'That war is a great evil, but it is chosen to avoid a greater. The practice of pressing is one of the mischiefs war brings with it; but it is a maxim in law and good policy too, that all private mischiefs must be borne with patience, for preventing a national calamity, &c.'

2. Supposing there is a defect of jurisdiction in the secretary of state, yet the defendants are within the stat. 24 Geo. 2, c. 44, and though not within the words, yet they are within the reason of it. That it is not unusual in acts of parliament to comprehend by construction a generality, where express mention is made only of a particular. The statute of *Circumspecte agatis* concerning the bishop of Norwich extends to all bishops. Fitz. Prohibition 3, and 2 Inst. on this statute, 25 Edw. 3, c. enables the incumbent to plead in *quare impedit*, to the king's suit. This also extends to the suits of all persons, 38 E. 3, 31. The act 1 Ric. 2, ordains that the warden of the Fleet shall not permit prisoners in execution to go out of prison by bail or baston, yet it is adjudged that this act extends to all goalers. Plowd. Com. case of Platt, 35 b. The stat. *de donis conditionalibus* extends to all other limitations in tail not there particularly mentioned, and the like construction has been put upon several other [1041] statutes. Tho. Jones 62. The stat. 7 Jac. 1, c. 5, the word 'constable' therein extends to a deputy constable. Moor 845. These messengers in ordinary have always been considered as officers of the secretary of state, and a commitment may be to their custody, as in sir W. Wyndham's case. A justice of peace may make a constable *pro hac vice* to execute a warrant, who would be within the stat. 24 Geo. 2. So if these defendants are not constables, yet as officers they have power to execute a warrant of a justice of peace. A constable may, but cannot be compelled to execute a warrant out of his jurisdiction. Officers acting under colour of office, though doing an illegal act, are within this statute. Vaugh. 113. So that no demand having ever been made of the warrant, nor any action commenced within six months, the plaintiff has no right of action. It was said, that a conservator of the peace had no more power than a constable has now. I answer, they had power to bind over at common law, but a constable has not. Dalton, cap. 1.

Counsel for the Plaintiff, in reply. It is said, this has been done in the best of times ever since the Revolution. The conclusion from thence is, that it is the more inexcusable, because done in the best of times, in an æra when the common law (which had been trampled under the foot of arbitrary power) was revived. We do not deny but the secretary of state hath power to commit for treason and other offences against the state; but that is not the present case, which is breaking into the house of a subject, breaking into his drawers and boxes, ransacking all the rooms in his house, and prying into all his private affairs. But it is said, if the secretary of state has power to commit, he has power to search, &c. as in the case of stolen goods. This is a false consequence, and it might as well be said he has a power to torture. As to stolen goods, if the officers find none, have they a right to take away a man's goods which were not stolen? Pressing is said to be a dangerous power, and yet it has been allowed for the benefit of the state. But that is only the argument and opinion of a single judge, from ancient history and records, in times when the lower part of the subjects were little better than slaves to their lords and great men, and has not been allowed to be lawful without an act of parliament since the time of the Revolution. The stat. 24 Geo. 2, has been compared to ancient statutes, naming particular persons and districts, which have been construed to extend to many others not named therein; and so the defendants, though no such officers are mentioned, by like reason, are within the statute of 24 Geo. 2. But the law knows no such officers as messengers in ordinary to the king. It is said the Habeas Corpus Act extends to commitments by secretaries of state, though they are not mentioned therein. True, but that statute was made to protect the innocent [1042] against illegal and arbitrary power. It is said, the secretary of state is a justice of peace, and the messengers are his officers. Why then did the warrant direct them to take a constable to their assistance, if they were themselves the proper officers? It seems to admit they were not the proper officers. If a man be made an officer for a special purpose to arrest another, he must shew his authority; and if he refuses, it is not murder to kill him. But a constable or other known officer in the law need not shew his warrant.

Lord Chief Justice. I shall not give any opinion at present, because this case, which is of the utmost consequence to the public, is to be argued again. I shall only just mention a matter which has slipt the sagacity of the counsel on both sides, that it may be taken notice of upon the next argument. Suppose a warrant which is against law be granted, such as no justice of peace, or other magistrate high or low whomsoever, has power to issue, whether that magistrate or justice who grants such warrant, or the officer who executes it, is within the stat. 24 Geo. 2, c. 44. To put one case (among an hundred that might happen): suppose a justice of peace issues a warrant to search a house for stolen goods, and directs it to four of his servants, who search and find no stolen goods, but seize all the books and papers of the owners of the house, whether in such a case would the justice of peace, his officers or servants, be within the stat. 24 Geo. 2.? I desire that every point of this case may be argued to the bottom, for I shall think myself bound, when I come to give judgment, to give my opinion upon every point in the case.

Mich. 6 Geo. 3.

Counsel for the Plaintiff on the second argument. If the secretary of state, or a privy counsellor, justice of peace, or other magistrate whatever, have no legal power to grant the warrant in the present case, it will follow, that the magistrate usurping such an illegal power, can never be construed to be within the meaning or reason of the statute of 24 Geo. 2, c. 44, which was made to protect justices of the peace, &c. where they made blunders, or erred in judgment in cases within their jurisdiction, and not to give them arbitrary power to issue warrants totally illegal from beginning to end, and in cases wherein they had no jurisdiction at all. If any such power in a secretary of state, or a privy counsellor, had ever existed, it would appear from our law-books. All the ancient books are silent on this head. Lambert never once mentions a secretary of state. Neither he nor a privy counsellor, were ever considered as magistrates. In all the arguments touching the Star-Chamber, and Petition of Right, nothing of this power was ever dreamt of. State-commitments anciently were either *per mandatum regis* in person, or by warrant of several of the privy counsellors in the plural number. The king has this [1043] power in a particular mode, viz. by the advice of his privy council, who are to be answerable to the people if wrong is done. He has no other way but in council to signify his mandate. In the Case of the Seven Bishops, this matter was insisted upon at the bar, when the Court presumed the commitment of them was by the advice of the privy council; but that a single privy counsellor had this power, was not contended for by the crown-lawyers then. This Court will require it to be shewn that there have been ancient commitments of this sort. Neither the secretary of state, or a privy counsellor, ever claimed a right to administer an oath, but they employ a person as a law-clerk, who is a justice of peace, to administer oaths, and take recognizances. Sir Barth. Shower, in Kendall and Roe's case, insisted they never had such power. It would be a solecism in our law to say, there is a person who has power to commit, and has not power to examine on oath, and bail the party. Therefore whoever has power to commit, has power to bail. It was a question formerly, whether a constable as an ancient conservator of the peace should take a recognizance or bond. In the time of queen Elizabeth there was a case wherein some of the judges were of one opinion and some of another. A secretary of state was so inconsiderable formerly, that he is not mentioned in the statute of *scandalum magnatum*. His office was thought of no great importance. He takes no oath of office as secretary of state, gives no kind of security for the exercise of such judicial power as he now usurps. If this was an ancient power, it must have been annexed to his office anciently; it cannot be now given to him by the king. The king cannot make two chief justices of the Common-Pleas; nor could the king put the great seal in commission before an act of parliament was made for that purpose. There was only one secretary of state formerly: there are now two appointed by the king. If they have this power of magistracy, it should seem to require some law to be made to give that power to two secretaries of state which was formerly in one only. As to commitments *per mandatum regis*, see Staunf. Pl. Coron. 72. 4 Inst. c. 5, court of Star-Chamber. Admitting they have power to commit in high treason, it will not follow they have power to commit for a misdemeanor. It is of necessity that they can commit in high treason, which requires immediate interposition for the benefit of the public. In the case of commitment by Walsingham secretary of state, 1 Leon. 71, it was returned on the Habeas Corpus at last, that the party was committed 'ex sententia et mandato totius concilii privati dominæ reginæ.' Because he found he had not that power of himself, he had recourse to the whole privy council's power, so that this case is rather for the plaintiff. Commitment by the High Commission Court of York was declared by parliament illegal from the beginning; so in the Case of Ship-Money the parliament declared it illegal.

[1044] *Counsel for the Defendants* on the second argument. The most able judges and advocates, ever since the Revolution, seem to have agreed, that the secretaries of state have this power to commit for a misdemeanor. Secretaries of state have been looked upon in a very high light for two hundred years past. 27 H. 8, c. 11. Their rank and place is settled by 31 H. 8, c. 10. 4 Inst. 362, c. 77, of Precedency. 4 Inst. 56. Selden's Titles of Honour, c. Officers of State. So that a secretary of state is something more than a mere clerk, as was said, Minshew verb. Secretary. He is 'e secretioribus consiliis domini regis.' Serjeant Pengelly moved, that sir William Wyndham might be bailed. If he could not be committed by the secretary of state for something less than treason, why did he move to have him bailed? This seems a concession that he might be committed in that case for something less than treason. Lord Holt seems to agree that a commitment by a secretary of state is good. Skin. 598. 1 lord Raym. 65. There is no case in the books that says in what cases a secretary of state can or cannot commit; by what power is it that he can commit in the case of treason, and in no other case? The resolution of the House of Commons touching the Petition of Right, [Selden last volume, Parliamentary History, vol. 2, p. 374.] Secretary Coke told the Lords, it was his duty to commit by the king's command. Yoxley's case, Carth. 291, he was committed by the secretary of state on the statute of Elizabeth for refusing to answer whether he was a Romish priest. The Queen and Derby, Fortescue's Reports, 140, the commitment was by a secretary of state, Mich. 10 Annæ, for a libel, and held good. (Note. Bathurst J. said he had seen the Habeas Corpus and the Return, and that this was a commitment by a secretary of state.) The King and Earbury, Mich. 7 Geo. 2, 2 Barnard 346, was a motion to discharge a recognizance entered into for writing a paper called The Royal Oak. Lord Hardwicke said it was settled in Kendall and Roe's case, that a secretary of state might apprehend persons suspected of treasonable practices; and there are a great number of precedents in the Crown-office of commitments by secretaries of state for libels against the government.

After time taken to consider, Lord Camden, Lord Chief Justice, delivered the Judgment of the Court for the Plaintiff, in the following words:

L. C. J. This record hath set up two defences to the action, on both of which the defendants have relied.

The first arises from the facts disclosed in the special verdict; whereby the defendants put their case upon the statute of 24 Geo. 2, insisting that they have nothing to do with the legality of the warrants, but that they ought to have been acquitted as officers within the meaning of that act.

[1045] The second defence stands upon the legality of the warrants; for this being a justification at common law, the officer is answerable if the magistrate has no jurisdiction.

These two defences have drawn several points into question, upon which the public, as well as the parties, have a right to our opinion.

Under the first, it is incumbent upon the officers to shew, that they are officers within the meaning of the act of parliament, and likewise that they have acted in obedience to the warrant.

The question, whether officers or not, involves another; whether the secretary of state, whose ministers they are, can be deemed a justice of the peace, or taken within the equity of the description; for officers and justices are here co-relative terms: therefore either both must be comprised, or both excluded.

This question leads me to an inquiry into the authority of that minister, as he stands described upon the record in two capacities, viz. secretary of state and privy counsellor. And since no statute has conferred any such jurisdiction as this before us, it must be given, if does really exist, by the common law; and upon this ground he has been treated as a conservator of the peace.

The matter thus opened, the questions that naturally arise upon the special verdict, are;

First, whether in either of these characters, or upon any other foundation, he is a conservator of the peace.

Secondly, admitting him to be so, whether he is within the equity of the 24th Geo 2.

These points being disposed of, the next in order is, whether the defendants have acted in obedience to the warrant.

In the last place, the great question upon the justification will be, whether the warrant to seize and carry away the plaintiff's papers is lawful.

First Question.

The power of this minister, in the way wherein it has been usually exercised, is pretty singular.

If he is considered in the light of a privy counsellor, although every member of that board is equally to it with himself, yet he is the only one of that body who exerts it. His power is so extensive in place, that it spreads throughout the whole realm; yet in the object it is so confined, that except in libels and some few state crimes, as they are called, the secretary of state does not pretend to the authority of a constable.

To consider him as a conservator. He never binds to the peace, or good behaviour, which seems to have been the principal duty of a conservator; at least he never does it in those cases, where the law requires those sureties. But he commits in certain other cases, where it is very doubtful, whether the conservator had any jurisdiction whatever.

His warrants are chiefly exerted against libellers, whom he binds in the first instance to [1046] their good behaviour, which no other conservator ever attempted, from the best intelligence that we can learn from our books.

And though he doth all these things, yet it seems agreed, that he hath no power whatsoever to administer an oath or take bail.

This jurisdiction, as extraordinary as I have described it, is so dark and obscure in its origin, that the counsel have not been able to form any certain opinion from whence it sprang.

Sometimes they annex it to the office of secretary of state, sometimes to the quality of privy counsellor; and in the last argument it has been derived from the king's royal prerogative to commit by his own personal command.

Whatever may have been the true source of this authority, it must be admitted, that at this day he is in the full legal exercise of it; because there has been not only a clear practice of it, at least since the Revolution, confirmed by a variety of precedents; but the authority has been recognized and confirmed by two cases in the very point since that period: and therefore we have not a power to unsettle or contradict it now, even though we are persuaded that the commencement of it was erroneous.

And yet, though the enquiry I am now upon cannot be attended with any consequence to the public, it is nevertheless indispensable; for I shall trace the power to its origin, in order to determine whether the person is within the equity of the 24th Geo. 2.

Before I argue upon that point, or even state the question, whether the secretary of state be within that act, we must know what he is. This is no very agreeable task, since it may possibly tend to create, in some minds, a doubt upon a practice that has been quietly submitted to, and which is of no moment to the liberty of the subject; for so long as the proceedings under these warrants are properly regulated by law, the public is very little concerned in the choice of that person by whom they are issued.

To proceed then upon the First Question, and to consider this person in the capacity of a secretary of state.

This officer is in truth the king's private secretary. He is keeper of the signet and seal used for the king's private letters, and backs the sign manual in transmitting grants to the privy seal. This seal is taken notice of in the Articuli super Chartas, cap. 6, and my lord Coke in his comment (2

Inst. 556,) upon that chapter, p. 556, describes the secretary as I have mentioned. He says he has four clerks, that sit at his board; and that the law in some cases takes notice of the signet; for a *ne exeat regno* may be by commandment under the privy seal, or under the signet; and in this case the subject ought to take notice of it; for it is but a signification of the king's commandment. If at the time my lord Coke wrote his 3d Institute he had been acquainted with the authority that is now ascribed to the secretary, he would certainly have mentioned it in this [1047] place. It was too important a branch of the office to be omitted; and his silence therefore is a strong argument, to a man's belief at least, that no such power existed at that time. He has likewise taken notice of this officer in the Prince's case in the 8th Report. He is mentioned in the statute of the 27th H. 8, chap. 11, and in the statute of the same king touching precedency; and it is observable, that he is called in these two statutes by the single name of secretary, without the addition, which modern times has given him, of the dignity of a state-officer.

I do not know, nor do I believe, that he was anciently a member of the privy council; but if he was, he was not even in the times of James and Charles the 1st, according to my lord Clarendon, an officer of such magnitude as he grew up to after the Restoration, being only employed, by this account, to make up dispatches at the conclusion of councils, and not to govern or preside in those councils.

It is not difficult to account for the growth of this minister's importance. He became naturally significant from the time that all the courts in Europe began to admit resident ambassadors; for upon the establishment of this new policy, that whole foreign correspondence passed through the secretary's hands, who by this means grew to be an instructed and confidential minister.

This being the true description of his employment, I see no part of it that requires the authority of a magistrate. The custody of a signet can imply no such thing; nay, the contrary would rather be inferred from the circumstance; because if his power to commit was inherent in his office, his warrants would naturally be stamped with that seal; and in this light the privy seal, one should think, would have had the preference, as being highest in dignity and of more consideration in law. Besides all this, it is not in my opinion consonant to the wisdom or analogy of our law, to give a power to commit, without a power to examine upon oath, which to this day the secretary of state doth not presume to exercise. Mr. Justice Rokeby, in the case of Kendall and Rowe, says, that the one is incident to the other; (5 Mod. 78,) and I am strongly of that opinion: for how can he commit, who is not able to examine upon oath?[4] What magistrate can be found, in

---

[4] See Leach's Hawkins's Pleas of the Crown, book 2, c. 16, s. 4.

our law, so defectively constituted? The only instance of this kind, that can be produced, is the practice of the House of Commons. But this instance is no precedent for other cases. The rights of that assembly are original and self created; they are paramount to our jurisdiction, and above the reach of injunction, prohibition, or error.[5] So that I still say, notwithstanding that particular case, there is no magistrate in our law so **[1048]** framed, unless the secretary of state be an exception. Now Mr. Justice Rokeby and myself, though we agree in the principle, form our conclusions in a very different manner. He from the assumed power of committing, which ought first to have been proved, infers the incidental powers of administering an oath. I on the contrary, from the admitted incapacity to do the latter, am strongly inclined to deny the former.

Again, if the secretary of state is a common law magistrate, one should naturally expect to find some account of this in our books, whereas his very name is unknown; and there cannot be a stronger argument against his authority in that light, than the unsuccessful attempts that have been made at the bar to transform him into a conservator. These attempts have given us the trouble of looking into those books that have preserved the memory of these magistrates, who have been long since deceased and forgotten. Fitz-herbert, Crompton, Lambard, Dalton, Pulton, and Bacon, have all been searched to see, if any such person could be found amongst the old conservators. It is not material to repeat the whole number, and to range them in their several classes; but it will be sufficient to enumerate the principal ones; because they may be referred to in some other part of the argument.

The king is mentioned as the first. Then come the chancellor, the treasurer, the high steward, the master of the rolls, the chief justice and the justices of the King's-bench, all the judges in their several courts, sheriffs, coroners, constables; and some are said to be conservators by tenure, some by pre-scription, and others by commission. But no secretary of state is to be found in the catalogue; and I do affirm, that no treatise, case, record, or statute, has ever called him a conservator, from the beginning of time down to the case of the King against Kendall and Rowe.[6]

The first time, he appears in our books to be a granter of our warrants, is in 1 Leonard 70 and 71, 29 and 30 Elizabeth, where the return to a Habeas Corpus was a commitment by sir Francis Walsingham, principal secretary, and one of the privy council. The Court takes this distinction. Where a person is committed by one of the privy council, in such case the cause of the commitment should be set down in the return; but on the contrary, where the party is committed by the whole council, there no cause need be alleged. The Court upon this ordered the return to be amended, and then the return is a commitment by the whole council.

---

[5] Ibid. Book 2, c. 15, s. 73.
[6] See Leach's Hawkins's Pleas of the Crown, book 1, c.60, s.1.

There is a like case in the 2 Leonard, p. 175, a little prior in point of time, where the commitment is by sir Francis Walsingham, one of the principal secretaries, &c. Because the warden of the Fleet did not return for what cause Helliard was committed, the Court gives [1049] him day to mend his return, or otherwise the prisoner should be delivered. Nobody who reads this case can doubt, but that the &c. must be supplied by the addition of privy counsellor, as in the other case.

These authorities shew, that the judges of those days knew of no such committing magistrate as a secretary of state. They pay no regard to that office, but treat the commitment as the act of the privy counsellor only; and to shew farther that the privy counsellor as such was the only acting magistrate in state matters, all the twelve judges two years afterwards were obliged to remonstrate against the irregularities of their commitments, but take no notice of any such authorities practised by the secretaries of state.

In the 3d year of king Charles the 1st, when the House of Commons started that famous dispute, upon the right claimed by the king and the privy council to commit without shewing cause, it is natural to expect, that the secretary's warrant should have been handled, or at least named among the state commitments. But there is not throughout that long and learned discussion one word said about him, or his name so much as mentioned; and the Petition of Right, as well as all the proceedings that produced it, is equally silent upon the subject.

Again, when in the 16th year in the same king's reign the Habeas Corpus was granted by act of parliament (16 Cha. 1, c. 10, s. 8,) upon all the state commitments, and where the omission of one mode of committing would have been fatal to the subject, and frustrated all the remedy of that act, and where they have enumerated not only every method of committing that had been exercised, but every other that might probably exist in after times; yet the commitment by a secretary of state is not found amongst the number. If then he had power of his own to commit, this famous act of parliament was waste paper, and the subject still at the mercy of the crown, without the benefit of the Habeas Corpus; a supposition altogether incredible: for who can believe, that this parliament, so jealous, so learned, so industrious, so enthusiastic of the liberty of the subject, when they were making a law to relieve prisoners against the power of the crown, should bind the king, and leave his secretary of state at large?

Whoever attends to all these observations will see clearly, that the secretary of state in those days never exercised the power of committing in his own right; I say, in his own right, because that he did in fact commit, and that frequently even at the time when the matter of the Habeas Corpus was agitated in the 3d of king Charles the 1st, will appear from a passage in the Ephemeris Parliamentaria, page 162. This passage, when it comes to be attended to, will throw great light upon the present enquiry. It is sufficient of itself to convince me, from what source this practice first arose. It was from a delegation of the king's [1050] royal prerogative to commit by his own power, and from the king devolved in point of execution upon the secretary of state. The passage I allude to is a speech of secretary Cook.

Whilst the parliament were disputing the king's authority to commit, either by himself or by his council, without shewing the cause, the king, who was desirous to pacify those discontents, and yet unwilling to part with his prerogative, sent a message to the House of Commons to assure them, that is they would drop the business, he would promise them, upon his royal word, not to use this prerogative contrary to law. Secretary Cook delivers this message, and then the book proceeds in these words. After speaking of himself and the nature of his place, he says, "Give me leave freely to tell you, that I know by experience, that by the place I hold under his majesty, if I will discharge the duty of my place and the oath I have taken to his majesty, I must commit, and neither express the cause to the goaler, nor to the judges, nor to any counsellor in England, but to the king himself. Yet do not think, I go without ground of reason, or take this power committed to me to be unlimited. Yea rather to me it is charge, burthen, and danger; for if I by this power commit the poorest porter, if I do not upon a just cause, if it may appear, the burthen will fall upon me heavier than the law can inflict; for I shall lose my credit with his majesty and my place: and I beseech you consider, whether those that have been in the same place, have not committed freely, and not any doubt made of it, or any complaint made by the subject."

To understand the meaning of this speech, I must briefly remind you of the nature of that famous struggle for the liberty of the subject between the crown and the parliament, which was then in agitation.

The points in controversy were these: whether a subject committing by the king's personal command, or by warrant of the privy council, ought to express the cause in the warrant, and whether the subject in that case was bailable.

The matter in dispute was confined to those two commitments. The crown claimed no such right for any other warrant; nor did the Commons demand redress against any other. The statute of Westminster the first, which was admitted on all sides to be the only foundation upon which the pretensions of the crown were built, speaks of no other arrests in the text, but the king's arrest only; and the comment of law had never added any other arrest by construction, but that only of the privy council. No other commitment whatever was deemed by any man to be within the equity of that act. The case, cited upon that occasion, speaks of no other commitments but these. Nay the House of Lords, who passed a resolution in the heat of this business in favour of the king's authority, resolves only, that the king or his council could commit, but meddle with no other commitment. Secretary Cook tells them [1051] in this public manner, that he made a daily practice of committing without shewing the cause; yet the House takes no notice of any secretary's warrant as such, nor is the secretary's name mentioned in the course of all those proceedings. What then were those commitments mentioned by the secretary? They were certainly such only, as were 'per speciale mandatum domini regis.' They could be no other. They were the commitments then under debate. They, and they only, were referred to by the king's message, and were consequently the subject matter of the secretary's apology; for no other warrant claimed that extraordinary privilege of concealing the cause.

This observation explains him, when he calls it a power committed to him; which I construe, not as annexed to his office, but specially delegated. This accounts too for his notion, that the law could not touch him; but that if he abused his trust, he should lose his credit with the king and his place, which he describes as a heavier punishment than the law could inflict upon him. Upon this ground it will be easy to explain the notable singularities of this minister's proceeding, which are not to be reconciled to any idea of a common-law magistrate. Such are his meddling only with a few state-offences, his reach over the whole kingdom, his committing without the power of administering an oath, his employment of none but the messenger of the king's chamber, and his command to mayors, justices, sheriffs, &c. to assist him; all which particularities are congruous enough to the idea of the king's personal warrant, but utterly inconsistent with all the principles of magistracy in a subject.

If on the other hand it can be understood, that he could and did commit without shewing the cause in his own right and by virtue of his office, then was his warrant admitted to be legal by the whole House, and without censure or animadversion. It was neither condemned by the Petition of Right, nor subject to the Habeas Corpus Act of 16th of Charles the First, (c.10.)

The truth of the case was no more than this. The council-board were too numerous to be acquainted with every secret transaction that required immediate confinement; and the delay by summoning was inconvenient in cases that required dispatch. The secretary of state, as most entrusted, was the fittest hand to issue sudden warrants; and therefore we find him so employed by queen Elizabeth under the quality of a privy counsellor. But when the attempt failed, the judges declaring, that he must shew the cause, and that they would remand none of his prisoners in any case but that of high treason, those warrants ceased, and then a new method was taken by making him the instrument of the king's *speciale mandatum*; for that is the form in which all warrants and returns were drawn, that were produced upon that famous argument.

Having thus shewn, not only negatively that this power of committing was not annexed to [1052] the secretary's office, but affirmatively likewise that he was notifier or countersigner of the king's personal warrant acting *in alio jure* down to the times of the 16th of Charles the first, and consequently to the Restoration, for there was no secretary in that interval, I have but little to add upon this head, but observing what passed between that time and the case of Kendall and Rowe.

The Licensing Act, that took place in the 13th and 14th of Charles the Second, (c.33) gave him his first right to issue a warrant in his own name; not indeed to commit persons but a warrant to search for papers. Whether upon this new power he grafted any authority to commit persons in his own right, as it should seem he did by the precedent produced the other day, is not very material. But it is remarkable, that during that interval he adhered in some cases to the old form, by specifying the express command of the king in this warrant.

With respect to the cases that have passed since the Revolution, such as the King against Kendall and Rowe, the Queen against Darby, and the King and Earbery, I shall take no other notice of them in this place, than to say, they afford no light in the present inquiry by shewing the ground of the officer's authority, though they are strong cases to confirm it.

But before I can fairly conclude, that the secretary of state's power was derived from the king's personal prerogative and from no other origin, I must examine, what has passed relative to the power of a separate privy counsellor in this respect. This is the more necessary to be done, because my lord chief justice Holt has built all his authority upon this ground; and the subsequent cases, instead of striking out any new light upon the subject, do all lean upon and support themselves by my lord chief justice Holt's opinion in the case of Kendall and Rowe.

I will therefore fairly state all that I have been able to discover touching the matter; and then, after I have declared my own opinion, shall leave others to judge for themselves.

In the first place it is proper to observe, that a privy counsellor cannot derive his authority from the statute of Westminster the first; which recites an arrest by the command of the king to be one of those cases that were irrepleviseable by common law. The principal commentator upon these words is Staundford, (Pl. fo. 72, b.) who says, as to the commandment of the king, this is to be understood of the commandment of his own mouth, or of his council, which is incorporate to him, and speaks with the mouth of the king himself; for otherwise, if you will take these words of commandment generally, you may say that every Capias in a personal action is the command of the king. Lambard in his chapter of Bailment, where he cites this act of parliament, gives it the same construction, by allowing a commitment by the council to be within the equity of these words, "commandment [1053] of the king." (Lamb. Eirenarch, & b. 3, c. 2, p. 335.) Thus far, and no further, did the crown lawyers in the third of king Charles the first endeavour to extend the text of the law; and it is plain from the cases before cited, that the judges in queen Elizabeth's time were of the same opinion, that the argument could not be extended in favour of the single counsellor; because they held, that he is bound to shew the cause upon his warrant, as distinguished from the other warrants, where they admit the cause need not be shewn.

If he is not then entitled by this statute, is he empowered by the common law? They, who contend he is, would do well to shew some authority in proof of their opinion. It is clear, he is not numbered among the conservators. It is as clear, that he is not mentioned by any book as one of the ordinary magistrates of justice with any such general authority.

The first place, in which any thing of this kind is to be found, is in the year-book of Henry the sixth, where the sheriff returns a detainer under the warrant of 'duos de concilio pro rebus regem tangentibus.' This proof has an unlucky defect in it; because the reading is doubtful, the word *dnos* as it is written standing as well for *dominos*, as for *duos*; so that till the reading is settled, which is beyond my skill, the authority must be suspended.

The next time you meet with a privy counsellor in the light of a magistrate is in the first of Edward the sixth, chap. 12, s. 19, where one of the privy council is empowered to take the accusation in some new treasons therein mentioned; and he is for this purpose joined with the justice of assize and justice of the peace. The like power is given to him by the 5th and 6th of the same king, c. 11, s. 10, in a like case; and I find in Kelyng, p. 19, that when the judges met to resolve certain points before the trial of the Regicides, they resolved, that a confession upon examination before a privy counsellor, though he be not a justice of the peace, is a confession within the meaning of the statute of the 5th and 6th of Edward the 6th. That act of parliament in the twelfth section had provided, that no person should be attainted of treason, but upon the testimony of two lawful accusers, unless the said party arraigned should willingly without violence confess the same.

It seems to me, that the ground upon which the judges proceeded in this resolution, was the express power given to the privy council in the clause next but one before that just mentioned, where the act enables them to take the accusation in the new treasons there mentioned.

Whether they reasoned in that way, or whether they conceived that the power there given was a proof of some like power which they enjoyed to take accusation in the case of treasons at the common law, the book has not explained; so that hitherto this authority in the case of high treason stands upon a very poor foundation, being in truth no more than a conjecture of law without authority to support it.

[1054] The next authorities are the cases already recited in Leonard, which to the present point prove nothing more than this; that the judges do admit a power in a privy counsellor to commit without specifying in what cases. They demand the cause, and a better return; whereupon sir Francis Walsingham, instead of relying upon his power as privy counsellor, returns a new warrant signed by the whole board.

Two years after this came forth that famous resolution of all the judges, which is reported in 1 Anderson 297, 34th of Elizabeth. There is no occasion to observe, how arbitrary the prerogative grew, and how fast it increased toward the end of this queen's reign. It seems to me, as if the privilege claimed by the king's personal warrant, and from him derived to the council-board, by construction, had some-how or other been adopted by every individual of that board; for in fact these warrants became so frequent and oppressive, that the courts of justice were obliged at last to interpose.

However they might be overborne by the terror of the king's special command either in or out of council, they had courage enough to resist the novel encroachments of the separate members; and therefore they did in the courts of King's-bench and Common Pleas set at large many persons so committed; upon which occasion a question being put to the judges, to specify in what cases the prisoner was to be remanded, they answer the question with a remonstrance of their own against the illegal warrants granted by the privy counsellors. The preamble relates entirely to these commitments, wherein they desire, that some good order may be taken, that her highness's subjects may not be committed or detained in prison by commandment of any nobleman, against the laws of the realm.

The question is this: In what cases prisoners sent to custody by her majesty, her council, or any one or more of her council, are to be detained in prison, and not to be delivered by her majesty's courts or judges.

The answer is, "We think, that if any person be committed by her majesty's command from her person, or by order from the council-board, or if any one or two of her council commit one for high treason, such persons so in the case before committed may not be delivered by any of her courts without due trial by the law and judgment of acquittal had. Nevertheless the judges may award the queen's writs to bring the bodies of such persons before them; and if upon return thereof the causes of their commitment be certified to the judges, as it ought to be, then the judges in the cases before ought not to deliver him, but to remand the prisoner to the place from whence he came; which cannot conveniently be done, unless notice of the causes in generality, or else specially, be given to the keeper or goaler that shall have the custody of such prisoner."

There is a studied obscurity in this opinion, which shews, how cautious the judges were obliged to be in those dangerous times; for [1055] whether they meant to acknowledge a general power in the king or his council to commit, as distinguished from a special power in one or more of his council to commit, only in the case of high treason; or whether this case of high treason is to be referred to all the commitments as the only unbailable case; or again, whether in the superior commitment by the royal person or his council, they would deliver the prisoner though no cause was specified; or if one of the council committed for offences below high treason where they declare they would not remand, yet whether they would absolutely discharge or only upon bail; is altogether either ambiguous or uncertain.

It is evident to me, that the judges did not intend to be understood touching these matters; and the only propositions, that are clearly laid down in this resolution, are these:

First, that they would never remand upon the counsellor's commitment but in high-treason.

Secondly, that the cause ought to be shewed in all cases.

This resolution grew to be much agitated afterwards in the third of Charles the first, and had the honour, like other dark oracles, to be cited on both sides.

Thus much it was necessary to observe upon this famous opinion; because it was upon this opinion, that lord chief justice Holt principally relied. At this time it is apparent, that all the privy counsellors exercised this right in common. Whatever it was, the complaint shews, it was a general practice, and a privilege enjoyed by all the menbers of that board; from whence it is natural to suppose, that if the power was well founded, the same practice would have continued to this time in the same way, seeing how tenacious all men are of those things that are called rights and privileges. Instead of this it doth not appear, that the council from that æra have ever asserted their rights; and now at last, when the secretary of state has revived the claim, for the common benefit, as it should seem, of the whole body, no other person has followed this example, or knows to this moment that he is entitled to such right. Any body who considers what the consequence must have been from these determinations of the judges, might venture to affirm, that the privy counsellor's warrant from this period ceased and grew out of use; for as the cause in this case was necessary to be specified, and the prisoner was never to be remanded but in the case of high treason, that warrant became at once unserviceable, and the crown was forced to resort to the royal mandate or the board-warrant, which, notwithstanding the case in Anderson, was still insisted to be unbailable and good without a cause.

Hence happened, that in the great debate in the third of king Charles the first, no privy counsellor's warrants do once occur; but instead thereof you find the secretary of state dealing forth the king's royal mandate, and the privy counsellor's authority at rest.

[1056] The only reason, why I touch upon these proceedings, is for the sake of observing, that no notice is taken in those arguments of the privy counsellor's right to commit; and yet the power of the king himself, and of his council, by the statute of Westminster the first, is largely discussed, and so fully handled, that if the warrant of one privy counsellor had then been in use, it must have been brought forth in the argument; for if it could have served no other purpose, it would have been material, in order to mark the distinction between that and the warrant of the whole board.

From these observations I conclude, that these warrants were then deceased and gone, and would probably have never made their appearance again even in description, if the bill in the 16th of Charles the first, c. 10, had not recalled them to memory, not as things either then in use or admitted to be legal, but as one of the modes of commitment which might be again revived because it had been formerly practised.[7] Therefore when this form of warrant appears, as it does in the catalogue of other forms, both legal and illegal, no argument can be raised from a pretended recognition of this particular warrant; since it was necessary to name every mode, that ever had been used by the king, the council, or the Star-Chamber, in order to make the remedy by Habeas Corpus universal.

But if there can be a doubt, whether this act of parliament is to be deemed a recognition of this authority, there is a passage in the Journal of the House of Commons, that proves the contrary in direct terms.

Whilst this bill was passing, the House makes an amendment, which appears by the question put to be this, whether the House should assent to the putting the word 'liberties' out of the bill.

But as the passage in the bill is not mentioned in the Journals, it must be collected by inferences. By the phrase 'left out of the bill,' I presume it was permitted to stand in the preamble. Now when you look into the preamble, the word 'liberties' is there to be found in that part of the preamble which recites this usurpation of the privy council upon the liberties, as well as the properties of the subject; whereas the enacting clause condemns only the jurisdiction of that board, so far as it assumed a jurisdiction over the property of the subject; from whence I collect that the word 'liberties' stood in that clause; and the passage that follows in the Journal does strongly confirm it.

The words are these: "Resolved upon the question, that this House does assent to the putting the word 'liberties' out of the bill concerning the Star-Chamber and Council pleadings; because the House has a bill to be drawn to provide for the liberty of the subject in a large manner. Mr. Serjeant Wild and Mr. Whitelock are appointed to draw a bill to that [1057] purpose upon the several points that have been here this day debated."

"Resolved upon the question, that the body of the lords of the council, nor any one of them in particular as a privy-counsellor, has any power to imprison any free-born subject, except in such cases as they are warranted by the statutes of the realm."

It is pretty plain from this passage, that the debate turned upon the meaning of the statute of Westminster the first, and the resolution of the judges in Anderson, about which it is not fit to give any opinion; my design by citing this passage being only to shew, that this act of parliament does not even prove the actual practice of such warrants at that time, much less does recognize their legality.

---

[7] See Leach's Hawkins's Pleas of the Crown, book 2, c. 15, s. 71.

What follows is still more remarkable touching this business, upon a doubt started in the trial of the Seven Bishops.[8] They were committed by a warrant signed by no less than thirteen privy counsellors; but the warrant did not appear to be signed by them in council. The objection taken was, that the warrant was void, being signed only by the privy counsellors separately, and not in a body. If any man in Westminster-hall at that time had understood, that one or more privy counsellors had a right to commit for a misdemeanor, that would have been a flat answer to the objection; but they are so far from insisting upon this, that all the king's counsellors, as well as the Court, do admit the warrant would have been void, if it could be taken to be executed by them out of council.

The solicitor-general upon that occasion cites the 16th of Charles the first, which statute is produced and read, and yet no argument is taken from thence to prove the authority of the separate lords, though the act is before them. Mr. Pollexfen in the course of the debate says, 'We do all pretty well agree, for aught I can perceive, in two things. We do not deny, but that the council-board has power to commit. They on the other side do not affirm, that the lords of the council can commit out of the council.'

Attorney General. 'Yes, they may as justices of the peace.'

Pollexfen. 'This is not pretended to be so here.'

L. C. J. 'No, no, that is not the case.'

The Court at last got rid of the objection, by presuming the warrant to have been executed in council.

There cannot be a stronger authority than this I have now cited for the present purpose. The whole body of the law, if I may use the phrase, were as ignorant at that time of a privy counsellor's right to commit in the case of a libel, as the whole body of privy counsellors are at this day.

The counsel on both sides in that cause were the ablest of their time, and few times have produced abler. They had been concerned in [1058] all the state-cases during the whole reign of king Charles the second, on one side or the other; and to suppose that all these persons could be utterly ignorant of this extraordinary power, if it had been either legal or even practised, is a supposition not to be maintained.

This is the whole that I have been able to find, touching the power of one or more privy counsellors to commit; and to sum up the whole of this business in a word it stands thus:

The two cases in Leonard do pre-suppose some power in a privy counsellor to commit, without saying what; and the case in Anderson does plainly recognize such a power in high treason: but with respect to his jurisdiction in other offences, I do not find it was either claimed or exercised.

In consequence of all this reasoning, I am forced to deny the opinion of my lord chief justice Holt to be law, if it shall be taken to extend beyond the

[8] See this Case, vol. 12, p. 183.

case of high treason. But there is no necessity to understand the book in a more general sense; nor is it fair indeed to give the words a more large construction: for as the conclusion ought always to be grounded on the premisses, and the premisses are confined to the case of high treason only, the opinion should naturally conform to the cases cited, more especially as the case there before the Court was a case of high treason, and they were under no necessity to lay down the doctrine larger than the case required.–Now whereas it has been argued, that if you admit a power of committing in high treason, the power of committing in lesser offences follows *a fortiori*; I beg leave to deny that consequence, for I take the rule with respect to all special authorities to be directly the reverse. They are always strictly confined to the letter; and when I see therefore, that a special power in any single case only has been permitted to a person, who in no other instance is known or recorded by the common law as a magistrate, I have no right to enlarge his authority one step beyond that case. Consider how strange it would sound, if I should declare at once, that every privy counsellor without exception is invested with a power to commit in all offences without exception from high treason down to trespass, when it is clear that he is not a conservator. It might be said of me, 'he should have explained himself a little more clearly, and told us where he had found the description of so singular a magistrate, who being no conservator was yet in the nature of a conservator.'

I have now finished all I have to say upon this head; and am satisfied, that the secretary of state hath assumed this power as a transfer, I know not how, of the royal authority to himself; and that the common law of England knows no such magistrate. At the same time I declare, wherein my brothers do all agree with me, that we are bound to adhere to the determination of the Queen against Derby, and the King against Earbury; and I have no right to [1059] overturn those decisions, even though it should be admitted, that the practice, which has subsisted since the Revolution, had been erroneous in its commencement.

The secretary of state having now been considered in the two lights of secretary and privy counsellor, and likewise as the substitute of the royal mandate; in the two first he is clearly no conservator; in the last, if he can be supposed to have borrowed the right of conservatorship from the sovereign himself, yet no one will argue or pretend, that so great a person, one so high in authority, can be deemed a justice of the peace within the equity of the 24th of Geo. 2.

However, I will for a time admit the secretary of state to be a conservator, in order to examine, whether in that character he can be within the equity of this act.

Second Question.

Upon this question, I shall take into consideration the 7th of James 1, c. 5, because though it is not material upon this record to determine, whether the special evidence can be admitted under the general issue of not guilty, the defendant having in this instance justified; yet as that act is made in *eadem materia*, and for the benefit of the same person, the rule of construction observed in that will in great measure be an authority of this.

The 24th of Geo. 2 is entitled, 'An act for the rendering justices of the peace more safe in the execution of their offices, and for indemnifying constables and others acting in obedience to their warrants.' The preamble runs thus: 'Whereas justices of the peace are discouraged in the execution of their offices, by vexatious actions brought against them, for or by reason of small and involuntary errors in their proceedings; and whereas it is necessary that they should be, as far as is consistent with justice and the safety and liberty of the subjects over whom their authority extends, rendered safe in the execution of the said office and trust; and whereas it is also necessary, that the subject should be protected from all willful and oppressive abuse of the several laws committed to the care and execution of the justices of the peace.' Then comes the enacting part.

The only granter of the warrant in the enacting part, as well as the preamble, is the justice of the peace. The officers, as they are described, are constables, headboroughs, and other officers or persons acting by their order, or in their aid. If any person acting in obedience to such warrant, and producing the said warrant upon demand, is afterwards prosecuted for such act, the statute says, he shall be acquitted, upon the production of such warrant. The counsel for the defendants say, the secretary and the messengers are both within the equity of this act. The first is a justice of the peace, because he is a conservator. If so the latter is his officer, which I will admit. The proposition then is, [1060] that conservators are within the equity of this act. They are clearly not within the letter; for justice and conservator are not convertible terms; and though it should be admitted, that a justice of the peace is still a conservator, yet a conservator is not a justice.

The defendants have argued upon two rules of construction, which in truth are but one.

First, where in a general act a particular is put as an example, all other persons of like description shall be comprized.

Secondly, where the words of a statute enact a thing, it enacts all other things in like degree.

In Plowden 37, and 167, and 467, several cases are cited as authorities under these rules of construction; as, that the bishop of Norwich in one act shall mean all bishops; that the warden of the Fleet shall mean all goalers; that justices of a division mean all justices of the country at large, that guardian in socage after the heir's attaining fourteen, shall be a bailiff in account; that executors shall include administrators, and tenant for years a tenant for one year or any less time; with several other instances to the like purpose.

In the first place, though the general rule be true enough, that where it is clear the person or thing expressed is put by way of example, the judges must fill up the catalogue; yet we ought to be sure, from the words and meaning of the act itself, that the thing or person is really inserted as an example.

This is a very inaccurate way of penning a law; and the instances of this sort are scarce ever to be found, except in some of the old acts of parliament. And wherever this rule is to take place, the act must be general, and the thing expressed must be particular; such as those cases of the warden of the Fleet and the bishop of Norwich; whereas the act before us is equally general in all its parts, and requires no addition or supply to give it the full effect. Therefore if this way of arguing can be maintained by either of the rules, it must fall under the second, which is, that where the words of a statute enact a thing, it enacts all other things in like degree.

In all cases that fall within this rule, there must be a perfect resemblance between the persons or things expressed and those implied. Thus for instance, administrators are the same thing with executors; tenant for half a year and tenant for years have both terms for a chattel interest, differing only in the duration of the term; and so of the rest, which I need not repeat one by one: and in all these cases, the persons or things to be implied are in all respects the objects of the law as much as those expressed. Does not every body see from hence, that you must first examine the law before you can apply the rule of construction? For the law must not be bent by the construction, but that must be adapted to the spirit and sense of the law. The fundamental rule then, by which all others are to be tried, is laid down in Wimbish and Tailbois, Plowden 57, 58, according [1061] to which the best guide is to follow the intent of the statutes. Again, according to Plowden, p. 205 and 231, the construction is to be collected out of the words according to the true intent and meaning of the act, and the intent of the makers may be collected from the cause or necessity of making the act, or by foreign circumstances.

Let us try the present case by these rules; and let the justice of the peace stand for a moment in this act as a magistrate at large; and then compare him as he is here described with the conservator.

The justice here is a magistrate intrusted with the execution of many laws, liable to actions for involuntary errors, and actually discouraged by vexatious suits; in respect of which perilous situation he is intended to be rendered more safe in the execution of his office.–He is besides a magistrate, who acts by warrant directed to constables and other officers, namely, known officers who are bound to execute his warrants.

Now take the conservator.–He is intrusted with the execution of no laws; if the word 'law' is understood to mean statutes, as I apprehend it is.–He is liable to no actions, because he never acts; the keeping of the peace being so completely transferred to and so engrossed by the justice, that the name of conservator is almost forgot. He is far from being discouraged by actions. No man ever heard of an action brought against a conservator as such;

unless you will call a constable a conservator, which will not serve the present purpose, because these persons can hardly be deemed justices within the act.–Again, how does it appear, that the conservator could either grant a warrant like the present, or command a constable to execute it? These powers are at least very doubtful; but I think I may take it for granted, that the conservator could not command a messenger of the king's chamber.

Did then this act of parliament refer to magistrates of known authority and daily employment, or to antiquated powers and persons known to have existed by historical tradition only? Did it mean it redress real grievances, or those that were never felt? 'Ad ea, quæ frequenter accidunt, jura adaptantur.'

From this comparison it may appear, how little there is to drag the conservator into the law, who hardly corresponds with the justice of the peace in any one point of the description. But further, it is unfortunate for the conservators upon this question, that one half of them are the objects of the statute by name, as constables, &c. and yet not one of their acts as conservators is within the provision.

And now give me leave to ask one question. Will the secretary of state be classed with the higher or the lower conservator? If with the higher, such as the king, the chancellor, &c. he is too much above the justice to be within the equity. If with the lower, he is too much below him. And as to the sheriff and the coroner, they cannot be within the law; because [1062] they never grant such warrants as these. So that at last, upon considering all the conservators, there is not one that does not stand most evidently excluded, unless the secretary of state himself shall be excepted.

But if there wanted arguments to confute this pretension, the construction that has prevailed upon the seventh of James the first, would decide the point. That is an act of like kind to relieve justices of the peace, mayors, constables, and certain other officers, in troublesome actions brought against them for the legal execution of their offices; who are enabled by that act to plead the general issue. Now that law has been taken so strictly, that neither church-wardens, nor overseers, were held to be within the equity of the word 'constables,' although they were clearly officers, and acted under the justice's warrants. Why? Because that act, being made to change the course of the common law, could not be extended beyond the letter. If then that privilege of giving the special matter in evidence upon the general issue is contrary to the common law, how much more substantially is this act an innovation of the common law, which indemnifies the officer upon the production of the warrant, and deprives the subject of his right of action?

It is impossible, that two acts of parliament can be more nearly allied or connected with one another, than that of 24 George 2, and the 7th of James 1. The objects in both are the same, and the remedies are similar in both, each of them changing the common law for the benefit of the parties concerned. The one, in truth, is the sequel or second part of the other. The first not being an adequate remedy in case of the several persons therein mentioned, the second is added to complete the work, and to make them as secure as they ought to be made from the nature of the case. If by a contrary construction any person should be admitted into the last that are not included in that first, the person, whoever he is, will be without the privilege of pleading the general issue, and giving the special matter in evidence, which the latter would have certainly given by express words, if the parliament could have imagined he was not comprized in the first.

Upon the whole, we are all of the opinion, that neither secretary of state, nor the messenger, are within the meaning of this act of parliament.

Third Question.

But if they were within the general equity, yet it behoved the messenger to shew, that they have acted in obedience to the warrant; for it is upon that condition, that they are intitled to the exemption of the act. When the legislature excused the officer from the perilous task of judging, they compelled him to an implicit obedience; which was but reasonable: so that now he must follow the dictates of his warrant, being no longer obliged to inquire, whether his superior had or had not any jurisdiction. The late decision of the Court of [1063] King's-bench in the Case of General Warrants[9] was ruled upon this ground and rightly determined.

This part of the case is clear, and shall be dispatched in very few words.

First, the defendants did not take with them a constable, which is a flat objection. They had no business to dispute either the propriety or the legality of this direction in the execution of the warrant; nor have their counsel any right to dispute it here in their behalf. They can have no other plea under this act of parliament, than ignorance and obedience.

Secondly, they did not bring the papers to the earl of Halifax, to be examined according to the tenor of the warrant, but to Mr. Lovell Stanhope. This command ought to have been literally pursued; nor is it any excuse to say now, as they do in their plea, that Mr. Lovell Stanhope was an assistant to the earl of Halifax. If he is a magistrate, he can have no assistant, nor deputy, to execute any part of that employment. The right is personal to himself, and a trust that he can no more delegate to another, than a justice of the peace can transfer his commission to his clerk.

I shall say no more upon this head. But I cannot help observing, that the secretary of state, who has not been many years intrusted with this authority, has already eased himself of every part of it, except the signing and sealing the warrant. The law clerk, as he is called, examines both persons

---

[9] Money and others against Leach, Mich. 6 Geo. 3, *ante*, p.1002.

and papers. He backs or discharges. This is not right. I could wish for the future, that the secretary would discharge this part of his office in his own person.

Fourth and Last Question.

The question that arises upon the special verdict being now dispatched, I come in my past place to the point, which is made by the justification; for the defendants, having failed in the attempt made to protect themselves by the statute of the 24th of Geo. 2, are under a necessity to maintain the legality of the warrants, under which they have acted, and to shew that the secretary of state in the instance now before us, had a jurisdiction to seize the defendants' papers. If he had no such jurisdiction, the law is clear, that the officers are as much responsible for the trespass as their superior.

This, though it is not the most difficult, is the most interesting question in the cause; because if this point should be determined in favour of the jurisdiction, the secret cabinets and bureaus of every subject in this kingdom will be thrown open to the search and inspection of a messenger, whenever the secretary of state shall think fit to charge, or even to suspect, a person to be the author, printer, or publisher of a seditious libel.

The messenger, under this warrant, is commanded to seize the person described, and to bring him with his papers to be examined before [1064] the secretary of state. In consequence of this, the house must be searched; the lock and doors of every room, box, or trunk must be broken open; all the papers and books without exception, if the warrant be executed according to its tenor, must be seized and carried away; for it is observable, that nothing is left either to the discretion or to the humanity of the officer.

This power so assumed by the secretary of state is an execution upon all the party's papers, in the first instance. His house is rifled; his most valuable secrets are taken out of his possession, before the paper for which he is charged is found to be criminal by any competent jurisdiction, and before he is convicted either of writing, publishing, or being concerned in the paper.

This power, so claimed by the secretary of state, is not supported by one single citation from any law book extant. It is claimed by no other magistrate in this kingdom but himself: the great executive hand of criminal justice, the lord chief justice of the court of King's-Bench, chief justice Scroggs excepted, never having assumed this authority.

The arguments, which the defendants' counsel have thought fit to urge in support of this practice, are of this kind.

That such warrants have issued frequently since the Revolution, which practice has been found by the special verdict; though I must observe, that the defendants have no right to avail themselves of that finding, because no such practice is averred in their justification.

That the case of the warrants bears a resemblance to the case of search for stolen goods.

They say too, that they have been executed without resistance upon many printers, booksellers, and authors, who have quietly submitted to the authority; that no action hath hitherto been brought to try the right; and that although they have been often read upon the returns of Habeas Corpus, yet no court of justice has ever declared them illegal.

And it is further insisted, that this power is essential to government, and the only means of quieting clamors and sedition.

These arguments, if they can be called arguments, shall be all taken notice of; because upon this question I am desirous of removing every colour or plausibility.

Before I state the question, it will be necessary to describe the power claimed by this warrant in its full extent.

If honestly exerted, it is a power to seize that man's papers, who is charged upon oath to be the author or publisher of a seditious libel; if oppressively, it acts against every man, who is so described in the warrant, though he be innocent.

It is executed against the party, before he is heard or even summoned; and the information, as well as the informers, is unknown.

It is executed by messengers with or without a constable (for it can never be pretended, that such is necessary in point of law) in the presence or the absence of the party, as the [1065] messengers shall think fit, and without a witness to testify what passes at the time of the transaction; so that when the papers are gone, as the only witnesses are the trespassers, the party injured is left without proof.[10]

If this injury falls upon an innocent person, he is as destitute of remedy as the guilty: and the whole transaction is so guarded against discovery, that if the officer should be disposed to carry off a bank-bill he may do it with impunity, since there is no man capable of proving either the taker or the thing taken.

It must not be here forgot that no subject whatsoever is privileged from this search; because both Houses of Parliament have resolved, that there is no privilege in the case of a seditious libel.

---

[10] "If a private person suspect another of felony, and lay such ground of suspicion before a constable, and require his assistance to take him, the constable may justify killing the party if he fly, though in truth he were innocent. But in such case, where no hue and cry is levied, certain precautions must be observed: 1. The party suspecting ought to be present; for the justification is, that the constable did aid him in taking the party suspected. 2. The constable ought to be informed of the grounds of suspicion, that he may judge the reasonableness of it. From whence it should seem that there ought to be a reasonable ground shewn for it: otherwise it would be immaterial whether such information were given to the constable or not, as to the point of his justification. And it was formerly supposed to be necessary, that there should have been a felony committed in fact, of which the constable must have been ascertained at his peril." East's Pleas of the Crown, ch. 5, s. 69.

Nor is there pretence to say, that the word 'papers' here mentioned ought in point of law to be restrained to the libellous papers only. The word is general, and there is nothing in the warrant to confine it; nay, I am able to affirm, that it has been upon a late occasion executed in its utmost latitude: for in the case of Wilkes against Wood, when the messengers hesitated about taking all the manuscripts, and sent to the secretary of state for more express orders for that purpose, the answer was, "that all must be taken, manuscripts and all." Accordingly, all was taken, and Mr. Wilkes's private pocket-book filled up the mouth of the sack.

I was likewise told in the same cause by one of the most experienced messengers, that he held himself bound by his oath to pay an implicit obedience to the commands of the secretary of state; that in common cases he was contented to seize the printed impressions of the papers mentioned in the warrant; but when he received directions to search further, or to make a more general seizure, his rule was to sweep all. The practice has been correspondent to the warrant.

Such is the power, and therefore one should [1066] naturally expect that the law to warrant it should be clear in proportion as the power is exorbitant.

If it is law, it will be found in our books. If it is not to be found there, it is not law.

The great end, for which men entered into society, was to secure their property. That right is preserved sacred and incommunicable in all instances, where it has not been taken away or abridged by some public law for the good of the whole. The cases where this right of property is set aside by positive law, are various. Distresses, executions, forfeitures, taxes, &c. are all of this description; wherein every man by common consent gives up that right, for the sake of justice and the general good. By the laws of England, every invasion of private property, be it ever so minute, is a trespass. No man can set his foot upon my ground without my licence, but he is liable to an action, though the damage be nothing; which is proved by every declaration in trespass, where the defendant is called upon to answer for bruising the grass and even treading upon the soil. If he admits the fact, he is bound to shew by way of justification, that some positive law has empowered or excused him. The justification is submitted to the judges, who are to look into the books; and if such a justification can be maintained by the text of the statute law, or by the principles of common law. If no such excuse can be found or produced, the silence of the books is an authority against the defendant, and the plaintiff must have judgment.

According to this reasoning, it is now incumbent upon the defendants to shew the law, by which this seizure is warranted. If that cannot be done, it is a trespass.

Papers are the owner's goods and chattels: they are his dearest property; and are so far from enduring a seizure, that they will hardly bear an inspection;

and though the eye cannot by the laws of England be guilty of a trespass, yet where private papers are removed and carried away, the secret nature of those goods will be an aggravation of the trespass, and demand more considerable damages in that respect. Where is the written law that gives any magistrate such a power? I can safely answer, there is none; and therefore it is too much for us without such authority to pronounce a practice legal, which would be subversive of all the comforts of society.

But though it cannot be maintained by any direct law, yet it bears a resemblance, as was urged, to the known case of search and seizure for stolen goods.

I answer, that the difference is apparent. In the one, I am permitted to seize my own goods, which are placed in the hands of a public officer, till the felon's conviction shall intitle me to restitution. In the other, the party's own property is seized before and without conviction, and he has no power to reclaim his goods, even after his innocence is cleared by acquittal.

[1067] The case of searching for stolen goods crept into the law by imperceptible practice. It is the only case of the kind that is to be met with. No less a person than my lord Coke (4 Inst. 176,) denied its legality; and therefore if the two cases resembled each other more than they do, we have no right, without an act of parliament, to adopt a new practice in the criminal law, which was never yet allowed from all antiquity.

Observe too the caution with which the law proceeds in this singular case.–There must be a full charge upon oath of a theft committed.–The owner must swear that the goods are lodged in such a place.–He must attend at the execution of the warrant to shew them to the officer, who must see that they answer the description.–And, lastly, the owner must abide the event at his peril: for if the goods are not found, he is a trespasser; and the officer being an innocent person, will be always a ready and convenient witness against him.[11]

On the contrary, in the case before us nothing is described, nor distinguished: no charge is requisite to prove, that the party has any criminal papers in his custody: no person present to separate or select: no person to prove in the owner's behalf the officer's misbehavior.–To say the truth, he cannot easily misbehave, unless he pilfers; for he cannot take more than all.

If it should be said that the same law which has with so much circumspection guarded the case of stolen goods from mischief, would likewise in this case protect the subject, by adding proper checks; would require proofs beforehand; would call up the servant to stand by and overlook; would require him to take an exact inventory, and deliver a copy: my answer is, that all these precautions would have been long since established by law, if the power itself had been legal; and that the want of them is an undeniable argument against the legality of the thing.

[11] See Leach's Hawkins's Pleas of the Crown, book 2, c. 13, s. 17.

What would the parliament say, if the judges should take upon themselves to mould an unlawful power into a convenient authority, by new restrictions? That would be, not judgment, but legislation.

I come now to the practice since the Revolution, which has been strongly urged, with this emphatical addition, that an usage tolerated from the æra of liberty, and continued downwards to this time through the best ages of the constitution, must necessarily have a legal commencement. Now, though that pretence can have no place in the question made by this plea, because no such practice is there alleged; yet I will permit the defendant for the present to borrow a fact from the special verdict, for the sake of giving it an answer.

If the practice began then, it began too late to be law now. If it was more ancient, the Revolution is not to answer for it; and I could [1068] have wished, that upon this occasion the Revolution had not been considered as the only basis of our liberty.

The Revolution restored this constitution to its first principles. It did no more. It did not enlarge the liberty of the subject; but gave it a better security. It neither widened nor contracted the foundation, but repaired, and perhaps added a buttress or two to the fabric; and if any minister of state has since deviated from the principles at that time recognized, all that I can say is, that, so far from being sanctified, they are condemned by the Revolution.

With respect to the practice itself, if it goes no higher, every lawyer will tell you, it is much too modern to be evidence of the common law; and if it should be added, that these warrants ought to acquire some strength by the silence of those courts, which have heard them read so often upon returns without censure or animadversion, I am able to borrow my answer to that pretence from the Court of King's-bench which lately declared with great unanimity in the Case of General Warrants, that as no objection was taken to them upon the returns, and the matter passed *sub silentio*, the precedents were of no weight. I most heartily concur in that opinion; and the reason is more pertinent here, because the Court had no authority in the present case to determine against the seizure of papers, which was not before them; whereas in the other they might, if they had thought fit, have declared the warrant void, and discharged the prisoner *ex officio*.

This is the first instance I have met with, where the ancient immemorable law of the land, in a public matter, was attempted to be proved by the practice of a private office.

The names and rights of public magistrates, their power and forms of proceeding as they are settled by law, have been long since written, and are to be found in books and records. Private customs indeed are still to be sought from private tradition. But whoever conceived a notion, that any part of the public law could be buried in the obscure practice of a particular person?

To search, seize, and carry away all the papers of the subject upon the first warrant: that such a right should have existed from the time whereof the memory of man runneth not to the contrary, and never yet have found a place in any book of law; is incredible. But if so strange a thing could be supposed, I do not see, how we could declare the law upon such evidence.

But still it is insisted, that there has been a general submission, and no action brought to try the right.

I answer, there has been a submission of guilt and poverty to power and the terror of punishment. But it would be strange doctrine to assert that all the people of this land are bound to acknowledge that to be universal law, which a few criminal booksellers have been afraid to dispute.

[1069] The defendants upon this occasion have stopped short at the Revolution. But I think it would be material to go further back, in order to see, how far the search and seizure of papers have been countenanced in the antecedent reigns.

First, I find no trace of such a warrant as the present before that period, except a very few that were produced the other day in the reign of king Charles 2.

But there did exist a search-warrant, which took its rise from a decree of the Star-Chamber. The decree is found at the end of the 3d volume of Rushworth's Collections. It was made in the year 1636, and recites an older decree upon the subject in the 28th of Elizabeth, by which probably the same power of search was given.

By this decree the messenger of the press was empowered to search in all places, where books were printing, in order to see if the printer had a license; and if upon such search he found any books which he suspected to be libellous against the church or state, he was to seize them, and carry them before the proper magistrate.

It was very evident, that the Star-Chamber, how soon after the invention of printing I know not, took to itself the jurisdiction over public libels, which soon grew to be the peculiar business of that court. Not that the courts of Westminster-hall wanted the power of holding pleas in those cases; but the attorney-general for good reasons chose rather to proceed there; which is the reason, why we have no cases of libels in the King's-bench before the Restoration.

The Star-Chamber from this jurisdiction presently usurped a general superintendance over the press, and exercised a legislative power in all matters relating to the subject. They appointed licensers; they prohibited books; they inflicted penalties; and they dignified one of their officers with the name of the messenger of the press, and among other things enacted this warrant of search.

After that court was abolished, the press became free, but enjoyed its liberty not above two or three years, for the Long Parliament thought fit to restrain it again by ordinance. Whilst the press is free, I am afraid it will always be licentious, and all governments have an aversion to libels. This parliament, therefore, did by ordinance restore the Star-Chamber practice; they recalled the licences, and sent forth again the messenger. It was against the ordinance, that Milton wrote that famous pamphlet called Areopagitica. Upon the Restoration, the press was free once more, till the 13th and 14th of Charles 2, when the Licensing Act passed, which for the first time gave the secretary of state a power to issue search warrants: but these warrants were neither so oppressive, nor so inconvenient as the present. The right to enquire into the licence was the pretence of making the searches; and if during the search any suspected libels were found, they and they only could be seized.

[1070] This act expired the 32d year of that reign or thereabouts. It was revived again in the 1st year of king James 2, and remained in force till the 5th of king William, after one of his parliaments had continued it for a year beyond its expiration.

I do very much suspect, that the present warrant took its rise from these search-warrants, that I have been describing; nothing being easier to account for than this engraftment; the difference between them being no more than this, that the apprehension of the person in the first was to follow the seizure of papers, but the seizure of papers in the latter was to follow the apprehension of the person. The same evidence would serve equally for both purposes. If it was charged for printing or publishing, that was sufficient for either of the warrants. Only this material difference must always be observed between them, that the search warrant only carried off the criminal papers, whereas this seizes all.

When the Licensing Act expired at the close of king Charles 2's reign, the twelve judges were assembled at the king's command, to discover whether the press might not be as effectually restrained by the common law, as it had been by that statute.

I cannot help observing in this place, that if the secretary of state was still invested with a power of issuing this warrant, there was no occasion for the application to the judges: for though he could not issue the general search-warrant, yet upon the least rumor of a libel he might have done more, and seized every thing. But that was not thought of, and therefore the judges met and resolved:

First, that it was criminal at common law, not only to write public seditious papers and false news; but likewise to publish any news without a licence from the king, though it was true and innocent.

Secondly, that libels were seizable. This is to be found in the State Trials; and because it is a curiosity, I will recite the passages at large.

"The Trial of Harris for a libel. Scroggs Chief Justice.

Because my brethren shall be satisfied with the opinion of all the judges of England what this offence is, which they would insinuate, as if the mere selling of books was no offence; it is not long since that all the judges met by the king's commandment, as they did some time before: and they both times declared unanimously, that all persons, that do write, or print, or sell any pamphlet that is either scandalous to public or private persons, such books may be seized, and the persons punished by law; that all books which are scandalous to the government may be seized, and all persons so expounding may be punished: and further, that all writers of news, though not scandalous, seditious, nor reflective upon the government or state; yet if they are writers, as they are few others, of false news, they are indictable and punishable upon that account." [See vol. 7, p. 929]

[1071] It seems the chief justice was a little incorrect in his report; for it should seem as if he meant to punish only the writer of false news. But he is more accurate afterwards in the trial of Carre for a libel.

"Sir G *Jefferies*, Recorder. All the judges of England having met together to know, whether any person whatsoever may expose to the public knowledge any matter of intelligence, or any matter whatsoever that concerns the public, they give it in as their resolution, that no person whatsoever could expose to the public knowledge any thing that concerned the affairs of the public, without licence from the king, or from such persons as he thought fit to intrust with that power."

Then Scroggs takes up the subject, and says, The words I remember are these. When by the king's command we were to give in our opinion, what was to be done in point of regulation of the press, we did all subscribe, that to print or publish any news-books or pamphlets, or any news whatsoever, is illegal; that it is a manifest intent to the breach of the peace, and they may be proceeded against by law for an illegal thing. Suppose now that this thing is not scandalous, what then? If there had been no reflection in this book at all, yet it is *illicitè* done, and the author ought to be convicted for it." [See vol. 7, p. 1127.]

These are the opinions of all the twelve judges of England; a great and reverend authority.

Can the twelve judges extrajudicially make a thing law to bind the kingdom by a declaration, that such is their opinion?–I say No.–It is a matter of impeachment for any judge to affirm it. There must be an antecedent principle or authority, from whence this opinion may be fairly collected; otherwise the opinion is null, and nothing but ignorance can excuse the judge that subscribed it. Out of this doctrine sprang the famous general search-warrant, that was condemned by the House of Commons; and it was not unreasonable to suppose, that the form of it was settled by the twelve judges that subscribed the opinion.

The deduction from the opinion to the warrant is obvious. If you can seize a libel, you may search for it: if search is legal, a warrant to authorize that search is likewise legal: if any magistrate can issue such a warrant, the chief justice of the King's bench may clearly do it.

It falls here naturally in my way to ask, whether there be any authority besides this opinion of these twelve judges to say, that libels may be seized? If they may, I am afraid, that all the inconveniences of a general seizure will follow upon a right allowed to seize a part. The search in such cases will be general, and every house will fall under the power of a secretary of state to be rummaged before proper conviction.–Consider for a while how the law of libels now stands.

[1072] Lord Chief Justice Holt and the Court of King's-bench have resolved in the King and Bear,[12] that he who writes a libel, though he neither composes it nor publishes, is criminal.

In the 5th Report, 125, lord Coke cites it in the Star Chamber, that if a libel concerns a public person, he that hath it in his custody ought immediately to deliver it to a magistrate, that the author may be found out.

In the case of Lake and Hutton, Hobart 252, it is observed, that a libel, though the contents are true, is not to be justified; but the right way is to discover it to some magistrate or other, that they may have cognizance of the cause.

In 1st Ventris 31, it is said, that the having a libel, and not discovering it to a magistrate, was only punishable in the Star Chamber, unless the party maliciously publish it. But the Court corrected this doctrine in the King and Bear, where it said, though he never published it, yet his having it in readiness for that purpose, if any occasion should happen, is highly criminal: and though he might design to keep it private, yet after his death it might fall into such hands as might be injurious to the government; and therefore men ought not to be allowed to have such evil instruments in their keeping. Carthew 409. In Salkeld's report of the same case, Holt chief justice says, if a libel be publicly known, a written copy of it is evidence of a publication. Salk. 418.

If all this be law, and I have no right at present to deny it, whenever a favourite libel is published (and these compositions are apt to be favourites) the whole kingdom in a month or two becomes criminal, and it would be difficult to find one innocent jury amongst so many millions of offenders.

I can find no other authority to justify the seizure of a libel, than that of Scroggs and his brethren.

If the power of search is to follow the right of seizure, every body sees the consequence. He that has it or has had it in his custody; he that has published, copied, or maliciously reported it, may fairly be under a reasonable suspicion of having the thing in his custody, and consequently become the object of the search-warrant. If libels may be seized, it ought to be laid down with precision, when, where, upon what charge, against whom, by

---

[12] Reported Carth. 407. 1 L. Raym. 414. 12 Mod. 299. 2 Salk. 417. 616.

what magistrate, and in what stage of the prosecution. All these particulars must be explained and proved to be law, before this general proposition can be established.

As therefore no authority in our books can be produced to support such a doctrine, and so many Star-Chamber decrees, ordinances, and acts have been thought necessary to establish a power of search, I cannot be persuaded, that such a power can be justified by the common law.

I have done now with the argument, which [1073] has endeavored to support this warrant by the practice since the Revolution.

It is then said, that it is necessary for the ends of government to lodge such a power with a state officer; and that it is better to prevent the publication before than to punish the offender afterwards. I answer, if the legislature be of that opinion, they will revive the Licensing Act. But if they have not done that, I conceive they are not of that opinion. And with respect to the argument of state necessity, or a distinction that has been aimed at between state offences and others, the common law does not understand that kind of reasoning, nor do our books take notice of any such distinctions.

Serjeant Ashley was committed to the Tower in the 3d of Charles 1st, by the House of Lords only for asserting in argument, that there was a 'law of state' different from the common law; and the Ship-Money judges were impeached for holding, first, that state-necessity would justify the raising money without consent of parliament; and secondly, that the king was judge of that necessity.

If the king himself has no power to declare when the law ought to be violated for reason of state, I am sure we his judges have no such prerogative.

Lastly, it is urged as an argument of utility, that such a search is a means of detecting offenders by discovering evidence. I wish some cases had been shewn, where the law forceth evidence out of the owner's custody by process. There is no process against papers in civil causes. It has been often tried, but never prevailed. Nay, where the adversary has by force or fraud got possession of your own proper evidence, there is no way to get it back but by action.

In the criminal law such a proceeding was never heard of; and yet there are some crimes, such for instance as murder, rape, robbery, and housebreaking, to say nothing of forgery and perjury, that are more atrocious than libelling. But our law has provided no paper-search in these cases to help forward the conviction.

Whether this proceedeth from the gentleness of the law towards criminals, or from a consideration that such a power would be more pernicious to the innocent than useful to the public, I will not say.

It is very certain, that the law obligeth no man to accuse himself; because the necessary means of compelling self-accusation, falling upon the innocent as well as the guilty, would be both cruel and unjust; and it should seem, that search for evidence is disallowed upon the same principle. There too the innocent would be confounded with the guilty.

Observe the wisdom as well as mercy of the law. The strongest evidence before a trial, being only *ex parte*, is but suspicion; it is not proof. Weak evidence is a ground of suspicion, though in a lower degree; and if suspicion at large should be a ground of search, [1074] especially in the case of libels, whose house would be safe?

If, however, a right of search for the sake of discovering evidence ought in any case to be allowed, this crime above all others ought to be excepted, as wanting such a discovery less than any other. It is committed in open day-light, and in the face of the world; every act of publication makes new proof; and the solicitor of the treasury, if he pleases, may be the witness himself.

The messenger of the press, by the very constitution of his office, is directed to purchase every libel that comes forth, in order to be a witness.

Nay, if the vengeance of government requires a production of the author, it is hardly possible for him to escape the impeachment of the printer, who is sure to seal his own pardon by his discovery. But suppose he should happen to be obstinate, yet the publication is stopped, and the offence punished. By this means the law is satisfied, and the public secured.

I have now taken notice of every thing that has been urged upon the present point; and upon the whole we are all of opinion, that the warrant to seize and carry away the party's papers in the case of a seditious libel, is illegal and void.

Before I conclude, I desire not to be understood as an advocate for libels. All civilized governments have punished calumny with severity; and with reason; for these compositions debauch the manners of the people; they excite a spirit of disobedience, and enervate the authority of government; they provoke and excite the passions of the people against their rulers, and the rulers oftentimes against the people.

After this description, I shall hardly be considered a favourer of these pernicious productions. I will always set my face against them, when they come before me; and shall recommend it most warmly to the jury always to convict when the proof is clear. They will do well to consider, that unjust acquittals bring an odium upon the press itself, the consequences whereof may be fatal to liberty; for if kings and great men cannot obtain justice at their hands by the ordinary course of law, they may at last be provoked to restrain that press, which the juries of their country refuse to regulate. When licentiousness is tolerated, liberty is in the utmost danger; because tyranny, bad as it is, is better than anarchy; and the worst of governments is more tolerable than no government at all.

[A great change of the king's ministers happened in the July before the judgement in the preceding case; particularly the marquis of Rockingham was placed at the head of the treasury. The judgment was soon followed with a resolution of the House of Commons, declaring the seizure of papers in the case of a libel to be illegal. Journ. Com. 22 April, 1766. At the same time the Commons passed a resolution [1075] condemning general warrants in the case of libels. The latter resolution was afterwards extended by a further vote, which included a declaration, that general warrants were universally illegal, except in cases provided for by act of parliament. Journ. Com. 25th April, 1766.–All these resolutions were in consequence of Mr. Wilkes's complaint of a breach of privilege above two years before. Journ. Com. 15th November, 1763. Two prior attempts were made to obtain a vote in condemnation of general warrants and the seizure of papers, one in 1764, the other in 1765. Journ. Com. 14th and 17th February, 1764; 29th January, 1765. [See, too, New Parl. Hist.] But they both had miscarried, and one of the reasons assigned for so long resisting such interposition of the House was the pendency of suits in the courts of law. This objection was in part removed by the solemn judgment of the Common Pleas against the seizure of papers, [1076] and the acquiescence in it. Whether the question of general warrants ever received the same full and pointed decision in any of the courts, it is not in our power at present to inform the reader. The point arose on the trial of an action by Mr. Wilkes against Mr. Wood; and lord Camden in his charge to the jury appears to have explicitly avowed his own opinion of the illegality of general warrants; but what was done afterwards is not stated. How a regular judgment of the point was avoided, in the case of error in the King's-bench between Money and Leach, by conceding that the warrant was not pursued, we have observed in a former Note, see p. 1028. As to the action, in which Mr. Wilkes finally recovered large damages from the earl of Halifax, it was not tried till after the declaratory vote of the Commons, which most probably prevented all argument on the subject. *Hargrave.*]

Index

Lightning Source UK Ltd.
Milton Keynes UK
UKHW02f1656070618
323864UK00004B/235/P